P9-DIJ-261

ALSO BY BILL SLOAN

The Darkest Summer: Pusan and Inchon 1950—The Battles That Saved South Korea—and the Marines—from Extinction

The Ultimate Battle: Okinawa 1945—The Last Epic Struggle of World War II

Brotherhood of Heroes: The Marines at Peleliu, 1944—The Bloodiest Battle of the Pacific War

Given Up for Dead: America's Heroic Stand at Wake Island

JFK: Breaking the Silence

JFK: The Last Dissenting Witness

Elvis, Hank and Me: Making Musical History on the Louisiana Hayride (with Horace Logan)

The Other Assassin (fiction)

The Mafia Candidate (fiction)

Unde

America's Heroic Fight for Bataan and Corregidor

feated

BILL SLOAN

Simon & Schuster Paperbacks
New York London Toronto Sydney New Delhi

Simon & Schuster Paperbacks
A Division of Simon & Schuster, Inc.
1230 Avenue of the Americas
New York, NY 10020

Credits for the photographic insert are on page 402.

First Simon & Schuster trade paperback edition June 2013

Designed by Jill Putorti

Manufactured in the United States of America

10 9 8 7 6 5 4 3 2 1

Library of Congress has cataloged the hardcover edition as follows:

Sloan, Bill.
Undefeated : America's heroic fight for Bataan and Corregidor / Bill Sloan.
p. cm.
1. Bataan, Battle of, Philippines, 1942. 2. World War, 1939–1945—Campaigns—Philippines—Corregidor Island. 3. Bataan (Philippines : Province)—History, Military. 4. Corregidor Island (Philippines)—History, Military. I. Title.
D767.4.S58 2012
940.54'25991—dc23 2011039887

ISBN 978-1-4391-9964-0
ISBN 978-1-4391-9965-7 (pbk)
ISBN 978-1-4391-9966-4 (ebook)

To those who came home and those who didn't

Contents

Undefeated

SOVIET UNION
OUTER MONGOLIA
MANCHUKUO
(MANCHURIA)
Hokkaido
Sapporo
Vladivostok
Hoten
(Mukden)
Sea of
Japan
Peking
CHOSEN
(KOREA)
Pyongyang
Keijo (Seoul)
JAPAN
Honshu
Tokyo
Nagoya
Yokohama
Hiroshima
Osaka
Kyoto
CHINA
Shikoku
Nagasaki
Kyushu
Hankow
Shanghai
East
China
Sea
Okinawa
Canton
Formosa
Pacific Ocean
Hong Kong
N
W
E
S
Lingayen Gulf
Luzon
FRENCH
INDO-CHINA
Subic Bay
Manila
South
China
Sea
Mindoro
PHILIPPINES
Samar
Panay
Negros
Leyte
0 100 200 300 miles
0 200 400 kilometers
Mindanao
Davao
The Far East, 1941-42

1

A $36-a-Month Paradise

As the 1930s faded into the 1940s, the growing aggregation of United States military bases clustered around the Philippine capital city of Manila ranked near the top of the list of most coveted overseas duty stations for officers and enlisted men of America's armed forces—and for lots of good reasons.

A young first lieutenant's salary of $143 per month supported a lifestyle in Manila that only the ultrawealthy could afford back in the States, where the Great Depression still held sway. Among the usual perks were a fashionable apartment, a full staff of servants, access to exclusive golf, tennis, polo, and drinking clubs—and plenty of leisure time to enjoy all this. General Douglas MacArthur, supreme commander of United States Army Forces, Far East (USAFFE), set the tone for his junior officers from the lavish penthouse atop the Manila Hotel, where he lived with his second wife and three-year-old son.

One junior officer who did his best to live up to his commander-in-chief's example was twenty-eight-year-old First Lieutenant Ralph E. Hibbs of the U.S. Army Medical Corps, who arrived in Manila aboard the liner-turned-troopship *President Coolidge* on June 20, 1941.

Assigned as a brand-new battalion surgeon in the 31st Infantry Regiment, Hibbs had suffered a double disappointment when he went to the dock at Fort Mason in San Francisco to board his ship.

First, he was refused permission to bring his spiffy, fire-chief-red Ford convertible aboard the *Coolidge* and forced to sell it at a considerable loss to a waiting used car dealer.

"The second incident," he recalled decades later, "was the loss of six bottles of Old Grandad whiskey. Rumor had it that no liquor would be allowed on the ship, so I secreted a cache in my golf bag. Unfortunately, it was dropped during loading, and all six bottles were broken. The baggage sergeant was in a tizzy trying to find the source of the aroma until I pointed to my own bag."

Replacing the car in Manila was impossible, and Hibbs had to settle for a rather drab Chevrolet sedan, but he had no reason to cry over spilled whiskey, as it turned out. Drinks at the Baroque Bar in the Army Navy Club cost 15 or 20 cents apiece, he soon discovered, "and the bartender kept pouring from the bottle until you signaled him to stop."

Hibbs's job involved the health of roughly 700 soldiers and meant that he would be on the front lines with them if war broke out. But as long as peacetime prevailed, his routine duties in the clinic at old Fort Santiago, built by the Spanish in 1565, took only about four hours a day.

"I was free by 11 o'clock for golf at Fort McKinley or Manila's lovely Wack-Wack course," he recalled. "Lunch might be at the Polo Club, which included Manila's social elite . . . and a chance for young American officers to meet gorgeous and eager señoritas."

By late afternoon, Hibbs and a small group of friends who called themselves the "Whiffenpoof Boys" were often found rolling dice for drinks at the Army Navy Club. Later in the evening, they might visit the Jai Lai Club for gambling and dinner, or they might return to the Army Navy Club for the free fifty-foot-long buffet.

Before the end of that summer, Hibbs had established a more or less steady romantic relationship with a beautiful, U.S.-educated woman named Pilar Campos, daughter of a prominent Manila family, who spoke five languages and held the position of society editor for the *Manila Herald*. They golfed together and spent their evenings drinking, dining, and dancing just as "Stateside Americans would."

In late November 1941, Hibbs took a moment out of his crowded social schedule to write a letter to his parents back in Iowa. "Things are peaceful here," he said. "Life in the Orient is easygoing with emphasis on the mañana and siesta ethic. . . . A Jap attack seems unlikely."

About ten days later, on December 5, Hibbs's regiment was placed on "red alert," and newspapers reported "enemy airplanes over Luzon for the second time this week." But Hibbs had assured his parents that "Nothing's going to happen here," and he still believed it.

With an exchange rate of two Filipino pesos to one Yankee dollar, even a lowly Army private could claim a share of the good life on his $21-a-month salary. A half-liter peck of gin cost about 15 cents, and a houseboy could be hired to keep the private's boots polished, his uniform pressed, and his bunk made for the equivalent of $1.50 per month.

Manila was known as "the Pearl of the Orient," and so coveted was a two-year tour there that most aspirants had to start at the bottom of a lengthy waiting list. More than a few—including Texas-born Corporal Louis Read, who had enlisted in June 1939 a couple of weeks after his high school graduation, even accepted a temporary reduction in rank to nail down such a plum assignment.

"Peacetime duty in the Philippines was great," Read recalled some seven decades later. "We worked in the mornings, napped during the heat of the afternoon, then took a cab ride for 7 centavos (about three and a half cents American) and went out on the town in the evening. I got to know the bars and nightclubs along main drags like Dewey Boulevard and Rizal Avenue very well."

PFC Walter Bell, a self-described "old native tarheel" from Sparta, North Carolina, had joined the Army at age nineteen on August 1, 1939. After an abbreviated thirty-day boot camp at Fort Slocum, New York, he sailed for Manila aboard the transport *President Grant* with forty other members of the Fourth Chemical Company. He was favorably impressed with the surroundings the moment he stepped ashore.

"It was an incredibly beautiful country," remembered Bell, who was originally stationed at Fort McKinley, about twenty miles from downtown Manila. "There were beautiful girls everywhere you looked and beer joints on every corner. We'd drill until noon, then have the whole afternoon off to drink beer and chase girls."

Complementing the relaxed pace and light duties were ample entertainment possibilities to fill the spare time of the rank and file. On the half-dozen major military bases in southern Luzon, air-conditioned theaters provided free first-run movies. Bowling alleys, sports fields, swimming pools, and tennis courts were also readily available. NCO clubs and an endless assortment of bars and dance halls in Manila proper served ice-cold beer for a nickel a bottle. Pristine beaches stretched as far as the eye could see, and the fragrance of bougainvillea, gardenias, and orchids filled the air. Local radio stations played the latest big-band tunes, and English-language newspapers and 5-cent orchid corsages were hawked on many major street corners. Beautiful women were everywhere, and on neon-lit side streets attractive prostitutes offered their services for as little as 50 cents.

"It was the closest thing to paradise any of us had ever seen," said Tech Sergeant Smith L. Green, who arrived in October 1939, well before serious war clouds began to gather over the islands. Green, who had joined the Army in 1935 to escape the throes of the Great Depression, was assigned to a communications unit in the 31st Infantry, the only all-American regiment in the Philippines, which operated a richly appointed NCO club on Dewey Boulevard overlooking Manila Bay. "I was single, I had $36 a month to spend, and I was happy as a lark," he recalled.

Even at Clark Field, some sixty miles north of Manila, the living was easy for members of the 19th Bomb Group's Seventh Materiel Squadron, who arrived there in October 1941 to perform routine maintenance on the field's growing flock of B-17 heavy bombers.

"Our work wasn't all that hard," recalled PFC Russell Gill, a native Oklahoman assigned to such jobs as emptying fifty-five-gallon drums of gasoline into the field's 4,000-gallon storage tanks and making sure that the big planes had plenty of oil for their 200-gallon crankcases.

"We got to go into Manila fairly often for supplies, and we had real nice quarters at Clark," Gill said. "The barracks were made out of mahogany and nipa, and each one was set up to house five guys. We had houseboys as servants to do our laundry and make our beds, and our meals were served on fine china. I'd have stayed there forever if not for the war."

By the spring of 1941, the Americanization of Manila's downtown area was virtually complete. Those who ventured far enough from the glitzy areas of the city could find plenty of squalor and slum shacks constructed of nipa leaves and bamboo. But it was possible to spend months in the city and never see those things if you didn't want to.

"Manila was different from anything I'd imagined," said Corporal Clemens Kathman, who landed there in September 1941 as a new member of the 200th Coastal Artillery Regiment. "The seafront was adorned with beautiful buildings, homes, and hotels surrounded by lush green lawns and palm trees. Wide paved streets that cut their way through the business district resembled any American city. It looked more like Southern California than the Far East."

By this time, however, rapid changes were taking place—all of them of an ominous nature. The last dependents of American military personnel and, in fact, the vast majority of all American civilians in the islands were scurrying to get out. Talk in the bars, clubs, and restaurants inevitably turned to the growing probability of a war with Japan, but most U.S. servicemen in the Philippines gave little credence to the talk, and many scoffed openly at the idea of the Japanese picking a fight with the United States.

Their typical response to such suggestions was laced with arrogance, bravado, and denial. "The Japs don't have the balls to attack us," they said, in essence, "and if they ever try it, it'll be the shortest war in history. We'll kick their asses and send 'em home in boxes in two or three weeks."

Unfortunately, the scoffers didn't understand how drastically Japanese-U.S. relations had soured over the preceding forty years. They failed to grasp the depth of Japanese anger toward the arrogant white intruders into Nippon's East Asia domain or to realize how much military muscle and advanced weaponry Japan had amassed since the early 1900s. If they had, the naysayers would have kept their mouths shut and started digging.

* * *

Compared to the massive conflicts that would convulse the world during the following century, the Spanish-American War of 1898 didn't amount to much—not on the surface, at any rate. It lasted barely four months, cost a mere handful of American casualties, and ended when Commodore George Dewey's U.S. Asiatic Squadron quickly destroyed the Spanish fleet in Manila Bay, suffering only nine wounded sailors in the process.

But from a broader perspective, this "splendid little war," as U.S. ambassador to Britain John Hay described it at the time, set the stage for the most horrendous cataclysm in human history slightly more than four decades later.

The easy victory over Spain established the United States as a genuine world power and gave it a chain of newly acquired possessions stretching from Cuba to Hawaii to the Philippines. Our inwardly focused, predominantly rural, and still young nation, where most citizens had never ventured more than a hundred or so miles from home—suddenly found itself with a vast Pacific domain half a world away from its major population centers. As the twentieth century dawned, the general public wanted little to do with anything that far away, and few American political leaders were eager to spend the hefty sums of money required to support these far-flung new interests, particularly those in the Far East.

One who *was* willing—even eager—was Spanish War hero Teddy Roosevelt. When he ascended to the White House in 1901, following the assassination of President William McKinley, one of Roosevelt's first priorities was to develop a "big stick" Navy that could hold its own in waters far from home. In late 1907, Roosevelt sent the sixteen new battleships of America's "Great White Fleet," with 14,000 sailors aboard, on a triumphal 43,000-mile, fifteen-month, around-the-world cruise to show off U.S. sea power.

Meanwhile, the Japanese navy—fresh from its resounding defeat of Czar Nicholas's fleet in the Russo-Japanese War of 1905—was flexing its own muscles in the Pacific. Although Japanese officials and citizens gave the American dreadnoughts an outwardly cordial welcome on their arrival in Tokyo Bay in October 1908, the country's militants resented the "provocative" presence of so many U.S. warships in Japan's own backyard.

* * *

Japan and the United States were nominal allies against Germany in World War I, but there was minimal cooperation between the two nations, and their goals were as different as night and day. While more than a million American doughboys were being sent to France to "make the world safe for democracy," Japan's chief concern was laying claim to certain German holdings in the Pacific following the kaiser's defeat. As early as 1920, U.S. military strategists identified Japan, now boasting the world's third largest navy and controlling a string of former German colonial possessions, as the likeliest potential adversary of the United States in a future Pacific conflict.

To counter the perceived threat from Tokyo, the United States and Britain tried using strong-arm diplomacy at the Washington Naval Conference of 1922 to limit the size and number of new Japanese warships, but Japan found its own clandestine ways to circumvent these attempts. Meanwhile, American military leaders formulated a top secret anti-Japanese strategy designated as War Plan Orange. With a few revisions, the same basic strategy was still favored by many U.S. military leaders, under the name WPO-3, when hostilities broke out in late 1941.

One of the two principal cornerstones of each version of Plan Orange would be the construction of massive U.S. fortifications in the Philippine Islands, particularly around Manila Bay and on southern Luzon. The other was the transfer of the U.S. Pacific Fleet and its formidable firepower from its traditional home port of San Diego 2,000 miles west to Hawaii. This, in theory, placed the fleet close enough to the Philippines to come to the rescue if besieged U.S. defenders could execute an orderly retreat into the Bataan Peninsula and hold out there for up to six months. Other remote fortified points of land scattered over the far western Pacific, including Wake Island, Midway, and Guam, were intended to add teeth to the plan.

Meanwhile, throughout the 1920s, seeds of mutual animosity and distrust were sown continuously between the United States and an increasingly bellicose empire of Japan. The seeds would flower into flaming disaster at Pearl Harbor on the balmy morning of December 7, 1941.

The first major attacks on American bases in the Philippines (on the other side of the International Date Line, where it was December

8) would follow about ten hours later. When they came, no American in the islands—from General MacArthur in his posh penthouse down to the lowliest private sleeping off a weekend drunk in his barracks—would be ready to respond.

Over the seven decades since, historians and students of military strategy have continued to wonder why.

During the period between the skirmish with Spain and World War II, most top-level diplomats and national political leaders studiously avoided such terms as "colonial empire" to describe America's far-flung Pacific holdings. They much preferred such designations as "territories" and "protectorates"—or in the case of the Philippines, a "commonwealth." And beginning in 1936, to the credit of the United States, the Philippine archipelago *was* set on a ten-year path toward full independence. Nevertheless, in the words of historian Duane Schultz, "These were truly the days of empire. These were lazy, luxurious, pampered days, and the white man lived like royalty, served well by his native subjects."

It seems likely that no white man on earth had more opportunities during this period to embrace the languorous aura of the Philippines—or to enjoy a more regal and pampered existence there—than General Douglas MacArthur.

After graduating at the top of his West Point class of 1903, MacArthur had proceeded directly to the Philippines, where his father, General Arthur MacArthur, a Civil War Medal of Honor winner, was serving a lengthy tenure as military governor. After the elder MacArthur's death there in 1912 from a tropical disease, young Douglas returned to the States in time to distinguish himself with the American Expeditionary Forces during World War I. As a field officer during the fierce trench warfare in France, he gained a reputation for battlefield courage and inspired leadership that earned him a Distinguished Service Cross and placed him among the nation's most revered heroes of "the war to end war."

By 1935, however, MacArthur had spent seventeen years further distinguishing himself as the Army's youngest general, youngest division commander, first-ever press officer, youngest superintendent of

West Point, and youngest chief of staff. Now he was fifty-six years old and too far along in age to be the "youngest" at much of anything anymore. It was also a dismal time for the nation's military with tightfisted isolationists controlling Congress and the Army seemingly withering on the vine.

In the meantime, MacArthur's personal life had also fallen into the doldrums. In 1929, his ill-advised marriage to wealthy socialite Louise Cromwell Brooks had ended in a nasty, much publicized divorce. Then, in 1932, his harsh treatment of destitute World War I veterans in breaking up their "Bonus March" on Washington had left a bad taste in the mouths of millions of Americans. Clearly, a change was in order for the nation's most colorful general, and his best opportunity to achieve it seemed to lie in the Philippines, where he was again spending considerable off-duty time.

In 1935, after five years as chief of staff, MacArthur was already flirting with the idea of retirement when he received an incredibly appealing proposition from Philippines president Manuel Quezon, whom the general had known since 1903. Quezon wanted to hire a world-recognized military leader to serve as commander-in-chief of the commonwealth's fledgling armed forces, and his old friend MacArthur was his first choice. In quickly accepting Quezon's offer, MacArthur not only became the only American general ever to hold the exalted rank of field marshal but also received a larger salary than Quezon himself. In return, MacArthur would be charged with building a Philippine Army capable of defending the archipelago from any external threat.

From all indications, this decision led to one of the most satisfying interludes of MacArthur's life. In 1937, he officially resigned from the U.S. Army, adding to the remoteness of his situation while emphasizing his displeasure with the state of America's military. That same year, he married Jean Marie Faircloth, a thirty-seven-year-old from Murfreesboro, Tennessee, whom he'd met in the Philippines several years earlier. In 1938, the new Mrs. MacArthur gave birth to a son, Arthur, and the general, now fifty-eight, enthusiastically embraced a new role as a doting first-time father.

Yet from a military standpoint, the arrangement with Quezon turned out to be studded with rare peculiarities as the 1930s wound down. Although Field Marshal MacArthur no longer had any official status with the U.S. Army, his views and recommendations on Philippine defense continued to weigh heavily with the U.S. War Department, the Army's new chief of staff, General George C. Marshall, and President Franklin Roosevelt. At the same time, however, considerable friction flared between Manila and Washington.

MacArthur was clearly nettled by what he considered his mother country's lack of financial commitment to build up the Philippines' military—so much so that, in 1939, he peevishly dismissed his trusted longtime aide, U.S. Army Major Dwight D. Eisenhower, and sent him back to the States. When asked what had caused the rift between himself and MacArthur, Eisenhower replied, "He thought I was stealing his publicity."

This breakup triggered lingering ill feelings between the two men destined to become the Army's two most powerful commanders during World War II. Where the prewar Philippines were concerned, it also deepened MacArthur's isolation from Washington's top military leadership as the conflict approached.

Nevertheless, growing concern about a war with Japan would bring an ever-widening stream of U.S. troops and armaments to the islands during 1940 and 1941. The all-American 31st Infantry Regiment had been permanently based in the Philippines since its inception two decades earlier, and it would remain as a mainstay of Philippine defense. The Philippine Scouts, made up of Filipino soldiers led by U.S. Army officers and established during an insurrection following the war with Spain, had long ago proved itself as another top-notch fighting organization. These two well-trained, well-equipped entities formed the nucleus of a defensive force still under the auspices of the U.S. Army but also within the full, on-the-scene jurisdiction of Field Marshal MacArthur, an employee of the Philippine government. The result was an unwieldy, if not paradoxical, situation.

Ironically, despite his urgings for more and faster assistance from Washington, MacArthur chose to follow an amazingly relaxed pace in preparing his new Philippine Army for combat. On one hand, he talked of defending "every inch of shoreline" in the Philippines against attack by outside forces. (The 7,100-plus islands in the archipelago have more total shoreline than the United States.) On the other hand, he repeatedly discounted the threat of Japanese aggression against the Philippines.

"It has been assumed, in my opinion erroneously, that Japan covets these islands," he said in 1939 in his usual verbose style. "Just why has never been satisfactorily explained. Proponents of such a theory fail fully to credit the logic of the Japanese mind. Economically, Japan would gain nothing by conquest [of the Philippines]. If committed to such an attack, the Japanese position would become desperate if . . . intervention should materialize on the part of a nation equipped with a powerful fleet."

In other words, MacArthur was insisting, Japan would be courting suicide if its aggression provoked the United States, and this argument, when repeated a sufficient number of times, had a distinct trickle-down effect on American servicemen in the Philippines. By late 1941, the opinions of most American officers and enlisted men serving under MacArthur would reflect these same cocksure misconceptions.

On paper during those final weeks of peace in the Pacific, the Philippine Army encompassed more than 80,000 troops, neatly formed into divisions and regiments. But—virtually to a man—it was made up of young, untrained draftees without a single minute of combat experience, the vast majority of whom had drilled only with wooden dummy rifles and never held an actual weapon in their hands, much less fired one. Most could neither speak nor understand the language spoken by their officers and noncommissioned officers.

"They were brave young men who sincerely wanted to defend their country," said Colonel John Olson, a West Pointer who had helped mold the Philippine Scouts into a superb fighting machine, "but they didn't know the first damn thing about being soldiers, and they were destined to die like flies for that reason."

It was much the same story with the Philippine Air Force. It boasted sixty planes, which sounded good on paper. But closer examination revealed that forty-two of these were ancient, unarmed P-13 primary trainers. Its "combat aircraft" consisted of twelve long obsolete P-26 pursuit planes and three lumbering B-10 bombers dating from the early 1930s.

In his communications with Washington, however, MacArthur continued to exude his special breed of impervious self-confidence.

Even after President Roosevelt sought to drive home the urgency felt by the rest of America's military establishment by ordering MacArthur back to active duty in July 1941 as commander of U.S. Army Forces in the Far East, the general remained unflappable and unperturbed.

While he was now willing to admit that war with Japan could happen—an eventuality he'd denied for a long time—MacArthur blithely assured the powers in Washington that there was "no reason to fear" any attack by the Japanese before April 1942 at the earliest. "And by then," he promised, "we will be fully prepared to meet whatever comes."

By then, Japan's domination of the Philippines would be virtually complete, and MacArthur's 80,000-man Philippine Army would no longer exist.

When war erupted in the Philippines on December 8, 1941, it would find 1,000 members of the Fourth Marine Regiment newly arrived from fourteen years of duty in Shanghai and billeted on Bataan to guard U.S. Navy facilities there. The "China Marines," as they were known, had been in the Philippines for only a week when the first Japanese attacks came.

As part of a small contingent of Marines stationed at the big Cavite Navy Yard on Manila Bay, however, PFC Otis H. King and his fellow Texan and best buddy, Private Ike Williams, had been stationed in the Philippines since the summer of 1940. At a strapping six-foot-one and 200 pounds, King looked about the same age as his nineteen-year-old friend, but he was, in fact, less than six months past his fifteenth birthday.

Earlier that same year, after fibbing his way into the Corps, King had been mistakenly shipped to Shanghai because of a glitch in his orders, but after he'd spent only a couple of weeks with the China Marines, the error had been discovered, and he'd been sent back to Manila. As fate would have it, Williams, with whom the underage King had struck up a rowdy friendship that landed both in the brig, was also transferred out of China as retribution by his angry commanding officer.

"The chemistry between us was what buddies are made of," King would recall decades later in explaining how the two Marines became an inseparable team. "We each seemed to know what the other was thinking and knew what to do in any given situation without verbal communication."

Although Cavite wasn't considered quite as choice a duty station as Shanghai, the "Gold Dust Twins," as their fellow Marines took to calling them, had ample opportunity to pull liberties together in Manila and gain a deserved reputation for drinking and carousing. Their only extended absence from the city's nightlife came during a few weeks of shared sentry duty on Corregidor, guarding the entrance to a top secret communications facility known as the Navy Radio Tunnel.

The sixteenth anniversary of King's birth found him in a Navy hospital recovering from an emergency appendectomy. On the evening of December 5, 1940, Ike Williams and some other buddies decided that King was sufficiently recovered to go out and celebrate what they thought was his twentieth birthday. He didn't argue or bother to correct them, and he had no problem matching them drink for drink as they made the rounds of half a dozen bars.

Later, feeling a slight twinge of guilt for withholding the truth from his best friend, King finally confessed his secret to Williams, but the latter's reaction was hardly more than a shrug. All he said was, "So what's that got to do with the price of cotton in China?"

For much of the following year, King and Williams were out on the town almost every night. Near the end of 1940, their easygoing lifestyle became even more so when they were assigned to "detached duty" doing what King termed "low-level counterintelligence work," in addition to their duties as guards and runners. They moved off base into a nicely furnished apartment, paid for by the office of Admiral Thomas Hart, commander of the Cavite-based Asiatic Fleet, and were handed the enviable assignment of prowling such popular spots as the Poodle Dog Bar & Grill, Scottie's Bar, and the Silver Dollar Saloon.

"Just keep your eyes peeled and your ears open for suspicious activity," said their CO, Lieutenant Colonel William Clement. "If you hear any of those Jap cocktail waitresses pumping drunk sailors about where their ships are headed, let me know."

Then, late in the summer of 1941, somber changes gradually

started dampening the party atmosphere in Manila. Dependents of men serving in Admiral Hart's small, mostly obsolete Asiatic Fleet were suddenly ordered stateside. Machine and ordnance shops at the Cavite Navy Yard began working overtime, and the base's antiaircraft batteries were dispersed to safer, camouflaged locations. The Cavite Marines' supplies of fuel and ammunition were moved to secluded dumps away from the navy yard to protect them from enemy air raids. Admiral Hart moved his staff from his flagship, the heavy cruiser *Houston*, to a nondescript building on Manila's waterfront.

For Williams and King, the strongest indication of how serious matters were getting came when they were called in by Colonel Clement and handed a new, more stringent set of instructions: From now on, even off duty, they were ordered to stay sober, report any suspicious activity immediately, and be especially alert to anything said in the bars by military personnel about fleet or troop movements.

Clement's concern was that many bars in Manila were owned by Japanese nationals who could be feeding critical information back to Tokyo. "For reasons of his own," King said, "the skipper would tell us which bars or night clubs we should visit with particular attention to Japanese bar maids in those establishments."

Suddenly, barhopping wasn't quite as much fun anymore.

On the night of October 16, 1941, Lieutenant Edgar Whitcomb's stomach was filled with butterflies as he looked down through the plastic nose of his B-17 and watched the Golden Gate Bridge disappear beneath him. Ahead lay only the yawning, unbroken blackness of the Pacific Ocean, and Whitcomb felt slightly weak in the knees at the awesome responsibility now facing him. As the plane's navigator, it was his job to guide it through that infinite black wall on the first leg of its 7,000-mile journey from San Francisco to Clark Field in the Philippine Islands.

Whitcomb knew that he and his plane—along with the other twenty-five Flying Fortresses of the 19th Bomb Group, commanded by Colonel Eugene Eubank—were taking part in a truly historic occasion on this night. Theirs was the first mass-formation flight in aviation history to attempt such a long, grueling trip. Their route would take them to Hawaii, Midway Island, Wake Island, New Guinea, Port Darwin in Australia, and finally to the plains of southern Luzon.

In years to come, Whitcomb would think back hundreds of times to his first sight of Clark Field and the lush, green countryside surrounding it. "From the nose of the plane I looked with eager eyes at the scenery below as it flashed past," he recalled. "Directly to the east of the field, a volcano-shaped mountain rose abruptly out of the flat country around it. As we circled for a landing, we could see the golf course spread out west of the field, a swimming pool, and a number of large frame houses. From the air, everything looked clean and fresh, and we were certain that this would be a wonderful place to spend the next few months."

Like most new arrivals to the Philippines, Whitcomb and his buddies were amazed at the luxuries available to them after they settled into spacious, well-appointed houses near the airfield. "It took us no time at all to find that life was impossible without a battery of servants to wash our clothes, keep our shoes polished, and fetch tall drinks at our beck and call—and all for a few cents a day," the young officer from Indiana marveled. "We could swim, play golf, or hike to the various villages near the field. On these walks, we saw beautiful groups of multicolored birds—parakeets, canaries, and parrots, all very much at home in the tropical vegetation of palms and banana trees."

The situation only seemed to get better when, in early November, the bomber crews were granted a lengthy leave in Manila, where Whitcomb and a close friend, Lieutenant Warner Croxton, bunked at the magnificent Manila Hotel and got their first close-up look at the city.

"Manila was a great and wonderful place," said Whitcomb. "There were modern theaters, hotels, and nightclubs, and I found one fine spot for a party—a club with good food and a good orchestra on top of the Avenue Hotel, six or seven stories above the heart of Manila."

Later Whitcomb and Croxton strolled through the hundreds of small shops in Manila's old Walled City. In the wee hours of the morning, they watched drunken American sailors racing down Dewey Boulevard in commandeered taxis with their Filipino drivers hanging on for dear life in the passenger seats. Then, finally, they returned to bask in the unexcelled luxury of the Manila Hotel.

"Too soon, it was time for us the board the train and head back to Clark Field," said Whitcomb, "but we knew now why they called Manila 'the Pearl of the Orient,' and we knew we'd have great times there once we were settled and better acquainted."

On their first day back at Clark, Whitcomb and Croxton were ordered to wear their .45 automatics and World War I–style steel helmets constantly while on duty and to keep their gas masks with them at all times.

They didn't know it at the time, but their Manila party plans were about to go on permanent hold. They'd made their last lighthearted foray through the "Pearl."

Sergeant Cletis Overton's arrival in Manila on November 20, 1941, bore scant resemblance to that of Ed Whitcomb and his fellow fliers. For Overton and other ground crewmembers of the 16th Squadron of the 27th Bomb Group, there was little fanfare or historical significance to the occasion.

Overton's three-week voyage from San Francisco had gotten off to a rocky start when the affable twenty-year-old from Malvern, Arkansas, came down with an acute case of seasickness. In a day or two, the queasy dizziness subsided, however, and he had an opportunity to enjoy a brief taste of luxury aboard his ship, the converted cruise liner *President Coolidge*.

"There was a live orchestra in the dining room," Overton recalled, "and we were served sit-down meals at fancy tables. We got to splash around in the swimming pools, and games of poker, blackjack, and shuffleboard sprang up all over the ship."

For the most part, though, Overton spent his time up on the top deck, watching schools of flying fish and thinking about Maxine Cox, a girl he'd been smitten with since the fifth grade. When they were both about thirteen, he'd started walking Maxine home from church, and they'd continued to date steadily all the way through high school.

After joining the Army Air Corps in August 1940, he'd written her regularly, and while he was stationed fairly close to home in Georgia and Louisiana, he'd visited her in Hot Springs, where she was attending nursing school. When his overseas assignment came through in the fall of '41, he'd written her a goodbye letter, telling her that he might never come back to Malvern and that she should forget about him and find somebody else.

"I knew at the time I didn't really mean it," he later admitted. "I guess I was just trying to play on her heartstrings."

As the *President Coolidge* carried him farther and farther away from her, he could only hope that Maxine hadn't believed him.

After docking in Manila, Overton's outfit was issued steel helmets, gas masks, and 1903 Springfield rifles still packed in Cosmoline. Then the men were bivouacked in six-man tents on the parade ground at Fort William McKinley, just outside the city, to await the anticipated arrival of their planes and equipment and pending the completion of their permanent base at the new Del Carmen Field.

In the interim, they had little to do while on duty other than performing routine camp chores and trying to avoid the afternoon heat, which was still fierce in late November, even for a young man accustomed to Arkansas summers. But in the evenings Overton and one of his tent mates, Charles Watson, often ventured into Manila to check out the nightclubs, watch the natives play a handball-style game called jai alai, and shop for such goods as 35-cent trousers and $1.50-a-pair dress shoes.

Overton also shot numerous photos of his fascinating new surroundings with a 35-millimeter camera that he'd bought during a one-night stopover in Honolulu. He even got Watson to take some shots of him while they were touring the hot spots in Manila—just to impress Maxine.

Unfortunately, though, not a single one of Overton's pictures ever made it back to Arkansas. Mail service from the Philippines was about to be suspended indefinitely.

At about the same time that Cletis Overton's ship sailed into Manila Bay, news came that the China Marines were evacuating Shanghai and being transferred to the Philippines aboard another converted luxury liner, the *President Harrison*. Escorted by a pair of U.S. submarines and two old Yangtze River gunboats, the *Harrison* arrived in the islands without serious incident on December 1.

Two days later, Otis King and Ike Williams happened to be in the flag offices of the Asiatic Fleet during a tense conversation among Admiral Hart, Colonel Sam Howard, commander of the Fourth Marines, and Admiral Francis W. Rockwell, commander of the 16th Naval District.

At this meeting, Colonel Howard's regiment was placed under Admiral Rockwell's command and ordered to protect naval installations on Luzon, principally at the small port of Mariveles at the extreme southern tip of Bataan and the Olongapo Naval Station. The Cavite Marines, of which King and Williams were part, would continue to guard the Cavite Navy Yard.

"Gentlemen," the two young Marines overheard Hart tell the others grimly as the meeting broke up, "I expect a war with Japan within a week, maybe sooner."

On December 5, King observed his seventeenth birthday in an atmosphere far more somber than the one he'd enjoyed a year earlier. Colonel Clement, apparently impressed with the job King and Williams had done collecting information in the bars, presented the pair with an unexpected "birthday present"—consisting of orders for them to return to the States for intelligence training. They were given five days to gather their gear and board the troopship *Chaumont* for the long trip home.

"You'll be sailing on December 10," Clement told them. "Bon voyage."

PFC Otis King—who preferred to be known as "Karl" rather than by the name he'd been given at birth—wasn't the only underage American enlisted man in the Philippines that fateful autumn. He also wasn't the only one about to be ordered stateside as war closed in on the island paradise—or who disliked the name he'd been born with.

Joseph Trejo, a Latino kid with a background as a brawler and troublemaker, would later have his name legally changed to Joseph Alexander and eventually be certified as the youngest individual ever to serve in the U.S. Army Air Corps. He'd been only fourteen years old when his grandmother had signed his enlistment papers on July 7, 1941, at Fort Sam Houston in San Antonio, Texas.

"They didn't ask for a birth certificate or any kind of personal records," he recalled. "All they did was ask if I wanted to join up. I said yes, and that was it."

After boot camp and six weeks of training as a maintenance ordnance technician, Trejo/Alexander became a member of the 440 Aviation Ordnance Squadron and was sent halfway around the world to Clark Field in the Philippines. His job was supposed to be loading 500-pound bombs into the bellies of new B-17s, the world's most formidable combat aircraft.

Joe was somewhat relieved when he learned he'd be stationed at Clark, which was separated from the fleshpots of Manila by sixty miles of mountains and jungles. If Manila was anything like San Antonio, he'd get into trouble there for sure, he thought. He'd always been in trouble in San Antonio.

"I was a mean kid, always in fights, always in trouble in school and everywhere else," he said. "I don't know where my mean streak came from or who I was mad at, but I always had a chip on my shoulder."

Some of his anger may have stemmed from the fact that he'd never known his father or his mother. His grandmother told him only that his mother was dead and that nobody knew—or cared—where his father was. And when Joe was at home, he could feel the hate that radiated from the only other person in his household, a woman who claimed to be his aunt.

"I was a mess," he recalled. "I'd probably have wound up dead if it hadn't been for Mr. Ramsey, one of my teachers in junior high. He kind of took me under his wing and helped me make better grades. I think it was him who gave me the idea of joining the service. I'm sure he didn't intend for me to do it until I was older, but I didn't feel like I could wait. If I stayed in San Antonio, I figured I was bound to kill somebody sooner or later—or get killed myself."

At the time, Joe Trejo had no way of knowing that he was jumping out of the frying pan into the fire. "People in my neighborhood wouldn't let their kids play with me because I was so mean," he recalled. "They said I'd end up in prison. I did, but not the kind of prison they were thinking of."

On the evening of December 7, 1941, PFC Cletis Overton and four buddies took the cheap taxi ride from Fort William McKinley into Manila to see one of the year's most popular movies. *Sergeant York*, starring Gary Cooper as the peace-loving conscientious objector from Tennessee who became a major hero of World War I, was playing at one of the big downtown theaters, and Overton had been eager to see it for weeks.

After the film was over and all the Germans had been subdued, the group persuaded Overton, who had already earned a reputation as a clean-living, early-to-bed kind of guy, into hanging around until an unusually late hour while they made the rounds of several nightclubs. In fact, they stayed until closing time at the last club they visited, and it was approaching 2:30 AM by the time they got back to their bivouac area at McKinley.

"Man, it's dang near breakfast time already," one of Overton's buddies muttered as they made their way past a busy mess tent, where the cooks were wrestling pots and pans and listening to dance music on a small radio. "But I don't think I'm gonna be very hungry this morning."

The others had just grunted in agreement when an urgent, tinny voice cut through the radio's big-band sounds, and they paused to listen.

"We interrupt this program to bring you a special news bulletin," the voice said. "Aircraft identified as Japanese have attacked the U.S. naval base at Pearl Harbor in Hawaii. Repeat, aircraft identified as Japanese—"

"Oh crap!" one of the guys blurted. "How stupid can the Japs get? If they want a war, they'll get one, all right—and it won't last six weeks!"

"Come on, let's hit the sack," another guy said. "It's probably just a false alarm anyway."

"Yeah, but they'll roust us out for another drill in the morning just the same. You wait and see."

Groggily, the young night owls stumbled back to their barracks. Within minutes, the radio report was forgotten, and all five of them were fast asleep.

That same evening of December 7, a few miles from Fort McKinley, an exuberant party dominated the scene at the Fiesta Pavillion of the Manila Hotel. The party was being thrown by the same 27th Bomb

Group to which Cletis Overton and his comrades were assigned. Its purpose was to celebrate the unit's recent arrival from the States and the expected delivery of its fifty-two single-engine Douglas A-24 dive-bombers within the next few days. Junior officers from many of the U.S. Army and Army Air Corps units stationed in the Manila area were among the invited guests, and Major General Lewis Brereton, commander of the U.S. Far East Air Force (FEAF), was the special guest of honor.

The party had been billed in advance as the "hottest show west of Minsky's," the famed New York strip club. In his Internet history of the 31st Infantry Regiment, Colonel Karl H. Lowe described the evening's activity as "marked by raucous laughter, off-key singing, tinkling glasses, and squealing girls." It would continue unabated into the wee hours of the next morning.

Enjoying the festivities from beneath the scarlet cascades of bougainvillea that framed the pavilion's Bamboo Bar were Lieutenant Ralph Hibbs and four other young officers representing a cross section of U.S. military personnel now massing in the Philippines.

"Hey, do you think these guys can fly B-17s any better than they can sing?" gibed First Lieutenant Dwight Hunkins of H Company, 31st Infantry, nodding toward a group of Air Corps crooners from various bomb groups.

"We'd better hope so," said someone else. "If not, our planes may be in one helluva lot of trouble."

Other kibitzers at the bar included George Williams, an infantry officer newly assigned to the Philippine Army; George McClellan III, an aviator and descendant of famed Civil War General George B. McClellan; and Bill Tooley, a Signal Corps officer. Along with Hibbs and Hunkins, the five of them had come to refer to themselves as the Whiffenpoof Boys. They all grinned and nodded as a willowy Filipina waitress brought another round of gin-and-tonics.

No one in the group ever actually learned the answer to Hunkins's question, however, because none of the scores of additional B-17s intended for the Philippines ever reached their destination—and many of those that were already there would never fly a single combat mission.

None of them realized it on that final carefree, boozy evening of peace in the Pacific, but the five Whiffenpoofs would never again be together in the same room, and four of the five would be dead before peace returned.

The first vague report of the Pearl Harbor disaster reached Far East Air Force headquarters in Manila at 2:30 AM on December 8, when Private Norman Tant, a night-duty cryptographer at Nielson Field, ripped an incoming message from Hawaii off the Teletype machine and hurriedly decoded it.

As the gist of the message became clear, Tant's eyes widened in shock: "*Attention all commanders. Japan has begun hostilities. Conduct yourselves accordingly.*"

Tant quickly relayed the message to the Fifth Interceptor Command and the FEAF's G-2 and G-3 sections. But it wasn't until 4:15 AM—an hour and forty-five minutes later—that Captain Charles "Bud" Sprague of the Fifth Interceptor Command telephoned Colonel Harold H. George, his chief of staff, to repeat the message.

"Jesus Christ!" George exclaimed. He turned to Captain Allison Ind and Captain Harold Eads, the two other officers with whom he shared quarters at Fort McKinley. "The Japs have hit Pearl Harbor," he said.

Shortly after four that morning, Lieutenant Ralph Hibbs was awakened in his Manila quarters by a ringing telephone and a loud outburst of cursing from a suite across the garden from Hibbs's apartment. The lieutenant recognized the voice as that of General Brereton, with whom he'd been partying a few hours earlier, and its tone left no doubt that Brereton was mad as hell.

"What? You've got to be kidding!" yelled the FEAF commander. "Well, I'll be damned! Those dirty sons of bitches!"

Hibbs heard Brereton bang the phone down, followed by a cacophony of strident sounds—racing footsteps, slamming doors, scattered shouts, car engines starting suddenly, tires squealing, and gears clashing. But having been asleep only a couple of hours and feeling more than a little hungover from the previous evening's festivities, the young medical officer scarcely gave the noises a second thought.

He groaned softly and pulled a pillow over his aching head. In less than a minute, he'd slipped back into a deep slumber, blissfully unaware that his country was at war or that this would be the last time he'd sleep in a bed for nearly four years.

2

Paradise Lost

The sky was still pitch-black shortly after 5 AM on December 8, when General Brereton's staff car pulled up to One Calle Victoria in Manila's old Walled City. No more than twenty minutes had passed since Brereton's angry outburst had awakened Lieutenant Hibbs, and the FEAF commander's nerves were still as taut as a steel spring. He slammed the car door behind him and hurried up a set of stone steps to the rambling wooden building housing USAFFE headquarters, where General MacArthur's chief of staff, General Richard K. Sutherland, was waiting.

"So the bastards have hit us," Brereton said, breathing heavily. "I need to see MacArthur right away. I want to mount all available B-17s at Clark Field for missions already assigned against Jap bases on Formosa."

"I agree that we need to act quickly," Sutherland replied, "so go ahead with your preparations, but you'll have to get MacArthur's approval before mounting any attacks. He's in conference now, but as soon as he's out, I'll ask him to authorize daylight missions."

Brereton felt his agitation growing. "Okay," he said, "but tell him we've got to get these planes on their way as soon as possible after sunup if we're going to have any hope of hitting the Japs before they hit our bases here."

He told Sutherland that he'd check back shortly for MacArthur's decision. Meanwhile, Brereton's first priority was to get the B-17s at Clark Field fueled and airborne by first light—not to prepare for the offensive action he was urging but for their own protection.

At about 6:30 AM, still having no idea what the earlier commotion outside his quarters had been about, Lieutenant Hibbs stepped out hesitantly into the morning, shielding his eyes against the light. He was freshly shaved and showered and had managed to eat a light breakfast of coffee and sliced mango, but he was still feeling the aftereffects of the night before.

He suppressed a yawn as he slipped behind the steering wheel of his old Chevrolet sedan. Then he pulled out of the parking area beside his apartment building and navigated his way through the quiet streets of Manila toward his Second Battalion's bivouac site fifteen minutes away on the southern outskirts of the city and a few stone's throws from the runways of Nichols Field.

Nichols was the largest pursuit plane base in the Philippines and one of five major military airfields in various stages of development across southern Luzon. The others included Nielson, a pursuit base adjacent to Nichols that also served as home for FEAF headquarters; Clark, where most of the vaunted B-17 bombers were concentrated; Iba, another pursuit base west of Clark; and Del Carmen, a primitive new facility still under construction south of Clark.

The Third, 17th, and 21st Pursuit Squadrons with a combined total of about fifty new P-40Es, the Army Air Corps's most modern fighter aircraft, were based at Nichols. But some of the planes had arrived in crates only three or four days earlier, and none was yet considered fully operational. In some cases, their .50-caliber wing guns had been installed and bore-sighted but not yet test-fired, partly because of a critical shortage of ammunition. In others, the P-40s' hydraulic charging systems had been deactivated in the process of armoring the planes, rendering their guns inoperable. Complicating matters further was the fact that few of the pilots assigned to the new planes had had more than a couple of hours' training in formation flying or interception techniques.

Being a surgeon in an infantry battalion, Hibbs had little intimate knowledge of these problems, of course, nor of the numerous other shortages and mechanical flaws faced by American pursuit squadrons in the Philippines. To Hibbs's casual eye, the U.S. planes looked sleek, well armed, and powerful. He would never have guessed, for instance, that the neat rows of P-35A Buffalos lined up at Nichols and other fields—and which the P-40Es were eventually intended to replace—were already classified as obsolete and "unsuitable for combat" or that some of their pilots caustically referred to them as "flying cordwood."

Many unpalatable truths about the U.S. military presence in the Pacific would manifest themselves before this day was over, not only to Hibbs but to every other American serviceman stationed there. The most stunning of these truths leaped out at the young medical officer as he paused at a downtown street corner and glanced out the car window at a news vendor waving a morning paper. When Hibbs saw the blaring black headline that filled the front page, his breath caught in his throat like a stone:

HAWAII BOMBED—WAR!

He blinked for an instant in disbelief, then pressed down hard on the accelerator, sending the old Chevy streaking away on squalling tires. A wave of nausea convulsed his midsection, and it had nothing to do with the gin-and-tonics he'd consumed the night before.

My God, he thought. *What a sneaky way to start a war! Can this really be happening?*

When Hibbs reached 31st Regiment headquarters, he encountered conflicting reports on the seriousness of the situation, but he went directly to the weapons racks that were open to all troops, including medics, and armed himself with a .38 Smith & Wesson revolver.

Later, at the bivouac area, he saw men frantically digging foxholes, and Major Lloyd Moffit, the stocky, balding commander of the Second Battalion, came running toward him with a grim look on his face.

"You're now a captain, Hibbs," Moffit said. "As of this morning, there's a war on, and all company grade officers are promoted one grade."

Nearby, First Sergeant Joe Wilson, who was handing out collapsible shovels, shook his head and shrugged. "Better start diggin' a hole for yourself, *Captain*," he said. "Promotion or not, the Nips are likely to be here any time now!"

Sixty miles north of Manila at Clark Field, Lieutenant Edgar Whitcomb, assigned as navigator of B-17 No. 87, was having breakfast and listening to his fellow officers in the 19th Bomb Group joking about a "silly rumor" that the Japanese had bombed Pearl Harbor. To a man, they refused to believe it.

"It didn't make sense to us that the Japs should attack Pearl Harbor and leave Clark Field unharmed," Whitcomb would later recall. "Also, if it *was* true, why hadn't we received official word of it? Why weren't we on our way to bomb Formosa? No, we decided, it couldn't be true."

Yet a short time later, an urgent phone call from FEAF headquarters at Nielson Field transformed the silly rumor into cold, hard fact. When it did, the Flying Fortresses parked in neat rows at Clark, the largest, best-equipped U.S. bomber base in the Far East, took off in a maelstrom of confusion and chaos. In the crews' haste to keep their planes from becoming sitting ducks, Lieutenant Whitcomb, who'd been delayed while running an errand for Lieutenant Ed Green, his pilot, was left on the ground.

"Hey!" he yelled at a ground crewman when he realized that his B-17 was gone. "What the hell happened to my plane?"

"It took off with only three engines turning," the enlisted man said, shaking his head. "Damndest thing I ever saw—P-35s, P-40s, and B-17s all taking off at once. Don't see how they kept from crashing into each other."

Whitcomb piled back into his jeep and drove to 19th Bomb Group headquarters. As he ran through the door, he almost collided with his friend, Lieutenant Croxton.

"What the hell's happening?" Whitcomb demanded.

"We got word that a Jap raid was coming, and everything was ordered off the field," Croxton said.

"Where's Ed Green?"

Croxton pointed skyward. "He took off like a bat out of hell. Guess he's flying around up there somewhere. You know, the crazy thing is, we can't seem to get orders to bomb Formosa."

"Why?" Whitcomb asked with a frown.

"Nobody seems to know," Croxton said.

Ranking high among those who didn't know was General Lewis Brereton. At 7:15 AM, when he returned anxiously to MacArthur's headquarters, General Sutherland's entire demeanor seemed to have undergone a drastic change.

"The General hasn't responded to your request," Sutherland said, his tone cool and aloof. "Until he does, you're not to take any offensive action."

By now, Brereton was unable to conceal his irritation. "Look, I want to see the General myself," he said, his voice rising a couple of octaves. "I want to talk to him directly about this situation. Is there someone with him now?"

"No, he's alone in his office, but he's not seeing anyone at the moment. I'll go ask him about it."

Sutherland disappeared through the door to MacArthur's inner office, but he returned in less than a minute. "The General says no," he said. "Don't make the first overt act."

Brereton stared at Sutherland for a moment in disbelief. Then he exploded. "Damn it, wasn't the bombing of Pearl Harbor an overt act? Can't the General acknowledge that we're at war?"

"You're to maintain a defensive stance until further notice," Sutherland told him icily. "I doubt that you have sufficient information on targets on Formosa to justify offensive operations at this time, anyway. Your instructions are to have your people remain on alert and await further orders."

Cursing under his breath, Brereton stormed out. By 8 AM, he was at his Nielson Field headquarters, where, according to observers, "his face was pale and his jaw hard" as he broke the bad news to his staff.

Less than half an hour later, a formation of seventeen Japanese Type 97 heavy bombers, led by Captain Ryosuke Motomura and flying at 13,000 feet, arrived over Camp John Hay, a U.S. Army outpost near the resort town of Baguio on Lingayen Gulf in the center of Luzon's west coast. During the 145-mile flight southward along the coastline, Motomura had been holding his breath, expecting to be challenged at any moment by American fighters. Now he felt a surge of relief because none had appeared.

At approximately 8:25 AM, on Motomura's signal, the planes unleashed scores of 220-pound bombs—the first of thousands of tons of Japanese high explosives that would fall on Luzon in weeks to come—on Camp Hay's barracks and other installations.

Almost simultaneously, twenty-five other Japanese twin-engine bombers struck the small U.S. airfield at Tuguegarao some sixty miles inland from Luzon's north coast. Like Motomura's group, these pilots had maintained a constant lookout for American pursuit planes, fully expecting to be intercepted but encountering no opposition whatsoever. As they looked down, they were chagrined, however, to discover that their target consisted of little more than two intersecting—and vacant—runways. Not a single U.S. plane could be seen, and there was no evidence of other military installations or activity.

Following orders from their leader, Captain Kiyosato Goto, the pilots dumped their bombs anyway, blowing numerous holes in both unoccupied runways, then veering north toward their base at Kato on Formosa.

At least two key factors may explain why the initial enemy air strikes on Luzon happened to occur against such obscure, low-value targets. The first was a Japanese intelligence report that General MacArthur was attending a USAFFE retreat at Camp Hay. If the report had been accurate, Motomura's raiders might have been able to kill America's top commander in the Far East while he was there, but MacArthur was many miles away at his Manila headquarters at the time.

The second factor—one beyond the control of the Japanese—was a heavy fog that blanketed many of their major airfields on Formosa, forcing indefinite postponement of missions originally scheduled to begin at daylight that morning.

(A third Japanese air attack on Philippine targets—and the earliest of the three—had been carried out at 6 AM on December 8 by thirteen bombers and six fighters, all from the aircraft carrier *Ryujo*, against an airstrip at Davao on Mindanao. A hangar, some gasoline storage tanks, and the field's radio station were damaged. But, again, the results were disappointing because no American planes were at the field.)

With their bomb bays empty, the Baguio raiders executed a wide right turn and streaked west over Lingayen Gulf, then north again along the Luzon coastline, retracing the route they had taken to their target. They spotted no U.S. planes, and all seventeen raiders returned unblemished from the attack.

As they exited Philippine airspace, approximately six hours had passed since the first Pearl Harbor report had been received at U.S. headquarters in Manila. The airwaves were filled with radio reports of mysterious aircraft allegedly approaching various points on Luzon—including Clark Field, where ground troops were rousted out to contest a feared attack by Japanese paratroopers. Aloft, cruising P-40s searched fruitlessly for the reported enemy planes but found only circling B-17s instead.

Meanwhile, at Nielson Field, General Brereton continued to wait for MacArthur's approval to take offensive action against Japan.

It was 9:45 AM before the heavy fog over Formosa lifted sufficiently for the scores of Japanese attack aircraft earmarked for raids on the Philippines to be cleared for takeoff. As he awaited his turn on the flight line at the controls of Zero fighter V-135, Flight Seaman First Class Masa-aki Shimakawa was relieved that the long wait to get airborne was almost over. Yet he was also apprehensive, even pessimistic, about what lay ahead.

Like the other pilots in his eight-plane squadron, Shimakawa had purposely left his parachute harness behind on the ground. None of them wanted to risk being captured if they had to bail out over enemy territory. If the worst happened, they much preferred to die with their planes, and they'd been warned that up to 90 percent of them weren't expected to return alive from their mission against Clark Field.

I'm in the hands of fate now, Shimakawa told himself.

At almost precisely the same time that Shimakawa and his comrades were taking off from Tainan Naval Air Base on Formosa, the all clear sirens were sounding at Clark and other principal U.S. bases, and the extreme tension that had characterized the morning thus far was easing a little.

At 10 AM, from his office at Nielson Field, a still fuming General Brereton had put in another call to General Sutherland, once more urging immediate offensive action by the 19th Bomb Group's B-17s.

"If Clark Field gets taken out by a Japanese attack," he warned, "the FEAF will be out of business offensively."

Sutherland's response, however, remained the same as before, and it left Brereton more incensed than ever.

"In case we ever get permission to strike back at the Japs," he told Colonel Eugene Eubank, commander of the 19th Bomb Group, by phone, "I want you to get your group bombed-up and ready for a mission to Formosa at the earliest possible moment."

"I know how you feel, sir, and I feel the same way," said Eubank, "but I don't think it's wise to load the bombs just yet. It could be dangerous to have fully loaded B-17s on the ground if the Japs should attack before we can leave."

Brereton sighed. "I guess you're right," he said. "Okay then, focus on preparations for that three-plane photo reconnaissance mission over southern Formosa that Sutherland's finally approved."

Surprisingly, however, at 10:14 AM—exactly fourteen minutes after Brereton had hung up from calling Sutherland—the phone on the FEAF commander's desk rang, and he found himself talking to General MacArthur in person for the first time that day.

"If you feel offensive action is in order, Lewis, the decision is yours to make," MacArthur said, countermanding Sutherland's recent order in a single sentence.

Brereton called his staff together immediately, and by 10:45 AM, a plan of attack had been developed and approved by Brereton, who insisted that the first mission against Formosa be carried out before the end of the day. Two squadrons of B-17s loaded with 100- and 300-pound bombs would attack airfields on southern Formosa "before darkness today," according to Brereton's order. Meanwhile, the two B-17 squadrons at Del Monte Field on Mindanao would be moved to Clark under cover of darkness "at the earliest practicable moment" to prepare for a follow-up raid the next morning.

"Let's go after the bastards and give 'em hell," Brereton told his staff as the meeting broke up.

Around 11:30 AM, after flying in circles for several hours, the 19th Bomb Group's B-17s returned to Clark to refuel and—their crews hoped—to take on loads of bombs for the anticipated strikes against Formosa. While these operations were under way, the fliers parked their planes in orderly rows and took a break for lunch.

Some fifteen minutes later, personnel in the Air Warning Center at Nielson Field in the suburbs of Manila found themselves deluged with incoming reports of unidentified planes crossing the northwest Luzon coast. Coming as thick and fast as they did, the rash of reports alarmed Colonel Alexander Campbell, the officer in charge. The planes seemed to be heading directly for Clark Field.

Campbell tried sending a Teletype warning to Clark but was unable to get through. He next tried a radio message, but the Clark radio operator was apparently out to lunch. In desperation, he grabbed the phone on his desk and managed to reach a junior officer at the airfield, who agreed to relay the message to the base commander's office as soon as possible.

At 11:56 AM, air raid sirens sounded at every military airfield on Luzon—except Clark. By 12:10 PM, all fighter aircraft at all other bases were either airborne or on full alert with engines idling and pilots in their cockpits. At Clark, by contrast, eighteen freshly refueled P-40s of the 20th Pursuit Squadron stood in silent formation at the edge of the field while their pilots milled about nearby awaiting orders to take off. Of these, only three would manage to get airborne. The rest would be engulfed by bombs and machine gun bullets before they could leave the ground.

"We were so naive, and we felt so safe," recalled PFC Henry H. King of the Seventh Materiel Squadron, who'd been stationed at Clark Field since arriving in the Philippines in October 1941. "The atmosphere at Clark was so relaxed that when I heard about the attack on Pearl Harbor, my first thought was, *Thank God I'm not there.*"

King, a native of Graham, Texas, was finishing his lunch in one of the Clark mess halls, along with some mechanics and B-17 crewmembers, when they heard the voice of Don Bell, a popular announcer on a Manila radio station, as he began his regular 12:30 newscast.

"We have no official confirmation at this time," Bell was saying, "but we've received reports that Japanese planes are bombing Clark Field at this very moment and inflicting heavy damage. Please stand by for further details."

The men in the mess hall looked at each other. Some frowned, then grinned and rolled their eyes. "We just laughed," said King, "and went on eating."

At about this same juncture, Lieutenant Ed Whitcomb, the navigator left behind when his plane took off without him early that morning, finished his own lunch and headed back toward 19th Group headquarters, where he'd been preparing map reproductions for the pending photorecon mission to Formosa.

"The sun was high in the heavens," he recalled. "The day was bright and clear, and everything at Clark Field appeared perfectly normal. It was as if the Japs didn't even know Clark existed, but that was impossible to believe."

Formosa's only three hours away, he thought. *Why do we have to waste time taking pictures on a reconnaissance mission? We know where their damn bases are. Why aren't we bombing them right now? Are we just waiting around for them to bomb us first?*

Gripped by growing uneasiness, Whitcomb reached the two-story wooden building that housed his headquarters shortly after 12:30 PM and found Colonel Eubank, the 19th Group commander, closeted in his office with several squadron leaders and operations officers. Noticing that his own pilot, Lieutenant Green, was among them, Whitcomb edged closer to the door, hoping to learn what was going on.

At that instant, he heard a shrill warning shout from another officer at the rear of the building:

"Here they come! Here they come!"

Realizing instantly who "they" were, Whitcomb whirled toward the back door of the building, rushed outside and down the steps, and made a wild dive into the nearest slit trench twenty feet away. Everyone else from the headquarters building was running, too—far more shelter seekers than the recently dug trenches could accommodate. Whitcomb felt bodies piling on top of him, jamming his face into the sand in the bottom of the trench and crushing the wind out of him.

As he struggled to free himself, he heard strange, crackling noises filling the air above him, sounding "like dry boards being broken." An ear-splitting explosion rocked the ground beneath him, followed by another. And another. And another . . .

Then everything went black.

PFC Victor Mapes, one of a group of 14th Bomber Squadron ground crewmen staring at the skies above Clark at that moment, saw considerably more than Lieutenant Whitcomb.

"Coming in over the mountains from the China Sea," he recalled "were these two beautiful 'V' formations of twenty-seven planes each."

Someone in Mapes's group speculated that the fifty-four approaching aircraft belonged to the U.S. Navy. Then Mapes spotted the flaming red "meatball" insignia on the undersides of their wings.

"It's an attack!" he yelled. "They're Japanese!'"

Seconds later, Mapes saw enemy bombs "walking up the runway" toward him—one of them hitting perilously close—as he and the others made a mad scramble for cover in a cement latrine. They cowered there while the raiders' direct hits gouged huge holes in the field and coughed up clouds of smoke, dirt, and debris.

The bombers had scarcely departed when thirty-seven Mitsubishi Type O fighters—soon to be universally known as Zeros—streaked in at treetop level. Their stuttering machine guns caused even greater damage than the bombs to the parked B-17s as their tracer rounds chewed into the big bombers' gas tanks, and they burst into flames.

"I saw a guy throw his shoe at a Jap plane," Mapes said. "Another was firing his .45. Everything was a holocaust. It seemed like it went on forever."

In the eerie silence following the explosions, Mapes and the others could hear a Manila radio station playing soft music as if nothing had happened. "Then the wounded started coming in," he said. "Most were cut up and bloody. All of them should've been in the hospital, but some stayed to fight the fires and carry the dead.

"When we limped back to our barracks, our clothes were hanging from the rafters. There was a big hole where the Japs had dropped one right through the roof. We saw a man in his '38 Ford lying there, shot. I guess he'd been trying to get off the base. Then there was a dead pilot in the cockpit of a burning B-17. You could hardly see him for the flames."

PFC Edward Jackfert, a mechanic in the 19th Bomb Group's 28th Bomb Squadron, had been working inside a hangar all morning on one of the obsolete B-18 bombers being refitted as cargo planes. At about 12:30 PM, he and several others decided to stop for lunch. They'd just walked outside when they heard the low roar of many approaching aircraft engines.

"None of us had made any plans about what to do in case of an attack," Jackfert recalled, "and the only air raid siren we had had to be cranked by hand, so we had no advance warning at all. At first, in my confusion, I started back toward the hangar where my airplane was—which was about the most foolish thing I ever did in my life. Then the first bomb hit about 300 yards away, and I ran back the other way, looking for some kind of shelter."

None of the recently dug slit trenches around Clark's perimeters were close enough to reach, but Jackfert spotted a concrete culvert in a nearby ditch and crawled inside as bomb blasts jarred the ground.

"One bomb hit our barracks and killed our adjutant," he recalled, "and our officers quarters were heavily damaged, too. But the worst thing was our planes. We lost a total of thirty-eight aircraft in a matter of minutes."

No man at Clark found himself in a more potentially deadly spot than Staff Sergeant J. S. Gray of the 27th Bomb Group's 454th Ordnance Squadron as the Japanese bombers began their attack.

"I was sitting right out in the middle of the field with five truck-loads of bombs," Gray recalled a half-century later. "I was in charge of all that ammunition, and we were getting ready to put the bombs on our planes and send them back up, but the Japanese caught us on the ground."

After Gray and others in his unit had put considerable distance between themselves and the bomb-laden trucks, he watched in fear and fascination as the raiders methodically destroyed the neat rows of American planes but totally ignored a dummy B-17 constructed mostly of bamboo.

"The Japs got every one of our real planes," he said, "and left that dummy—which looked exactly like the real B-17s—untouched."

Fifteen-year-old Private Joe Alexander was standing outdoors with other members of the 440 Aviation Ordnance Squadron when the first explosions rocked the field. Like Sergeant Gray, Alexander had also been waiting to start loading 300-pound bombs into the bellies of the B-17s. But fortunately he and his comrades were still a considerable distance from the planes—and the bombs to be loaded—when the raid started.

"Guys were running off in all directions, and I was out in the open with almost no cover at all and not knowing which way to go," Alexander remembered many years later. "The only protection I could see anywhere near was a very small tree, and I ran as hard as I could and jumped behind it. I lay there hugging the trunk of that little tree like it was my best friend in the whole world. At the time, I guess it was. There were pieces of planes and buildings flying all around me, and then the Zeros came in low, strafing everything in sight. I tried to lie totally still so maybe they'd think I was dead, but it was still a miracle I didn't get hit."

The carnage went on for more than an hour with the Zeros making pass after pass in an almost leisurely fashion. When it was over, the toll at Clark stood at fifty-five dead and more than 100 wounded. Of the seventeen B-17s based at Clark, only three survived. Fifty-three P-40s at Clark and other fields were destroyed that day, along with thirty other U.S. aircraft. The Japanese raiders lost seven fighter planes.

Even before the raid ended, a stream of wounded from Clark began showing up at the hospital at Fort Stotsenburg, adjoining the airfield. But the smallish facility was totally inadequate to handle the bloodbath, and by afternoon many of the wounded had been transferred to Sternberg Hospital in Manila.

General Jonathan M. Wainwright, commander of the Army's North Luzon Force, who maintained his headquarters at Stotsenburg, dodged stray pieces of shrapnel as he watched the destruction at Clark from the Stotsenburg parade ground with a feeling of sheer helplessness.

As soon as the all clear sounded, Wainwright ordered every available truck in the fort's fleet to get to Clark in a hurry to pick up and transport the wounded. It was obvious that there weren't enough ambulances to handle the job. Then Wainwright called for his horse, and accompanied by his aide, Lieutenant Thomas Dooley, the longtime cavalry officer rode over to Clark to see if there was anything he could do to help.

There wasn't much, and what he saw at the airfield merely added to the sick and sinking feeling in his gut.

When the bombing and strafing finally ended, Ed Whitcomb extricated himself from the overcrowded trench, cleared the sand from his eyes, nose, mouth, and ears, and stared across Clark Field at scenes of abject horror.

The bombing pattern laid down by the Japanese had started with the mess hall where Whitcomb had eaten lunch, then spread diagonally across the field to the southeast. An undetermined number of officers had been killed by the direct hit on the mess hall, and the bodies of others were strewn over the field and along the flight line.

"I couldn't see even one plane that hadn't been hit," he said, "and many were still blazing furiously. Our fighters had been knocked down as they tried to take off. Crews standing by their planes were destroyed along with the ships."

Yawning craters had been blasted in the wreckage-littered runways, and virtually every building within Whitcomb's field of vision lay in ruins. Huge clouds of oily smoke obscured the sky and blotted out the sun. Nearby, Colonel Eubank stood silent and slack-jawed as his eyes swept over the devastation.

Whitcomb found the charred, unrecognizable bodies of four of his crewmates lying beside what was left of B-17 No. 87. A fifth member of the crew, Lieutenant George Berkowitz, who had jokingly asked at breakfast that morning for someone to tell him there was a war on "so I can start doing what soldiers are supposed to do in war," had lost a leg to a large chunk of shrapnel but was still alive.

At 2:30 PM, a meeting of all officers of the Second Battalion, 31st Infantry, was called by battalion CO Major Lloyd Moffit. His voice was calm but to the point as the small group of officers sat in a circle on the ground at a bivouac area near Nichols Field.

"Clark Field was bombed two hours ago, and the Japs are expected here momentarily," he said. "The regiment's in the field to stay, so each of you needs to go to Manila, gather up your personal belongings, take care of your personal business, and get back here on the double—before the Japs do if you can. Any questions? End of meeting."

Moments later, medical officer Ralph Hibbs heard his friend, now Captain Dwight Hunkins, commanding H Company, Second Battalion, yell at him from the driver's seat of an open command car. "I'm headed for Manila," he said. "Climb in and let's get going."

At the courtyard of the strangely silent San Carlos Apartments, where Hibbs had lived for the past five months, he found his number one houseboy, Dominador, standing in a doorway.

"What's going on, sir?" the Filipino asked. "Tell me what to do."

"It's war now," Hibbs told him. "You've got to get the hell out of the city and go to the hills. You've got to do it now."

"But what about the furniture, the table service, golf clubs, liquor . . . ?"

"It's all yours. Just get your wife and get out of this mess."

Dominador burst into tears as he followed Hibbs from room to room, begging to be allowed to "do something."

Hibbs emptied his wallet of all the pesos it contained and gave them to Dominador. "Divide these with Rosita," he said, referring to the laundress, then handed the houseboy the keys to the old Chevy, his most prized possession. "God will protect you while we kick the shit out of these dirty bastards," Hibbs said as he climbed back into the command car with Hunkins. "Goodbye. God bless you."

As Hunkins drove away, Hibbs realized that he was saying goodbye to a lot of things that would be terribly missed. There'd be no more evenings at the Baroque Bar at the Army Navy Club, no more rolling the dice for drinks or eating from the free fifty-foot buffet. No more dancing the night away with beautiful Pilar Campos at the Manila Hotel. No more leisurely rounds of golf at the manicured Wack Wack course. That much was for sure.

He wondered where Pilar was at this moment. He wondered what would happen to her—and to him.

Hours later, as dusk descended over the ruins of Clark, the men who had called the big base home wandered dazed through the wreckage. Adding to the confusion, the planes of the 17th Pursuit Squadron, based at Nichols Field, were ordered to move to Clark before dark for fear of similar devastation at Nichols that night.

Second Lieutenant John Poston, a pilot in the 17th, described the scenes that confronted his squadron when it arrived: "Everything was confusion. The hangars were still burning, and every once in a while a lot of stored ammunition would go off. Automobiles, trucks, and planes were wrecked and burning all over the place. All the wounded had been taken away, but the dead were still lying where they fell."

At Iba Field, due west of Clark, the raiders had paused long enough to virtually wipe out the Third Pursuit Squadron based there. "They got a few planes off, but most of them, including pilots and support personnel, were killed or wounded on the ground," said Lieutenant Poston.

"The question of why our bombers weren't sent on a mission before they were destroyed on the ground has never been satisfactorily answered," a still troubled Whitcomb would recall decades later. "Our generals and leaders committed some of the greatest errors possible for military men by letting themselves be taken so totally by surprise.

"For reasons only he knew, MacArthur wanted the Japs to strike the Philippines first, before we struck them, and Washington was so mesmerized by MacArthur that they believed he was infallible. But there was also plenty of blame to go around. Our intelligence was terrible. None of us at Clark took the Japanese threat seriously enough. We had no idea that Japan was capable of sending fifty-four heavy bombers and thirty-seven Zeros against us on December 8."

And that was only the beginning. Over the next two days, every major U.S. naval and military installation would feel the wrath of the Japanese aerial juggernaut.

The attackers had mostly ignored Nichols Field on December 8, but Captain John S. Coleman Jr., commander of the 27th Materiel Squadron and the officer in direct charge of ground defenses at Nichols, realized that the base was living on borrowed time. During the confused, frantic hours after the Pearl Harbor attack, he tried to take maximum advantage of the brief calm before the inevitable storm.

Coleman, a 1929 graduate of Texas A&M College, had sailed from San Francisco on August 28, 1941, aboard the *President Pierce*, leaving behind a ten-year-old daughter, a six-year-old son, and his wife, Ethel, who was "practically sick" with fear that he would never return.

Coleman tried hard to keep his thoughts from dwelling too much on his family. He missed them terribly, but he was indescribably thankful that Ethel couldn't see him now.

Like other matériel squadrons assigned to various Army Air Corps bases, the 27th had a wide variety of responsibilities. They ranged from procuring and transporting many types of supplies to preparing and serving meals to assembling new P-40s that arrived from the States in crates to maintaining and expanding the airfield's physical facilities. Other work details from the 27th were doing similar jobs at Clark Field, Del Monte Field on Mindanao, and an auxiliary airstrip under construction at Lipa on Luzon.

"We had twenty shoeshine boys on duty that morning [December 8], and I put them all to digging slit trenches near our squadron headquarters," Coleman recalled. "I knew trenches would be of more help than shined shoes."

Expecting Nichols to be bombed no later than the night of the

8th, Coleman moved his men to an area about three miles northwest of the airfield, where they could sleep in relative safety, and his cooks could go about their job of preparing food without dodging bombs or strafing Zeros. Coleman himself, however, elected to remain at the officers quarters on the base.

At 1:30 AM on December 9, the air raid sirens blared at Nichols, sending all personnel rushing to their assigned posts. But half an hour later, the all clear sounded, and everyone went back to bed. Then, at about four o'clock, the sirens shrieked again across the blacked-out airfield, followed almost immediately by the sound of heavy motors approaching from the west.

Coleman and a fellow officer jumped into one of the newly dug slit trenches moments before bombs began falling on the officers quarters and in the hangar areas. Seven .50-caliber machine gun emplacements built around the field by Coleman's troops opened fire on the attackers. Fire trucks raced across the field, their sirens wailing. Wounded men began flooding into the base aid station.

After the all clear sounded again, Coleman went back to his room to check out the damage. A bomb had hit squarely on his front porch, riddling everything in the building with shrapnel and blowing the contents of his room into the adjacent quarters. When he investigated further, he made a gruesome discovery.

"I went into the room just south of mine to see if I could find some of my clothes," he recalled, "and I found a headless lieutenant in a sitting position in a chair. Evidently, he'd started to put on his shoes to go to his foxhole because he had one shoe on. The concussion from the bomb apparently snapped off his head."

After full daylight on December 9, Coleman paid a brief visit to base headquarters, located in Nichols's only bomb shelter and about fifty yards from where a platoon of the 27th was digging foxholes and additional machine gun emplacements, to confer with Colonel Bill Maverick, the base commander.

"Just as I stepped out the door to go back to where my men were, I heard a terrible roar," Coleman recalled. "I looked up and counted ninety-six heavy bombers flying at about 21,000 feet. Our anti-aircraft shells were exploding just below them. We just didn't have weapons that were capable of reaching that altitude."

Within the next few minutes, dozens of 500-pound bombs fell on Nichols Field. They set fire to the base's post exchange and the now vacated 27th Materiel barracks, damaged a large water storage tank, and blasted a king-sized hole in the center of Coleman's office. Remarkably, however, none of Nichols's runways was hit, and none of its grounded fighter planes was damaged. Many of the bombs struck along Manila's bay side, causing numerous civilian casualties.

By the end of the day on December 9, every U.S. Army and Army Air Corps base on Luzon had been blasted repeatedly by hundreds of Japanese planes. Yet, in one of the peculiarities of warfare, U.S. Navy facilities in the same area had largely been spared thus far, and the sprawling Cavite Navy Yard on the south shore of Manila Bay had received only a few glancing blows.

All that was about to change, however, with heart-stopping finality.

Before noon on December 10, a radar operator with the Marine Air Warning Unit on the beach near the Luzon town of Batangas picked up a large blip on his screen. It indicated several dozen aircraft approaching Manila Bay from about 120 miles to the southwest. The operator first tried, without success, to notify the Navy radio station at Sangley Point. He then tried to warn Army radio operators on Corregidor, but the information never reached Army headquarters.

Marine PFCs Karl King and Ike Williams were at Cavite that morning with their seabags packed and preparing to leave for Manila to board a ship for the States, where they were scheduled to attend intelligence school.

"Before we could leave our barracks," King recalled, "we heard bombs exploding across the bay as Japanese bombers struck at harbor installations in Manila."

Explosions flared all along the Manila waterfront, but within minutes it became clear that the bombers' primary objective was Cavite itself as fifty-four of them streaked toward the navy yard in their now familiar V formations.

One eyewitness to the attack, seeing brightly flickering objects falling from the planes, was heard to shout, "Look, they're dropping leaflets!"

"Leaflets, hell!" several other onlookers yelled in reply. "Those are bombs! Hit the deck!"

The first wave of attackers approached at about 15,000 feet, low enough to be within range of Cavite's antiaircraft batteries, and realizing this, they veered away to regroup. The second wave released their bombs prematurely, and they exploded in the bay short of their targets. But once the raiders climbed above 20,000 feet, they were impervious to the American batteries, and they hung around indefinitely with calamitous results.

"The bombers continued their bombing runs unmolested," said King, who watched the destruction helplessly but in no immediate danger. Cavite's gunners accounted for only one attacking plane and it was a dive-bomber that swooped in low enough to be hit by .50-caliber machine guns. Not a single P-40 appeared to challenge the raiders. Dozens of the American fighters were now useless junk, and those that remained flyable were assigned to provide air cover for their own bases. Cavite was on its own.

The raid lasted for almost two hours. When the enemy planes finally departed, the massive fires they left behind could be seen from Manila thirty miles away, and they would continue to burn for days. The U.S. submarines *Sealion* and *Seadragon*, undergoing repairs at Cavite, both took direct hits that killed one officer and wounded several. One of the most spectacular explosions occurred when a bomb struck a warehouse containing more than 200 torpedoes. The fires also reached a small-arms warehouse, where stored ammunition exploded in sporadic bursts far into the night.

Nearly 1,000 civilian workers at the navy yard were killed in the raid, and streets around the base were littered with bodies. The only Marine to lose his life, however, was PFC Thomas Wetherington, the first of many to die in defense of the Philippines.

That evening, Admiral Hart reported to Washington that Cavite—which only that morning had been the largest and best equipped U.S. naval facility in the Far East—was finished as a viable American base. Even if some relief ships miraculously managed to reach Cavite, he said, they could expect to find neither supplies nor services there. The destruction was that complete.

The only possible bright spot was that Hart had already sent most of the surface ships in his little Asiatic Fleet out of Philippine waters to temporary safety in seas to the south. Two of his cruisers, the flagship *Houston* and the decrepit old *Marblehead*, were on their way to the Java Sea and Borneo, and the light cruiser *Boise* was bound for Australia. All but two of the fleet's twenty-nine submarines were at sea at various points around the archipelago and also avoided the Cavite debacle. Lieutenant John Buckeley ordered the six fast boats of his Patrol Torpedo Squadron Three out into Manila Bay where their speed, maneuverability, and small size made them less vulnerable to Japanese dive-bombers that zoomed down to within 200 feet of the water. The ancient four-stack destroyer *John D. Ford*, anchored near Cavite, was somehow missed by the raiders and escaped that night to the Sulu Sea.

As Buckeley's squadron zigged and zagged, he observed the perfectly shaped V of enemy bombers circling Cavite "like a flock of well-disciplined buzzards" and wondered why none of the Army's P-40s were there to intercept them. "I hadn't heard anything about the destruction of Clark Field and the other airfields," he recalled later. "All I knew was that the P-40s never showed."

In their first crack at enemy targets, the PT boats used their .50-caliber guns to send one of the raiders splashing into the bay, but it was insignificant consolation for the damage the planes inflicted.

Roughly ten kilometers away, Lieutenant Ralph Hibbs had a panoramic view of Cavite's doom from "a seat on the fifty-yard line" in his foxhole near Nichols Field.

"I could see the bomb bay doors open and the bombs glistening in the sun," he would write decades afterward. "[At first] they seemed to tumble wildly. [But] soon, as if on command, like puppets, they lined up in the sky in perfect formation, plunging earthward with a spine-chilling crescendo."

Long after the sound and fury had ebbed away, a reflective Hibbs was still struck by incredulity at what had happened to American forces in the Philippines over a period of less than sixty hours.

"We had just witnessed the complete and final destruction of our primary naval and air bases in the islands," he said, his frustration and disgust boiling over. "I thought that the destruction of just one airfield, not the whole damn air force, would have been sufficient. A second Pearl Harbor was unnecessary. The 'don't shoot first' policy ruined us. No counterattack was ever carried off, and also, according to a Navy file, half of Cavite could have been saved with a good fire department."

Amid the confusion of the raid, First Lieutenant James W. Keene, commanding D Company of Cavite's Marine contingent, located PFCs King and Williams to remind them of their orders to report for stateside transportation.

"You don't want to miss your ship," Keene said, "assuming it's still afloat. You need to get out of here as soon as you can."

When the bombing stopped, the pair located a Filipino taxi that was still in running condition, tossed their seabags inside, and headed for Asiatic Fleet headquarters in Manila's dockside Marsman Building. As the taxi picked its way past the corpses, debris, and roaring flames of Cavite, dump trucks and a bulldozer began the job of collecting the hundreds of dead and temporarily depositing them in a common grave.

At the bomb-damaged Marsman Building, Williams and King found only a skeleton crew on duty in the flag offices. When they inquired about their ship, the *Chaumont*, a radioman broke the bad news.

"Looks like you're shit out of luck, boys," he said. "The *Chaumont*'s been diverted south to Australia, and she won't be coming back. If you're gonna go stateside, you may have to swim."

"Well, do you know where we can find our CO, Colonel Clement?" Williams asked.

"Yeah, he's gone to Olongapo on Bataan to meet with Colonel Howard," the radioman said. "He probably won't be back for several days. Hell, the way things are going, he may never be back."

Williams and King looked at each other and shook their heads. Then the two crestfallen Marines hefted their seabags and turned away. Obviously, there was no one around to give them orders, and they could only guess when there might be. So what were they supposed to do now?

"After discussing the matter," King recalled many years later, "we decided the only logical thing to do was go back to our apartment and finish off our supply of San Miguel beer while we mourned our lost chance to get back to the States."

By the afternoon of December 10, Fort Stotsenburg had still suffered only minimal damage in comparison to other major U.S. bases. The Japanese had bombed the stables there, killing or wounding several cavalry horses. The fort's ice plant had been knocked out of commission, and there were a few bomb craters in the parade ground, but General Wainwright's headquarters was virtually untouched.

As the day wore on, however, the general received unsettling reports that the fight for the Philippines had entered a dangerous new phase. Japanese amphibious assault troops had come ashore at three points on Luzon—the first at the little village of Aparri on the north coast of the island, the second at Vigan on the west coast, and a third at Legaspi on the Bicol Peninsula at the northeastern tip of Luzon.

This was not an invasion in strength, with only a brigade-size force of about 3,000 landing at Aparri, about 2,000 at Vigan, and fewer still at Legaspi. The worse news was that the invaders had met almost no opposition from Philippine Army troops, who fled inland in disarray, and that the airfield at Aparri had quickly fallen into enemy hands as had a smaller airstrip near Legaspi. This meant that Japanese planes could now launch air attacks from Philippine soil instead of from distant Formosa or carriers at sea.

The pockets of localized activity by enemy ground troops were too far away to pose an immediate threat to major American installations, and Wainwright was rightly more concerned about the possibility of a much larger invasion against his thinly stretched beach defenses at Lingayen Gulf on Luzon's central west coast. He was convinced that the three small Japanese landings were actually a feint designed to lure him into dividing his already inadequate force at Lingayen, and he decided to drive there on the afternoon of the tenth to check on the disposition of his troops.

He was less than pleased with what he found, and he was even

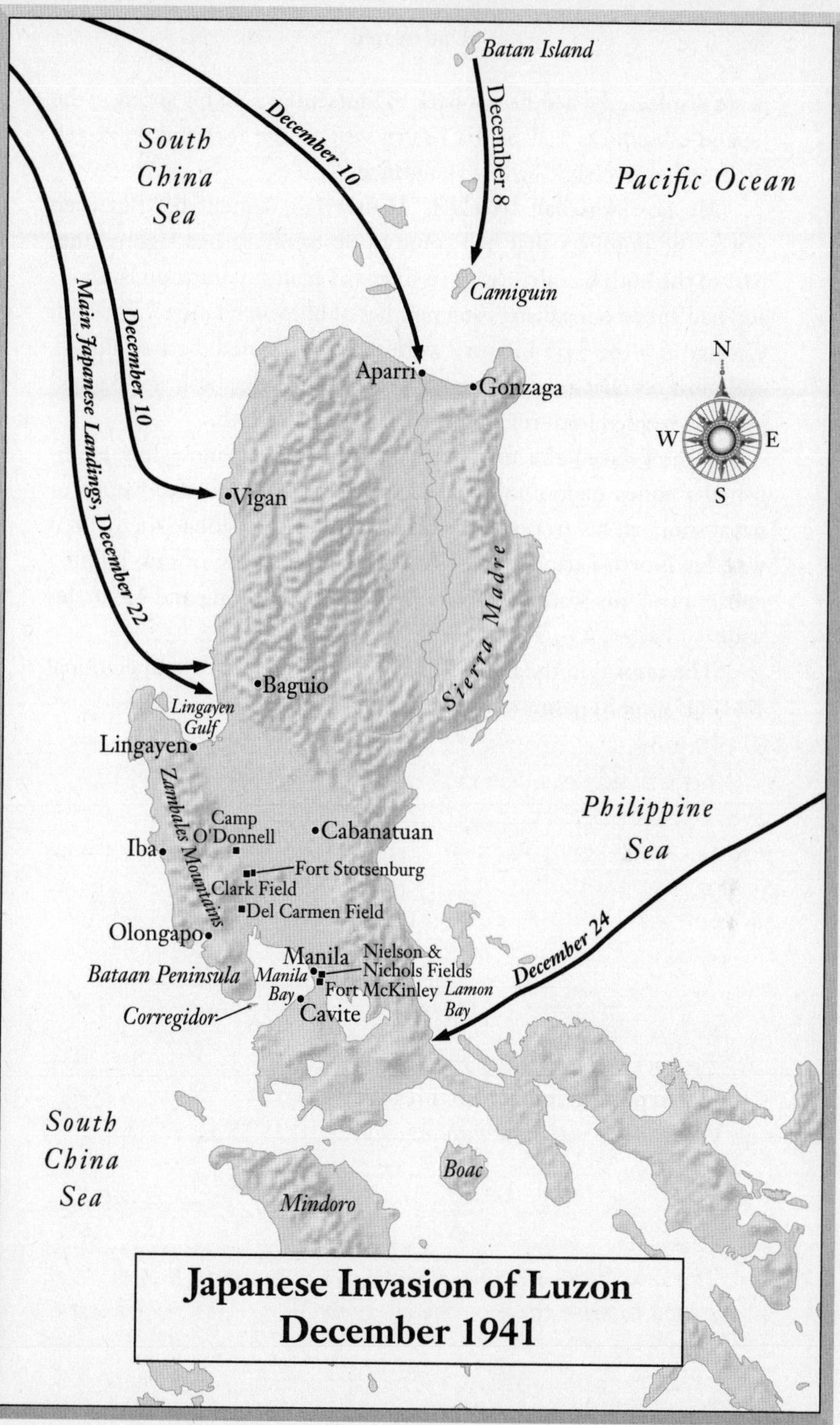
Batan Island
December 8
December 10
South China Sea
Pacific Ocean
Camiguin
December 10
Main Japanese Landings, December 22
Aparri
Gonzaga
N
W
E
S
Vigan
Sierra Madre
Baguio
Lingayen Gulf
Lingayen
Zambales Mountains
Philippine Sea
Camp O'Donnell
Cabanatuan
Iba
Fort Stotsenburg
Clark Field
Del Carmen Field
Olongapo
December 24
Manila
Nielson & Nichols Fields
Bataan Peninsula
Manila Bay
Fort McKinley
Lamon Bay
Corregidor
Cavite
South China Sea
Boac
Mindoro
Japanese Invasion of Luzon
December 1941

more displeased when he got back to Stotsenburg. In his absence, the Japanese bombers had paid a return visit to the fort and corrected their earlier oversight with a vengeance.

"My post was half wrecked," Wainwright lamented. "But even worse, the bombers that had come to Stotsenburg had sighted that part of the 26th Cavalry assigned to guard against paratroop landings and had wiped out a distressing number of horses and men." The 26th Cavalry and the 31st Infantry were the best-trained, best-equipped, and most combat-ready troops at Wainwright's disposal, and he desperately needed both regiments to be at full strength.

He now faced the unhappy facts that the Japanese had established a series of footholds on Luzon, and without effective air or naval support, his troops lacked the strength to dislodge them. As it was, his North Luzon Force—mostly a paper army of raw Filipino conscripts—was scattered over an area 625 miles long and 125 miles wide.

"The rat was in the house," as Wainwright put it. And operational rat traps were in pathetically short supply.

3

A Black-and-Blue Christmas

In the days following the nightmare of December 8–10, American and Filipino troops floundered in uncertainty, and a state of shock seemed to immobilize much of the U.S. command structure. Despite all the years of planning and the belated but frenzied preparations for war, military decision makers on both sides of the Pacific struggled to respond to the Japanese onslaught.

"We knew we were at war, but we didn't know what to do or where to go," said Sergeant Cletis Overton of the 27th Bomb Group. "We knew something was screwed up, and the very idea of our leaders being slipped up on and caught shorthanded made us nervous. We couldn't understand why we weren't on the alert as soon as the Japs bombed Pearl Harbor. Why weren't our pilots ready to go when they hit the Philippines? Why didn't we attack? I never heard any explanation for all that."

While thousands of U.S. troops were sent out on patrols to guard against enemy paratroop attacks that never came, their bases were obliterated by high-level bombers that American antiaircraft guns couldn't reach and Japanese fighter planes that could outrun and outshoot their U.S. counterparts. Personnel at some of the bombed-out airbases took to the hills and refused to return unless they received assurance that the Japanese weren't in control. While General Wainwright concentrated his forces at Lingayen Gulf and the Zambales coast of Luzon—for totally sound military reasons—enemy troops landed at three other points and seized two important airstrips. And when three surviving B-17s tried to attack the invaders, they were swarmed by Japanese Zeros that shot down two of them. The good guys, as the old saying goes, simply couldn't win for losing.

Meanwhile, the stories of American victories that appeared almost daily in stateside newspapers during this period were often gross exaggerations or complete fabrications. One example of such tainted reporting was the celebrated, but utterly false, account of how a B-17 piloted by Captain Colin Kelly of the 14th Bomb Group supposedly sank the Japanese battleship *Haruna* on December 10 off the north coast of Luzon.

Kelly was a heroic young officer whose bomber was riddled by gunfire from a flock of pursuing Zeros as it left the scene of the attempted bombing. After ordering his crew to bail out, Kelly became the first West Pointer to die in combat in World War II when an oxygen tank exploded aboard his plane. Kelly's body was found in the wreckage, yet the fiction persisted for years that he'd purposely crashed his doomed bomber into the Japanese battleship, and he was posthumously awarded the Distinguished Service Cross. Later research showed that the *Haruna* was nowhere near the Philippines that day, and that, in fact, Kelly's bombs had failed to sink *any* Japanese ship.

A perennially tightfisted Congress that had refused throughout the 1930s to appropriate enough money to update a U.S. military still operating with World War I leftovers was a major villain in the disaster that befell the Philippines. And despite mitigating circumstances, a portion of blame rightfully rests with President Roosevelt and his military advisers in Washington. At the urging of British prime minister Winston Churchill, Roosevelt had agreed months earlier to a wartime grand strategy of "Europe First," giving top priority to halting the Nazi blitzkrieg on the other side of the Atlantic and relegating the Japanese Pacific threat to secondary status. Yet during the agonizing weeks when the defenders of Bataan and Corregidor were fighting valiant delaying actions against a vastly superior foe, Roosevelt and his War Department tacitly nurtured the false hope that relief was on its way to the Philippines. To the contrary, no genuine attempt was ever made to resupply or reinforce the garrison there, and, in fact, shipments of vital matériel were already being diverted to Australia even before the outbreak of war.

"There were ships carrying planes and supplies in the convoy with us," said Sergeant J. S. Gray of the 27th Bomb Group, recalling the Pacific voyage that brought him to Manila on November 20, 1941. "But when we were about five days west of Pearl Harbor, the ships that didn't have troops aboard turned south. Some of us stood on deck and watched them turn away, and we wondered where they were going. They were carrying our planes that we were supposed to use against the Japanese. I understand now that they went to Brisbane, Australia, and I guess it was planned that way. We didn't know. We were just peons in the big scheme of things."

Deep-seated disagreement within America's military establishment and the naive nationalism of Philippines president Quezon also played key roles in the chaos that lay ahead for American and Filipino defenders once the rumors of impending hostilities exploded into reality. One War Department faction urged scrapping War Plan Orange, arguing that it was categorically impossible to defend the Philippines or the chain of other U.S. bases in the far western Pacific. For more than three decades, some Army and Navy brass had branded the archipelago as "indefensible against any foe" intent on its conquest. In the late 1920s, well after the development of War Plan Orange, General Johnson Hagood, outgoing commander of the Army's Philippine Department, told President Herbert Hoover: "It is not within the wildest possibility to maintain or to raise in the Philippine Islands a sufficient force to defend it against any probable foe."

A dozen years later, faced with the likelihood of a two-ocean war, a high-ranking U.S. military board favored replacing the current version of War Plan Orange (WPO-3) with what they considered a more realistic alternative called Rainbow Five. Under the new plan, if the United States was drawn into the conflict, its offensive capabilities would be focused on the eastern Atlantic and aid to Great Britain. A strong defense would be aimed at protecting territory in the Western Hemisphere, but defensive needs in the Pacific would be relegated to a backseat until other wartime priorities were met.

This meant that most of the responsibility for defending the Philippines would fall on the Filipinos themselves while the United States and its Allies concentrated their strength against Nazi Germany. And while no one in authority was saying so, it also meant that the Filipino-American garrison, along with other U.S. defensive forces at Wake Island, Guam, and Midway, would, in effect, be declared expendable in the event of a heavy Japanese offensive. For obvious reasons, Rainbow Five was held in closely guarded secrecy, not merely from potential U.S. adversaries but from military personnel being sent into harm's way in the Pacific and America's general public as well.

Even after Rainbow Five was adopted as official War Department strategy, many military leaders continued to support the more hopeful scenario of WPO-3, which envisioned Filipino and American defenders on Bataan and Corregidor holding out for up to six months until a relief force could arrive from Hawaii.

By December 11, 1941, however, Japan held absolute rule over the sea lanes and airways of the western Pacific. The U.S. Pacific Fleet lay in shambles at Pearl Harbor, and America's accumulated airpower west of California had largely ceased to exist.

"The Japs were so far ahead of us in aircraft design that we never really had a chance, but we didn't know that going in," said Iowa-born Tech Sergeant Robert B. Heer, who had aspired to be a flying cadet but ended up as a carpenter with the 19th Bomb Group at Clark Field.

"We laughed at the Japanese pilots and planes," Heer said. "Then the Jap Zeros shot down our P-40s like chunks of firewood, and they caught us flatfooted at Clark because we'd never been taught what to do in case of an actual air raid."

Hence, to military brass in Washington and Hawaii, the odds of American forces being able to rescue or reinforce the Philippines within a six-month period, as outlined in WPO-3, appeared virtually nil. Naval experts estimated that it would take at least two years for the U.S. Navy to fight its way across the Pacific to the Philippines. Meanwhile, on Luzon and Mindanao, direction-deprived U.S. unit commanders could do little but send their soldiers into hiding and cling to the fragile hope that they weren't being abandoned by their government.

Complicating matters was a massive communications breakdown in which USAFFE headquarters and its staff lost touch with troops freshly ousted from established bases and forced into makeshift temporary bivouac areas where they languished with no clear plan of action. Many radar and radio installations were damaged or destroyed. Only public telephone service was available to the military, and it was disrupted in many outlying areas. There was also strong evidence that Japanese fifth columnists had somehow gained control of commercial telegraph service to spread wild scare stories about fictitious landings and mass marches involving tens of thousands of enemy troops and mechanized vehicles.

Under such circumstances, confusion and uncertainty could be expected for a period of hours or even a few days. But in this instance, the malaise was deeper, more contagious, and harder to cure than it should have been. It may have been worsened by the fact that Christmas was approaching, and the troops were lonely, homesick, and demoralized. Whatever the reason, the ill effects spread throughout Manila and across Luzon, and they dragged on for more than two weeks.

Fortunately for the Americans, Lieutenant General Masaharu Homma, commander of Japan's 14th Army, who was under intense pressure from Tokyo to complete the conquest of the Philippines by January 15, 1942, wasn't forceful or confident enough to take full advantage of this opportunity. If he had been, he might well have met his deadline. As it turned out, he would miss it by almost four months.

Many individuals may justly deserve a share of the blame for the American forces' massive loss of cohesion and coherent strategy as the dismal Christmas season of 1941 unfolded. But without doubt, General Douglas MacArthur, the one person with full authority to control the situation, failed miserably to do so throughout the crucial period between December 8 and Christmas Eve.

"The confusion created by poor communication, misinformation, and unwillingness to digest bad news affected MacArthur's judgment," wrote historian Gerald Astor, one of many observers who later castigated the general for his indecisive response to the crisis.

"MacArthur's vacillation did not end with the Clark Field raid," added historians Richard Rovere and Arthur Schlesinger Jr. in their 1950s book, *The MacArthur Controversy and American Foreign Policy*. "He reacted slowly and uncertainly to the new situation. His mind seemed still to be fixed on his grandiose plan for the defense of the entire Philippines. He refused to acknowledge the necessity of preparing for an eventual retreat to . . . Bataan and the island fortress of Corregidor."

Even William Manchester, a friendly MacArthur biographer, described the general's mental state as verging on "catatonia" and his physical condition as "gray, ill, and exhausted" after he learned of the Pearl Harbor attack. Manchester blamed these conditions on an "overload" of conflicting demands on MacArthur, paramount among which was President Quezon's persistent belief that the Philippines could somehow declare neutrality in the war and persuade Japan to honor its declaration.

At 3:40 AM, Manila time, on December 8, Brigadier General Leonard T. Gerow, chief of the Army's War Plans Division, had phoned MacArthur from Washington and formally confirmed the Pearl Harbor attack. Roughly half an hour later, a cable from Army Chief of Staff General George Marshall directed MacArthur to implement the Rainbow Five plan at once. (On November 19, 1941, Rainbow Five had been amended to include orders for Far East Air Force planes to attack Japanese targets "within range," which clearly included the enemy bases on Formosa.)

But what British historian John Costello called a "fatal paralysis" born of sharply conflicting loyalties apparently held MacArthur's command in a state of suspended animation during this crucial period. MacArthur dreaded the thought of abandoning the charming city of Manila, as WPO-3 specified, fearing that, as long as Quezon clung to the hope of neutrality, this would be seen by his old friend as a personal betrayal. But at the same time, the Far East commander was under direct orders from Washington to take immediate action against the Japanese.

While no one living today can say for sure, it seems a near-certainty that MacArthur and Quezon talked by telephone early on the morning of December 8 and that during their conversation Quezon emphasized his hope that the Philippines could claim neutrality. Any such hope would have died instantly, of course, if Philippine-based American bombers had carried out raids against Japanese bases on Formosa—which could explain why MacArthur refused General Brereton's repeated requests for offensive action that morning.

One fact is clear, however. In this pressure situation, MacArthur committed two grave blunders: First, he forfeited the opportunity for his B-17s to strike a decisive blow against the Japanese and save themselves from destruction on the ground in the process. And second, he ordered General Wainwright's raw, inept Philippine Army divisions to attack and destroy the Japanese landing force on the beaches of Luzon. He might as well have ordered them to fly to the moon.

Among MacArthur's most outspoken on-the-scene critics was Colonel Clifford Bluemel, who had the misfortune to command the grossly ill-prepared 31st Philippine Army Division, charged with defending the coastline of Luzon. Bluemel described his troops as "untrained rabble" and was infuriated when he learned what MacArthur expected him to do with them.

"MacArthur and [General] Sutherland were trying to draw up a plan in a few days after discarding the one [WPO-3] that had been worked on for twenty-five years—which, to me, shows an inability to command," Bluemel said. "MacArthur had no transportation for us. He was too busy thinking about meeting them [the Japanese] at the beaches. Our artillery was old [and] wooden-wheeled . . . and I had nothing to tow it. We had to portage it . . . because the wooden wheels would fall off if we went at truck speed. . . . It's something MacArthur should have known."

General Wainwright was well aware of the condition of Bluemel's division, even if MacArthur wasn't, but he was powerless to correct its deficiencies because of lack of time, the geography involved, and the fact that, for weeks prior to December 8, MacArthur's staff repeatedly disregarded Wainwright's requests for essential supplies and equipment. According to Wainwright:

> Bluemel's infantrymen trained an average of only three or four weeks before being forced to fight. His engineers got no training at all. His artillery never fired a practice shot; indeed, its first shot was aimed in the general direction of the approaching enemy.
>
> We were terribly short then, and understandably shorter later, of hand grenades, .50-caliber machine-gun and infantry mortar ammunition. We were poverty-stricken, too, in ammunition for 2.95 howitzers, for these were obsolete guns, and the ammunition for them was no longer being made.
>
> What I'm saying is this: the Philippine Army units with the North Luzon Force were doomed before they started to fight. They never had a chance to win.

Throughout his military career, MacArthur had gained a reputation for exuding confidence in combat situations, and he continued to do so—to blatant extremes, some say—even as his reeling forces sought to compose themselves in the face of the Japanese onslaught. When he received reports of the initial enemy landings on Luzon, his orders to General Wainwright consisted of a single sentence—simple, straight to the point, and utterly beyond Wainwright's ability to carry out.

"In the event of a [Japanese] landing," the orders read, "attack and destroy the landing force."

After the war, "Skinny" Wainwright scrupulously avoided voicing anything resembling harsh criticism of his old boss and West Point classmate. But in his autobiography, published in 1946, Wainwright sought to explain in the mildest possible language why MacArthur's order broached on the absurd.

"It was not possible to attack, even if trained troops had been available," Wainwright said. "There was no room to deploy any considerable force between the mountains and the beaches in the landing area. I intensified the patrol activities around the landings to delay their advance as much as possible while I maneuvered my divisions into positions from which a counterattack could be launched."

Years later, MacArthur's supreme confidence remained unshaken, at least in retrospect. In his own postwar memoir, *Reminiscences*, he perpetuated the myth that a December 11 enemy landing attempt at Lingayen Gulf had been "repulsed with severe loss by a Philippine Army division." In fact, the alleged enemy defeat at Lingayen was "sheer fantasy"—historian Gerald Astor's words—because no such landing ever took place.

When *Life* photographer Carl Mydans hurried to Lingayen from Manila in search of enemy corpses, wrecked landing boats, and the telltale residue of combat, he was met on a quiet, deserted beach by an obviously chagrined Army major, who told Mydans: "There are no bodies and no boats, but God only knows why we aren't all dead. There was no battle. A green division has just been shooting the hell out of shadows all night long. First one let go and then another until the whole gulf was blazing, but there was never any enemy."

While MacArthur dallied over his illusions of victory on the beaches and disdained WPO-3 as a "defeatist" strategy, preparations for an orderly withdrawal into Bataan Peninsula were ignored and left in limbo. Even worse, the opportunity to procure sufficient food, munitions, medical supplies, and other matériel to sustain a six-month defense and deliver them to Bataan—as specified in WPO-3—was totally squandered.

(The truth was that Rainbow Five was far more "defeatist" than WPO-3 because it assumed that no relief could be sent to American forces in the Far East until the Nazi threat in Europe had been alleviated. Rainbow Five was, in fact, more of a broad strategic philosophy than a detailed tactical plan of action, and military leaders on both sides of the Pacific were lukewarm, at best, in supporting it. MacArthur's temporary embrace of Rainbow Five probably stemmed from his unrealistic concept of meeting and defeating the Japanese on the beaches, primarily with Filipino troops.)

By ruling out the use of WPO-3 before hostilities began, MacArthur had derailed any concerted effort to move critical supplies, especially food, to Bataan. The garrison at Corregidor, while less than one-eighth as large as the one that ultimately ended up on Bataan, was allotted a disproportionately larger share of food, and, in fact, Bataan got no food at all until Corregidor's quotas were met—a situation that continued unchanged from December 8 until Bataan's surrender. As one of MacArthur's own staff officers noted in his diary: "Our high command, I believe, was prepared to sacrifice the Bataan forces to starvation rather than to take the risk of being starved out on Corregidor."

The Army's 1,300-man Quartermaster Corps in the Philippines, commanded by Brigadier General Charles C. Drake, had amassed huge quantities of food from the United States in Manila and was empowered to augment these stocks from local sources. But Drake warned that even under optimal conditions, it would take two weeks to transfer sufficient supplies to Bataan.

By December 9–10, with Japanese bombers pounding Manila's port facilities, conditions were hardly ideal, but even at that late date, if MacArthur had made the decision to activate WPO-3, Drake's men would have had the two weeks they needed to get adequate food supplies to Bataan.

"In the Tondo District of Manila were stored large supplies of rice, owned mostly by Chinese merchants," wrote Captain Harold A. Arnold of the Quartermaster Corps in a postwar report described by Arnold as "a saga of too little and too late."

"Much of this rice was obtained for Army use," the report states, "and was delivered to the port area for distribution to units in the field. [But] this work was very difficult because of almost continuous air-raid alarms. . . . It was not uncommon to have an entire convoy of vehicles stranded in the middle of Manila because all the [native] drivers and other workers had fled. Despite these difficulties, thousands and thousands of cabanas (125-pound sacks) of polished rice were delivered to the port area."

Virtually none of these ever reached Bataan, however.

Large stocks of food supplies from the United States had previously been placed in war reserve at various strategic points on Luzon, but most of the supply depots were in the northern part of the island

and many miles from Bataan. A combination of Philippine government bureaucracy and the chaos accompanying MacArthur's belated decision to retreat into Bataan caused almost all of these supplies to be left behind and lost.

The Manila railroad, which was capable of hauling many of these supplies, had no crews to man its trains because the civilian workers had deserted, and the Philippine government refused to let U.S. troops take their places. Red tape requiring advance government permits to move commodities from one Luzon province to another also created a bureaucratic logjam.

"At one depot," wrote historian Duane Schultz, "some fifty million bushels of rice had to be abandoned, only to be burned later by the Japanese. Not one sack of it could be moved to Bataan. As little as twenty percent of that rice would have been sufficient to feed every soldier on Bataan for almost a year. . . . And in the end, it was the lack of food more than the military efforts of the Japanese that would lead to the fall of Bataan."

The first faint indication that even MacArthur's confidence was starting to ebb came on December 12 when he sent word to President Quezon to prepare to move himself and his government into the tunnels of Corregidor on four hours' notice. MacArthur explained that he was also making similar preparations for moving his own headquarters.

"Do you mean that tomorrow you will declare Manila an open city and that some time during the day we shall have to go to Corregidor?" asked the startled president.

"No, no, there's no immediate cause for concern," MacArthur assured Quezon. "I just want to be prepared for the worst in case the Japanese should land in great force at different places. At the moment, it's only a contingency strategy, and I merely wanted to make you aware of the possibility."

Three days later, on December 15, MacArthur did start transferring the USAFFE staff into Corregidor's rocky fastness, but it wasn't until December 22 that he moved his own headquarters there. Finally, on December 23, he made his official decision to change war plans and advised his subordinates, with what seemed to be thunderclap suddenness, that "WPO is in effect." And it would be Christmas Eve—sixteen long days after the first Japanese raids—before orders for the helter-skelter retreat into Bataan (where virtually no essential supplies had yet been stockpiled) finally trickled down to most of the rank and file. By then some 43,000 more Japanese troops had joined the advance parties of invaders on Luzon to establish an impregnable beachhead at Lingayen Gulf and launch a powerful drive southward toward Manila.

The main battle for Bataan was still to come, but, in essence, the fate of its defenders had already been sealed.

A few dozen yards from the panorama of death and destruction that had been Clark Field, the displaced members of permanently grounded flight crews took refuge in jungle glades and grassy fields after the December 8 raid. At night, they rolled up in blankets on the ground with their steel helmets still on their heads, clutching gas masks and .45-caliber pistols and trying to make sense of the cataclysm that had engulfed them.

"We were all weary from lack of sleep and food," said Lieutenant Ed Whitcomb, "and the following days were filled with confusion. We established our headquarters farther to the south in a thicket, where we aircrew members learned about bivouac areas, command posts, and message centers. We also learned a lot about the soil of Pampanga Province as we rooted deeper and deeper into our foxholes with each successive air raid. The whole affair from the beginning of the war until Christmas was like a nightmare—a maze of utter confusion."

Ground crews patched the craters in Clark's runways enough to allow some B-17s to fly in from Del Monte Field on Mindanao, but none of the big planes tarried for long. They came only to refuel or haul away personnel and equipment. By December 15, all surviving B-17s in the Philippines had been ordered to Australia, narrowly escaping the same fate as their counterparts at Clark. Four days after the last Flying Fortress departed Del Monte, a massive series of Japanese raids obliterated the field.

A handful of P-40s also operated out of Clark for several days, flying missions against the Japanese landing forces in northern Luzon. But for all practical purposes, Clark was finished as a major base, and all surviving U.S. warplanes—by mid-December the number of flyable combat aircraft was down to about thirty—were moved to hastily constructed smaller airstrips where they would be less obvious targets.

"Our situation became more grave day by day, as we learned of the loss of more and more of our planes," Whitcomb said. "But the biggest blow of all came when returning fighter pilots reported spotting a convoy of eighty-four Japanese ships heading for the beaches of Lingayen Gulf just sixty miles away."

By December 20, it was obvious that the Japanese were about to make their major landing exactly where General Wainwright had anticipated. The U.S. submarine *Stingray* had confirmed the reconnaissance planes' report of a huge convoy of enemy ships. Now, however, the invasion fleet was only forty miles north of Lingayen Gulf and closing.

A week earlier, to attain better access to his front-line troops at Lingayen and better communication with their commanders, Wainwright had moved his headquarters from heavily damaged Fort Stotsenburg to a new command post ten miles north at the town of Bamban, site of a major highway. He and his field officers were having to make extensive use of couriers because the public telephone system had become totally unreliable, and by operating out of Bamban, the couriers had considerably shorter distances to cover.

"That was the day [December 20] when I realized for all time the futility of trying to fight a war without an air force," Wainwright would later comment. "What targets those eighty-four [enemy] transports would have made!"

Private Joe Alexander and the rest of his 440th Ordnance Squadron had been transferred out of the ruins of Clark Field and taken by ship 500 miles south to Mindanao in time to witness the ensuing destruction at Del Monte from the surrounding jungle.

Alexander had been at his new duty station only a few days when his first sergeant summoned him to his tent and directed a quizzical stare in his direction.

"You're not eighteen years old, are you, kid?" the sergeant asked.

Joe started to sweat as he stood at attention. "No sir," he admitted quietly.

"Well, how old *are* you?"

Joe lowered his eyes. "I just turned fifteen a while back."

"Jesus Christ," the sergeant exclaimed. "How the hell did you get in the Army Air Corps?"

"My grandma signed for me, and that was all it took," Joe told him.

The sergeant shook his head. "Well, you're not supposed to be here in this war zone. There's a ship due in Manila soon to evacuate American civilians, and you're going to be on it when it sails, so get your gear packed. This is no damn place for a kid your age."

Joe felt a surge of relief rush over him. He had no idea how the Army had discovered that he was underage, but he felt like falling on his knees and thanking God that it had.

"I never did find out how they knew, and I didn't care," he recalled decades later. "I was just overjoyed at the thought of going home."

But as it turned out, Alexander wasn't going anywhere. A day or two later, he got word that the ship on which he was berthed had been bombed and sunk by Japanese planes. He was in the war zone for the duration—and he was terrified.

"After coming so close to getting away, I couldn't believe it," he said. "I'd enlisted because I thought I needed a change, but not like this!"

After several days, the supply of beer ran out at the Manila apartment shared by PFCs Karl King and Ike Williams, but the limbo surrounding the almost vacant Asiatic Fleet headquarters in the Marsman Building continued unabated.

The two young Marines, now resigned to the fact that their planned voyage to the States had been permanently canceled by the Japanese naval blockade now surrounding Luzon, had still seen no sign of Colonel Clement, their commanding officer, so they were without orders or direction. They'd speculated that they might be assigned to the Marine contingent aboard the cruiser *Houston*, but the days dragged on, and the *Houston*—now cruising in dangerous waters off Java—failed to appear, so they started to consider other options.

Making their way back to the Marsman Building, they found the flag offices deserted. But as they studied a map of the Philippines on an office wall, they spotted the bony finger of Bataan jutting down between Manila Bay and the South China Sea, and they began to wonder how they might manage to get there.

"We remembered Admiral Hart saying that the battle plan for the defense of the Philippines called for American forces to withdraw to Bataan and set up lines across the narrow, mountainous peninsula," King recalled. "Hart believed the veteran Fourth Marines would occupy the left side of the line, and we thought it was time to take action on our own to get to Bataan and find where the regiment was bivouacked."

As they set out through the city toward MacArthur's headquarters, where they hoped to find a naval attaché who could arrange transportation for them, all the charm and glamour had been bled out of Manila, and the Philippine capital resembled an abandoned ghost town. The streets were pocked with bomb craters and lined with damaged buildings and boarded-up businesses.

Then, as they neared the old Walled City, they came upon a stroke of sheer luck. Parked at the curb on a side street was an Army staff car bearing a brigadier general's one-star flag on its left front fender.

Williams and King looked at each other with raised eyebrows.

"What do you think?" Williams asked.

"I figure the general's driver must've abandoned the car rather than try to steer around all these bomb craters," King replied.

"I don't think we've got much of a chance getting past Army MPs into MacArthur's headquarters anyway," Williams said. "I say let's take the car and head for Bataan."

While King kept an eye out for MPs, it took Williams only a couple of minutes to hot-wire the ignition and get the car started. The gas tank was full, assuring that they'd have plenty of fuel to reach their destination. It was like a godsend.

"As we drove along, we saw streetcars that had been hurled into nearby buildings, leaving their tracks curled over the bomb craters like the ribs of a ship," King remembered. "Clouds of billowing smoke from burning buildings hung over the city. The streets were jammed with Army trucks and commandeered buses filled with Filipinos and supplies, all moving north out of the city."

In the glove compartment of the staff car, King found a map that allowed him to direct Williams through less-traveled streets to bypass the traffic and reach Highway Three, a main route that circled northwest around Manila Bay toward Bataan.

At the moment, King and Williams were still convinced that good luck was riding with them. But as King would recall nearly sixty years later: "The road to hell lay before us."

At Nichols Field, where the devastation of December 9–10 was comparable to that at Clark, Captain John Coleman, commanding the 27th Materiel Squadron, found his life further complicated by a fractured leg, suffered as he slogged through a buffalo wallow to dodge strafing enemy planes.

The doctor who treated Coleman at the Fort McKinley hospital assigned him a bed there, but after two members of the 27th located a pair of crutches, Coleman insisted on returning to his unit, temporarily bivouacked in a brushy area a mile or two from the ravaged airfield.

"All my officers were out on assigned details," he recalled, "so I had to operate the squadron from the bed for about two weeks."

On the first night after the fracture, the bed in question was outdoors and protected from the elements only by a leaky tarp. "I was miserable," Coleman said. "It rained most of the night, and it was cold. The water kept trickling through on me and running into my blanket. I would try to turn over, but my leg was very painful every time I moved. The next day my men set up a pup tent under some bushes to conceal me from planes and found a good mattress for me to lie on. From there, I kept in phone contact with each of my platoons."

While Coleman was convalescing, he received an order from MacArthur's headquarters that most Americans in the Philippines that Christmas season would have been overjoyed to obey. "I was told to take the three cargo planes that I had left to Australia [two others had been destroyed on the ground in the raids], but under the conditions we were in, I didn't feel I could leave my squadron," Coleman said.

The following day, three more than willing pilots volunteered to fly the planes out. They took with them one critically ill soldier and another with a much more severe leg fracture than Coleman's while Coleman himself remained at his post in the brush.

He never knew whether the planes arrived in Australia or not.

On Christmas Eve, as his order for all American and Filipino troops to move to Bataan with all possible speed was reaching individual units on the peninsula, MacArthur formally declared Manila an open city in hopes of sparing it from further destruction. By this time, about 7,000 additional Japanese troops had landed at Lamon Bay seventy miles south of the city, and with next to no opposition facing them, advance elements of this force were expected to reach the capital within two or three days.

Meanwhile, in Manila's once glittering venues, amid a bizarre mixture of doomsday foreboding and giddy revelry, many civilians prayed and cried. Some listened intently to the muted sound of Christmas carols echoing in the ghostly streets. Others drowned their fears and sorrows in a final series of drunken parties. No one knew how much time remained before the conquerors' arrival signaled Manila's final last call.

Sergeant Sidney Stewart, an Army medic from Oklahoma, and a comrade—both of them flat broke and faced with a distasteful set of orders that would place them among the last American soldiers to vacate the city—drove down Dewey Boulevard and dropped in at the Manila Hotel in search of free drinks and female companionship. They'd never felt they could afford to visit the famed hotel before, but tonight they didn't care.

They were admitted by an impeccably uniformed doorman who smiled, bowed, and opened the ornate door with a flourish, admitting them into a lobby crowded with elegantly gowned women and men in white sharkskin dinner jackets and ringing with laughter and music. Everyone seemed to pause and watch the two soldiers in grubby uniforms as they crossed the room.

"Joe, how about a drink?" Stewart's friend asked a bartender behind a polished bar. "We haven't got any money, though. Uncle Sam's been too busy to pay us lately."

"Anything you wish is on us," the bartender said.

"Yep, you can just about have the house," a lithe young blonde in an off-the-shoulder yellow dress interjected from an adjacent barstool. "You fellows aren't staying for the reception, I hope."

"What reception?" Stewart asked innocently, before realizing that she meant the impending arrival of the Japanese.

"Oh, don't act naive," she said, stubbing her cigarette out on top of the gleaming bar. "We know what's going on. We know where we're headed in a few days. Won't I look pretty behind barbed wire?"

Stewart stared wordlessly at her, not knowing how to reply.

Captains Ralph Hibbs and Dwight Hunkins were also among the many Americans who couldn't resist a final Christmas Eve visit to Manila before the axe fell. They arrived at mid-morning and encountered a sorrowful panorama of almost empty streets, barricaded stores, devastated piers, and fires burning out of control. Out in the bay, the hulls and masts of thirty or forty sunken ships jutted from the oily, debris-littered water.

The quartermaster's office was still in operation in the dock area, and Hunkins had been told that Christmas rations, including a supply of frozen turkeys, were available there. But Hibbs had a far more urgent reason than turkeys for coming to the stricken city. He was hoping—with held breath—that, despite the prevailing end-of-the-world atmosphere, he might find Pilar Campos working as usual at her desk in the *Manila Herald* newsroom.

As Hunkins pulled up in front of the *Herald* building, only a few dozen yards from the dock area, Hibbs jumped out of their borrowed command car, armed with his gas mask, .38-caliber sidearm, steel helmet, and a hand grenade that Hunkins had insisted he fasten to his belt.

"I'll pick you up later at your old apartment," Hunkins yelled as he drove away.

Hibbs felt more than a little foolish as he ran up the steps to the building's main entrance, looking, he thought, like a refugee from the set of *Sergeant York*, then burst into a large room filled with people pounding on typewriters. With heart racing, he searched among them for Pilar's familiar face. Then he heard her call his name and saw her rushing toward him.

She grabbed his hand, pulled him behind a convenient bamboo curtain, and hugged him fiercely.

"Boy, it's good to see you, Petie," he said.

"Let's go," she whispered. "My work's about finished. Besides, the building will be cleared soon because of our daily bomb raids."

After a short drive in Pilar's car, they were sitting together at a small table in the exclusive Spanish Club, where her parents were charter members. Hibbs found it hard to talk, even after downing a gin-and-tonic and with a lone bartender as their only company. His tongue seemed frozen in his mouth, and he was afraid if he tried to say anything, he'd start blubbering, so he sat there, silently biting his lip and squeezing her hand.

He was glad when they left the club and drove to his apartment, where he found the premises almost bare except for a few pieces of rattan furniture and some wall hangings. There was no sign of Dominador, his houseboy.

"What happened?" he asked.

"I loaded up all the valuables in your footlocker and hid them in my attic," she said, lowering her eyes. "Is that okay?"

"Sure, Petie, that's fine. It was great of you to do it." He tried to keep his voice calm, but he felt alarm rising in his chest. Stories were already circulating about the brutality meted out by the Japanese to female civilians in occupied territory who were found with opposing servicemen's belongings. Boldly stenciled on top of his footlocker, he clearly remembered, were the words "Lt. Ralph Hibbs, M.C., U.S. Army."

"You'd better take off for the hills, Pilar," he said heavily. "Don't get mixed up in this mess."

She stared at him soulfully but said nothing. The silence between them was broken only when they heard Hunkins honking the car horn out in the street.

He could feel her tears on his face when she kissed him goodbye. "Be careful," she whispered. "I want you to come back."

His mouth was dry, and his voice broke as he replied. "Don't worry about me," he said. "Take care of yourself, Pilar."

Then he was gone.

* * *

Captain John Coleman was still limping along on one crutch when his 27th Materiel Squadron, now scattered in small details near the ruins of Nichols Field and at various other points, became one of the first Army units to get official word from MacArthur's headquarters that a major move was impending.

The call came at about 1 PM on December 23, and the caller left no doubt that there was a major rush on. "How long will it take you to get your squadron down to Pier Five in Manila?" he demanded.

"I don't have a single truck in camp right now," Coleman said, "but I think we can get to Pier Five by five o'clock."

"Five o'clock, hell!" the caller snapped. "Make it four o'clock."

"Very well, sir," Coleman replied. As he hung up, he had no idea how he could possibly meet this unexpected deadline—or, for that matter, where he and his men were going. He quickly phoned Lieutenant Morton Deeter, a platoon leader who was thirty miles away at Lipa with two of the squadron's trucks, and told him to get to Pier 5 on the double. Then Coleman had the squadron clerk contact other details with the same message while Coleman himself ran out to the highway to commandeer the first truck he saw, which fortunately happened to be a large moving van.

The van's driver was agreeable enough after Coleman handed him a receipt for the vehicle, and he pitched in to help the 27th's cooks load up as much equipment and canned goods as the van would carry.

True to his word, Coleman was standing on Pier 5 by 4 PM, but many members of his squadron didn't reach the pier until up to an hour later, then immediately began loading their equipment aboard a waiting interisland ship.

As they worked, two U.S. submarines surfaced nearby to take on battery water, but after about fifteen minutes, the air raid sirens sounded, and the subs left in a hurry. They were half-submerged when a small flock of Zeros streaked over, flying close to the water and sending Coleman's troops scurrying for cover but not attacking. In the distance, thick plumes of black smoke rose from a Navy storage area between Cavite and Nichols Field, where a million gallons of American oil were being destroyed to keep them out of Japanese hands.

"By dark, we'd loaded about 1,500 men and our essential belongings on the ship," Coleman recalled. "There were so many of us that no one aboard had room to lie down. We still hadn't been told where we were going, and we hoped we were going to run the blockade on our way to Australia. This being a very dark night, we thought we had a good chance to get through."

Hopes of Australia vanished during a long night of waiting, however, and at dawn on Christmas Eve morning, the men of the 27th found their ship bogged down in a mudflat a quarter-mile off the pier at the small port of Mariveles on the south end of Bataan. At this point, a barge was sent out, but it wasn't large enough to hold all the men and their cargo. After a lengthy argument, Coleman managed to have a second barge sent, but soon after the two barges had reached shore and unloaded, Japanese dive-bombers appeared.

"The first flight [of enemy planes] set fire to our ship, and it sank in thirty minutes," said Coleman. "Had we not secured a second barge, half of the men would have still been on the ship waiting to unload. Most of our equipment was still on the pier when the bombing started, and we had to flee for protection, leaving it there."

Only after the raid was over did Coleman and his men finally learn what they were expected to do next. The Rainbow Five plan to defend the Philippines on the beaches had been abandoned, they were told, and replaced with the WPO-3 plan to defend only Bataan and Corregidor.

"This didn't look good to us," Coleman said. "[We] hadn't been briefed or given any details of this new plan, and we still hadn't been issued a full complement of infantry equipment. None of my men had raincoats, and only about a fourth of them had shelter halves [components for two-man tents]."

The squadron's first orders were to move eight miles north and secure a campsite where its members were to continue training for combat duty. The men were expected to march to their destination, and Coleman decided to march with them, despite the still healing fracture in his leg.

There was, however, no transportation for the heavy equipment until Coleman flagged down a courteous Filipino driver and commandeered his old Ford truck.

Lieutenant Deeter, who went ahead in the borrowed truck, picked out a favorable campsite. It was close to a heavily wooded area, and a clear creek nearby provided plenty of fresh water. It was also a considerable distance from Bataan's most notorious areas of heavy mosquito infestations. The major problem confronting Coleman's men was obtaining an adequate supply of food. Tons of C rations and other staple goods were stored in depots and warehouses in Manila's port area, but that now seemed much farther away—and getting there and back was far more dangerous—than it had been a few days earlier.

For Bataan's defenders, the food problem had scarcely begun. It was destined to grow steadily larger and more unsolvable with every passing day. Eventually, it would become worse than any man headed for Bataan or already there that Christmas Eve could yet imagine.

Of all the nervous, unhappy Americans on the island of Luzon as Christmas approached, none was stuck with a more futile assignment than Lieutenant Ed Whitcomb—and none received a more unwanted "Christmas present."

One of a small detachment of Army Air Corps personnel left at wrecked and otherwise abandoned Clark Field with the pointless mission of guarding against a Japanese parachute drop, Whitcomb had lost count of the times they'd been bombed and strafed. But for the last several days, a void of inactivity had settled over them as they huddled in the jungle near the field, eating and sleeping on the ground, and praying for someone to tell them they could leave.

At mid-afternoon on December 23, Whitcomb was sitting outside the small trailer housing the radio station that linked them with the outside world when his friend, Lieutenant Croxton, suddenly appeared in the doorway.

"Let's get this station torn down," Croxton said excitedly. "We're moving out!"

Whitcomb's mood brightened instantly at the news. "Where are we going?" he asked.

"Can't tell you."

"You *can't* tell me, or you *won't* tell me?" Whitcomb pressed.

"Can't tell you. Let's just get this thing down and get the hell out of here."

By the time the sun was slipping behind the mountains to the west of Clark, Whitcomb's group had left the ruins of the airfield behind to join a convoy of vehicles moving slowly southeast in the general direction of Manila, but their destination was still unknown.

"As far as I could tell, Croxton was the only one who knew where we were going, and I wasn't so sure that he knew, either," Whitcomb recalled.

It was dark when the convoy reached the town of San Fernando, where, instead of continuing on toward Manila, it veered off to the west and picked up speed. "We passed truck after truck that had stalled or run off the road and overturned," Whitcomb remembered, "and there were long stops with nobody knowing where we were."

At about 2 AM on Christmas Eve, the convoy was ordered off the road and into a brushy area where the vehicles couldn't be spotted from the air after sunup. Whitcomb and his comrades ended up sitting there all day, and although they set up their radio station to be on the alert for any important messages, their frequency stayed dead until late afternoon.

"It was as if the war had ended and left us stranded in the jungle," Whitcomb recalled. "Then, as we whiled away the time in the radio trailer, I looked up to see Lieutenant Jim Dey, another friend from the 19th Bomb Group, standing in the doorway, and he motioned me to come outside."

"Hey Whit," Dey said in a whisper, "did you hear about it? The whole damn outfit's shoving off tonight."

"Shoving off for where?" Whitcomb inquired.

"Del Monte pineapple plantation on Mindanao," Dey said.

"Man, that's really good news," Whitcomb said. "Maybe we can get back to flying." Then he frowned. "But I haven't had any word about it, and it'll take at least half an hour to get this radio station knocked down."

Dey grinned uneasily, and Whitcomb could tell that something was amiss.

"You don't have to worry about that, pal," Dey said. "You and Croxton aren't going anyplace. This boat's reserved for aircrew members, and you guys are signal slingers now. But, hey, I'll drop you a nice, juicy pineapple sometime when I'm flying over this way."

Dey started to turn away, but Whitcomb pulled him back. "Just a damned minute," he flared. "Are you saying that just because I volunteered for this radio work while you guys sat on your fat asses, I'm getting rewarded by having to stay here? Where the hell did this cheerful information come from?"

"Major Miller told me," Dey said. "He's on his way up here now. I thought I'd drop by and prepare you for the shock."

"Well, thanks at lot," Whitcomb said coldly.

"It's not as bad as it sounds," Dey assured him. "They say the boat'll be back to pick up the rest of the squadron later."

Thus, while most of his former squadron mates cruised away to Mindanao, Whitcomb spent Christmas Day sitting forlornly in a mango grove deep in the Bataan jungle and trying to avoid the searing Philippine sun. Later, he had no clear recollection of what he had for Christmas dinner—mangoes, in all likelihood—but for the most part he spent the holiday figuratively eating his heart out.

His sole consolation was that his taunting buddy Jim Dey had been bumped from the Mindanao passenger list at the last minute and was now stuck in the same boat with Whitcomb, Croxton, and a few other unfortunates.

"Actually, I was damned glad that Jim was still with us," Whitcomb later admitted. "He was one of those rare individuals who could make fun of the darkest situation, and we had a great need for that kind of talent."

Meanwhile, many other U.S. military units were also converging on Bataan in unseemly haste and extreme disarray during the last hours before Christmas.

"On Christmas Eve night, shortly after the chow truck had made its rounds, orders came down from regimental headquarters," recalled Sergeant Clem Kathman of the 200th Coastal Artillery, a New Mexico National Guard antiaircraft outfit. "We were told to destroy anything we couldn't take with us, and we emptied what we could from our footlockers into our barracks bags. The footlockers and their remains were buried in the fields adjoining our gun position. I don't think any of us thought we'd be digging them up again—ever."

Marching orders were issued at about 10:30 PM, signaling the start of what Kathman characterized as "one of the most hectic nights imaginable."

"Traveling forty-five miles an hour, driving a right-side-of-the-road vehicle on the left side, blacked out, in convoy, and with the enemy supposedly hot on your tail can get pretty hairy," he noted. "Sometime during the night, the kitchen truck tried to straddle a concrete road marker and ripped the whole underside out, and the cargo was spread out over the other vehicles. Heretofore, I'd managed to doze some, but with a frozen side of beef as a bed partner, sleep was out of the question."

Early Christmas Day, the caravan pulled into a cane field near the town of Hermosa with orders to deploy its 37-millimeter guns as antiaircraft defense against anticipated enemy air attacks on a vital bridge over which U.S. troops were withdrawing toward Bataan.

What irony, Kathman thought. *This is supposed to be a day of peace on earth, good will toward men. What peace? What good will? Bah, humbug!*

"We spent most of the day digging foxholes," he recalled, "and setting up and trying to camouflage our gun positions. Instead of turkey and cranberry sauce, we had to content ourselves with C-rations and biscuits for lunch. But that evening, the cooks outdid themselves, and my frozen bed partner became a beautiful piece of roast beef with gravy and the usual trimmings. It was a feast!"

After dinner, Kathman and his foxhole mates received a visit from their platoon commander, Captain Jack Ashby, who came armed with his last bottle of orange gin. The group killed most of the bottle by the time everyone except Kathman either left or drifted off to sleep.

The soft strains of "Silent Night" floated through the darkness from some soldier's harmonica in a nearby foxhole as Kathman gazed up at the millions of stars overhead. For a moment, he felt himself being drawn back through time to the porch of his grandparents' little homestead shack in New Mexico, where he'd sat on many nights as a boy, listening to the crickets chirping and the horses snorting in the shed out back.

He was struck by the incredible realization that the stars above him now were the same ones that had shone down so long ago on that boy and that shack 8,000 miles away. Suddenly, he felt himself shaking with uncontrollable sobs, and warm tears were streaming down his cheeks.

"Maybe hardened soldiers aren't supposed to cry," he observed many years later, "but I had no regrets and felt no shame. This was my first Christmas away from home."

He couldn't have known it at the time, but if not for the grace of God and Kathman's own quick feet, it also would have been his last Christmas anywhere.

4

The Last Bridge to Nowhere

While American troops in the Philippines were caught up in a melee of fright, flight, and confusion at Christmastime 1941, the only immediate physical peril for most came from the skies above them, and they had yet to face any significant danger from the enemy on the ground.

It was a different story, though, for General Wainwright's North Luzon Force. In addition to ongoing air attacks, the predominantly Filipino NLF was beset by sudden firefights, nocturnal infiltrators, mortar and artillery fire, and hand-to-hand combat. By December 26, units of Wainwright's command had already spent ten days fighting—and generally losing—a series of close-quarter run-ins with pockets of Japanese invaders intent on pushing south, either by force or stealth, toward Manila.

Now, as the final week of 1941 began, the two divergent groups of defenders found themselves drawn together in a single urgent cause. Most U.S. troops evacuated from the immediate Manila area had been shipped directly across the bay to Bataan, so they were essentially already where they needed to be. But those based far to the north and south of the peninsula were expected to fight delaying actions even as they withdrew toward Bataan through enemy-infested territory. Wainwright's force and the South Luzon Force commanded by General Albert M. Jones faced a particularly daunting job in reaching the defensive enclave. The landing of 10,000 Japanese on Christmas Day at Lamon Bay, sixty miles southeast of Manila, threatened to cut off the SLF's route of escape to the north while Jones's men were tied down in delaying actions to allow other converging USAFFE troops to reach Bataan.

Even without this added problem, the SLF had a long, difficult road to travel—up to 120 miles, including a northward curve around Manila Bay, then a sharp turn south toward Bataan. The SLF's situation was worsened by having only two battalions of infantry and no artillery in the area to oppose the new enemy invaders. In addition, a smaller Japanese force that had landed earlier on the Batangas Peninsula, south of Manila on the west coast of Luzon, was also in a potential position to block the SLF's withdrawal route. Wainwright tried to send help, but he could offer little of substance until Jones's force retreated past Manila and reached central Luzon.

Fortunately, Jones was able to lead his forces out of a potential death trap by loading them on civilian buses and rushing them north to set up a defensive line between the invaders and Manila. Meanwhile, a team of Army engineers destroyed all rail and highway bridges in the path of the Japanese to delay their advance for an additional day or two.

As Wainwright later summed up his own difficulties during this crucial period: "MacArthur's orders to withdraw my men to Bataan came at a time when my North Luzon Force of approximately 28,000 men—25,000 of them still untrained—were scattered over a considerable area. The average distance we had to withdraw was close to 150 miles. But first those units had to be rounded up to present the kind of semi-solid front we'd need for the delaying actions."

Wainwright fully expected many of his Filipino soldiers to desert their posts and flee as soon as they came under fire for the first time—and they did. By January 6, 1942, when the withdrawal into Bataan was considered complete, the NLF had lost more than 12,000 men to casualties and desertion in twenty days of sporadic combat. Jones's smaller SLF had lost only about 1,000 personnel during the same period.

A key problem in the four undersized Philippine Army divisions making up the bulk of the NLF was a woeful lack of experienced leadership. In an effort to provide at least a partial remedy, numerous noncoms in

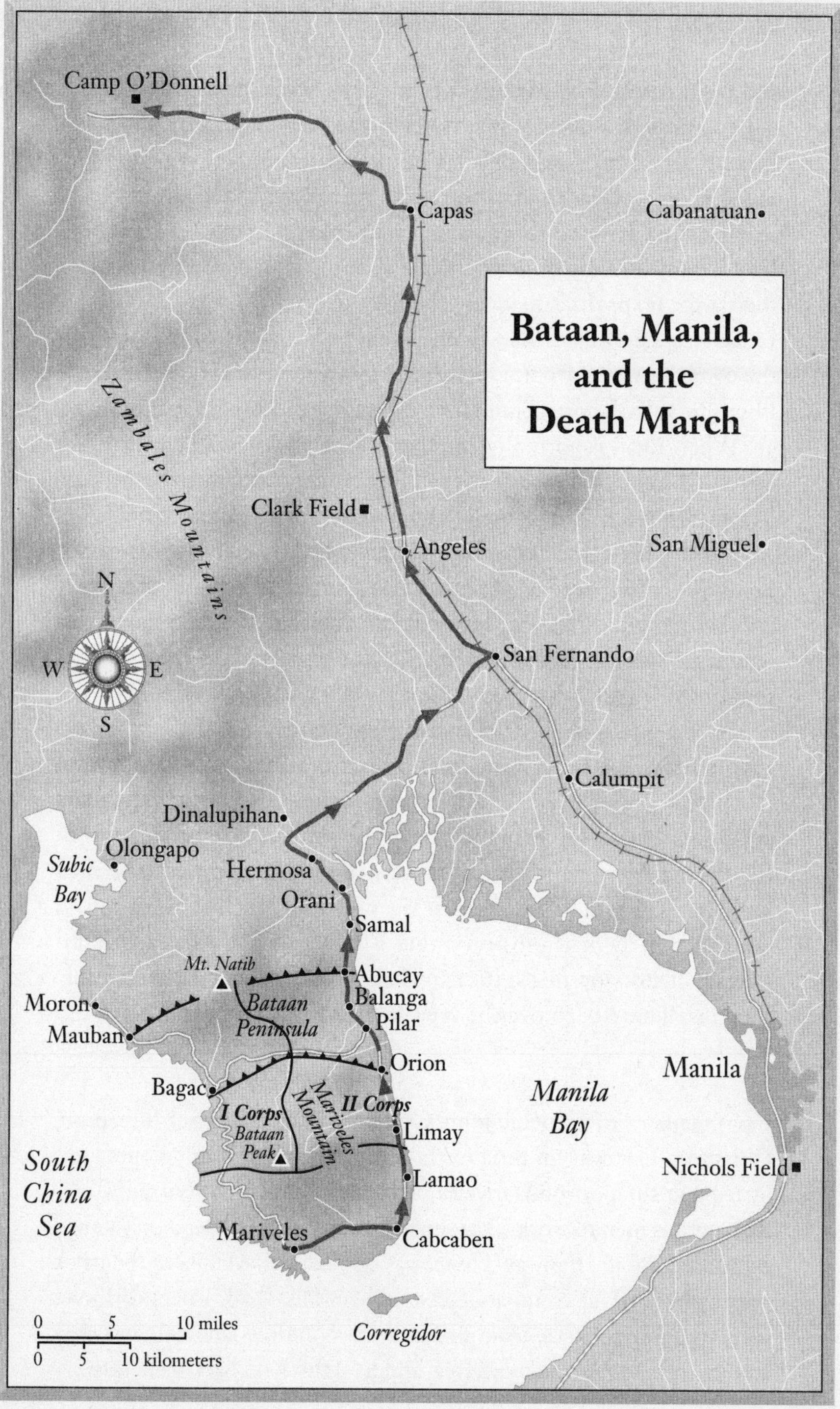

Bataan, Manila, and the Death March
Camp O'Donnell
Capas
Cabanatuan
Zambales Mountains
Clark Field
Angeles
San Miguel
N
W
E
S
San Fernando
Calumpit
Dinalupihan
Olongapo
Subic Bay
Hermosa
Orani
Samal
Mt. Natib
Abucay
Balanga
Moron
Bataan Peninsula
Pilar
Mauban
Orion
Manila
Bagac
Mariveles Mountain
I Corps
II Corps
Manila Bay
Limay
Bataan Peak
South China Sea
Lamao
Nichols Field
Mariveles
Cabcaben
Corregidor
0
5
10 miles
0
5
10 kilometers

the all-American 31st Infantry Regiment were offered second lieutenant commissions to serve as advisers in the Philippine Army divisions. Among them was now-Sergeant Louis Read, who had temporarily forfeited a corporal's stripe to win an assignment to the Philippines in 1939.

"I turned the offer down, as did many others, despite the fact that I had literally nothing to do in my job at regimental headquarters since there were no payrolls to meet or records to keep," said Read. "Instead, I asked Captain Robert Barker, my company commander, to let me join the company at the front. I'd been trained as a rifle squad leader in the Ninth Infantry before coming to the Philippines, so Barker agreed."

When Read reported to the front lines, he made a stunning discovery. "I was the only one in my antitank company who'd ever seen a round of live ammo for our obsolete 37-millimeter guns, much less ever fired one. Our high-explosive shells just bounced right off the Jap tanks. If you were lucky, sometimes you could blow the tracks off and kill the tank that way, but unfortunately, most of our hand grenades and mortar shells were left over from World War I, and a large percentage were duds."

Yet despite the chaos in which they floundered, the American-Filipino forces on Luzon enjoyed one intangible advantage during this period in that General Homma and other Japanese commanders apparently failed for a time to grasp the shift in U.S. strategy from Rainbow Five to WPO-3. As it was, the invaders initially seemed far more intent on brushing past weak Allied resistance to seize and occupy Manila than on preventing a USAFFE withdrawal toward Bataan. If not for this critical mistake, the fight for the peninsula might well have been over by New Year's Day.

For members of Captain John Coleman's 27th Materiel Squadron, Christmas Day was no time for holiday celebrating. Only hours after arriving at the port of Mariveles on the southern tip of Bataan, Coleman put his men to work. One small group, traveling over a threatened but still passable Highway Three, was sent back to Manila in the truck that Coleman had commandeered earlier. They had orders to locate four additional trucks, load all five with C rations and other staples from warehouses in the port area, and haul the food back to Bataan.

Most of the rest of the Army Air Corps squadron spent the day learning the rudiments of infantry combat training under Coleman's direction. All of the now planeless air units were to be rolled into a single new organization known as the Provisional Air Corps Infantry Regiment, which would take its place on the front lines alongside regular infantry units.

At about four o'clock that afternoon, after drilling in the heat for several hours, the trainees were allowed to go down to the bay for a refreshing swim. The water was shallow, and it was necessary to venture out about fifty yards from shore before it was deep enough for swimming.

"We'd just gotten out in water three or four feet deep when we heard a flight of Japanese fighter planes," Coleman recalled. "There were about 100 of us in the water, and some started to run toward shore. I shouted for them to dive under the water as the planes swooped down on us like hawks. We could hear the bullets popping on top of the water as they strafed us, but not a single man was hit."

This put an abrupt end to daylight swimming and bathing in the bay—just one of many essential adjustments for Coleman's men. It was unusual to see thirty-five-year-old former aircraft mechanics drilling with bayonets and taking target practice with machine guns. But as a onetime infantry officer, Coleman was well qualified as an instructor, and he would soon be pressed into service training several other Air Corps squadrons in addition to his own.

As New Year's Eve approached, Coleman made his last trip into Manila to check military supply depots for any remaining food. He found a few bags of wheat flour and cooking starch, but the other foodstuffs that had been so plentiful a short time earlier were now gone, and the depots were stripped to the bare walls.

Accompanying Coleman on the trip was Master Sergeant Brennison, the squadron's supply sergeant, whose wife was still hospitalized in Manila after giving birth to a baby boy.

A stoic Brennison left his wife $500 in cash and promised to return to her and the baby as soon as possible. There was nothing else he could do.

"The sergeant had never seen his son until that night, and it was also the last time he ever saw him," Coleman remembered.

* * *

The makeshift Air Corps Infantry that Coleman helped train was to become a vital part of Bataan's front-line defense. And no single individual was more active in that defense than Sergeant J. S. Gray, who had started the war as one of the top ordnance men in the now-inactive 27th Bomb Group's 16th Ordnance Squadron.

In the early going on Bataan, Gray was assigned as crew chief for a group of shell handlers whose job was delivering 105- and 155-millimeter shells to artillery batteries. But as the fighting grew heavier, Gray moved onto the front lines more or less permanently, and he became a prolific and remorseless killer of enemy soldiers.

"When they told me I was going to the infantry, I found me a Thompson submachine gun," the Louisiana native recalled a half-century later. "It shot .45-caliber bullets, and when those bullets hit a human head, they busted it wide open like you were shooting a watermelon."

Even fifty years after the fact, Gray clearly remembered the tactics he used with the tommy gun. "At first, it gave me kind of a funny feeling to kill another person, but that didn't last long," he said, "because there was always another one real close by, and you had to get him before he got you. I always tried to be the first one to shoot. I had enough country boy left in me that it was just like when I used to shoot squirrels with a .22 rifle. I would always try to shoot them in the head, and I wanted to shoot those Japanese the same way. When I got one, I wanted to mangle his head."

Sergeant Cletis Overton, one of Gray's best buddies in the old 16th Ordnance Squadron, didn't share his friend's relish for killing Japanese soldiers face-to-face. Instead, for the first time in his life, he embraced the Christian faith and began to pray regularly and read the Bible his mother had given him for his twenty-first birthday.

"One day I realized I was probably praying for my physical well-being while God was more interested in my spiritual welfare," he recalled. "When I did, this great burden of fear I'd been carrying around rolled away, and there was a deep sense of peace in my heart."

During his months on Bataan, Overton never fired a shot at an individual enemy soldier. But his newfound faith didn't keep him from accepting assignment as an ammo handler on the two-man crew of a .50-caliber machine gun salvaged from a downed American plane.

"There were five guns set in pits about three feet deep at a makeshift airfield hastily built by the Corps of Engineers about two miles back in the jungle," Overton remembered. "Almost every day, the Japanese dive-bombers raided the field, coming in so low I could see the pilots' goggles, and once in a while, we'd shoot one down. I never knew for sure if it was my gun that did it, but it wouldn't have bothered me much if it was. You did what you had to do in a situation like that, and I figured God would understand."

Although General MacArthur relayed an entirely different set of figures to Washington, the raw numbers of troops on Luzon actually favored the USAFFE with Filipino and American defenders handily outnumbering the invaders. As of Christmas Day, General Homma's Japanese 14th Army had put a total of about 58,000 troops ashore at four different locations on Luzon. Opposing them were approximately 80,000 defenders, including 14,000 Americans. In the Philippines as a whole, MacArthur probably had close to twice as many men in uniform as Homma. But in reporting the situation to his boss, Army Chief of Staff General George Marshall, over a distance of nearly 10,000 miles, MacArthur basically reversed these figures to portray the defenders as the numerical underdogs.

What Homma failed to understand was that capturing the Philippine capital without subduing U.S. forces on Bataan and Corregidor was, in itself, pointless. Unless the Japanese could also gain control of Manila Bay, they could never utilize its superb port and harbor facilities to bring in the men and matériel necessary to complete their conquest of the archipelago. And as long as the giant U.S. coastal batteries on Bataan and "the Rock" dominated the bay, it would remain an American shooting gallery where no Japanese ship could survive.

"The enemy might have the bottle," MacArthur remarked, "but I've got the cork."

The essential first step toward maintaining this advantage was to gather all friendly troops into a cohesive force capable of manning a series of defensive lines across Bataan's twenty-five-mile-long and up to twenty-mile-wide "thumb" of land. Unless that could be accomplished by early January, as both Wainwright and MacArthur knew, it most likely would never happen at all.

For Wainwright's forces, the shooting war had started on December 16 when two busloads of Japanese troops, trying to move south from their small beachhead at Vigan on the northwest coast of Luzon, had been ambushed by a platoon of Filipino infantry. By most accounts, the Filipinos, led by an American lieutenant, had the best of the skirmish, killing several dozen enemy soldiers as they piled out of the buses. But having temporarily halted the Japanese advance, the Filipinos then withdrew to the south, setting a pattern for what was to follow repeatedly on an ever-widening scale.

As Wainwright later put it: "It was the beginning of endless days and nights of killing Japs, getting killed, and withdrawing. Not that we didn't try, with everything we had, to hold whatever we had."

The fifty-four M-3 tanks of Company A of the 194th Tank Battalion, a National Guard outfit based at Brainerd, Minnesota, were among the first American armor to face the Japanese in pitched battle.

"On our way to Bataan, we were diverted north to intercept the Jap invaders," recalled Staff Sergeant Kenneth J. Porwoll, who commanded one of those tanks and its four-man crew. "It's hell to be the first ones out there, I can tell you, and we took some heavy casualties. We lost our company commander, Captain Ed Burke, early on. His tank was hit, and he was wounded and captured by the Japs, but we regrouped and gave a good account of ourselves."

Many of the men in the company had known each other since childhood and gone to school together in Brainerd, a Mississippi River town of 12,000 in central Minnesota. "We were a close-knit bunch, and we cared about each other," said Porwoll. "Our morale was great, and each time we stopped the Japs, it got better."

After the initial enemy landings on December 10, Porwoll's company and the other two companies of the 194th—B Company out of St. Joseph, Missouri, and C Company from Salinas, California—fought a series of fierce delaying actions that held up Japanese attempts to advance south for more than a month.

"Going in, the 194th had 150 tanks in all, and we took up blocking positions along various holding lines," Porwoll said. "For several weeks we were able to stop the Japs in their tracks. That bought our infantry units enough time to make a fairly orderly retreat into Bataan. God knows what would've happened if we hadn't been there."

(According to official U.S. Army records, more than 55 percent of the members of Company A died during the war, either in battle or as POWs.)

The 26th Cavalry Regiment formed part of the proud "heart" of the Philippine Scouts, but it was actually a regiment in name only, and, in fact, not even a full traditional battalion, since it consisted of only fifty-four officers and 784 enlisted men when the war began. As one of the world's last horse cavalry units in an era of 400-mile-an-hour aircraft and monstrous mechanized vehicles, it seemed an "absurd anachronism" to some. But to old cavalryman Wainwright, it was, without question, the finest fighting outfit in the islands—and maybe anywhere.

The withdrawal into Bataan by tens of thousands of USAFFE troops was as chaotic and confused as any large-scale military operation in America's history, but it might never have been accomplished at all if not for the hard-riding heroics of the 26th's relative handful of men and mounts.

The legendary "horse soldiers," who had once personified the best of the U.S. Army, were a vanishing breed by late 1941. But Wainwright knew, perhaps better than any other active American commander of the time, what skilled cavalrymen could accomplish on the battlefield—and he lost no time in sending them out to do it.

Six years earlier, in 1935, the Army had discarded the flashing sabers that had served for centuries as the cavalry's trademark and primary attack weapon. In their place, the few remaining mounted units were equipped with .45-caliber automatic pistols attached to lanyards that ran from each rider's left shoulder to right hip to prevent the weapons from being dropped. While the sabers may have been more intimidating, the pistols were far more deadly, and the men of the 26th—mostly Filipino troopers led by American officers—knew how to use them as efficiently as any cavalry unit in the world.

As of Christmas night, the riders and horses of the 26th had already been locked in a life-and-death struggle with the Japanese invaders for five days. Their role was inevitably to protect the flank of Wainwright's constantly retreating foot soldiers. In near-continuous action, they had inflicted deep wounds on the enemy but suffered grievous losses of their own—more than 300 riders and fully half the regiment's horses. (Among the dead horses was Wainwright's own beloved personal mount, Little Boy, killed by an enemy rifle bullet to the head.)

"The ill-prepared pair of Philippine Army divisions assigned to block entry at Lingayen folded quickly, although an occasional unit fought bravely and inflicted casualties before being overrun," wrote historian Gerald Astor. "The Filipino soldiers streamed backward in an ever-deepening rout. The chief resistance to the enemy advance came from . . . the 26th Cavalry, Philippine Scouts, mounted on horses."

In the words of Wainwright himself, the performance by troopers of the 26th was "a true cavalry delaying action, fit to make a man's heart sing."

Despite their consummate skill and unflinching courage, the men and steeds of the 26th were nevertheless expected to be mere cannon fodder for the Japanese armored column that spearheaded the drive south from the enemy beachhead at Lingayen on the morning of December 22.

The Japanese tanks mounted 47-millimeter guns when the 26th confronted them at the town of Binalonan on the Agno River. Wainwright had asked for a detachment of sixteen American tanks to provide support for the cavalry against the Japanese armor. But when only five thinly armored M-3 light tanks showed up, mounting nothing heavier than single-shot .37-millimeter cannons and unreliable air-cooled machine guns, Colonel Clinton Pierce, the cavalry CO, reacted with disdain.

"Get your damn tanks out of the way," he reportedly yelled at one tank crew. "They're scaring my horses!"

Lieutenant Edwin Price Ramsey, a platoon commander in the 26th, credited the skeletal regiment with delaying the enemy tank column for more than two hours that day, enabling Wainwright to establish a crucial defensive line along the Agno River.

"With no antitank weapons, the troopers halted the Japanese armor with fanatical feats of heroism," Ramsey said, "throwing themselves on the tanks, dropping grenades down the hatches, and firing into the gunports. Then, as they fell back, they gave ground grudgingly and at a terrible cost."

At the end of the day, the surviving 450 troopers of the 26th were exhausted, gaunt with hunger, and hollow-eyed from lack of rest. Colonel Pierce, a thirty-year cavalry veteran, was so spent that he could scarcely speak. "We took one helluva beating," he confided to Ramsey, who reached the scene shortly after the battle.

(For the record, the American tanks fared no better than the horse soldiers that day against the tougher Japanese armor and its heavier guns. Every U.S. tank was hit by enemy shells that tore through them, according to one eyewitness, "like a hot knife through butter." Several American tankers were killed, and at least one entire tank crew was captured.)

Ramsey recalled barely recognizing Lieutenant Steve Graves, an old friend from Fort Stotsenburg and one of the first survivors of the battle that he saw face-to-face. "He was frighteningly thin, and his eyes were sunk into his head like those of a dead man," Ramsey said. "But he was not unique. Nearly all the men were prostrate with exhaustion and shock."

Still, the 26th had only begun to fight. After a few hours' rest, they were on the move again to protect the vulnerable flanks of the Philippine Army's floundering infantry units and hold the fragile lines of defense that would allow the rest of the USAFFE to reach the defensive bastion of Bataan.

The horsemen's most historic action was still several weeks away, however. When it came, Lieutenant Ramsey would be the man giving the orders.

Shortly before dawn on Christmas morning, after spending almost three days and nights inching their way through the massive traffic jam on Highway Three, PFCs Karl King and Ike Williams had crossed the Layac bridge over the Culo River and driven their borrowed Army staff car onto Bataan Peninsula. The two young Marines were still searching for the Second Battalion of the Fourth Marine Regiment, but they had only the foggiest idea of where to find it.

"According to our map, the town of Abucay was about ten miles south of the Layac bridge," King recalled. "The next town was Balanga, and about three miles farther on, the map showed a road cutting west across Bataan to the fishing village of Bagac on the coast of the South China Sea."

Williams and King didn't know it at the time, but Abucay, the Layac bridge, Balanga, and Bagac would all become the scenes of fierce battles in days to come.

"The road we were on led to Mariveles at the tip of Bataan and was pretty heavily traveled," King said. "We decided we'd better get off that road before we met any Army units that might question why two enlisted Marines were in an Army general's staff car."

The road to Bagac was little more than a rough trail barely wide enough for one vehicle. It wound through dense jungle, crossed a saddle between two mountains, and didn't appear to have been traveled by anyone else in weeks. But at a clearing along the way, King and Williams happened upon a veritable gold mine in the form of a small supply dump, now apparently forgotten and overgrown with vines.

The two Marines helped themselves to a pair of backpacks, several changes of Army-issue khakis, boxes of .45-caliber ammunition, and bandoleers of rifle ammo. A few miles farther on, they left the staff car beside the trail and walked the rest of the way to Bagac, where they received a rousing welcome from townspeople who insisted that the Americans join their holiday celebration.

"Since we were aware of Admiral Hart's idea for the reinforced Fourth Marines to man the western line of defense, we assumed the regiment would come up from Mariveles to take up its positions nearby," King said, "so we decided to wait for the regiment to come to us."

King and Williams were destined to be bitterly disappointed, however. Because of animosity toward their Corps by General MacArthur, there would be no Marine units assigned to the front lines on Bataan. Instead, one of the three best-trained, most combat-ready American fighting forces in the Philippines would be relegated to beach defense on Corregidor, where it would never fire a shot in anger until the final Japanese amphibious assault on the Rock more than four months later.

"The Marines got more than their share of glory in World War I," MacArthur reportedly told one of his staff officers. "They're not going to do that in this war."

* * *

The fifty-one American and Filipino nurses who clambered aboard buses and trucks in Manila on Christmas Eve as the first assigned staff members of a new 1,000-bed hospital on Bataan—to be known simply as Hospital No. 1—had no clue what to expect when they reached their destination. Some envisioned a neat red-brick building equipped with all the amenities of modern medicine. At the very least, they expected a fully equipped military surgical facility, including an operating pavilion, an emergency room, multiple postoperative wards, a well-stocked pharmacy, laundry, mess, and adequate staff quarters.

It wasn't as if many of these first nurses to arrive on Bataan hadn't already seen their share of war wounds. As members of the staff at Sternberg General Hospital in Manila, they'd been flooded with hundreds of critically wounded men in the wake of the enemy air raids. As Army Lieutenant Juanita Redmond, an attractive young RN from South Carolina, put it: "They came in trucks, ambulances, buses, carts, anything that had wheels. They were brought in on blood-crusted litters, many of them still bleeding, some with shrapnel lodged in their wounds, or arms dangling, or partially severed legs, and many were dead when they reached us."

But at least at Sternberg they'd had access to the most advanced state-of-the-art medical facilities. When they saw what awaited them on Bataan, they may have yearned to return to Manila and take their chances in an open city.

When the buses stopped briefly at a small village en route to the hospital site, nurse Redmond got a hint that her former life as a civilized medical professional—one who enjoyed frequent afternoon rounds of golf and evenings of fine dining and dancing under the stars—was now a thing of the past.

Not having had an opportunity to eat all day, Redmond was hungry, but she lost her appetite when she saw one of the soldiers accompanying the buses wolfing down handfuls of wild rice cooked by the villagers.

"That stuff's contaminated or worm-infested or both," another nurse warned the man.

"Listen, sister," he said, wiping his mouth with the back of his hand, "you'll be eating worse than this before this party's over, and you'll be damn glad to get it!"

The nurses merely laughed. *How silly*, they thought. *Surely, no one's going to go hungry in the United States Army.* In a few weeks, they would realize how prophetic the soldier's words had been.

Several hours later, nurse Leona Gastinger stared in disbelief at a ramshackle aggregation of twenty-nine open-sided bamboo and nipa sheds—the abandoned Philippine Army training camp that now served as the makeshift wards of Hospital No. 1.

"*This* is a hospital?" she gasped.

Although certainly not by Gastinger's definition, it *was* indeed a hospital—and the only one currently available to the defenders of Bataan. Someone had spread out several bedsheets on the ground in the compound outside the sheds and painted a large red cross on them. The symbol was hopefully intended to keep Japanese bombers away, but Gastinger wasn't so sure how effective it would be.

"Welcome, ladies," said one of the doctors who had arrived the previous day. "Make yourselves at home."

A few minutes later, Gastinger, Redmond, and the others were busily setting up cots, scrubbing the dirt off the crude facilities, and generally trying to make the best of a bad situation that they feared could only grow worse.

On December 26, a second group of nurses arrived at Hospital No. 1. By that evening, they were treating their first crop of more than 200 casualties.

From Christmas night until New Year's Eve, Sergeant Clem Kathman's home was a cane patch near the village of Hermosa. Then another marching order arrived, and Kathman and his comrades moved a few hundred yards into a rice paddy, where they dug the obligatory foxholes but left them vacant, preferring to retire to some straw stacks for the night.

On New Year's Day 1942, dawn arrived at about the same time as a skyful of Japanese dive-bombers. With brief intervals of quiet in between, the raids continued until afternoon as the bombers tried—but consistently failed—to demolish a nearby bridge.

"I'll always remember that day," said Kathman, "the same as I'll always remember December 8, 1941. After about the umpteenth raid, our telephone went dead, and I figured a Jap bomber must've hit the wires we'd strung across the river bottom below the bridge. All the other guys were busy manning our AA guns, so I shouldered my '03 Springfield, grabbed a test phone, wire cutters, and tape and went to fix the phone line, hoping the Japs would lay off for a few minutes."

Finding the break in the lines was easy enough since a large bomb crater marked the spot where the wires had crossed the streambed. With trembling fingers, sweat running down his face, and one eye on the sky, Kathman got the wires spliced and taped in short order. He'd just plugged in the test phone when the AA guns opened up again.

"Glancing up, I saw dive-bombers heading my way with 500-pound bombs hanging from their bellies," he recalled. "I ran like hell for some boulders and barely reached them when I heard a whistling sound, and a bomb hit not twenty feet from where I'd been working fifteen seconds before. It plunged into a Filipino shack and blew it—and the family that lived there—into a million pieces. I had the very same terrible, end-of-the-world feeling that I'd had that day at Clark Field."

To add to Kathman's discomfort, the bomb that he so narrowly escaped had severed the phone wires again. "I had to do the whole thing over a second time," he said. "Same trembling. Same sweating. Same eye on the sky. I'm sure my communications instructor would've been downright disgusted with the job I did."

For Lieutenant Ed Whitcomb, the final days of 1941 and the first days of the new year were spent deep in the heart of the Bataan jungle, where a man could walk for miles at midday under an unbroken canopy of foliage and never see the sky. Whitcomb still yearned to fly again, but he'd learned to accept—for the moment at least—his new job as a communications officer in charge of a small radio station and a primitive telephone system linking his headquarters with a new airstrip called Cabcaben Field. His friend, Lieutenant Croxton, had been assigned to a higher headquarters a mile or so down the road, but Whitcomb was still sharing quarters with another friend, Lieutenant Jim Dey.

Carved by Navy engineers out of a series of rice paddies, Cabcaben was one of several of tactical airstrips intended to accommodate the dozens of new U.S. fighters and dive-bombers reportedly en route to the Philippines. Toward this goal, officers and enlisted men of the old 19th Bomb Group were working around the clock to build camouflaged revetments for the anticipated aircraft. At the moment, however, Cabcaben had the distinction of being the only "active" airfield on Bataan without a single plane.

At twilight on an evening in early January, Whitcomb was walking back to his bivouac area from the airstrip after receiving an especially discouraging piece of news. The ship that was supposed to return to Bataan to pick up Whitcomb and other former aircrew members of the 19th and take them to Del Monte Field on Mindanao had been spotted and sunk by a Japanese patrol plane.

"I was still feeling glum when I got to camp and saw Jim Dey standing on a big boulder in the middle of a stream, stark naked, and singing 'When Johnny Comes Marching Home' at the top of his voice," Whitcomb remembered.

"Hey, what's with you and all the merriment?" Whitcomb demanded.

"Christ, Whit, haven't you heard the news?" Dey yelled. "A big convoy's coming through the San Bernardino Straits right this minute. Aircraft carriers, battle wagons, the whole works. It's only a matter of hours till—"

"I think this rumor's an honest one, Whit," interjected the voice of another friend, Lieutenant John Renka. "Jim picked it up down at the Navy base at Mariveles today. The Navy's betting two to one that there'll be planes in here within twenty-four hours."

"We've had rumors from the Navy before," Whitcomb said, shaking his head, "and from the chaplain, and from Corregidor. I'll believe there's reinforcements on the way when I see 'em coming. I'm gonna get an early chow and go back to the airstrip to monitor the radio. I'll let you know if I hear anything good."

On his way to the mess area, Whitcomb wondered in spite of his better judgment if this latest rumor could conceivably be true. Unfounded reports of relief forces and imminent reinforcements that momentarily boosted morale, then vanished like puffs of smoke, were a dime a dozen on Bataan, and Whitcomb had no intention of getting excited prematurely about this one.

At the field kitchen, he found the chow the same as it had been for days—rice and canned tomatoes, and not nearly enough of either, and to make the situation even less palatable, each minimal meal came with a dose of quinine doled out by a mess sergeant to reduce the risk of malaria.

After dinner, in a dismal frame of mind, Whitcomb joined a small group of comrades in a bamboo thicket, and the same inevitable questions began popping up: "What the hell are we doing in this godforsaken place, anyway? So we defend the Philippines. So what? What damned difference does it make to any of us Americans unless we own a sugar plantation, a pineapple plantation, or a mine out here?"

When the phone rang in the operations shack, Whitcomb headed over to listen in on the conversation. But before he got there, the wide-eyed operations officer burst through the doorway.

"Planes coming in sometime tonight," he said excitedly.

Whitcomb's mood immediately brightened. "How many planes? Where from?"

"Don't know," said the operations guy, "but we've got to be ready for them."

"Hey, this confirms the rumor Jim Dey got from the Navy today," Whitcomb said, feeling his own pulse quicken.

"Lord, I hope so," said the other officer. "I better get my crews together! We're all set for 'em!"

Everybody was laughing and joking about their last night in San Francisco when they first heard the sound of approaching aircraft engines. Then, as the field lights flashed on and the first plane touched down, the small crowd at the edge of the field started cheering and punching the air with their fists.

"We thought for sure that help had arrived," Whitcomb recalled. "We were safe, we thought, and we'd soon be flying missions again."

Moments later, though, the onlookers identified the new arrivals as three battle-scarred P-40s, then gaped open-mouthed as a fourth plane missed the runway and crashed into the trees as it attempted to land, scattering its wreckage over 500 feet of jungle. Fortunately, the pilot escaped serious injury, but the same couldn't be said for the hopes and dreams of the watchers on the ground.

"We'd received our reinforcements, all right!" Whitcomb recalled many years later, his voice still tinged with disappointment. "Three beat-up P-40s from another Bataan field three kilometers away!"

* * *

On New Year's Day, only nine days after the main enemy landings on Luzon, advance units of General Homma's 14th Army marched into the open city of Manila, touching off wild celebrations by Japanese troops. From Corregidor, officers at USAFFE headquarters could see the "flaming asshole" Japanese flag hoisted above the Manila Hotel, where General MacArthur and his family had made their home slightly more than three weeks earlier.

"Homma was still unconcerned about the massed withdrawal into Bataan," wrote historian Duane Schultz. "He believed that victory lay in the occupation of Manila, now undefended and only twelve miles south of his main units. Once the city was in Japanese hands, Homma thought, the Philippine campaign would be almost over. . . . He was wrong."

As Homma would later discover to his dismay, the most important action that day was taking place a long way from Manila at the small town of Calumpit on the Pampanga River south of San Fernando. To reach Bataan, the weary troops of both the NLF and the SLF would have to cross the river at Calumpit over the same bridge on Highway Three.

"The bridge was a serious bottleneck," Wainwright would observe years later. "The Japs knew it and started for it, bent on trapping a large part of the South Luzon Force. We had to protect that bridge."

There were two major problems in doing so, however. One was that the only troops available to counter the oncoming enemy were 500 survivors of the decimated 91st Philippine Division, a regiment of the beaten-up 71st Philippine Division, a single artillery battalion with six old howitzers, and a handful of tanks from the 192nd Tank Battalion.

The other problem was that the Japanese almost got there first.

A major enemy attack came at 10:30 AM on December 31, but with what reinforcements Wainwright could muster, the 91st managed to hold its position all day in bitter fighting while General Jones's South Luzon troops "ran what amounted to a gauntlet," in Wainwright's words. By midnight, most of Jones's force had made it through San Fernando to safety, thanks to a courageous stand north of the town by the 11th and 21st Philippine Divisions. Wainwright himself crossed the Calumpit bridge at about that same time.

At 1 AM on January 1, the ominous rumble of approaching tanks gave Wainwright an anxious moment, but when he discovered that the sound came from American armor of the 192nd Tank Battalion, he relaxed a little.

"I welcomed in the New Year by ordering the plucky 91st to begin its own withdrawal over the Calumpit bridge—and to be done with it before daylight," Wainwright said. "I was at the bridge at dawn as the last elements of the 91st crossed."

Soldiers in the 91st's final truck jerked to a stop at Wainwright's end of the bridge to warn him that they 'd been fired on by a Japanese patrol at a crossroad only 500 yards away. Through field glasses, the general could clearly see the enemy patrol, the lead element of a large Japanese advance guard moving rapidly toward the bridge.

Wainwright jerked a thumb toward the Calumpit highway bridge. "Blow it!" he yelled to Lieutenant Colonel Harry Skerry, his chief engineer.

But Skerry hesitated. "Sir, about a platoon of the 14th Engineers [a crack Philippine Scouts outfit] are still detonating bridges between here and Manila. If we blow this one, we'll cut off their escape."

Wainwright stared back toward the approaching Japanese column, then glanced at his watch, knowing he had only seconds to make a decision. It was exactly 6:15 AM when he repeated his order.

"Sorry, but we can't wait any longer," he said. "Blow it now."

Seconds later, eight tons of dynamite exploded in one thunderous blast as both the highway and railroad bridges across the wide, unfordable Pampanga River came crashing down, leaving the pursuing Japanese stranded on its eastern bank.

The next-to-last approach to Bataan from the east was now closed. Of the 184 bridges that had initially been defended to enable the Allied retreat toward the peninsula, 183 had now been destroyed to hold the Japanese at bay. Only one remained intact.

The Layac bridge over the Culo River northwest of the town of Abucay represented the last gateway to Bataan. Once General Jones's troops crossed the Culo, they would fall back, along with Wainwright's force, to a pre-established main line of resistance stretching across the width of Bataan but broken in the center by an impassable mountain range dominated by 4,000-foot Mount Natib on the north and 5,000-foot Mount Bataan on the south. MacArthur's defensive plan called for Wainwright to take command of the newly created I Corps on the west side of the mountains and General George Parker to command II Corps on the eastern front. Jones's South Luzon Force was to take up positions in Parker's sector.

At 2 AM on January 6, moments after the exhausted riders and skin-and-bones mounts of the 26th Cavalry followed other rear-guard elements of Wainwright's force across the Culo, the Layac bridge was blown. Its destruction slammed the door in the faces of the pursuing Japanese, but it simultaneously bottled up an estimated 80,000 American and Filipino troops—along with 25,000 or more Filipino refugees—in a sanctuary with no escape hatch.

From this point on, hunger was to be a constant companion of Bataan's defenders. WPO-3 had envisioned a force of no more than about 40,000 men falling under siege on the peninsula. Even for this number, the food supply would have been inadequate, but with close to three times as many mouths to feed, semi-starvation would quickly begin taking its toll.

Only a day earlier, on January 5, MacArthur had approved a recommendation by Lieutenant Colonel Irvin Alexander, his Bataan quartermaster, to place the garrison on half-rations of about 2,000 calories per day per man. This amount was marginally enough to sustain a sedentary individual but totally inadequate for a combat soldier working or fighting up to twenty hours a day. Furthermore, the calories available, consisting mostly of rice, canned fish, and canned vegetables, lacked many of the nutritional elements essential to human health, and even the lower rate of consumption couldn't be sustained for long, Alexander warned. Unless stringent additional belt-tightening was ordered, he estimated that the defenders' food supply would run out in sixty days or less.

Personnel in the field were already supplementing their short rations with canned foods scrounged in Manila or at scattered depots during the retreat, as well as with anything remotely edible that they came across in the wilds. As Alexander put it: "Any carabao [a type of water buffalo used extensively as domestic beasts of burden in the Philippines] encountered in the jungle was classed as wild, and neither his ancestry nor his ownership was investigated."

Thus, despite their failure to block the American-Filipino withdrawal into Bataan, the Japanese commanders had ample reason to remain outwardly confident. Lieutenant General Sasumu Morioka of General Homma's staff compared the U.S. withdrawal to "a cat entering a sack." Wainwright, on whose thin shoulders would rest the chief burden in the struggle to come, described Bataan with brutal candor as "a symbol of forlorn hope."

As the original framers of War Plan Orange had realized more than two decades before Pearl Harbor, Bataan was a near-ideal place for mounting a military defense. But this was true only if its defenders were adequately supplied and equipped in advance, and the garrison on Bataan was critically short of everything an army needed to survive a siege. The rugged terrain and thick vegetation offered excellent protection against air attacks, but it also made ground movement slow and difficult.

The coastal waters of Manila Bay on the east were generally too shallow to accommodate troopships or landing barges, and Bataan's west coast was studded with cliffs and promontories that made amphibious operations difficult—but not impossible, as the Japanese would shortly prove. Communications, meanwhile, were strictly of the Dark Ages variety. Telephone lines were nonexistent; only a handful of radios were available; and messengers had a distressing habit of getting lost amid the maze of thickets, ridges, and streams.

Only two roads worth the name existed on the peninsula. Route 110 was a paved two-lane highway whose route formed a large horseshoe, running south along the coast of Manila Bay from Layac to Mariveles at the lower tip of Bataan, then following the west coast north to the town of Moron, where it ended. The other road (the one that Marine PFCs King and Williams had traveled in their borrowed staff car) was the only direct east–west route across the peninsula. But it was little more than a cobblestone trail through a rugged wilderness and was barely wide enough to accommodate a single car or truck.

MacArthur's designated first line of defense was manned and fully fortified by January 7. Known as the Abucay–Mauban line, it extended from the east coast town of Abucay to the west coast village of Mauban with a five-mile gap for the mountains in the middle. Its in-depth defenses included a chain of forward outposts entrenched ahead of the main line and a system of secondary defenses well to the rear. Eight miles south of the main defensive line was a second—and last—line of defense that ran from Bagac on the west to Orion on the east. Preparations along the Bagac–Orion line were just getting started on January 7, the day the struggle for Bataan officially began.

Five days earlier, on January 2, the Japanese high command had unwittingly done a tremendous favor for the troops of MacArthur, Wainwright, and Parker. Because of the invaders' relatively easy success in advancing thus far, plus faulty intelligence reports placing total Allied strength on Bataan at only 25,000 physically spent troops, Tokyo decided to pull some of General Homma's best units out of the Philippines and send them to join the invasion of Java.

Instead of attacking the U.S. bastion with a nucleus of experienced, battle-hardened veterans, Homma was forced to rely on the newly arrived 65th Independent Brigade, consisting primarily of 6,500 conscripts with barely a month of training under their belts. The brigade's own commander, Lieutenant General Akira Nara, a 1927 graduate of the U.S. Army's Infantry School, described his troops as "absolutely unfit for combat," and they immediately proved him right.

On the afternoon of January 9, the Japanese launched their first concerted effort to overrun Bataan's defenders with a two-pronged attack on both sides of the peninsula. Elements of the 65th Brigade drove south down the east side of Bataan toward a defensive line manned by Parker's troops at Mabatang near Manila Bay.

The inexperienced enemy soldiers marched with seeming unconcern in a column of fours, followed by several batteries of horse-drawn artillery, until a half-dozen U.S. 155-millimeter howitzers opened fire on them at point-blank range from nearby hillsides, tearing bloody gaps in their ranks. Instead of retreating when the barrage lifted momentarily, the Japanese soldiers simply re-formed their columns and continued marching into the teeth of the guns, leaving scores of dead and wounded on the field.

About two hours later, a second group of Japanese moved west on an undefended road from Layac toward Olongapo on Subic Bay. Wainwright's forward positions were primed and ready for them, and Wainwright himself expected an attack at any moment. But the Japanese force bogged down amid a labyrinth of tortuous terrain and destroyed bridges, and it would take the better part of a week for the enemy troops to cover eleven miles and reach Wainwright's front line. For the moment, a deceptive quiet fell over the western sector of the front.

By the time MacArthur paid his first—and last—visit to the combat zone on January 10, it was clear that the defenders had scored no worse than a draw in round one of the Battle of Bataan. Over the ensuing decades, scorn and ridicule have often been directed at "Dugout Doug" for remaining holed up in his subterranean headquarters on Corregidor while the ailing, half-starved Bataan garrison fought the Japanese to a standstill. But MacArthur's appearance at the front lines—brief and perfunctory though it was—unquestionably provided a major morale boost for "his" men.

When the USAFFE commander's four-car entourage arrived at I Corps headquarters at mid-morning on the 10th, after first calling on General Parker's II Corps on the east side of the front, Wainwright and his entire staff were lined up and waiting.

MacArthur was all smiles as he climbed out of his car and extended his hand to Wainwright. "I'm glad to see you back from the north, Jonathan," he said warmly. "The execution of your withdrawal and your mission in covering the withdrawal of the South Luzon Force were as fine as anything in history."

In the course of their conversation, Wainwright suggested that MacArthur take a short walk to see a nearby battery of 155-millimeter howitzers in action and talk with members of the gun crews, but MacArthur declined.

"No, Jonathan," he said. "I don't want to *see* them. I want to *hear* them."

In a meeting with several dozen I Corps officers, MacArthur virtually oozed optimism and confidence. Japanese air superiority was only temporary, he said. New planes were on the way from the States to airfields on Mindanao, and the 20,000 U.S. troops on Mindanao were available to reinforce the Bataan defenders for a major counter-offensive to reoccupy Manila in the near future. Finally, he assured his listeners that the valiant resistance by Bataan's garrison had touched the hearts of the American people and set a courageous example for the rest of the nation's armed forces. Most who heard the speech were bolstered and inspired by it.

From troops on the line, however, MacArthur's appearance received sharply mixed reviews. PFC Richard M. Gordon, who had come to the Philippines on the same ship with Wainwright and who had often exercised the general's horses during the peaceful interlude before the war, was angered by the contrast in appearances between the visitors from Corregidor and the officers on Bataan. Not only were MacArthur and his entourage "overdressed" in their sharply creased uniforms, neckties, and, in some cases, jackets but were also overbearing in their manner, Gordon complained. It was Wainwright and his staff in their dirty, wrinkled, sweat-stained khakis "who impressed the troops at the CP [command post] with their command of the situation," he concluded.

Yet for other front-line officers and enlisted men, the reaction was totally opposite, and they came away from their encounter with MacArthur with unconcealed admiration.

Earlier that morning, for example, as Japanese dive-bombers were plastering the area east of the mountains where troops of the 31st Infantry were dug in, Corporal Paul Decker, a medic, spotted an impressive figure approaching across a treeless hillside.

"My God, look over here!" he yelled to Captain Ralph Hibbs, commander of the Second Battalion aid station.

When Hibbs turned to look where Decker was pointing, he was amazed to see General MacArthur strolling casually toward them, accompanied by General Jones and his staff.

"I jumped out of the foxhole and gave a rather clumsy salute without thinking," Hibbs later recalled. "MacArthur waved to stay put, and swinging his riding crop vigorously with great strides, moved across the open meadow as more Zeros came winging in. A couple of his aides were tugging on his shirt and telling him to get down, but he shrugged them off and kept walking. The bombs landed fairly close, but the general was completely oblivious to them. Me—I was in my foxhole! 'There is really a brave man,' I thought."

After MacArthur's party had moved on, Hibbs turned to Decker. "If I ever stumble into another war," he said quietly, "I just hope MacArthur's on my side."

Although the Japanese had no knowledge of MacArthur's January 10 tour of Bataan's defenses, either before or during his visit, they picked that same day to drop thousands of propaganda leaflets on American and Filipino positions along with their bombs. The message they conveyed, addressed to the USAFFE commander and signed by General Homma, constituted an ominous rebuttal to MacArthur's pep talks to the defenders. It began:

> You are well aware that you are doomed. The end is near. The question is how long you will be able to resist. You have already cut rations by half. I appreciate the fighting spirit of yourself and your troops who have been fighting with courage. Your prestige and honor have been upheld.
>
> However, in order to avoid needless bloodshed and to save the remnants of your divisions . . . you are advised to surrender. In the meantime . . . our offensive will be continued with inexorable force and will bring upon you only disaster.

The message drew no direct reaction from MacArthur's headquarters. Some of the troops at the front did, however, find a highly practical—and appropriately derisive—use for the Japanese leaflets. As with many other kinds of supplies, there was an acute shortage of toilet paper on Bataan.

5

Victory, Retreat, and a Final Charge

Shortly after MacArthur & Company departed aboard a PT boat on their return trip to Corregidor, the Japanese launched the first in a series of attacks in II Corps's eastern sector of the front against the Third Battalion, 57th Regiment, Philippine Scouts.

The battalion commander was Lieutenant Colonel Philip Fry, an old Philippines hand who had returned to the islands for a second tour in November 1941. At the time, he'd regretted having to leave his wife in the States along with other evacuated military dependents because they'd shared so many great times on his first tour. Now, of course, he was relieved to know that she was safe on the other side of the Pacific.

Like the 26th Cavalry, the 57th was among the Scouts' most highly regarded units. It was also one of the few armed with the new Garand M-1 semiautomatic rifles. In meeting and savagely repulsing what may have been the first Japanese "banzai charges" of the Pacific war against U.S. forces on the afternoon of January 10, the regiment would more than live up to its reputation.

As Fry later described the action: "It was slaughter. All of our guns had been carefully sighted for mutual support, and the Japs were caught by terrific fire, both frontal and flanking. Even now, I can't understand why the Japs launched an attack of this kind against modern weapons. My only explanation is that they hadn't faced trained troops before and thought if enough noise were made, the opposition would simply fade away. The attack was smashed before it got under way."

(In future Pacific battles on other islands, many U.S. field commanders would be as puzzled as Fry by such suicidal tactics. But as part of their Bushido code, Japanese soldiers had been trained to believe that their screaming infantry charges with fixed bayonets would strike panic and paralysis into their enemies. It would take many months of fierce combat and tens of thousands of Japanese deaths before they abandoned the banzai approach.)

The men of the 57th were justifiably elated once the attack was broken, especially after they counted only five wounded among their own ranks. But Fry warned them sternly against any premature celebrations. The battle was far from over, he told them, and another, stronger Japanese assault of the same type could be expected at any time.

He was right on all counts. The toughest fighting yet faced by American-Filipino forces lay just ahead.

As Fry had predicted, the frantic afternoon charge by the Japanese was merely a preview of what was coming. The enemy's first all-out effort to pierce Bataan's newly established main line of resistance between the towns of Abucay on the east and Mauban on the west began in General Parker's eastern sector shortly after one o'clock the following morning.

It was kicked off by a furious barrage from Japanese mortars and tank-mounted artillery against positions held by Fry's Third Battalion. The entire battalion front took a pounding, but Captain Herman Gerth's I Company absorbed the worst punishment.

The battalion had left its own light mortars behind during the evacuation of Fort McKinley because the ammunition for them had never arrived. So Fry, whose men had no means of replying to the enemy shelling, called Colonel George Clarke, the regiment's notoriously nervous CO, to request artillery support. But to Fry's consternation, Clarke refused to authorize a barrage.

"We ended in a furious exchange of words," Fry recalled years later, "but still no artillery!"

(Major Harold K. Johnson, executive officer of the 57th, blamed Clarke's refusal on a "phobic" fear that any use of his artillery would draw retaliatory air strikes against his gun emplacements and his command post. When reports of Clarke's nonaction reached USAFFE headquarters a few days later, he was relieved of his command.)

In growing frustration, Fry tried desperately to rally his troops. By now, both K and I Companies were drawing fire from snipers armed with submachine guns, who were slipping through an adjacent sector of American lines held by the Philippine Army's 41st Infantry and circling behind Fry's companies, threatening to cut them off.

Finally, the battalion was forced to fall back, but instead of the sort of full-scale retreat the Japanese had so often seen in the past, Fry's men stiffened and reestablished their lines a few hundred yards to the rear, where they held for the rest of the day.

About ten o'clock that night, the sound of tanks signaled an impending Japanese mechanized attack. But this time Fry was able to obtain the support of a battery of 75-millimeter howitzers, several 37-millimeter antitank guns, and a half-dozen .50-caliber machine guns, although it came with a stipulation that none of these weapons would open fire until the enemy armor was in plain sight.

"The attack was broken up even before the tanks could be used," Fry said. "The Japanese opened up with heavy and light mortar fire . . . [but] not much damage was done, thanks to excellent foxholes. Soon everything we had was in action. The firepower of a battalion armed with modern weapons is something. The Garand rifle is beyond my descriptive powers."

Intent on a major breakthrough and despite horrendous losses, the Japanese continued to pour fresh troops into the fight, sending many of them through the darkness as infiltrators. For several hours, the tide of battle surged back and forth with units of the 57th Regiment being forced to give ground under crushing pressure, then fighting like fiends to regain it.

One key reason that the attackers were largely held in check was the creation of company-level anti-sniper parties—particularly the one led by Lieutenant Alexander "Sandy" Nininger, a young West Pointer from Georgia attached to the First Battalion of the 57th. When an all-volunteer patrol from Nininger's A Company was being formed to track down and kill infiltrators in one heavily infested area, the boyish lieutenant asked for, and received, permission to lead it.

Soon after the heavily armed eight-man party vanished into the gloom, men in the foxholes behind them heard sharp exchanges of gunfire and teeth-rattling blasts from grenades. After a few minutes, the patrol returned intact with all its weapons empty of ammunition.

"We did pretty well," Nininger said, "but we need to go again." On this second foray, however, the lieutenant selected only three other men to accompany him. After a time, Nininger and the others returned to their lines, and Nininger ordered his three comrades to stay there. Then he grabbed a fresh supply of grenades and a bandoleer of ammo for his Browning automatic rifle and ran back into the jungle alone.

"He was never seen alive again," said then Captain John Olson, regimental adjutant of the 57th. "His body was found later leaning against a tree with three dead Japanese lying around him." Nininger was posthumously awarded the Medal of Honor, the first American soldier of World War II to be so honored.

A crucial turning point in the battle came when Major Johnson, executive officer of the 57th, bypassed Colonel Clarke's authority and finally ordered the regiment's heavy artillery into action against concentrated Japanese infantry and armor in a series of cane fields directly facing Fry's I and K Companies. One enemy tank was destroyed, and two others beat a hasty retreat.

After a brief lull along the front, the end of the invaders' offensive came when Fry borrowed E Company from regimental reserve and sent it, plus small groups of men from other units, to support I and K Companies in a coordinated counterattack. Several other companies provided machine guns to counter any enemy attempts to pull back and regroup.

"The attack was a beautiful one—an inspiring sight to see," Fry later commented. "The Scouts had been trained for years in attack, and it was a model of precision. If this attack had been staged at Fort Benning to show visiting firemen the mechanics, it could not have been improved upon. I knew the outcome at once."

As the Japanese tried to withdraw, their ranks were cut to pieces by the machine guns painstakingly positioned for that precise purpose. "The picture that greeted the sleepless eyes of the surviving Scouts as the sun rose was one of utter chaos and devastation," said Captain Olson. "Broken and bloody bodies were sprawled all over the foxholes and open ground throughout the I Company sector and to the left of

K Company. Forward of the front lines, mangled Japanese corpses were strung on the barbed wire like bags of dirty laundry. Abandoned weapons were strewn everywhere."

Most importantly, there had been no American or Filipino retreat. When the shooting was over, the 57th again stood astride its original line. For the first time in the Philippines campaign, a major attacking Japanese force had been soundly defeated, and not a foot of ground had been lost.

Although casualties to the 57th totaled more than 100, Japanese losses probably approached five times that number. Yet the deaths of several young American unit commanders and platoon leaders were keenly felt because they were essentially impossible to replace. Besides Nininger, they included Lieutenants Arthur Green, John Compton, and Kenneth Wilson. Captain Gerth of I Company suffered serious wounds.

For the better part of four days, relative calm had prevailed on General Wainwright's western side of the front. Meanwhile, the I Corps commander had monitored the action by Parker's men on the other side of the mountains with admiration tempered with a bitter dose of realism. II Corps had kept the Japanese in check in vicious fighting, and their artillery had inflicted heavy casualties in each enemy attack. Several times, the Japanese seemed on the brink of a breakthrough, but in each instance Parker's troops had counterattacked and held tenaciously to their position.

But Wainwright knew that few units in Parker's force had the training or fighting ability of the 57th Regiment, which, along with the 31st Infantry, had formed the bulwark of the II Corps defense. Under continuing heavy pressure from the invaders, the less capable troops on the eastern front could eventually be expected to give ground and retreat. Wainwright had seen the same scenario played out too often to believe otherwise.

On January 12, I Corps headquarters was visited by Brigadier General Richard Marshall, commander of the USAFFE's forward echelon on Bataan. After inspecting Wainwright's portion of the front, Marshall repeated the complaints voiced two days earlier by General Sutherland, MacArthur's chief of staff.

"I'm concerned that the gap between your forces and II Corps is too wide across the mountains, General," Marshall said. "If the Nips manage to slip through that gap in strength, there could be hell to pay."

Wainwright shook his head and told Marshall the same thing he'd told Sutherland: "I don't see any way the enemy could attack in force across that mountain range. If he did, he'd have to weaken the main part of his line drastically, and I don't think he's willing to do that. I still believe his main assault will come against Parker's sector."

By all accounts, Wainwright was a highly competent battlefield strategist, one who seldom, if ever, underestimated his foe. This time, however, he was wrong about the ability of Japanese troops to move through the heavily wooded foothills below towering Mount Natib—and his error almost condemned Bataan's defenders to an early doom.

Despite MacArthur's announced intention to relegate all of the approximately 1,000 U.S. Marines in the Philippines to guard duty and beach defense on Corregidor, approximately 200 combat Leathernecks were still on Bataan as of mid-January 1942. They were there primarily because of an order issued by Admiral Hart, commander of the Asiatic Fleet, that, in effect, countermanded MacArthur's directive, at least where the Marines originally assigned to protect the naval station at Olongapo were concerned.

And while PFCs Ike Williams and Karl King were still officially unattached and didn't necessarily fit into any of these categories, they remained on Bataan as well. When the pair finally reached the southern tip of the peninsula after their long, circuitous journey from Manila, they found one mixed group of Marines and sailors manning a salvaged antiaircraft battery in a rice paddy near the port of Mariveles. Another group of Bluejackets and Marines was dug in on the hills above the port with nine .50-caliber machine guns.

"The first familiar face we spotted," King recalled, "was that of Platoon Sergeant Robert A. 'Duke' Clement." After they told Clement how they'd missed their transportation to the States and wound up on Bataan, he snorted, then laughed.

"Only a damn Marine would pull a stunt like that," he said when they recounted the part about their "joy ride" in the Army general's staff car.

Clement seemed genuinely glad to see King and Williams, and so did Navy Commander Francis Bridget, who was forming a "Naval Battalion" for front-line combat and welcomed the addition of two more Marines to help train his 130 sailors in ground warfare.

"His urgency in getting the sailors trained was to make sure they were up to the task when—not if—the Japanese attempted a landing on the undefended China Sea coast," King explained.

Commander Bridget, who had once served as a naval attaché in the U.S. embassy in Tokyo, was well acquainted with Japanese battle tactics, and he was convinced that the enemy would try a flanking invasion on southern Bataan's west coast. At the moment, the sailors in his command were far from ready to meet such a threat, and most of the other naval and former air units assigned to beach defense were equally unprepared.

"Each ill-equipped and untrained unit was thinly spread along its assigned sector," King said. "Apparently, the high command on Bataan discounted the idea of an enemy landing because of the high cliffs and rugged terrain."

In later battles across the Pacific, American fighting men and their leaders would learn from painful experience the almost limitless tenacity of the Japanese soldier. Unfortunately, Bataan's defenders didn't have the benefit of such experience. They still believed that some mountains were impassable, some jungles impenetrable, and some coastlines unassailable.

The U.S. submarine tender *Canopus* had been a semi-permanent fixture in Far Eastern waters since late 1924, shuttling back and forth between Manila Bay and Tsingtao, China, and serving as flagship to the Asiatic Fleet's submarine squadron.

Luckily, the *Canopus* had been docked several miles away in Manila when the Japanese holocaust obliterated the Cavite Navy Yard on December 10, and she'd escaped with only a few dings and scratches. But between December 27 and January 7, after reaching Mariveles harbor on Christmas Day, she was struck in multiple raids by enough enemy bombs to sink most ships and left listing and leaking. Yet even in this seemingly helpless condition, the aging sub tender became perhaps the most valuable remaining ship of the now scattered Asiatic Fleet and a sustaining symbol of comfort and hope for Bataan's defenders.

"Some of her compartments were flooded so that she heeled over and looked abandoned, and the Japs left her alone after that," recalled Radioman First Class Randall Edwards, a Nebraska native who'd joined the Navy in 1935 and served aboard the *Canopus* since 1940. Strategically placed smoke pots were also kept burning aboard the ship to increase her resemblance to a smoldering hulk. But beneath this subterfuge, the twenty-two-year-old vessel was still loaded to the gunwales with many kinds of supplies and still possessed a functional galley, machine shops, foundries, and living quarters. She also remained capable of servicing the occasional U.S. submarines that slipped into the harbor under cover of darkness. Each night, belowdecks, she became a hotbed of dusk-to-dawn activity.

Six *Canopus* crewmen had been killed and another fifteen wounded in the Japanese attacks, but the rest of the tender's 516-man complement helped form the nucleus of the Naval Battalion headed by Commander Bridget. Others continued to work long hours aboard the ship at a wide range of jobs.

Ironically, while troops a few miles away were existing on scant and continually shrinking rations, the ship's substantial stock of food was shared with many of those stationed nearby and served in a genteel manner that was all but forgotten elsewhere.

"If a GI was lucky, he could wrangle an invitation aboard the *Canopus* for an evening meal," recalled Private Lester Tenney of Company B, 192nd Tank Battalion, in a memoir published decades later, "and what a meal it was rumored to be . . . fried chicken, mashed potatoes, carrots and peas, hot strong coffee, and for dessert a piece of freshly baked chocolate cake a la mode."

"The *Canopus* was spoken of almost reverently," added Madeline Ullom, a nurse at Bataan's Hospital No. 1. "A standing invitation to dinner was issued to the nurses. Delicious dinners on white linen tablecloths with silver seemed like another world."

As Radioman Edwards said fondly of his ship more than sixty years after the war, "She was one fine old lady, and she went right on dishing out ice cream until the day before Bataan fell."

* * *

On January 15, MacArthur attempted to rally Bataan's defenders with an upbeat message that struck many of its recipients as a fanciful pipe dream. It was accompanied by orders to his field commanders to read it to their troops in its entirety:

> Help is on the way from the United States. Thousands of troops and hundreds of planes are being dispatched. The exact time of arrival is unknown as they will have to fight their way through Japanese attempts against them. It is imperative that our troops hold until these reinforcements arrive.
>
> No further retreat is possible. We have more troops in Bataan than the Japanese have thrown against us; our supplies are ample; a determined defense will defeat the enemy's attacks. It is a question now of courage and determination. Men who run will merely be destroyed, but men who fight will save themselves and their country.

(In MacArthur's defense, his reference to "thousands of troops and hundreds of planes" being on the way to the Philippines merely echoed a message cabled a short time earlier by President Roosevelt to Philippines president Quezon. "Although I cannot at this time state the day that help will arrive in the Philippines," the cable read, "I can assure you that every vessel available is bearing to the Southwest Pacific the strength that will eventually crush the enemy and liberate your native land.")

MacArthur's admonition appeared genuinely encouraging to the Filipinos, many of whom held the general in almost worshipful esteem. But among many American enlisted men, it drew jeers, derisive laughter, and gestures of contempt, and even some officers found it impossible to conceal their disbelief. "Hell, it's just another one of MacArthur's ghost stories," snapped a company commander in Parker's II Corps.

Historian John Toland captured the prevailing mood on the front lines when he wrote: "Ample supplies? They were already on half-rations. Their grenades were no good, only one in four or five exploding. Their old Stokes mortars were more dangerous to them than to the enemy. Six out of seven rounds failed to detonate on landing, and too often the ill-fitting shells burst the [weapons'] barrels."

So, too, did the anonymous balladeer who jotted down the lyrics to a ditty soon to be sung by many of the Americans on Bataan to the tune of "The Battle Hymn of the Republic":

Dugout Doug MacArthur lies a-shaking on the Rock,
Safe from all the bombers and from any sudden shock.
Dugout Doug is eating of the best food on Bataan,
And his troops go starving on . . .

But the angst, disgust, and betrayal felt by Bataan's rank and file may have best been expressed by United Press correspondent Frank Hewlett, one of the few American journalists who ventured onto Bataan after the siege began, in a blunt-spoken verse that he overheard and sent back to the States.

We're the battling bastards of Bataan,
No mama, no papa, no Uncle Sam;
No aunts, no uncles, no nephews, no nieces;
No pills, no planes, no artillery pieces;
And nobody gives a damn.

It seems the bitterest kind of irony that, within hours after MacArthur's message was received, General Homma's forces launched their largest and most relentless offensive thus far—a two-pronged attack against both the east and west sectors of the Allied front. It came by land, sea, and air—along the coast of the South China Sea, across the mountains, through the jungles, and by planes operating from abandoned American bases on Luzon—and it left no doubt that its goal was to crush the last vestiges of resistance on Bataan once and for all.

The lull in General Wainwright's sector ended with a determined advance by the Japanese down the west coast from Olongapo toward the fishing village of Moron (sometimes spelled "Morong"), barely three miles north of Wainwright's forward positions. Some of the enemy troops picked their way along a narrow, winding coastal trail. Up to 1,200 others defied conventional U.S. military wisdom by boarding small boats and aiming an amphibious assault at the narrow beach below the "unassailable" cliffs. Hundreds more slipped through the gap between Wainwright's right flank and the mountains, just as Generals Sutherland and Marshall had worried and warned they would.

"They came as silently as snakes," Wainwright lamented, "hugging the opposite sides of Mount Silanganan and infiltrating between my right flank and the mountain and Parker's left flank and the mountain."

Almost immediately, Wainwright's concerns about the holding power of Parker's forces were borne out. II Corps was badly flanked on the left, and Wainwright had to send one of his own infantry regiments around the mountain to try to stabilize the line. But by the time this help arrived, a sizable Japanese force had slipped through to attack Parker's troops from the west, and by the end of the day on January 15, the enemy had driven a dangerous wedge between I Corps and II Corps, requiring Wainwright to rush his entire 31st Division to Parker's aid.

Meanwhile, an even more perilous situation was developing on the west side of Wainwright's own lines north of Moron. Some 5,000 Japanese troops had made their way south through the precipices and gorges overlooking the West Road, the only north–south supply route on the west side of Bataan. Now they were massing along the narrow Batalan River and threatening a ruinous breakthrough. If the enemy force could fight its way as far south as the town of Bagac, it could not only seize half the length of the West Road but also wheel east on the peninsula's only east–west road to menace the flank of Parker's II Corps.

Falling back from Moron before the advancing Japanese, to Wainwright's extreme agitation, was the First Philippine Division, considered the best of his all-Filipino units. On the morning of January 16, Wainwright ordered the division back to Moron to make a stand. But before the main body of the division could get there, the task of holding the village would fall to the skeletonized 26th Cavalry's E Troop, commanded by Captain John Wheeler.

Considering the circumstances, Wainwright's orders to Wheeler were almost ludicrous. He and his troopers were told to halt a major

Japanese force at Moron and keep it pinned down there until the First Philippine Division could arrive—or else. And Wheeler's force was expected to accomplish these feats with only three platoons of cavalry—fewer than ninety battle-worn riders and bone-weary horses.

It sounded like a bad practical joke, but it was a matter of life-or-death urgency for Bataan's defenders. Unless Wainwright's troops could firm up at least a temporary defensive line in the vicinity of Moron, he had plenty of reasons to doubt that the powerful Japanese assault now gathering steam could be stopped before it overran the entire peninsula.

Far from feeling jubilant or sensing that his troops now stood on the brink of ultimate victory, Japanese General Homma was deeply distressed at the condition of his 14th Army. The middle of January—the deadline imposed by Tokyo for completing the conquest of the Philippines—had arrived, and the Americans still held Corregidor and were fighting furiously for every inch of Bataan. This was particularly true in the eastern sector of the front, where a series of head-on infantry attacks had produced only windrows of Japanese casualties.

By January 16, it was obvious that the deadline couldn't be met. The American artillery fire was horrendous, far more lethal than Homma had expected, and despite an alleged shortage of ammunition, the defenders' guns kept firing almost constantly. Yet Homma's field commanders continued to order one costly charge after another. Then, with hundreds of dead Japanese soldiers littering the battlefield, reports from the same officers described the American and Filipino positions as "impregnable."

"I am thoroughly disappointed," Homma wrote in his diary. He had every right to be. The 14th Army had suffered close to 7,000 casualties since the ground fighting began, and the losses kept mounting. As they did, men of the attack-leading Summer Brigade, commanded by General Akira Nara, began losing their warrior spirit and failing to follow their officers' directions in battle. So many of Nara's experienced field officers in the reinforced 13,000-man brigade had been killed or wounded that Nara was forced to order those remaining to curtail their blatant risk taking in favor of a more cautious approach.

"A person who cannot lead his men if not in a standing position is not a hero but a fool," Nara admonished them. "There have been actual examples where three persons, the company commander and the platoon leaders, were killed at the same time."

Like the Americans and Filipinos, Japanese troops had also begun running short of food, water, and ammunition, and because of the rough terrain in which they were traveling, they were often without artillery and air support. Neither were the Japanese soldiers immune to the tropical diseases now sickening their foes. (Some U.S. medical authorities, in fact, later expressed the belief that the terrible malaria epidemic that swept across Luzon in early 1942 was actually touched off by Japanese soldiers who had been infected elsewhere.) By mid-January, at least half the invaders were suffering from tropical diseases, and nine out of ten Japanese front-line troops had contracted dysentery from polluted drinking water.

When troopers of the 26th Cavalry had stopped Japanese tanks at Christmastime at the town of Binalonan, armed with little other than hand grenades, .45-caliber pistols, bare hands, and sheer guts, Lieutenant Edwin Ramsey had arrived on the scene too late to take part in the fighting. But on the afternoon of January 16, Ramsey's twenty-seven-man First Platoon of E Troop was destined to be the lead unit of the three dispatched to Moron by Wainwright to contest a strong enemy force already in the process of fording the Batalan River to continue its march south.

The young lieutenant from Wichita, Kansas, had bedded down with his platoon the night before, near exhaustion from a long ride on a reconnaissance mission. The next morning, after supervising the feeding and watering of the horses, he'd accompanied his friend and senior officer, Captain Wheeler, to a hurriedly called meeting with Wainwright.

The I Corps commander had come to deliver a pointed reprimand to General Fidel V. Segundo, the West Point–educated commander of the First Philippine Division, for pulling his troops out of Moron in the first place. It was clear to Ramsey and Wheeler, who were standing only a few yards away, that Wainwright was in an ugly mood as he climbed out of his old Packard sedan and addressed Segundo face-to-face.

"You gave up a good defensive position along the only river between us and the Japanese," Wainwright said. "It was a line we can't afford to abandon, and I'm ordering you to move your division forward at once and reoccupy Moron. I'll send an advance guard of cavalry to secure the town until you get there, but I want you to get moving without delay."

After Segundo, who was widely known for swearing at his troops, had saluted and hurried away, probably preparing to swear some more, Wainwright turned toward Wheeler and Ramsey, and a spark of recognition flashed in his eyes.

"Ramsey, isn't it?" he asked.

"Yes, sir," the lieutenant replied.

"You played in that last polo match at Stotsenburg, right?" Wainwright inquired, referring to a grudge match the previous December, when an elite Manila team had defeated Wainwright's favorite team from Fort Stotsenburg, which had included Ramsey and his treasured gelding, Bryn Awryn.

"Yes sir, I did," Ramsey admitted.

Wainwright's response left no doubt that he was still fuming, but Ramsey was never sure whether the source of the general's anger was Segundo's ill-advised withdrawal or the lost polo match.

"Ramsey, you take the advance guard to Moron," Wainwright snapped. "Now move out!"

Ramsey knew the coastal road that led to Moron by heart, which was a main reason that Wheeler had wanted him to come along. "It was scarcely more than a jungle track," Ramsey said, "deeply rutted and thick with dry-season dust that irritated the eyes, clogged the nostrils, and coated the throat. The underbrush tangled up closely on either side, so dense that you couldn't see three feet into it. It was a dark, dangerous place, virtually an invitation for an ambush."

He assigned PFC Pedro Euperio, one of his most trusted Scouts, and two other troopers to take the point thirty or forty yards ahead of the main body of riders. "Column of twos," he shouted to the rest, "and spread out. We don't want to make easy targets."

At the eastern edge of the village, three trails branched off the road to the left and toward the sea, and Ramsey signaled the column to take the middle one, then divided the column into three eight-man squads. He positioned himself in the lead of the middle squad and about fifty yards behind the riders on the point.

"Raise pistols," he ordered.

Moron looked deserted as the point riders entered the town, and a deafening silence filled the air. As Ramsey recalled decades later, "The huts stood empty on their bamboo stilts, the pens beneath them long stripped of livestock by the retreating Allied army. Beyond lay thick groves of coconut palms inclining through a swamp toward the sea, while to our right, crossed by a rickety wooden bridge, was the narrow Batalan River, the line that Wainwright wanted to occupy."

As the column proceeded slowly toward the center of Moron, marked by a square and the village's only stone structure, a small Catholic church, Ramsey momentarily lost sight of the point riders. Then a sudden burst of rifle and automatic weapons fire broke the silence, and Ramsey spotted scores of enemy soldiers firing from the village center and a Japanese advance guard of several hundred others wading toward him across the river. Within minutes, he realized, the main Japanese force would be storming across the Batalan bridge to seize Moron.

At that moment, the point riders came galloping back with PFC Euperio badly shot up. He was still gripping his pistol and clinging to the reins, but his blood was streaming across his horse's neck and flanks. Ramsey dismounted long enough to help Euperio to a sheltered position behind one of the huts, but there was nothing else he could do for the wounded man at the moment. Right now, he could think of nothing but the approaching Japanese.

"Over the rattling gunfire," Ramsey recalled, "I ordered my troopers to deploy as foragers with their horses all lined up abreast with me, and I raised my pistol. A charge, I believed, would be our only hope to break up the body of Japanese troops and survive against their superior numbers. For centuries, the shock of a mounted charge had proved irresistible; now the circumstances and all my training made it instinctual."

Ramsey glanced to his left, then to his right. He jabbed the air with his pistol, then brought his arm forward and down.

"Chaaaarge!" he shouted.

The next few moments were a flurry of sheer madness that seemed to last an hour as a solid line of screaming riders and wild-eyed horses stunned—and thoroughly shattered—a Japanese force estimated to be at least a dozen times larger.

"Bent nearly prone across our horses' backs," Ramsey remembered, "we flung ourselves at the Japanese advance, firing our pistols full into their startled faces. A few returned our fire, but most fled in confusion. Some dashed into the swamp. Others ran on through the village toward heavy underbrush on the other side. Those closest to the river turned and waded back across to the dense jungle on the opposite bank. We killed and wounded a lot of them and scattered the rest."

The charge overwhelmed the enemy advance unit and carried all the way to the swamp. There, the troopers dismounted and pulled their rifles from their scabbards. One squad formed a skirmish line along the river to keep the main body of Japanese from crossing while Ramsey led the rest back into the village to hunt down snipers hiding in the huts and underbrush.

Moments later, a new burst of gunfire signaled the arrival of Wheeler's other two platoons. As the newcomers fought their way into the village, Wheeler dispatched one platoon to reinforce Ramsey's men at the river, and the other platoon fanned out to join the sniper hunt. Sporadic Japanese mortar fire from across the river had little impact on the troopers, but several horses that had broken free in the confusion were killed.

As the men of the 26th Cavalry hunkered down to maintain a steady rate of rifle fire to keep the enemy at bay, Ramsey was startled to look over his shoulder and find a grievously wounded PFC Euperio standing behind him, still clutching his pistol and "weaving like a drunken sailor" from shock and loss of blood.

"What the hell are you doing here?" Ramsey demanded. "You've got to get to the rear and get something done with those wounds."

"But sir, I cannot go back," Euperio mumbled. "I . . . I am on guard."

The trooper's left side was riddled by four bullet wounds, three to his chest and shoulder and another through his left arm. "I thought for sure he was a goner," Ramsey said. "I got him over against the church and on the ground until the battle was over and he could be evacuated. One of my first actions after that was to cite this man for the Distinguished Service Cross. It looked like the award would have to be posthumous, but much to my surprise and relief, Euperio lived. He received his medal after the liberation of the Philippines."

In bitter house-to-house fighting, Troop E's intrepid band of cavalrymen held Moron under continuous enemy mortar, artillery, and small-arms fire until late afternoon when General Segundo's division arrived and reoccupied the town. Incredibly, only one member of Ramsey's platoon had been killed. Six others, including PFC Euperio, had been wounded severely enough to be evacuated. "As for the Japanese," Ramsey would note some forty years later, "dozens lay dead and wounded all over the village and across the open fields toward the river." While no official body count was made, Japanese casualties probably totaled more than one hundred.

Ramsey and Wheeler both suffered minor shrapnel wounds during the melee, but neither realized it until they reached a safe area where other wounded were being tended, and their adrenaline rush subsided.

"Ramsey," Wheeler said, "you've got blood on your leg."

Ramsey glanced down at a broad brown stain on his trousers where a piece of shrapnel had knifed into his left knee.

"Look who's talking," he said, pointing at Wheeler, whose knee-high riding boot was oozing blood from a bullet hole in his calf. "What do you call that?"

The action by the First Platoon, Troop E, 26th Cavalry, Philippine Scouts, at Moron on January 16, 1942, is generally recognized by today's military historians as the world's last authentic battlefield charge by mounted cavalry.

Unfortunately, the positive effects of the charge and the subsequent stand by men of the 26th would be short-lived. Late in the afternoon of January 17, the First Philippine Division would again be forced to withdraw from Moron to positions about a mile and a half south, where it would make another stand. On January 19, after incurring heavy losses, the division would retreat once more, but at this point Wainwright's entire main line of resistance was in a state of flux and in growing danger of falling apart.

In addition to the 5,000-man force advancing down the west coast and pushing past Moron toward Mauban, at least two other segments of Japan's 14th Army were posing major trouble in Wainwright's sector. One was a 700-man force under Colonel Hiroshi Nakanishi that somehow hacked its way through the jungles on the slopes of Mount Silanganan, a shorter peak west of Mount Natib, to circle behind Wainwright's forward units on his right flank and set up a roadblock that cut off the beleaguered First Philippine Division.

Farther south—well behind Wainwright's second main line of defense, running from Bagac on the west coast to Orion on the east coast—a 1,200-man amphibious force tried to land at Caibobo Point on the early morning of January 23. Fortunately for the defenders, the landing barges were blown severely off course by stiff winds and treacherous currents, and many of the enemy troops were annihilated when American spotlights and machine guns found them as they tried to land elsewhere. Those who escaped took refuge in the jungle and most were eventually hunted down by Marines and sailors of Commander Bridget's Naval Battalion.

Not far away from the positions held by the 57th Regiment, the all-American 31st Infantry had been used primarily since January 10 as an "emergency reserve," assigned to plug holes in the Allied line wherever they were gouged by the Japanese. But on January 15, the 31st received orders to fill its own designated spot on the line near the village of Abucay at the eastern terminus of the II Corps sector of the front.

"On the night of January 16, we moved up and deployed in a thicketed ravine with complete, readymade foxholes nearby," recalled Captain Ralph Hibbs, medical officer of the Second Battalion. "This was about the sixteenth move and fifteenth foxhole that I'd had so far."

By the following dawn, the regiment was prepared to launch a counterattack aimed at pushing the main line of resistance (MLR) north of Abucay to positions overlooking the Balantay River on the eastern slopes of Mount Natib.

The morning quiet was soon shattered by a thunderous American barrage and an equally thunderous response from Japanese 105s that brought shrapnel raining down in all directions, "covering the area like an umbrella for a couple of hundred meters," in Hibbs's words.

In the adjoining Third Battalion position, a large chunk of shrapnel struck Captain Tom Bell, commander of M Company, in the left groin, severing his leg and his femoral artery, which gushed a thumb-size stream of blood with every beat of Bell's heart. He would have died in a matter of seconds if Captain Jim Brennan, the battalion surgeon, hadn't grabbed and clinched the artery with his bare fist until he managed to get a forceps on it. As it was, Bell lost his leg but survived, and Brennan was awarded a Silver Star for his quick thinking and bravery under fire.

Thus began ten straight days of almost constant combat for the 31st Infantry. Nightfall on the 17th brought an eerie silence, broken only by the moans of wounded men on both sides. The Japanese had also suffered numerous casualties, and their usual night assault never materialized.

"The ravine was full of our wounded with a few drifting to the rear," said Hibbs. "The unconscious or dying were segregated in their own terminal thicket . . . [and] ambulances began moving up the narrow roads in the dusk, crossing the open slopes, making contact with our litter teams, so that after an hour or two of darkness, most of the wounded had been evacuated."

Hibbs was proud of his medics' performance during their first taste of front-line action. One medic had been killed, shot through the head as he tried to help a wounded soldier, and another was seriously wounded, but they'd never once let the constant danger keep them from their duties.

"The Second Battalion had been badly mauled," Hibbs said, "but the enemy in front of us was annihilated. The number of our dead and wounded had been high, about 100 casualties, with just over 600 effective soldiers remaining—[a loss of] almost 15 percent in one day."

Deep in the silent darkness after a bizarre day, Hibbs's thoughts drifted to Pilar Campos, the girlfriend he'd left behind in Manila. He didn't want to think that she might still be in the Japanese-occupied city. He preferred to picture her somewhere in the back country, safe in a small house surrounded by her family. He envisioned a crucifix on the wall illuminated by a candle and a coconut-oil lamp, a mahogany bowl filled with fruit on a table with smiling family members seated in a circle around it.

Finally, he fell asleep, only to awaken to the renewed sound of artillery shells whistling overhead.

By mid-morning, the 31st Infantry's advance was stalled again. At noon, a dozen or more Japanese Val dive-bombers streaked in, catching Hibbs in the open. As he raced for the nearest foxhole, he could actually see the pilot above him release a bomb. Then he watched the bomb falling straight toward him, and for an instant he was sure he was going to die.

"My heart pounded wildly," he recalled. "The explosion pushed up a mushroom of earth which almost caved in my foxhole. Fortunately, the shrapnel was buried in the soft ground."

Shortly after the Vals departed at mid-afternoon, a medic appeared carrying a complete human leg, still clad in a Gl-issue khaki pant leg and an infantry combat boot. Hibbs guessed that the leg's owner had been a member of the Second Battalion's E Company. "We made out the battle casualty tag as 'unknown soldier,'" he said, "and buried it in an unmarked grave just to the rear of our area."

Meanwhile, in the II Corps sector east of the mountains, a thrown-together force including the Air Corps Infantry Regiment and various retreat-prone Philippine Army units was also trying to stem the Japanese tide, but the situation was clearly deteriorating.

Troops of Captain John Coleman's 27th Materiel Squadron—part of this amalgamation—were ordered to take up positions on the main East Road near Orion and stop all southbound traffic to check for Japanese infiltrators.

"The first truck I stopped was full of dead bodies," Coleman recalled. "There were some Filipino soldiers hitchhiking . . . on the fenders and bumpers of the truck. After questioning the driver about his cargo, I flashed a light into the rear of the truck . . . [and] it had what looked like twenty-five or thirty bodies stacked in it."

Coleman let the driver proceed but detained the hitchhikers, who told him their lieutenant had been killed in action, along with most of the other soldiers in their unit. In all, Coleman's men stopped 127 fleeing Filipino soldiers during the night, all of them hungry, thirsty, and dead on their feet from lack of sleep.

Two days later, Coleman received an order by radio to move his men north to the vicinity of Abucay, where front-line combat was raging. When they got there, early on January 20, the men bivouacked in the open, without tents, and tried to catch an hour's sleep, but they couldn't rest easy after learning that their squadron had been designated as the advanced point unit.

"This meant that my men would be the first to come in contact with the advancing Japanese Army in this sector," Coleman said. "We were to contact them in the rough mountain area [to] keep our main force, in the level land, from being out-flanked."

After a brief firefight with a Japanese patrol and an encounter with the only two Filipino soldiers to survive an enemy ambush of their squad, Coleman called in artillery against Japanese troops running along a mountain trail to attack the Allied left flank. Before the day was over, the 27th received new orders to fall back about four miles and make camp for the night. The following dawn, Japanese dive-bombers came calling, but Coleman's men kept under cover and the planes failed to spot them.

"We could see flashes of artillery in the northeast along the Abucay line," Coleman recalled. "The battle for Bataan had begun in earnest [and] our whole army didn't have a good defensive position at this time."

That night brought another four-mile withdrawal order, followed by yet another the next morning. By January 24, Coleman and his troops were part of a force manning a pre-prepared defensive line just west of Orion. This was the Bagac–Orion line, the second—and last—main line of resistance for Bataan's defenders. If the Japanese breached it, there would be nowhere left to make another unified stand. The defenders would be broken up into small pockets of troops that could be wiped out one by one.

From his command post that night, Coleman could see Japanese soldiers moving about 300 yards away across a no-man's-land of rice paddies and a bamboo thicket. Later, U.S. artillery pounded the bamboo thicket to splinters, and Coleman watched an engineer unit erecting barbed wire entanglements in front of his foxhole. The sight gave him little comfort.

At the time, Coleman and his men were unaware that the series of seemingly disorganized shifts in the American-Filipino front was the direct result of an order from USAFFE headquarters to withdraw all front-line troops to the Bagac–Orion line.

Early on the afternoon of January 22, General Sutherland had come to Bataan from Corregidor to assess the situation, and he'd been deeply troubled by what he found. More Japanese troops had infiltrated across the mountains in the gap between I Corps and II Corps, and intense enemy pressure was growing against both sectors of the front. If defenders on the Abucay–Mauban line continued trying to hold, they risked being flanked, surrounded, and annihilated—and that risk was growing by the minute. As if this weren't enough, new amphibious landings to the south of Bagac–Orion were expected at any time.

On Corregidor, MacArthur was sufficiently shaken by the enemy gains to warn Washington that "impending doom" faced Bataan's defenders. "My diminishing strength will soon force me to a shortened line [Bagac–Orion] on which I shall make my final stand," he informed General George Marshall. "With its occupation, all maneuvering possibility will cease. I intend to fight it to complete destruction. This will leave Corregidor.

"I wish to take this opportunity, while the army still exists and I am in command, to pay my tribute to the magnificent service it has rendered. No troops have ever done so much with so little."

As the general withdrawal of I Corps unfolded over a two-day period, Wainwright stayed on the road day and night, urging the troops to move faster, breaking up traffic jams, and clearing a path for bogged-down artillery and heavy equipment. The bulk of the trapped First Philippine Division managed to escape to the south only by avoiding the blockaded West Road and clambering down steep trails to the narrow beach, then fleeing on foot toward Bagac.

But all their vehicles and artillery had to be destroyed, leaving I Corps with only four 75-millimeter guns and a single pair of 155s.

By the morning of January 25, the First Division's rear guard, charged with holding back the enemy while the rest of the division hurriedly headed south, was almost out of ammunition and food, and many of its members were wounded. At about 10:30 AM, Colonel Kearie L. Berry, the rear guard commander, felt that he could wait no longer, and he told his exhausted men to withdraw, despite the fact that he had no authorization from Wainwright to do so. Carrying their casualties on makeshift litters, the troops followed the same route taken by the rest of the division. By early the next day, they were on a cliff overlooking the West Road and Bagac. Most were barefoot, and many had discarded their guns and uniforms during a grueling twenty-hour march, much of it under a fierce tropical sun.

Wainwright drove out to meet them, and Colonel Berry was worried about how the general would react to the unauthorized retreat, but a relieved Wainwright greeted him warmly. "Berry," he said simply, "I'm damned glad to see you."

By noon on January 26, all Allied units were in place on the new fourteen-mile-long Bagac–Orion line. Their fighting retreat had been a qualified success in that the most serious U.S. losses had been vehicles and artillery. No major combat units had been lost, and General Segundo and his First Philippine Division had largely redeemed themselves as a fighting force. General Homma's troops arrayed against them had suffered heavy losses—1,500 casualties in the 65th Brigade alone.

Still, there was no cause for jubilation, and even if there had been, the Americans and Filipinos were too worn-out and battle-weary to recognize it. As Lieutenant Henry Lee, a poetic young eyewitness, would observe in a verse titled "Abucay Withdrawal":

Supplies to move, and guns to sight,
A whole new line must be built tonight—
Another line in a losing fight . . .
Rifles spatter, machine guns spray,
As the weary doughboys take up the fray,
Bataan is saved for another day,

Save for hunger and wounds and heat;
For slow exhaustion and grim retreat;
For a wasted hope and a sure defeat.

The leg wound suffered by Lieutenant Ramsey at Moron had seemed no more than a minor irritation at first, but complications soon set in. At Mauban, south of Moron on the west coast, where Ramsey was sent for a few days' rest, he awoke each morning feeling weaker than the day before, and his eyes and skin took on a yellowish cast. The condition was diagnosed as jaundice, caused partly by the wound and partly by a grossly inadequate diet that now consisted almost entirely of rice.

"I was sent to Hospital No. 2 near Mariveles," he recalled, "a ramshackle affair of tents and flies stretched beneath the luan trees. There were rows of men on metal bedsteads hung with mosquito nets, suffering from every kind of wound and sickness. Their screams were terrible, and the stench hung thick in the air."

Ramsey hadn't been there long when he received a visit from Captain John Wheeler, who'd also contracted jaundice from his leg wound at Moron but had quickly recovered and was now on his way back to rejoin what was left of the 26th Cavalry.

"Is there anything I can do for you when I get there?" Wheeler asked.

"Just look after my mount," Ramsey told him. The last time the lieutenant had seen Bryn Awryn, he'd been tethered with other cavalry horses in a grove of trees near the river at Moron, where he couldn't be recovered because of heavy sniper fire. Ramsey had had to make the long, weary hike to Mauban on his wounded knee.

"Oh, I guess you haven't heard," Wheeler said uneasily. Then he frowned and glanced quickly away.

Ramsey felt a slight chill pass through him. "Heard what?"

"All the horses are gone," Wheeler said, still not meeting Ramsey's questioning gaze. "The quartermaster confiscated the ones that were left a day or two after the fight at Moron. Must've happened just after you went to Mauban. They were . . . uh, butchered for meat for the troops. You know how scarce food is."

"All of them?" Ramsey persisted.

Wheeler nodded. “Yeah, all of them, Ed. They were going to die anyway. I mean, there was no fodder left for them, and the men were starving.”

“Of course,” Ramsey agreed. He closed his eyes, remembering the days he’d spent schooling Bryn Awryn in polo and how the sleek chestnut gelding with the white blaze across his forehead had carried him through the opening weeks of the war. Always giving every ounce of his strength, never shying or flinching, no matter how hard the ride or how savage the fighting.

“I can’t imagine they got much meat from them, though, as scrawny as they were,” Wheeler said. “Still, it’s a sad end, don’t you think?”

“Yes,” Ramsey muttered, “a sad end.”

After Wheeler had left, Ramsey tried to tell himself that none of it mattered. How could he mourn a horse when wounded and dying men lay all around him? In the midst of such tragedy, what difference could one horse possibly make?

Besides, he thought, *the cavalry was finished long ago. The Army knew it, but we resisted out of pointless pride. Now the horses are gone, and we’re all alike.*

He glanced down at his sallow arms and legs, feeling as if the jaundice in his body was seeping inexorably into his spirit and his soul.

6

Abandoning the Battling Bastards

The newest and most serious enemy threat of late January and early February 1942 came in four coordinated amphibious incursions along the coast of the South China Sea.

For Wainwright, such landings by General Homma's forces behind the lines on the west side of Bataan had been a constant source of worry. If the Japanese should manage to break out of one or more of these beachheads while simultaneously pressing strong frontal attacks against the new Bagac–Orion line before the defenders were well dug-in, Bataan could soon be lost.

It took two weeks of brutal ground fighting, much of it miles behind the defenders' main line of resistance—plus all the help that the Navy's PT boats and the Air Corps's few remaining planes could provide—to choke off these combined assaults.

The most potentially dangerous landing was at Longoskawayan Point near the southern tip of Bataan, where Japanese troops came ashore on the early morning of January 23. The landing placed them within two or three miles of the port of Mariveles, the main service and supply center for Allied troops, as well as the only jumping-off point still in friendly hands for trips back and forth to Corregidor. Unless Mariveles could be held securely, the West Road, the only supply route between the port and the front, would become virtually useless. Fortunately, the enemy invaders were strongly contested by a battalion of the 45th Infantry, Philippine Scouts, and 450 sailors and Marines of Commander Francis Bridget's Naval Battalion.

The second landing was near Quinauan ("Quinine") Point, northwest of Longoskawayan, where the Japanese established a firm beachhead but were then held in check by a tough group of former Air Corps personnel and the Third Battalion of the 45th Infantry, commanded by Major Dudley Strickler. Nevertheless, one enemy position was only about a mile from the West Road, putting the supply route in imminent jeopardy.

A third landing, originally intended to reinforce the Quinauan Point beachhead but made by mistake on a small peninsula some 2,000 yards north, ended up posing yet another serious threat to the supply route.

The fourth—and least successful—of the landings came at Agloloma Point, where, as Wainwright later put it: "The Japs hardly touched the beach. Troops along the beach defenses shelled and machine-gunned them as they neared the shore, and our P-40s, happy to be rid of reconnaissance duty, strafed the landing boats, sinking and scattering them."

For the time being, all four landings were relatively well defended. But by the afternoon of January 27, Wainwright was sufficiently concerned about the simultaneous strikes against his main line and from the sea to send an urgent message by courier to General MacArthur at USAFFE headquarters on Corregidor. In it, he suggested another rearward adjustment of the main line of resistance to further shorten the front for both Bataan corps and "greatly strengthen" the Allied defense.

"My coastal flank is very lightly held," Wainwright emphasized, "so lightly that the Japs appear to infiltrate through it at night at points selected by them. If I take troops off my front to thicken the coast defense, they will certainly crash through the front. . . . The landings on the West Coast, so far accomplished, can and probably will be handled. Our experience, however, indicates such landings to be only a prelude to landings of much greater force. With reliable troops, the situation would not be particularly serious, but with the majority of troops available, it becomes distinctly serious. One battalion of the Philippine Army ran away last night from the front lines without having a shot fired at it."

MacArthur's reply to Wainwright's request for another tactical withdrawal to shorten the front, delivered on January 28, was a resounding "No!"

"We have now reached our last ditch," said the USAFFE commander. "Our only safety is to fight the enemy off. He is not in great strength, and if you can once really repulse him, you will obtain relief from his pressure. . . . You must, however, hold on your front, and there is no better place we can find than the one you are now on. . . . I am aware of the enormous difficulties that face you. Am proud, indeed, of the magnificent efforts you have made. There is nothing finer in history. Let's continue and preserve the fair name that we have so fairly won."

Over in General Parker's II Corps sector of the front, the fighting was also fierce, and the retreat southward by American and Filipino troops from the Abucay line on the night of January 25 was painfully slow over a route clogged with wounded and dying men who had to be carried by their comrades.

"Don't leave any wounded along the road," Captain Ralph Hibbs, commander of the 31st Infantry's Second Battalion medical unit, shouted repeatedly to the plodding, hollow-eyed soldiers. "Don't pass anyone who needs help!"

In Hibbs's view, the pace was too snail-like to excuse leaving behind any soldier who was still breathing, but he was also praying for a long night to improve the column's chances of reaching the new line of resistance at Orion before daylight brought another wave of enemy air attacks.

"Father, you've got to give us more darkness," he whispered. "Please God, don't let the sun come up yet."

At about 3 AM on January 26, the last of the column's covering force—rifle and machine gun platoons from E Company, Second Battalion, supported by the cannons of the 194th Tank Battalion and a few 75-millimeter self-propelled guns—pulled back. "They staggered out of their positions looking like walking dead men," Hibbs recalled, "[but] they kept the enemy hordes in check, and I gave them an overwhelming thanks. The dive-bombers were too late. We had escaped."

The combined effects of the night-long withdrawal and thirty-six hours without food or sleep lingered afterward, however. By now, rations had been cut to one-third of normal at best, and even that had been unavailable during the retreat. Along with their hunger and exhaustion, the men were also emotionally drained and dry-mouthed with the bitter taste of defeat.

At eleven that same morning, with Hibbs's medical unit squatting under nipa huts in the town of Balanga on the shores of Manila Bay, Major Lloyd Moffit, the battalion commander, sent out a runner to summon all his offices to an urgent meeting.

"How many effective soldiers do we have left?" Moffit asked as the meeting opened. The question was directed at Hibbs, who, as battalion surgeon and chief medical officer, was supposed to have the most up-to-date count of dead and wounded.

Hibbs bit his lip. "Somewhere around 350," he said, meaning that roughly 50 percent of the battalion's strength of a few days earlier had been lost to casualties. "I can't be sure of the exact number."

Shaking and obviously fighting to keep his composure, Moffit began to pace. He wiped clumsily at tears streaking his face, and the other officers could hear him swearing brokenly under his breath. When he tried to speak, his words came in hoarse, quavering bursts.

"We've *got* to hold this main road," he said. "It's our only chance to establish another line, and the survival of the whole corps depends on it. There are no effective troops between us and the Japs—only stragglers."

In a convulsive series of motions, as his officers watched in stunned silence, Moffit whipped out his revolver and jabbed the air with it. "Damn it," he yelled, "this time we mustn't fail!"

Then he jerked his pistol down toward the ground and fired a single shot, the muzzle blast from which almost bowled Hibbs over as he squatted a few feet away beside his friend, Captain Dwight Hunkins. A split second later, Hibbs spotted what appeared to be a neat, round hole in the toe of Moffit's right boot.

After the echo of the shot faded, there was dead silence for a second or two. "You've got to hold!" Moffit shouted then, still gripping the revolver and clenching his free fist. "There's no other choice! That's all!"

Most of the group drifted quietly away, seemingly unaware of what had happened, but Hibbs hung around, wondering whether to ignore a possible self-inflicted gunshot wound to his commanding officer or discreetly offer to treat it. He and the major stared at each other for a moment. Then, his face flushing bright red, Moffit blurted: "I just shot my damn toe off!"

"Well, let's take a look at it," Hibbs said, surprised at his own calm tone. When the boot was unlaced and the wound exposed, the medical officer found that the bullet had severed part of Moffit's right second toe. Using compression, he stopped the bleeding, applied a bandage small enough to accommodate the major's boot, and offered some pain pills.

"Naw, I don't need any," Moffit said, his drawn face and pained expression clearly disputing his words. "It really doesn't hurt that much." Then he limped away.

In Hibbs's estimation, as he later put it, Moffit "grew a foot and a half" that day as a leader. As far as Hibbs knew, no one else in the battalion ever found out about the wound, and it healed promptly without a single complaint from Moffit, who, for obvious reasons, never applied for a Purple Heart.

And the Second Battalion *did* hold that road.

For a dozen straight days, what became known on Bataan as the "Battle of the Points and Pockets" raged without respite in Wainwright's sector of the front. The "points" were the landing sites on the west coast where the Japanese had established beachheads. The "pockets" were a pair of jungle enclaves where a total of about 1,000 Japanese soldiers dug in after first slashing through an area held by exhausted troops of the battered First Philippine Division, then separating into two groups of infiltrators.

The smaller group, numbering about 200 men, took up positions atop a hill some 400 yards behind the front in a location soon to become known as the "Little Pocket." The larger group, some 800 soldiers, moved quickly east through dense undergrowth to fortify the "Big Pocket," situated well behind Allied lines and near the intersection of two trails used to move U.S. troops and supplies.

The enemy's intention was to create near-impregnable strongholds behind American and Filipino units, blocking off their path of escape and opening them up to attack from both front and rear. Instead, the infiltrators themselves were surrounded and sealed into their pockets, but they entrenched with skill and determination, constructing a labyrinth of deep, tunnel-connected earthworks that were virtually impervious to artillery fire.

"The shells exploded against trees . . . and not even reaching the enemy," wrote historian Duane Schultz. "The only way to clear out the Japanese was with rifle and bayonet, the dirtiest kind of war."

Toward the end of January, Colonel Samuel L. Howard, commander of the Fourth Marines, approved the unusual step of sending two platoons of Leathernecks, commanded by First Lieutenant Michael Peshek, across the bay from Corregidor by boat to help reduce a trouble spot near Mariveles. One platoon was armed with a pair of 81-millimeter mortars—heavier and more accurate than the weapons available to Army troops on Bataan—and Texas-born Marine Gunner Harold M. Ferrell, a former star athlete at Baylor University, was given the job of positioning them. With their high trajectories, the 81s were capable of hitting targets that howitzers simply couldn't reach, and they were far more reliable than the World War I relics normally used on Bataan.

"The Japs had two strategically placed machine guns on Lapiay Point [a small peninsula north of Longoskawayan Point] that were giving our guys fits," Ferrell recalled to family members many years later. "In one morning's work, we were able to take out both those guns, but then they sent us right back to Corregidor, where we were assigned to man the beach defenses, and we never went back to Bataan again."

The Marines' brief visit, however, was instrumental in breaking the enemy's grip on Longoskawayan Point. As PFC Karl King, a member of the Naval Battalion who witnessed the mortar barrage at close range, later recalled: "After the bombardment lifted, a patrol couldn't find any live enemy soldiers [in the target area]. A few survivors had made their escape into the jungle growth."

A day or two later, most of the 300 Japanese troops holding the beachhead on Longoskawayan Point were annihilated in a massive thirty-minute barrage by 12-inch mortars firing from Corregidor and commanded by Colonel Paul Bunker, accompanied by the 5-inch guns of the U.S. minesweeper *Quail.* Afterward, an infantry force of Philippine Scouts assaulted the enemy positions and took no prisoners. By January 31, the invading force had been destroyed to the last man.

Troops of the First Philippine Division, who had lost all their trenching tools during the retreat from the first main line of resistance, had been using mess kits to dig foxholes and bayonets to clear brush when the enemy broke through their lines. Now they were sent to wipe out the Japanese force in the Little Pocket, and in a week of bitter hand-to-hand fighting, with help from the 11th Philippine Division, they atoned for their earlier lapse by doing exactly that.

"It was a savage ferreting job," said Wainwright. "Rifle fire and machine-gun bursts were of little use, for the Japs were underground. We had so little infantry mortar ammunition left that we couldn't lob a suitable barrage into their holes. So we had to go up and practically breathe in the faces of the dug-in Japs. . . . Junior officers, sitting on the hoods of our few remaining tanks, drove up to the enemy positions with sacks of grenades and pegged them right down the foxholes."

At one point during the fighting, Wainwright himself escaped death only when Sergeant Hubert Carroll, his orderly, grabbed "two handfuls of the seat of my pants and yanked me down," causing a burst of enemy fire to miss Wainwright by inches.

"God damn it, General," Carroll admonished his commander sternly, "get down or you'll get your damn head shot off!"

The long, bloody ordeal didn't end until mid-February when Wainwright informed USAFFE headquarters that all enemy strongholds among the points and pockets had been blasted into oblivion. Allied losses had been heavy, but the Japanese threat from the rear was eliminated.

"I was able to report to MacArthur that I Corps now held every foot of ground it had first occupied on arrival at the reserve battle position," said Wainwright. "Yet we knew that things would get worse. Portions of the Bagac–Pilar road within our lines began to come under heavy fire from large artillery pieces the Japs were bringing south on the railway they now owned. A detachment of the 14th Engineers therefore cut a narrow, sheltered road across Bataan about six miles south of the Bagac–Pilar highway, and in this makeshift way we were able to maintain contact with Parker's force to the east of us."

Wainwright remained convinced that when the final Japanese offensive came, Parker's II Corps would receive the brunt of it, simply because of the geography involved. The coastal area on the east side of southern Bataan was more of a plain than the central and western areas now held by Wainwright's troops, and streams on the east side usually ran in a southwesterly direction, while in the I Corps area, they ran mainly due west and emptied into the South China Sea. Enemy advances against I Corps were thus handicapped by a series of stream crossings and east–west ridges whereas Japanese troops could advance parallel to most of the streams in Parker's sector.

Unknown to either Wainwright or Parker at this juncture, however, the battle-weary defenders of Bataan were about to receive an unexpected respite from constant combat.

The enemy drive that had breached the Abucay–Mauban line and the tenacious Allied counterattacks between mid-January and mid-February had bled away so much of the strength of Japan's 14th Army that it was no longer capable of launching an all-out offensive on either side of the front. Consequently, the struggle for Bataan was about to come to a temporary standstill as General Homma's depleted forces licked their wounds, attempted to regroup, and awaited resupply and reinforcements.

"While the defenders had begun to feel the effects of short rations, fatigue, and disease," wrote historian Gerald Astor, "the enemy had also succumbed to the brutal conditions of combat in Bataan, where the temperature averaged ninety-five degrees and the terrain was inhospitable to an attacking army."

Under ordinary conditions, Japanese combat soldiers received a ration of sixty-two ounces of food per day, but as of mid-February, they were subsisting on just twenty-three ounces daily—slightly more than one-third of normal. Coupled with the near-starvation diet, a critical shortage of medical supplies helped trigger raging epidemics of malaria and dysentery among the Japanese troops.

But, undeniably, the main reason that the invaders had failed to achieve Tokyo's goal of total victory on Bataan—first by mid-January, then by the end of the month—was the hellacious beating they'd taken from a thrown-together American-Filipino force that had evolved into a fearsome fighting machine.

Considering the initial disorganization and lack of discipline among the defenders, the losses inflicted on the Japanese since late December had been nothing short of incredible. As one example, General Homma's proud 16th Division had arrived on Luzon with 14,000 troops; now it could count only 700 combat-capable soldiers. The 65th Brigade, meanwhile, had been carved down from its original strength of 6,500 men to fewer than 1,000 effectives.

The month-long lull in the fighting that stretched from mid-February to mid-March 1942 might have enabled a healthy, well-nourished, adequately supplied defensive force to withstand an enemy siege indefinitely in a place like Bataan. But by this time, the defenders—almost to a man—were feverish with tropical diseases, weak and emaciated from lack of food, and desperately short of almost everything.

In sharp contrast to the invaders, for whom the respite brought rest, rejuvenation, fresh troops, and a vast influx of food, ammunition, and other essentials, it meant only more long days of hunger, disease, and suffering for the defenders. The reprieve from combat was welcome, but the sick still needed medicine, and everyone needed food.

"Rations were reduced from sixteen ounces a day to eight and then to four," said Colonel Glen Townsend, commander of the 11th Regiment. "Twice a week, we got small amounts of carabao, mule, or horse meat. There was no flour, vegetables, or sugar. The quinine was exhausted, malaria rampant. Almost everyone had dysentery."

The men were hungry enough to try to devour any substance that seemed remotely digestible. "I saw soldiers squatting beside trails, boiling a piece of mule hide or carabao hide in a tomato can and chewing away at the hide, trying to get some nourishment," said Major Harold Johnson of the 57th Regiment. "The soldiers never really complained, but all the time you could see the question in their eyes: 'What in the world have you done to us?'"

Looking back from a distance of nearly seven decades, Sergeant

Louis Read of the 31st Infantry still clearly recalled every item on the menu for his infantry company—down to about 100 men at this point. It was an extremely short list. "For one day," he said, "the ration for our entire company was thirty pounds of unhulled rice, one can of salmon, and a mule head with no neck attached."

Captain Hibbs, also of the 31st, ranked the palatability of the meats available, all in meager quantities, in the following order: "Calesa pony was first, mule second, horse third, carabao fourth, and monkey a poor last. . . . The troops didn't complain about [eating] geckos, iguanas, or snakes, but there was a real bitterness generated . . . by the food disappearing in transit from the quartermaster. The weight loss of the front-line troops had been dramatic—from 20 to 30 percent of their body weight. A 180-pound soldier would now weigh 125 to 130 pounds. This wasn't necessarily so with the military police, quartermaster, and service units in the rear."

More than 7,000 sick and wounded men were jammed into Hospitals No. 1 and No. 2, each of which was intended to accommodate no more than 1,000 bed patients, and their numbers were growing daily. By the end of March, the total at the two hospitals would reach 11,000. Regimental and battalion aid stations and smaller makeshift infirmaries were overrun with hundreds more, while countless others remained at their posts.

"Our troop strength was decreasing at the rate of three or four per day from malaria, dengue fever, dysentery, jungle rot of the feet, and starvation," said Captain Hibbs.

"When our men had a malarial chill, they would just lie around for a few days until the fever left," recalled Captain John Coleman, commanding the 27th Materiel Squadron, now part of the Army Air Corps Provisional Infantry, "and then they'd go back on duty. They weren't sent to the hospital."

"We ran out of quinine and nearly all other medicines," said Major Alva Fitch, a battery commander in the 23rd Field Artillery, Philippine Scouts. "I ran a forty-bed hospital in my battalion, and it was always full. Actually, when a man became strong enough to walk, he was returned to duty to make room for another who couldn't walk."

Even men who managed to stay relatively healthy grew noticeably thinner and steadily weaker from lack of food. "We had to forage on the land for most of the food we received," recounted Coleman. "Our men would go out into no man's land at night and get rice from what straw stacks they could find, bringing it back and threshing it out in the daytime. For a while, we could find some of our Army mules or horses that had been turned loose. Due to our lack of refrigeration, we only killed what we could eat in a day."

After the troops were put on quarter-rations in early March, Sergeant Cletis Overton of the Air Corps Infantry watched men kill and eat many things that would have defied his imagination a few months earlier. "We hunted the woods for anything that ran loose," he said, "but I drew the line at the small monkeys that some of the men killed and roasted over an open fire. To me, they looked too much like human babies, and I just couldn't handle that."

To others, however, dining on monkey meat was far preferable to starving. "The Japs bombed us every day," recalled Staff Sergeant Henry G. Stanley, originally of the 454th Ordnance Company but now also assigned to the Air Corps Infantry, "and the bombs scared the monkeys so bad that they crawled into our foxholes with us. The meat was tough, but we ate a bunch of them. Pythons and lizards, too."

Despite widespread illness, steady loss of weight, increasing weakness, and omnipresent hunger, the Bataan garrison's morale remained amazingly high well into March. To some extent, it was nurtured by the daily *Voice of Freedom* broadcasts from Corregidor's radio station, and even the tauntings of Tokyo Rose, Tokyo Radio's composite propaganda queen, did more to arouse the men's fighting spirit than to depress them.

But rumors of rescue and salvation, as baseless as all of them eventually turned out to be, also served as temporary morale boosters and sources of misplaced hope. At this point, virtually every American on Bataan had heard—and been bitterly disappointed by—more than one phony tidbit of scuttlebutt. Yet the rumor mill kept right on grinding, fed by wishful dreams that, for many, became an obsession.

"Our feeling about help coming from home had gotten to be a

constant, nagging, almost unconscious thought in the back of our minds," wrote nurse Juanita Redmond at Hospital No. 1. "Of course, we talked about it. . . . Every day, the doctors, nurses, corpsmen, and patients made bets with each other as to how many hours, days, weeks—we didn't dare make it any longer than that—it would be before our boats reached us. . . . We were working harder than we ever had, and we couldn't spare the strength to face the real possibility that help might never come."

At dawn one February morning, Lieutenant Ed Whitcomb was psychologically swept away by the kind of feelings that Redmond described. He awoke to the sound of loud cheering from the center of his camp area adjoining virtually deserted Cabcaben Field, where Whitcomb supervised a crude telephone system. Knowing that the uproar could mean only one thing—good news—he dressed hurriedly and rushed outside.

"There's a helluva big convoy steaming into Manila Bay," shouted the first person Whitcomb encountered, "and I know it ain't no rumor 'cause I saw it with my own eyes!"

Whitcomb ran as fast as he could go toward the top of a nearby hill, where he could get an unobstructed view of the bay. The trail was steep and about a quarter-mile long, and en route he passed men who'd been forced to stop and catch their breath. Halfway to the top, an eyewitness on his way back to camp provided Whitcomb with a fresh burst of energy.

"They're American ships!" the man shouted. "I saw them myself! It's a big convoy coming around Corregidor!"

A moment later, Whitcomb reached the crest of the ridge and saw the ships for himself. They were still four miles away, but they were definitely large American transports. "It looked as if the whole U.S. fleet had sneaked in without being noticed by the Japanese," Whitcomb later recalled, "and each time another ship rounded the eastern tip of Corregidor, another wild cheer rang out."

What a day! he thought. *The day we've been waiting for so long! It's not just another rumor—it's true! Now we'll have food and airplanes and mail from home and relief from all our worries! Nothing so wonderful has ever happened to any of us before!*

Whitcomb stumbled back down the hill, searching for his friends,

Lieutenants Jim Dey and John Renka, but when he found them, they showed none of the exuberance he was anticipating.

"The colonel wants to see you in his tent right away," Dey said grimly.

Whitcomb frowned. "Hey, it's a real convoy," he yelled over his shoulder as he headed for the colonel's tent. "I saw it with my own eyes."

The colonel greeted him with a cold stare. "What the hell's wrong with those telephone operators of yours, Whitcomb?" he demanded. "Why the hell are they sending out false messages about an American relief convoy?"

"But sir," Whitcomb protested, "I've just been to the top of the ridge, and I saw those ships for myself. There were—"

"What you saw were ships that have been lying south of Corregidor since the war started," the colonel said. "They're simply being moved to the north side so they'll be out of range of the Jap artillery on the Cavite shore. Now tell your operators to knock it off, and see that it doesn't happen again."

Whitcomb stood there for a moment, totally crestfallen and, by his own admission, embarrassed beyond belief. "Yes sir," he finally muttered. "I'll tell them."

Whitcomb, nurse Redmond, and their comrades on Bataan weren't the only Americans clinging to the hope that a miraculous happy ending was still possible.

At about the same time that the former Air Corps troops at Cabcaben Field were cheering the illusionary rescue convoy, General Wainwright was celebrating his troops' success against the enemy points and pockets and citing some optimistic "ifs" in an interview with Associated Press correspondent Clark Lee.

"Right now we've got the Japs stopped, and our position is more favorable than it's been since December 8," Wainwright told Lee. "If the United States will send me two divisions of American troops, or two trained Filipino divisions, and just enough planes to keep the Japs off our heads, I'll guarantee to drive the Japs off Luzon in short order."

Across the bay in Lateral No. 3 of Corregidor's labyrinthine Malinta Tunnel, MacArthur, too, was waxing optimistic in a radiogram to Army Chief of Staff General Marshall—and again urging Marshall to send reinforcements. "MacArthur spoke of the opportunity . . . to strike the Japanese a staggering blow," wrote historian Duane Schultz. "He called for the U.S. Navy to attack in force at the enemy's weak line of sea defenses. He said that if the Japanese fleet engaged the American Navy and lost, the war would be over."

But Marshall, President Roosevelt, and Secretary of War Henry Stimson had no way of providing fresh divisions to Wainwright or a fleet of U.S. warships to MacArthur. On the contrary, the decision had already been made in Washington that the defenders of Bataan and Corregidor were expendable—with one notable exception.

Washington's power brokers had decided that Douglas MacArthur, the epic, larger-than-life hero of the Philippines, whose face and name jumped almost daily from the front pages of America's newspapers, had to be saved. Although he'd made only one three-to-four-hour visit to the Bataan combat zone since the war began, the collective mind of the American public pictured him as *always* being there. MacArthur's name was the focal point of every press dispatch from the Philippines. To a news-hungry public, he seemed to be leading every counterattack by "his" tanks and infantrymen, directing every bombardment by "his" artillery, and flying along on every mission by "his" ragtag air force.

At the same time, the public was gradually being conditioned to accept the fact that Bataan's defenders were fighting a losing battle. But if MacArthur should be lost along with them, the damage to home front morale and the advantage to Japan's propaganda machine would be incalculable. Irreparable. Intolerable. Or so the thinking went in Washington. For this reason, Roosevelt and Marshall had begun in early February in their communications with MacArthur to broach the idea of his evacuation to Australia.

Philippine president Quezon and U.S. High Commissioner to the Philippines Francis Sayer and their families had already been spirited by the U.S. submarine *Swordfish* to the comparative safety of Mindanao, from which, after a brief interval, they would be flown to Australia. MacArthur and his wife, Jean, declined an invitation to join the *Swordfish* entourage but sent along a footlocker containing various memorabilia and personal items.

On February 23, after MacArthur had failed to accept several tactfully worded overtures from both Marshall and FDR advising him to leave the Philippines for safer environs, Roosevelt officially ordered the USAFFE commander to evacuate with his family. His top secret message read in part:

> The president directs that you make arrangements to leave Fort Mills [Corregidor] and proceed to Mindanao. You are directed to make this change as quickly as possible. . . . From Mindanao, you will proceed to Australia, where you will assume command of all United States troops.

Of all the difficult decisions of FDR's presidency, issuing this order surely ranks among the most agonizing. As author and presidential adviser Robert Sherwood described it: "It was ordering the captain to be the first to leave the sinking ship."

For weeks, the president had come under tremendous pressure from influential members of Congress, his own key advisers, and countless ordinary citizens to save MacArthur. But by ordering "Dugout Doug" to become "Bugout Doug," Roosevelt was making a clear admission to friend and foe alike—and most especially to the garrisons on Bataan and Corregidor—that the United States was renouncing its military commitment to the islands. Once the news was out, troops in the combat zone would have every reason to lose whatever heart they had left and quit fighting.

The miracle was that they didn't. Poetic young Lieutenant Henry Lee probably summed up the feelings of many when he wrote:

> *Though the thrill, the zest, and the hope are gone,*
> *Something within me keeps me fighting on.*

In recent days, MacArthur had blustered to aides and staff members that he would never consider such a move. He vowed to AP reporter Clark Lee that he would "fight to his own destruction" rather than desert the men on Bataan and Corregidor. And in his memoirs, published two decades later, he wrote: "My first reaction was to try to avoid the latter part of the order, even to the extent of resigning my commission and joining the Bataan force as a simple volunteer." This assertion struck historian Gerald Astor as "improbable fantasy."

Without doubt, MacArthur must have been beset by brutally conflicting emotions at this time. He knew as well as anyone that, without vast infusions of American men and arms, Bataan was doomed. He also knew that within a matter of days after the Japanese gained control of the entire peninsula and devoted the full attention of their bombers and heavy artillery to Corregidor, the island would become indefensible—and possibly uninhabitable—despite its warren of deep tunnels.

Yet no serious student of MacArthur's psyche and personality would identify fear or cowardice as major motivating factors for his departure. In Astor's words, "MacArthur's orders stipulated resistance as long as humanly possible, and he expected to die with his boots on." As the situation on Bataan deteriorated, the general displayed a loaded derringer pistol to one of his aides, Sidney Huff, and declared, "They'll never take me alive, Sid!"

MacArthur's monumental ego was also at stake here. The role of gallant loser had no appeal for him. Above all else, he wanted to be remembered by history as a victor, a conqueror, and regardless of how nobly "his" forces had acquitted themselves in battle on Bataan, their defeat had become a glaring certainty that he, as their commander, had to share.

Now, however, with Roosevelt and Marshall offering him supreme command of all U.S. forces in the Pacific, MacArthur sensed a huge, historic opportunity within his grasp. It could redeem his reputation as a military genius, free him from the fate of his Battling Bastards, lift him to even greater glory and stature, and allow him to strike back at the Japanese with a force fully capable of total victory.

Besides, he had received a direct order from the president of the United States, his commander-in-chief, and his aides warned him that refusal to obey that order could mean court-martial. He *had* to go to Australia. He had no choice. It was his duty as an American soldier—in many minds, the *ultimate* American soldier.

To the thousands of starving, disease-ravaged troops he was leaving behind, he would offer one final MacArthuresque assurance:

I shall return!

He didn't tell them—and, in all fairness, certainly had no way of knowing himself—that it would take him more than thirty months to make good on this promise, or that tens of thousands of "his" men would be murdered and maimed as POWs in the interim. Indeed, given his boundless self-confidence, MacArthur probably believed that his return could be accomplished much sooner, and his staff officers were apparently unanimous in reinforcing this belief.

As he insisted in his memoirs, "They felt that the concentration of men, arms, and transport . . . being massed in Australia would enable me almost at once to return at the head of an effective rescue operation."

With this in mind, MacArthur agreed to go, and preparations for his departure began immediately and in utmost secrecy. But he asked Roosevelt to let him set his own timetable. "At the right time, I believe they [the people and government of the Philippines] will understand it, but if done too soon and too abruptly, it may result in a sudden major collapse. Please be guided by me in this matter."

Roosevelt agreed, and MacArthur chose to remain in his Corregidor headquarters until the night of March 11. He didn't bother to tell even General Wainwright what was about to transpire until about thirty hours before departure time.

When the phone rang on the late evening of March 9 at Wainwright's makeshift command post in a small clearing just south of Bagac, the caller was General Sutherland, MacArthur's chief of staff.

"The general wants to see you," Sutherland said. "He has something important to tell you. We're sending a boat over to pick you up. It'll be at Mariveles at noon tomorrow."

"All right, I'll be there," Wainwright said. He was too tired to ask what the "something important" was.

The next morning, during a tour of the front, Wainwright narrowly escaped death when a strafing Japanese Zero put seventy-two bullet holes in the staff car in which he and two aides, Captain John R. Pugh and Lieutenant Tom Dooley, were riding. They were forced to bail out and take cover in some bushes, but fortunately, after the Zero left, the car was still sufficiently drivable to get them to the Mariveles dock, where they were met by a cabin cruiser with Lieutenant James Baldwin at the controls.

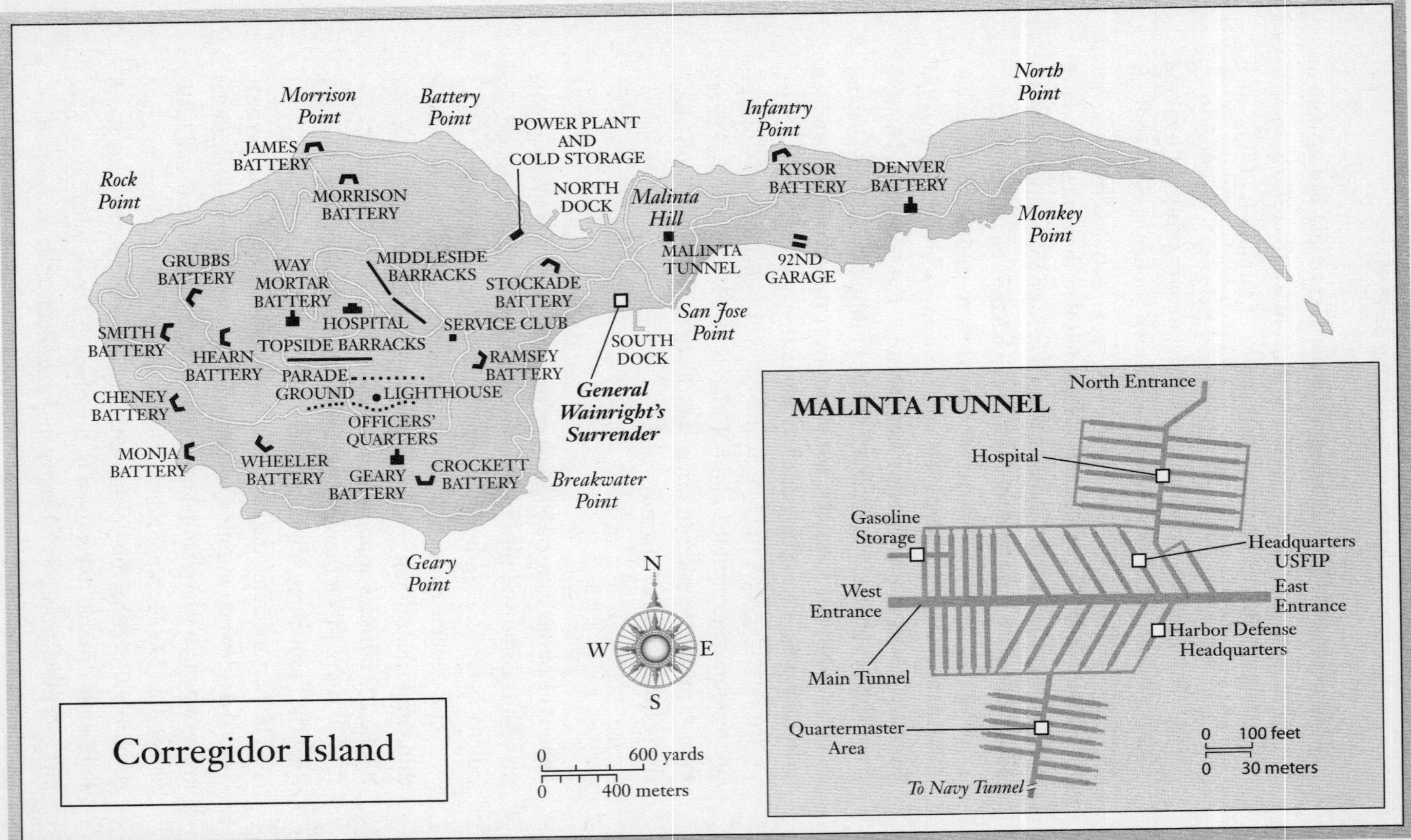

Corregidor Island
Rock Point
Morrison Point
Battery Point
JAMES BATTERY
MORRISON BATTERY
POWER PLANT AND COLD STORAGE
NORTH DOCK
Malinta Hill
MALINTA TUNNEL
Infantry Point
KYSOR BATTERY
DENVER BATTERY
North Point
Monkey Point
92ND GARAGE
San Jose Point
GRUBBS BATTERY
WAY MORTAR BATTERY
MIDDLESIDE BARRACKS
STOCKADE BATTERY
HOSPITAL
SERVICE CLUB
SOUTH DOCK
SMITH BATTERY
HEARN BATTERY
TOPSIDE BARRACKS
RAMSEY BATTERY
PARADE GROUND
LIGHTHOUSE
CHENEY BATTERY
OFFICERS' QUARTERS
General Wainright's Surrender
MONJA BATTERY
WHEELER BATTERY
GEARY BATTERY
CROCKETT BATTERY
Breakwater Point
Geary Point
N
W
E
S
0
600 yards
0
400 meters
MALINTA TUNNEL
North Entrance
Hospital
Gasoline Storage
Headquarters USFIP
West Entrance
East Entrance
Harbor Defense Headquarters
Main Tunnel
Quartermaster Area
To Navy Tunnel
0
100 feet
0
30 meters

A few minutes later, the boat tied up at Corregidor's north dock, and Wainwright went directly through the vast subterranean maze of Malinta Tunnel to USAFFE headquarters in crowded Lateral No. 3, where he was met by Sutherland.

"General MacArthur is going to leave here and go to Australia," Sutherland said quietly when they were out of earshot of the gaggle of officers working at desks in the corridor. "He's up at the house now and wants to see you, but I'll give you a fill-in first."

Over the next few minutes, Sutherland briefly outlined a list of command changes decreed by MacArthur to take place after he left. Wainwright was to take command of all troops on Luzon, with General Albert Jones replacing him as I Corps commander. A separate commander, General William F. Sharp, was appointed for Mindanao, and another, General Brad Chynoweth, for the Visayan group of islands. Yet another, General George Moore, was designated to command the fortified islands of Manila Bay. MacArthur himself would remain in overall command of all forces in the Philippines from his new headquarters in Melbourne, some 4,000 miles away. (All of these directives, however, would be changed within a few days by orders from the War Department that greatly expanded Wainwright's authority.)

After the briefing, Sutherland escorted Wainwright to MacArthur's home a quarter-mile from the Malinta Tunnel entrance. The departing USAFFE commander was waiting on the front porch.

"Jonathan," MacArthur said, "I want you to understand my position very plainly. I'm leaving for Australia pursuant to repeated orders of the president. Things have gotten to such a point that I must comply with these orders or get out of the Army. I want you to make it known throughout all elements of your command that I'm leaving over my repeated protests."

"Of course, I will, Douglas," Wainwright said.

"We're alone, Jonathan. You know that as well as I do. If I get through to Australia, you know I'll come back as soon as I can with as much as I can."

They stared silently at each other for a long moment. "You'll get through," Wainwright said then.

"And back," MacArthur said.

* * *

The original evacuation plan called for MacArthur, his wife, Jean; their young son, Arthur; the boy's Chinese amah, or nursemaid, Ah Cheu; and a sizable group of other Army and Navy officers to leave Corregidor by submarine on the evening of March 14. When the news leaked that MacArthur was taking command of all U.S. forces in Australia, however, the plan had to be changed for security reasons. The Japanese would have liked nothing better than to capture such a high-profile prize as he tried to escape, but killing him would have been almost as satisfying.

Under a revised plan, the departure date was moved up to the moonless night of March 11, with the same group traveling aboard the four surviving Navy PT boats still operating in Philippine waters, whose small size and fifty-knot top speed gave them greater ability to avoid enemy attack. The MacArthur family, Ah Cheu, and General Sutherland were assigned to *PT-41*, commanded by Lieutenant John Buckeley. All others in the party would be passengers on boats *32*, *34*, and *35*.

Far away in Washington, General Marshall was surprised when he learned how large a group had been handpicked by MacArthur to accompany him to safety, and the inclusion of Arthur MacArthur's nursemaid drew enough negative comments to prompt the general to jump to her defense.

"Few people outside the Orient know how completely a member of the family an amah can become," MacArthur explained. "Because of her relationship to my family, her death would have been certain had she been left behind."

As he recalled in his memoirs, MacArthur was in a pensive mood as he stood in the darkness on the Corregidor dock that evening and took a farewell look over the battle-scarred face of the Rock.

"Gone was the vivid green foliage with its trees, shrubs, and flowers," he noted. "Gone were the buildings, the sheds, every growing thing. The hail of relentless bombardment had devastated, buried, and blasted. Ugly, dark scars marked smoldering paths where the fire had raged from one end of the island to another. Great gaps and forbidding crevices still belched their tongues of flame."

From the gloom nearby, MacArthur heard a pair of bystanders talking quietly between themselves.

"What's his chance of getting through, Sarge?" one of them asked the other.

"I dunno," the other said with a shrug. "He's lucky. Maybe one in five."

MacArthur turned away and stepped aboard the waiting PT boat. "You may cast off when you're ready, Buck," he told Lieutenant Buckeley.

Buckeley saluted. "Aye, sir," he said.

Later, Buckeley recalled being confident of his and his crew's ability to carry their famous passengers safely across the 560 miles of enemy-infested waters to Mindanao. "I'd been in the Philippines for a long enough time and gone through the islands many times," he said. "I never doubted success, and I was damn glad to get out of Corregidor."

During the trip, *PT-32* developed mechanical problems and was forced to drop out of the little convoy and transfer its passengers to boats *34* and *41*, but early on March 13 the remaining three boats docked on schedule at Cagayan on Mindanao.

Army Air Corps Tech Sergeant Robert Heer of the 19th Bomb Group was assigned as a guard for the MacArthur party's arrival. Heer was waiting on the dock a few feet from General William Sharp, commander of U.S. forces on Mindanao, when *PT-41* came into view.

"I've got 'em dead in sight!" Heer heard Sharp declare as he stared northward out to sea.

"There on the horizon," Heer later recalled, "I could make out a small gray object traveling at a high speed. It was soon close enough to recognize as a Navy PT boat, and I could make out the Stars and Stripes fluttering on its mast."

A few hundred yards out, the boat's engines were throttled, and the craft glided smoothly up to the dock, where two crewmembers secured it to pilings.

"I'll never forget the events of the next few minutes," Heer said. "Exiting the cabin door of the boat was General MacArthur, followed by his wife Jean, his son Arthur, his Chinese nurse Au Cheu, and General Richard Sutherland. All of them were visibly wet and looked seasick."

Three B-17s were supposed to be available immediately to fly MacArthur and his party to Darwin on Australia's north coast, but an outbreak of interservice bickering about whether Air Corps or Navy planes would be used delayed the planes' arrival. Further delay developed when one B-17 was forced to turn back because of engine trouble, and the passengers had to crowd into two planes and leave much of their baggage behind. As they neared their destination, they were diverted to a field fifty miles from Darwin because the city was under attack by Japanese dive-bombers—possible evidence that the enemy was still stalking MacArthur.

At a stop in Adelaide on the final leg of his journey—the long train trip from Darwin to Melbourne at the other end of the Australian continent—he officially voiced the pronouncement for which he would forever after be both deified and reviled.

"I shall return," he told the press corps assembled at the Adelaide railway station. By the next day, these words were emblazoned across newspaper front pages around the globe. Shortly thereafter, MacArthur was awarded the Medal of Honor "for gallantry and intrepidity above and beyond the call of duty."

Back on Bataan, all this was received by the Battling Bastards with sharply mixed emotions. The reaction of Filipino soldiers in the combat zone to MacArthur's promise was mostly positive, and the Filipino public at large—helped along by explanatory leaflet drops by American pilots over Manila and other areas—seemed to take MacArthur at his word.

"Of course, there was a great deal of resentment among those left behind," said Colonel Irvin Alexander, the quartermaster on Bataan, "and the expression 'ran out on us' was on many tongues. But if there was a single officer who wouldn't have given his right arm to have gone with him, he would've at least given his left."

There was some sentiment among other American officers accompanying MacArthur to change his statement to "*We* shall return." But as Lieutenant Colonel Carlos Romulo, himself a native of the islands, a former newspaper publisher, and a close friend of MacArthur's who handled the general's news releases, put it: "If *he* says he is coming back, he will be believed."

But to then Major John Olson, a fellow West Pointer who had served as an honorary aide to MacArthur when the latter inspected Olson's 57th Regiment, Philippine Scouts, the news was "depressing and discouraging," but it was also fully characteristic.

"The statement 'I shall return' was typical of his extreme egotism and aloofness," said Olson. "MacArthur was never a team player, and he wasn't troop-related at all."

Where the troops in his 31st Philippine Division were concerned, now–Brigadier General Clifford Bluemel tried to put a positive spin on MacArthur's departure, but he personally viewed it as highly damaging to the fighting spirit of his men.

"I think it hurt morale all the way down to the front-line people," Bluemel said. "I had to tell them, because if I didn't, the Japs had loudspeakers . . . telling and begging them to desert. I told them, 'Help is going to come. He's going to bring it back.' I had to lie a little bit. I didn't believe it."

But no one condemned MacArthur's flight and his pledge to return more caustically than General William Brougher, commander of the 11th Philippine Division, who called it "a foul trick of deception . . . by a commander-in-chief and a small staff who are now eating steak and eggs in Australia. God damn them!"

Regardless of how they felt about MacArthur's exit from the scene, the men of Bataan were too exhausted, sick, and hungry to spend much time dwelling on it. The respite they'd been given since mid-February, when General Homma had called a time-out in his offensive to reinforce, resupply, and regroup his 14th Army, was about to come to an end. The air units that had been taken from Homma's command and sent to the Dutch East Indies were back now, bolstered by additional planes and pilots, and the total strength of his combat forces on the ground had been increased to 43,000 men.

Rumors that Homma had been so severely disgraced by the defeats suffered by his troops in January and February that he had committed hara-kiri circulated briefly on Bataan in mid-March. But like so many other rumors that reached the Battling Bastards, these proved to be totally unfounded. On the contrary, Homma had regained a measure of confidence. His troops were either fresh or well rested. They were again well fed, disease-free, and the new arrivals among them were receiving intensive training. They were better armed than ever before, with masses of new artillery.

On March 19, Homma sent Wainwright an ultimatum. It arrived in hundreds of beer cans dropped by planes across southern Bataan. The message inside the cans was addressed to "His Excellency Major General Jonathan Wainwright." It read in part:

> We are . . . now in position to state that with the men and supplies which surpass both numerically and qualitatively those under your leadership, we are entirely free to attack and put to rout your forces or to wait for the inevitable starvation of your troops within the narrow confines of the Bataan Peninsula.
>
> Your Excellency must be well aware of the future prospects of the Filipino-American forces under your command. To waste the valuable lives of these men in an utterly meaningless and hopeless struggle would be directly opposed to the principles of humanity. . . .
>
> Your Excellency, your duty has been performed. Accept our sincere advice and save the lives of those officers and men under your command. The International Law will be strictly adhered to by the Imperial Japanese Forces, and your Excellency and those under your command will be treated accordingly.
>
> If a reply to this advisory note is not received from Your Excellency through special messenger by noon, March 22nd, 1942, we shall consider ourselves at liberty to take any action whatsoever.

The final battle for Bataan was about to begin, and as MacArthur had predicted to two American war correspondents shortly before leaving for Australia, the end would be "brutal and bloody."

7

Chaos on a Collapsing Front

On the evening of March 20, General Wainwright received official notification from the War Department of his promotion to lieutenant general. At the same time, he was also informed that, contrary to General MacArthur's wishes, he'd been designated as commander of all American and Filipino forces in the Philippines.

MacArthur's plan to appoint four separate commanders in the archipelago, with himself maintaining overall authority from Australia, had been quickly vetoed by General Marshall and Secretary of War Stimson, who termed MacArthur's idea of conducting the Philippines campaign from a distance of 4,000 miles a "violation of all sensible policy."

The morning after his promotion, Wainwright turned over command of the troops on Bataan to Major General Edward P. "Ned" King, an old friend who had formerly served as artillery adviser to MacArthur. Then, after a short boat ride from Mariveles, Wainwright made his first appearance in his new capacity at the Corregidor headquarters of what would be known henceforth as United States Forces in the Philippines (USFIP) in Lateral No. 3 of Malinta Tunnel.

Wainwright's spirits that morning were higher than they'd been in weeks. He'd had nothing more than brief naps since the war started, and he was hoping for quieter, more peaceful conditions than those he'd endured for nearly three months on Bataan. "Here's where I finally get some sleep," he told himself.

He was destined to be sorely disappointed. Within a few hours, he would be exposed to the first of the Japanese bombing raids that shook the island at regular intervals each day, making the walls of his headquarters tremble and showering him with streams of dust from the ceiling. When he ventured outside on a brief tour the following day, he narrowly escaped death twice within a matter of minutes at the hands of enemy dive-bombers. At this point, Corregidor had endured close to 100 Japanese air raids since the war began, and much worse was yet to come.

"Bataan is nothing at all," Wainwright told General Charles Drake, his quartermaster on the Rock, after his brushes with death. "Corregidor is right in the middle of a bull's eye."

It's no exaggeration to say that virtually every person who survived the relentless air and artillery attacks on Corregidor between late March and early May 1942 owes his or her life to the two obscure American engineering officers who conceived and created Malinta Tunnel and its intricate network of laterals. Without them, it seems highly unlikely that any human being could have lived through the continuous bombardment directed at the island during this period by the Japanese.

The main tunnel was the brainchild of Major General Charles Evans Kilbourne Jr., a front-line commander of American troops in France in World War I and a Medal of Honor winner in the Spanish-American War. As commander of the Coast Artillery District of Manila and Subic Bay from 1929 to 1932, Kilbourne had to use subterfuge to obtain funds from Washington to start constructing the tunnel. It was originally intended to serve as a supplemental route for moving troops and supplies to the east end of the island, where the only road was often blocked by landslides. When Kilbourne asked for money to build an underground passage, he was turned down, but when he changed his request to funds for "quarrying," it was approved.

After Kilbourne left the Philippines and returned to Washington,

Brigadier General S. D. Embick took over the project while serving as commander of the harbor defenses in Manila Bay in 1933–34. Later hailed for his "prophetic vision and great energy," Embick added a north entrance and some two dozen lateral tunnels, each fifteen feet wide and 400 feet long. Most of these were originally planned for various types of storage, but when war broke out, a large portion were transformed into a well-equipped 1,000-bed hospital, headquarters and living quarters for military personnel, a quartermaster area for food storage, and other facilities. The main tunnel was eventually connected to a separate Navy Radio Tunnel with an entrance on the island's southern coast.

The main tunnel, completed in 1938, was approximately 850 feet long from its eastern entrance to its western entrance. At its center beneath 460-foot Malinta Hill, its roof of dirt, rock, and concrete was more than 100 feet thick, and its central portion measured about twenty-five feet wide with arched ceilings thirty feet high.

The overall result was an architectural marvel described by Wainwright—quite accurately—as "a godsend [that] saved thousands of us on Corregidor."

Unfortunately, however, there were no bombproof tunnels available to the troops manning front-line positions on Bataan.

The Japanese had spent most of the first half of March hauling in new and heavier artillery, establishing new battery positions, preparing bases for scores of new attack aircraft, and disembarking 25,000 fresh troops. At the same time, the enemy moved huge quantities of supplies into Bataan from the north, and more enemy warships joined those already crowding Philippine waters, tightening the grip of the Japanese blockade of Luzon. By the end of the third week of the month, it was obvious that General Homma's forces were through licking their wounds and ready to bring the siege of Bataan to a crushing conclusion.

On March 22, at about the same time that MacArthur and his entourage were getting settled in Melbourne, Allied patrols on Bataan began running into what Wainwright described as "furious opposition." Two days later, the most awesome combination of artillery barrages and saturation dive-bomber attacks yet seen in the Pacific signaled the start of Homma's make-or-break offensive.

"The final battle for Bataan had been shaping up for a couple of weeks with increased infiltration and sniper attacks—and now it was here," recalled Sergeant Louis Read, a 31st Infantry squad leader anchoring the line in the II Corps sector on the east side of the peninsula. "The Japanese artillery fire was vastly increased, and so was their air coverage. But we were reinforced by the 194th and 192nd Tank Battalions, which had a bunch of Stuart light tanks and a lot of half-tracks with .50-caliber machine guns mounted on them, so we hoped we could hold. I heard that the tankers shot down close to 200 Jap planes over the next few days, but they just kept coming."

On March 24, fifty-four Japanese heavy bombers, of a type that the American garrison hadn't seen before, also unleashed their fury on Corregidor. The devastation they wreaked on the island's surface structures, coupled with a simultaneous bombardment by enemy batteries on Cavite, persuaded Wainwright to abandon the small house he'd inherited from MacArthur and move his living quarters into two seven-by-nine-foot spaces in one of the laterals.

The size and intensity of the raid also drove home the vulnerability of Corregidor's huge coastal batteries to attacks from the air. A total of fifty-six 10- and 12-inch guns and mortars studded the cliffs around the portion of the island known as Topside, so-called because of its comparatively high elevation. Some of these weapons dated from the 1890s, but they had the power to hurl shells up to ten miles. They were backed up by smaller, permanently emplaced 3- and 6-inch batteries as well as by dozens of mobile field pieces, including twenty-four 155-millimeter guns and forty-eight 75-millimeter guns, all of World War I vintage.

Three other small islands south of Corregidor in Manila Bay—Fort Drum, Fort Frank, and Fort Hughes—were also fortified with coastal artillery.

This vast amalgamation of weaponry, assembled in an era when planes capable of carrying tons of bombs at a time were unknown, made Corregidor nearly impregnable to attack by sea, and the Japanese were careful to keep their ships out of range. But the big guns provided no protection whatever against bombing raids by modern military aircraft—either for the island as a whole or for themselves. In their permanent concrete emplacements, they were brutally susceptible to destruction from above. Corregidor's total air defenses, meanwhile, consisted of only twenty-four 3-inch antiaircraft guns and forty-eight .50-caliber machine guns. This wasn't nearly enough. Twenty times that much wouldn't have been enough.

Beginning in late March, even as they aimed a mortal blow at Bataan's defenders, the Japanese would exploit this disadvantage to the utmost. When Wainwright arrived on the Rock to assume command, none of the big batteries had yet been disabled by the bombers. A month later, all but two would be permanently silenced.

On March 29, Palm Sunday, the Japanese served notice that no quarter would be given Bataan's defenders when an enemy plane emptied its bomb bays—deliberately, it seemed to many observers—on Hospital No. 1, now located at the town of Little Baguio and clearly marked with Red Cross symbols.

Shrapnel from the bombs ripped through some of the outdoor wards, killing twenty-three people, wounding seventy-eight others, and destroying the main operating room, officers quarters, headquarters tent, and mess hall.

The Japanese issued an apology, broadcast over Manila radio, claiming that the bombing was "unintentional," and some Americans, including hospital commandant Colonel James Duckworth, were initially willing to accept it as an accident caused by an inexperienced Japanese pilot.

But only hours after the expression of regret was aired—at 10:17 AM on March 30—a second load of bombs struck the hospital, one of them exploding squarely in the middle of a crowded ward. Nurse Madeline Ullom, an eyewitness, vividly described the scene: "Devastation was everywhere. Trees were uprooted. Fragments of clothing and parts of bodies were in the tree branches. Roofs were pulverized. Sides of buildings were splintered. Beds were twisted. Dead and wounded were partially buried in debris. Many died of shock."

No act of apparent savagery by the enemy infuriated Wainwright as much as this one. "It was so shocking it made one cry with rage," he would later write, "and want to wade in and simply throw fists at the perpetrators."

To remove any remaining doubt about Japanese intentions, the attackers planted one of their bombs squarely on top of a large Red Cross emblem in the hospital yard. In all, ten bombs ravaged the hospital, killing seventy-three people and wounding 117 others.

"This time, they scored a direct hit on the wards," recalled nurse Juanita Redmond. "A thousand-pound bomb pulverized the bamboo sheds, smashed the tin roofs into flying pieces; iron beds doubled and broke jaggedly like paper matches. . . .

"Only one small section of my ward remained standing. Part of the roof had been blown into the jungle. There were mangled bodies under the ruins; a blood-stained hand stuck up through a pile of scrap; arms and legs had been ripped off and flung among the rubbish. Some of the mangled torsos were almost impossible to identify. One of the few medics who had survived unhurt climbed a tree to bring down a body blown into the top branches."

The unmitigated viciousness of the blitzkrieg-style offensive that was about to roll down the length of Bataan notwithstanding, no American on the peninsula could justifiably accuse the Japanese of striking without repeated warnings. For more than two weeks before the enemy launched his final drive, the defenders were inundated with leaflets dropped by planes inviting them to surrender, exacerbating the hunger and despair of the troops, promising humane treatment for prisoners, and, conversely, trying to incite murderous rebellion among the Filipino soldiers.

"Throughout the siege," recalled Major Alva Fitch, a battery commander in the 23rd Field Artillery, Philippine Scouts, "we were showered with propaganda leaflets. They included restaurant menus, lascivious pictures, fictitious letters from happy Filipinos who had escaped, tickets to be given the Japanese, showing they had authorized your surrender, etc. In March, this became more bitter and contained instructions for the Filipinos to shoot their American officers."

There were no reports of Filipino soldiers actually following these instructions. By and large, the native troops remained loyal to their American commanders and comrades-in-arms. But unfortunately, the Philippine Army's raw recruits were never able to curb their tendency to flee under fire—and the fire they were about to face was like nothing any of them had ever seen before.

General Homma's climactic infantry assault on the eastern sector of the Allied front at the northern foot of Mount Samat was set to jump off at 3 PM on April 3, Good Friday. Beginning that morning, it was preceded by five hours of the most devastating combined air-artillery bombardment ever seen on Bataan.

"The enemy's 150 artillery pieces facing Mount Samat were spaced thirty yards apart in a one-mile area near Balanga," said Marine PFC Karl King, who observed from a distance. "The target area was a 1,000-yard section of the American line in front of Mount Samat. Estimates indicated that Japanese aircraft dumped over seventy tons of explosives during nearly 200 passes over the target area."

Initially, the defenders managed to hold their ground against the tidal wave of high explosives. But when the raiders topped off their attacks with dozens of incendiary bombs along the narrow front, they triggered an inferno in which no human life could survive.

"The jungle became a furnace," King said. "Men were cremated in their foxholes. When the bombardment let up, Japanese troops poured through a gap in the lines created by the concentrated barrage."

Major John Olson of the 57th Infantry, Philippine Scouts, witnessed from uncomfortably close range as the 41st Philippine Army Division's portion of the front in General Parker's II Corps sector first vanished amid the conflagration, then collapsed into chaos.

"The uninterrupted five-hour barrage literally blew a gaping hole in the 41st Division's sector and the ongoing explosions and raging fires prevented reserves from moving up to reinforce the line," Olson said. "The terrified survivors became a dazed, fleeing mob, and there was nothing the American officers or Philippine Scouts could do to stop them. A major rupture had been torn in the eastern half of our line."

When early reports of the enemy breakthrough reached Wainwright on Corregidor, he instantly recognized the gravity of the situation. The collapse had occurred exactly as he'd been expecting for more than three months.

"The Bataan battle took on a new, sinister note on the morning of April 3," he later recalled, "when the Japs tore holes in the middle of Parker's corps and buckled the right flank of I Corps. Knots of trapped Jap troops of forward elements were wiped out in toe-to-toe fighting, but others held their gains, and we gave ground slowly—our artillery shooting point-blank at waves of advancing [enemy] troops."

Losses were horrendous on both sides, but the Filipinos definitely took the worst of it. Over the next few days, repeated counterattacks by disease-ridden, hunger-ravaged U.S. troops would slow but fail to stop the relentless Japanese advance down the east coast of Bataan. Each torturous retreat was followed by another, and the splintered front refused to solidify.

For the Battling Bastards, the beginning of the end had finally arrived.

At dusk on April 4, Major Lloyd Moffit of the Second Battalion, 31st Infantry, approached Captain Ralph Hibbs, his head medical officer, with a worried look and a troubling question.

"How many men out of the 225 on the morning roster could march one mile with battle gear?" Moffit wanted to know.

Hibbs frowned hesitantly. "Possibly two-thirds—somewhere around 150 to 175," he said. "Forced all-night marches are just beyond the capacity of most of these men."

"Well, the final big Jap offensive all along the line opened yesterday," Moffit said. "You'll have to count the effectives. We can't evacuate anyone who can walk and fight. There's no tomorrow in this jungle."

Hibbs went to bed that night dreading the task of sorting out the sick from the not-so-sick. He knew that fewer than one man in ten among the approximately 77,000 live troops left in the Bataan command could be classified as fully fit for duty.

As it turned out, Hibbs never got a chance to do the sorting. In the middle of that night, orders came for the battalion to move forward. "Help was needed now; the situation was desperate," Hibbs recalled. "Out of the original 700 men in the battalion, 128 volunteers stood up, put on their packs, and moved out for the front. Some fell out after a few kilometers. Others left their hospital beds and joined us. They said, 'Let's die at the front instead of in a hospital.'"

By April 6, the disintegration of the eastern front had reached crisis proportions. At this point, every man in Captain John Coleman's 27th Materiel Squadron was sick with malaria, but almost none of them went to the hospital voluntarily. They realized that the hospital had nothing to give them to relieve the chills and fever, and weak as they were, they preferred to stay on the line with their buddies.

"Every night, some of our tanks would come up to help us hold the line," said Coleman. "They couldn't stay there during the daylight hours for fear of being destroyed by Jap artillery. . . . We felt more secure with them there to help us. Nearly all of our artillery batteries had been silenced by the 500-pound bombs the Japs were using."

Coleman and his men were surrounded by ominous signs that the end was near. Among them was a sausage-shaped observation balloon floating high above the Japanese lines and beyond the range of any weapons now available to the defenders.

When Coleman awoke that morning and saw the balloon, his first thought was, "Well, this is it. They can see every move we make and where we are, and there's nothing we can do about it."

A short time later, Coleman received a call from Colonel Bill Maverick, a fellow Texan who commanded the First Battalion of the Air Corps Infantry Regiment, asking Coleman to come to his headquarters.

"You need to pick someone else to command the 27th Materiel Squadron," Maverick told Coleman when they met. "I want you to come up here and be my executive officer. I've been flying for twenty years, but I don't know much about maneuvering troops, and you've proved to us that you know the infantry business."

Coleman's first assignment in his new role was to withdraw the battalion to the regimental reserve line and prepare it for machine gun duty with a collection of .50-caliber weapons salvaged from wrecked P-40s and mounted on tripods for infantry use. The guns were cumbersome for exhausted men to move, but they possessed formidable firepower that could wreak havoc on charging enemy infantry. Unfortunately, though, Coleman's men would never get a chance to fire them.

"Supper on April 6 was the last time I was to eat with my old squadron," Coleman recalled. "That night the mess sergeant told me we had only enough food for one more meal, and it would all be rice. We didn't know where we could get any more food, and this was the situation with all the rest of the Air Corps Regiment."

Intelligence sources reported that veteran enemy combat troops from Singapore, known as the "Shanghai Division," were leading the attack in the First Battalion's area. Their artillery was concentrating on the Philippine troops to Coleman's left, shelling them day and night.

By daylight on the morning of April 7, the Japanese had punched another hole in the Allied lines on Coleman's left and penetrated up to seven kilometers to the south, overrunning the kitchen area of the 27th Materiel Squadron in the process.

When Coleman and Maverick climbed a knoll near their headquarters to survey their situation through field glasses, they saw thousands of Japanese troops spread out in skirmish formation across their front for at least half a mile.

"My God, Captain," Maverick said softly, "we'll never be able to overcome this!"

Moments later, hundreds of Filipino civilians, accompanied by numerous Philippine Army troops who had discarded their rifles, ran into the American lines shouting, "Tanks! Tanks!"

"Many of them had been wounded," Coleman said. "Some had arms dangling; some were lame, with fresh blood on them. I couldn't see any tanks, but I could hear motors, see trees and brush shaking, and hear the machine-gun fire."

"We've got to do something!" Maverick yelled. "Captain, you take charge of this regiment. We're about to be surrounded!"

Off to his left, Coleman spotted a deep ravine studded with large boulders that would deny the approaching enemy armor immediate access to the rear of his lines. Then, calling his runners together, he scribbled messages to each of his unit commanders telling them to move east at double time to put themselves on the opposite side of the ravine from the tanks.

The entire regiment was soon on the move to the south as fast as the men could travel, retreating in good order while avoiding a road clogged with civilians and under almost constant strafing attacks by enemy planes. At the first ridgeline that offered favorable defensive positions, Coleman ordered his troops to deploy in a thick growth of small trees and scrub brush, but the enemy tanks and infantry were still unnervingly close behind.

"We didn't have a single weapon that could knock out a tank, and I was at a loss to know what to do," Coleman said. "If we were surrounded, we wouldn't be able to move, and I knew we were outnumbered by probably fifty to one."

His only option, he decided, was to keep pressing south and try to shake free of the enemy attempt to encircle the regiment.

At five o'clock that afternoon, the regiment crossed the Mamala River without benefit of a bridge and slipped into a heavy forest on the south side of the stream. Finally, deep among the trees, where they were safe for the moment from the Japanese dive-bombers and strafers, Coleman gave the men a break and told them to get rid of all nonessential equipment. They poured the water out of their shoes and wrung out their socks after wading the river. They threw away the omnipresent gas masks they'd carried for four months but never used. They discarded their extra clothing, blankets, shaving gear, and digging tools but kept their rifles, bayonets, bandoleers of ammo, canteens, and first-aid kits. They also kept their mess kits, although they'd had nothing to put in them for almost twenty-four hours, and prospects for the foreseeable future were equally bleak.

As Coleman later remembered the interlude: "There wasn't much talk. I'm sure they had a lot on their minds and were wondering just what might be our fate in the next two days. I knew they realized that, the way things were going, something different had to happen [but] I heard no complaint from the men."

* * *

In late March, during his last visit to the diseased and battered remnants of the 26th Cavalry, General Wainwright had warned of the coming Japanese onslaught. Then he'd called on the now dismounted cavalrymen to do what they'd done so often in the past—be ready to plug the holes that would inevitably be ripped in the defenders' fragile line.

On April 3, Lieutenant Edwin Ramsey and other survivors of the 26th watched from a rear area as Wainwright's warning became reality. The massive Japanese air-artillery assault shook the Bataan Peninsula to its core that day, and much of the eastern sector of the front vanished in a pall of flame and smoke. Then the hordes of Japanese infantry came pouring through the gap.

"After two desperate days, II Corps collapsed and began streaming back toward . . . the town of Mariveles, bending I Corps backward to protect its naked flank," Ramsey recalled. "Report after frantic report reached us of penetrations all along the front. On April 6, Wainwright threw us forward into the center of the shredding line."

This time, the 26th was forced to charge on foot and in pitifully small numbers. Eighty percent of its troopers were sick with malaria; three-fourths suffered from dysentery, and a third had mild cases of beriberi. Their orders were to counterattack, but they'd scarcely started when word came that the enemy had broken through on their right, and all roads to II Corps had been cut. The entire center of the front had simply disintegrated.

"Wainwright ordered us to circle back around Mount Mariveles and then cut across country northeastward to the coastal town of Limay," Ramsey said. The order in itself indicated sheer desperation at the command level, since Limay was about eight miles south of Orion, which had been the eastern anchor of the front about seventy-two hours earlier.

The 26th was told to report to General Clifford Bluemel, commander of the 31st Philippine Division, but when the cavalry troops found Bluemel, he explained that his entire force, along with the 45th and 57th Infantry Regiments, Philippine Scouts, were falling back in confusion through the jungle. Bluemel, who had lost most of his headquarters staff in the fighting, commandeered some of the 26th's staff and ordered its Second Squadron forward to stall the Japanese advance as long as possible.

"We didn't have to move far to find them," said Ramsey, "and we opened a fierce firefight to force them to deploy. We held for ten minutes, then fifteen, then thirty, giving Bluemel's men time to withdraw. Then, as the Japanese began to turn our flank, we pulled back, still firing."

Ramsey and the others found themselves atop a steep bluff that fell several hundred feet to a stream below. As they started across a clearing along a dusty trail, a flight of Zeros spotted their dust cloud and immediately launched an attack.

"Some fled for the jungle, while those of us closest to the bluff had no choice but to dive over the edge," Ramsey said. "It was terrifying. Dozens of us hung there, grasping at vines and shrubs, flattened against the cliff face as plane after plane roared in, bombing and strafing."

The attack lasted until dusk, when the Zeros finally departed, and the survivors pulled themselves up over the edge of the bluff.

"The carnage was horrible," Ramsey remembered. "Most of our staff and rear guard had been wiped out. Men and vehicles were ground into the earth or flung among the trees. The wounded were everywhere, moaning or screaming curses. Some had limbs torn off. Others groped at gashes that exposed splintered bones. . . . One man sat with his back against a tree, staring at the open pit of his stomach, from which the intestines coiled out onto his thighs."

Ramsey called for his men to assemble, and those that were able to do so formed a line, then started back along the trail, moving woodenly and in a state of shock. But one of the troopers paused to point at the scattered bodies of the gravely wounded littering the clearing atop the bluff.

"What about them?" the man asked.

"There's nothing we can do!" Ramsey snapped. "We've got to get under cover."

He felt a surge of pity, shame, and helpless anger as the column stumbled slowly away and the moaning of the injured and dying gradually faded behind them.

* * *

Late on the afternoon of April 7, Brigadier General Arnold Funk, chief of staff for General Edward King, made a hurried, harried trip across Manila Bay to bring a message of despair to General Wainwright in his office in Lateral No. 3.

"General," Funk said, "General King sent me here to tell you that he might have to surrender."

Wainwright stared back at the messenger for a long moment. Funk's face, he recalled much later, was "a picture of weariness." Then Wainwright lowered his gaze to his desktop, where his most recent message from General MacArthur lay staring back at him.

"*When the supply situation becomes impossible, there must be no thought of surrender*," it read. "*You must attack.*"

"Arnold, you go back and tell General King that there will be no surrender," Wainwright said softly. "Tell him he will attack. Those are my orders."

There was another lengthy moment of silence, and tears came to Funk's eyes as he spoke. "General," he said, "you know what the situation is over there. You know what the outcome will be."

"I do," Wainwright replied, in a voice barely above a whisper. "God be with all of you over there. I've done all I can."

With most of the Philippine Army units in Parker's II Corps sector now in full, disorganized flight, only a few hundred U.S. troops were left to oppose the onrushing Japanese on the east side of Bataan. Besides the remnants of the 26th Cavalry, they included the remaining men of the 31st Infantry, the 192nd and 194th Tank Battalions, the clipped-wing Air Corps Infantry, plus a few Americans and Filipino Scouts attached to various artillery units.

"When masses of Japs broke through the Filipino lines on our left, it was all over," said Sergeant Wayne Carrington, a native North Carolinian manning a front-line post with the Air Corps Infantry. "We were lucky to hold them as long as we did. At least we bought our forces in Australia some time to get organized."

"It was an impossible situation," added Sergeant Clem Kathman of the 200th Coast Artillery, who watched the steady streams of retreating soldiers from his gun position high on a ridge overlooking the main East Road. "Outnumbered up to 100 to one, there was no way any of us could hold for long. As we watched, we knew that the front line would soon come to us, and we'd be the next bunch to withdraw."

After spending the day on April 8 in suspense, Kathman and his comrades were growing increasingly nervous by late afternoon. "We decided to call battery headquarters and see what was going down," Kathman said. "Instead, headquarters got through to us with orders to destroy our guns and equipment and fall back to Kilometer 162 near Cabcaben Airfield."

At this point, Kathman's unit was down to a single truck still in running condition. All the rest had been wrecked, worn out, or commandeered by other units. After disabling all weapons except their rifles—and with only about 200 rounds of ammunition per man—they loaded their barracks bags onto the battered truck and moved out, heading south like everyone else.

"About an hour after dark, our battery commander called us together and informed us that we were no longer an ack-ack outfit but an infantry unit and that we should govern ourselves accordingly," Kathman recalled. "He also told us that, outside of a few tanks and half-tracks, there was nothing between us and the Japs. In short, we *were* the front line."

And that wasn't all the bad news, either.

The "front" of the moment was a ridge running along the edge of Cabcaben Field and extending all the way from Manila Bay to the Mariveles Mountains, a distance of approximately ten miles. To cover it, the defenders had, at most, 1,500 men. As Kathman remembered:

> For the third time since December 8, I got a certain feeling in the pit of my stomach. It wasn't so much that I was afraid. It was more a feeling of uncertainty, of not knowing what was going to happen. Against an onslaught of tanks, artillery, mortars, bombers, and everything else at the Japs' command, we had about as much chance as a snowball in hell.

We spent the dragging hours of that night amid the rumble of the big 12-inch rifles on Corregidor, firing round after round over our heads into the advancing Japs to the north of us. Our battery commander finally found a position for us to dig in for the inevitable last stand. From where we sat, it looked like another Custer massacre, but by now, we'd committed ourselves to extinction, or so we thought.

We'd heard from the beginning that the Nips didn't take prisoners, so we had two options: Stay and fight to the death or risk desertion charges and take to the hills. Anyway, we stayed—all of us—glued to our rifles and waiting for the unknown.

Somewhere to the north of Kathman's position, what was left of the 31st Infantry had broken up into small, disorganized groups after the two Philippine Army divisions on both their flanks simply disappeared, leaving only confusion and hopelessness in their place.

"As darkness fell in the jungle, we just lost contact with each other," recalled Sergeant Louis Read. "I found myself alone in a tiny clearing surrounded by bushes and Jap soldiers. I could hear them jabbering all around me. I knelt with the butt of my rifle against the ground and its fixed bayonet pointing upward at an angle, hoping they'd all go on without spotting me. Suddenly, with a loud cry, a Jap jumped out of the bushes at me and landed squarely on my bayonet."

Read extracted his blade from the enemy soldier's motionless body and turned away, looking for someplace to hide. But other nearby Japanese had been alerted by their comrade's scream, and Read could feel—rather than see—them rushing toward him.

"The next thing I knew, I was stuck in the side with a Jap bayonet," he said. "I fell to the ground, and the Japs, apparently thinking I was dead and also probably in a hurry, took off. I didn't seem to be hurt badly, but the wound was bleeding quite a bit. I tore off a piece of my shirt and stuffed it into the hole in my side."

Moments later, as Read staggered down a seemingly deserted jungle trail, he heard a single shot, and a sniper's bullet slammed through his steel helmet. Luckily, the bullet only grazed his skull, but this wound, too, bled profusely, and he felt himself growing weak and extremely tired.

When he paused in a mango grove and sank to the ground, trying to catch his breath, he heard a sudden, staccato roar and looked up in disbelief to see a Japanese dive-bomber come zooming in over the grove at treetop level. When it was directly above him, its pilot released a bomb, possibly suspecting that an American tank was hiding there. Read saw a flash of fire, felt the force of a deafening explosion, and thought for sure he was going to die. But after the plane was gone, he pulled himself to a sitting position, surprised that he was still alive.

"I was hit by shrapnel fragments in several places, including one that broke the bridge of my nose," said Read. "This caused more bleeding, and now I was really getting worried. I thought I remembered the way to Hospital No. 1 at Little Baguio, but I wasn't sure if it was still there—or if I had enough strength left to make it that far."

Unknown to thrice-wounded Sergeant Read as he dragged himself toward Hospital No. 1, all the female nurses serving in that battered facility were being ordered to drop everything and leave—immediately—for the port of Mariveles and evacuation to Corregidor.

Dusk was approaching on April 8 when Colonel Duckworth, the hospital commandant, called First Lieutenant Edith Shacklette, his chief nurse, to the shattered remains of his office and broke the grim news to her.

"The word is that Bataan will surrender tomorrow, and we're going to get the nurses over to Corregidor," Duckworth said. "We don't want to have women around when the Jap soldiers come in. Go and tell everybody to stop what they're doing and take what possessions they can. A bus will be down here in about thirty minutes."

For a moment, Shacklette tried to protest. What about the 1,800 defenseless patients in her wards? How could the nurses just walk out and leave them?

Through tight lips, Duckworth simply repeated the order and told her there was no time to argue.

"Of course, there was crying," Shacklette said. "We hated to leave our patients, hated to leave our group." The nurses wrote out hurried instructions for the doctors and medics who were staying behind, grabbed a few personal belongings, and ran to the bus, where some of the doctors had gathered to say goodbye.

"We'll be seeing you," they all told each other, but nobody believed it.

If anything, the scene at Hospital No. 2 was even more frantic. The nurses there got a slightly later start than those at Hospital No. 1, and they were given barely fifteen minutes by Colonel James O. Gillespie, their commandant, to get ready to go.

"Tell your American nurses to get down here to my office by 2000 hours [8 PM] and only take whatever they can carry in their hands," he instructed his chief nurse, Lieutenant Josephine Nesbit.

"What about my Filipino nurses?" she asked.

"Only the American nurses," Gillespie said.

Nesbit balked and whirled to face her commander. "If my Filipino nurses don't go," she said, staring at Gillespie defiantly, "I'm not going, either!"

Out of respect for "Mama Josie," as the Filipino nurses called Nesbit, Gillespie took time to relay her demand to USFIP headquarters on Corregidor. He received a quick okay from someone there, and all the nurses and other female hospital workers raced to the waiting trucks, some carrying nothing more than a toothbrush and a comb.

"Walking out in the middle of an operation with hundreds of patients lined up under the trees waiting for surgery was devastating to me," recalled nurse Lucy Wilson, who was forced to leave an overflowing operating room at No. 2 when the order came. "This I have to live with for the rest of my life."

Sergeant Charlie James, a native of Carlsbad, New Mexico, had been toughened by years of hard work on his family's 225-section cattle ranch before his National Guard unit was called up in the summer of '41. As the man in charge of a communications section of the 200th Coast Artillery, he'd supervised the laying of countless miles of telephone wire to scattered outposts on Bataan, but virtually all of those phone lines were dead and useless now—and James felt useless, too.

He was only a stone's throw from the overflowing Hospital No. 2 and wondering, like everyone else, what to do next when an Army major pulled up in a jeep and told him the Americans had surrendered.

"He told us to destroy all our arms and anything else the Nips might be able to use," James recalled. "We drained all the oil out of the recoil systems of our 3-inch guns so they'd tear themselves apart if they were fired. That at least made us feel like we were doing something to hurt the enemy. Then we just sat down and waited."

Despite the fact that he was only eighteen years old, Private Charles Baum, who'd come to the Philippines with the 19th Bomb Group, had developed into one of the most seasoned machine gunners on Bataan during the long siege.

"On that last day of the fighting, I was using a .50-caliber gun out of a wrecked P-40," recalled the youngster from Whitesboro, Texas, "and I was more or less in charge of six other guns—all .30-caliber, three air-cooled and three water-cooled—that we'd set up out in no-man's-land. I had three men on each gun to begin with. I lost some of them as the day went on, but Lord knows how many Japs we killed."

Baum recalled firing "several thousand rounds" from his .50 over a period of about nine hours on the morning of April 9 before he and the other gunners were forced to abandon their position.

"The other guys fell back fast when the Japs broke through," he said. "I was the last one to go, and by then I knew it was all over."

At 3 AM on April 9, General Wainwright made what would be his last telephone call to General King, repeating, in essence, an order relayed to him earlier by General MacArthur and knowing full well that it was impossible to carry out.

"Launch a counterattack at dawn with [General] Jones's I Corps northward toward Olongapo," Wainwright said. "This will help relieve the pressure on II Corps."

As Duane Schultz, Wainwright's biographer, pointed out: "Everyone [present at King's command post] understood the hopelessness of the situation, but King dutifully went through the motions, just as Wainwright had done. He contacted Jones and passed on the order."

Jones's response was short, simple, and utterly realistic. "Any attack is ridiculous," he said. "Out of the question. My men are too weak."

King didn't argue the point. He realized that, even if Jones could mount some semblance of an attack, it would be doomed to failure and could only result in pointless further slaughter. About a half-hour later, King called his staff together to break the bitter news.

"I haven't asked you here to get your opinion or advice," he told them evenly. "I don't want any of you saddled with any part of the responsibility for the ignominious decision I feel forced to make. I haven't communicated with General Wainwright because I don't want him to be compelled to assume any part of the responsibility. I'm sending forward a flag of truce at daybreak to ask for terms of surrender. I feel that further resistance would only uselessly waste human life. We have no further means of organized resistance. There's just no way we can continue the fight."

King's quartermaster, Colonel Irvin Alexander, who attended the meeting, remembered the crestfallen Bataan commander adding that, if he lived to return home, he "fully expected to be court-martialed" for his decision. "He was certain," said Alexander, "that history could not deal kindly with the commander who would be remembered for having surrendered the largest force the United States had ever lost."

After King finished speaking and turned away, an oppressive silence fell over the command post. Virtually to a man, the entire staff was weeping.

Throughout the night of April 8, as the handwriting on the wall loomed larger and its meaning became unmistakably clear, a floodtide of humanity formed on and along either side of the road leading south from what had been the front lines toward the port of Mariveles. Its components were a pitiful mixture of the sick, the lame, the starving, and the lost—ragged American military of every rank and service, frightened Philippine Army conscripts, hard-eyed Philippine Scouts, and bewildered Filipino civilians. But all shared a common objective: to put as much distance as possible between themselves and the pursuing Japanese army.

Almost none of those who traveled this route had any clear idea what might await them when they reached their destination—even if they knew what that destination was. Many had received vague orders to rendezvous with other units at a certain kilometer post or some other landmark, only to find themselves among a milling mob of strangers when they arrived there.

"They told us to load up on trucks and head for Mariveles," said Sergeant Cletis Overton of the Air Corps Infantry. "We could hear explosions booming in all directions, including some really gigantic ones that somebody said was our main ammunition dumps being destroyed. We even got hit by a strong earthquake that night, and it seemed to me the whole world was crumbling around us."

Overton hid the fine camera he'd bought in Honolulu on the trip across the Pacific, along with all the photos he'd taken since and never had a chance to send back to Arkansas and the Bible his mother had given him, among the gnarled roots of a huge cypress tree. He covered them awkwardly with a piece of canvas—never to see them again—and ran back to where the trucks were waiting.

Progress on the road was painfully slow, coming in fits and starts, and it took more than four hours to travel a distance that could normally be covered in forty-five minutes. At one point, a small caravan of vehicles, led by MPs on motorcycles and including a command car carrying General King's surrender emissaries, passed Overton's truck, heading north against the crushing flow of southbound traffic. A white flag fluttered from the staff on the car's front fender.

It was after daylight on April 9 when Overton and his comrades reached Mariveles, but once they got there, they could only wonder why they'd bothered to come. The truck stopped at a desolate, bombed-out airstrip marked by a few wrecked planes and listless groups of hollow-eyed Americans and Filipinos. Sporadic gunfire could still be heard in the distance, but when Overton looked up toward a nearby string of hills, he saw long lines of Japanese soldiers surrounding the airstrip.

"The scene was total chaos," Overton would recall many years later. "We saw officers ordering their men to destroy their weapons. Other guys were crying or cursing and yelling that they'd fight to the death. Everywhere you looked, there were white flags made from bedsheets, pillowcases, and handkerchiefs. It was a sad, sad day, and I had this terrible feeling that everything was lost. We'd gotten to Mariveles, all right, but now there was no place left to go."

More than a few of Bataan's defenders, however, refused to believe that Mariveles was the end of the line. While the majority of Americans slumped on the ground, faint from hunger, feverish with illness, glassy-eyed with exhaustion, and numbed by defeat, many others frantically sought a means of escape from the peninsula they'd fought for and lost.

Virtually every fishing boat and small craft capable of floating was launched from the east coast of Bataan that morning, along with numerous makeshift rafts, and hundreds of men waded out into the bay, determined to swim the two and a half shark-infested miles to Corregidor. Most who made these attempts in daylight would be killed by relentless strafing attacks by Japanese planes and enemy sharpshooters firing from shore. But against all odds, an estimated 2,000 defenders would succeed in getting off the peninsula alive to avoid capture—or at least postpone it.

Among them were Marines Karl King and Ike Williams. Aware that a surrender was in progress and hoping to avoid being swept up in the attempted mass exodus, the two buddies paused long enough to help staff officers at the Marines' Bataan headquarters destroy documents and records, then followed an obscure trail to the edge of Manila Bay while it was still fully dark.

"Aided by a log large enough to support our packs and rifles," King recalled, "we swam to Corregidor. The waters were bombarded by fragments from the explosions and falling debris, which probably kept the sharks away. We had to do some hard talking to convince the Marines guarding the rocky beach that we weren't Jap infiltrators."

* * *

Late on the afternoon of April 8, former B-17 crewmen John Renka, Ed Whitcomb, and Jim Dey, along with a few other grounded Air Corps personnel, made their way south on foot along a trail from their last assigned posts near abandoned Cabcaben Airfield. Their orders were to proceed to a highway marker at Kilometer 184 on the East Road, where other troops were gathering. No one had bothered to tell them that they were going there to surrender.

After hiking for a while, they hitched a ride on a truck loaded with military personnel, including several nurses from Hospital No. 2, who told Whitcomb and the others they were headed for the Mariveles docks, then across the bay to Corregidor.

"Better come along to Corregidor with us," one of the nurses invited.

"Sure like to," Whitcomb replied, "but we've got to meet the rest of our outfit north of Mariveles."

"What're you going to do there?" the nurse asked.

"Looks like we'll set up a last-ditch stand and hold on till reinforcements arrive," Whitcomb said, still trying to sound a note of optimism amid the catastrophe unfolding around them.

"Well, good luck!" the nurses shouted as the truck reached the main road and the three young airmen jumped off to head north while the truck and its other passengers continued south.

Early on the morning of April 9, Whitcomb and his comrades reached a small cement road marker that read "KM 184." Beside the road was an open field where several hundred dispirited men were assembled and waiting. As they left the road and started into the field, they were met by two colonels, neither of whom the new arrivals recognized.

"General King drove to the Japanese lines this morning to surrender the forces on Bataan," one of the colonels told them. "Nothing's been heard from him since, but the troops here will be prepared for an orderly surrender to the Japanese when they arrive." (Many Americans were under the mistaken impression that King had gone in person to meet the Japanese, but this didn't happen until several hours later.)

Whitcomb, Dey, and Renka frowned uneasily at each other. "It struck us suddenly," Whitcomb recalled, "that the white flags we'd seen along the way were surrender flags, and we hadn't recognized them. Now we felt as if we were being guided into a trap by our own people—and we didn't like it."

"Put your .45s in this pile and your ammo in that pile over there," the colonel instructed, pointing to two large separate stacks of weaponry and ammunition on the ground nearby.

Several of the group obeyed, but Whitcomb walked to the edge of the field as though he hadn't understood the colonel's order. When he was some distance away, he unbuckled his gun belt and hid his .45 automatic under a clump of bushes. Then he made his way back to where Jim Dey was sitting on the running board of a truck, staring at the ground.

"What do you make of this, Jim?" Whitcomb asked.

"I think we ought to get the hell out of here, Whit," Dey said.

"I'm all for it," Whitcomb said, "but where can we go from here?"

"Don't know, but wherever it is, it'll be as safe as this damn place."

At that point, Renka walked up and stopped in front of his two friends, studying their faces without saying anything.

"We're getting out of here, John," Dey whispered. "Grab yourself a .45 and come along."

"Mine's hidden over here," Whitcomb said, nodding toward the bush where his pistol was stowed. "I'll meet you guys at the main road as soon as we can get there."

As the three young officers turned back south and trudged resolutely toward Mariveles, Whitcomb could feel their entire perspective changing with every step they took. They had no idea where they might end up, but they shared a single, clearly defined goal: to reach the shore of Manila Bay, find a boat, and get off Bataan before Japanese soldiers came streaming over the hills to take them captive or shoot them in their tracks.

"No longer did we have to remain in one place to be bombed and shelled and starved," Whitcomb said. "We were free to move, and we moved quickly."

Who knows? he thought, speeding up his pace. *Maybe we'll be joining those nurses on Corregidor, after all.*

* * *

At dawn on April 9, similar ideas were racing through the minds of two officers of the dismounted 26th Cavalry. Lieutenant Ed Ramsey and Captain Joe Barker now found themselves among a ragtag collection of about sixty Philippine Scouts with the Japanese closing in on them from three sides and no sense of purpose or direction.

"We were surrounded, cut off, and lost," Ramsey recalled. "We weren't so much soldiers now as fugitives, seeking lines that we doubted existed, trying to rejoin a fight that we suspected was already over."

The morning was strangely silent—no artillery fire in the immediate area for the first time in weeks; no enemy planes on treetop-level strafing and bombing runs. To Ramsey, the silence bristled with sinister implications. The only explanation was an American surrender, but no such order had reached the survivors of the 26th.

"You think it means what I'm thinking?" he asked Barker as they breakfasted on a can of salmon, part of a forgotten cache of food they'd accidentally stumbled across the previous day.

"I don't see how it could be anything else," Barker said. "We'll find out soon enough."

"What'll you do?"

Barker shrugged. "Don't suppose I'd last long in a prison camp. How about you?"

"Me neither," Ramsey said. "Guess I'll take my chances."

"If it comes to it, I guess I will, too. Try for the southern islands, then maybe New Guinea and Australia."

"What do you think our chances *are*?"

"Slim to none," Barker said, smiling wanly. "Surrendering doesn't appeal to me, though."

"You want to try for it together?" Ramsey asked.

Barker thought about it for a moment, then stuck out a hand so thin and bony that he now wore his West Point ring on his thumb.

"You're on," he said.

But the two young cavalry officers didn't turn south toward the town of Mariveles, as almost all the other would-be escapees were doing. Instead, carrying only scant rations, their canteens, and a .45 automatic apiece, they began picking their way north through dense jungle and past heavily armed Japanese patrols toward the summit of

4,000-foot Mount Mariveles. Between them and safety in the remote wilds of northern Luzon lay tens of thousands of enemy troops and many miles of some of the most inhospitable terrain on earth.

"Our goal was to reach the Bagac–Pilar road, cross it, and get out of Bataan," recalled Ramsey. "As the main east–west road across the peninsula, we knew it would be thick with Japanese, but crossing it was the key to our escape—and our survival."

At about 6 AM on April 9, three hours after he'd last spoken with General King, a bone-weary General Wainwright sagged in a chair in a small sitting area off Malinta Tunnel. He'd spent most of the night on the phone, issuing orders that he knew couldn't be obeyed to his commanders on Bataan and searching for some small bit of positive news.

What Wainwright didn't know was that King had intentionally avoided contact with his commander after that last conversation. As King had confided to his staff when he called them to his tent at about 3:30 AM to inform them of his decision to surrender: "I haven't communicated with General Wainwright because I don't want him to be compelled to assume any part of the responsibility."

Now, as Wainwright hovered near the edge of unconsciousness, he was jarred awake by the urgent voice of his night duty officer, Colonel Jesse T. Traywick.

"Sir!" Traywick said in a tone harsh with shock. "General King is going to surrender! He's sent emissaries to the Japanese under a flag of truce to discuss terms."

Wainwright jerked himself to an upright position. "Go back and tell him not to do it!" he yelled.

Traywick scrambled back to the phone, repeating Wainwright's words into the mouthpiece and listening for a moment. Then he returned, shaking his head.

"It's too late, sir," he said. "They're already gone."

"They can't do it!" Wainwright groaned. "They can't do it!"

But they *had* done it. In that instant, the commander of U.S. Forces in the Philippines realized with crushing finality that Bataan was gone, too.

8

Through One Hell to Another

For a period of several hours, the gut-wrenching task of surrendering Bataan proved almost as difficult and dangerous as defending it had been.

Colonel Everett C. Williams and Major Marshall H. Hurt Jr., a pair of bachelor staff officers, had volunteered to serve as General King's emissaries, and while they had no reason to expect their assignment to be easy, they might well have had second thoughts if they'd foreseen the bodily risks involved.

By the time they left on their mission, shortly after 3:30 AM on April 9, widespread destruction of American equipment was already under way. Depot and warehouse commanders had been alerted the previous noon to prepare for demolition, and a general order to that effect had gone out about midnight. The Navy had kicked off the fireworks even earlier at Mariveles, where explosions began rumbling at about 10:30 PM on April 8, and towering flames lit the skies above the town. Among the targets for destruction was the gallant old sub tender *Canopus*, which was scuttled in eighty-four feet of water.

Williams and Hurt began their journey in a reconnaissance car with a motorcycle escort, but they ran into numerous delays, which may have been fortunate because their first encounter with enemy soldiers didn't come until after daybreak. If it had happened in darkness or semidarkness, the Americans would likely have been killed before they could deliver their surrender message. As it was, they came perilously close to being cut to pieces by a screaming, bayonet-wielding Japanese infantry platoon. The two officers and their driver avoided death only by frantically waving a white bedsheet and using sign language to persuade an enemy soldier to let them speak to his commander.

This tension-charged reception was mild, however, compared to the one that greeted General King when he put on his last clean uniform and went forward some three hours later to meet with General Kameichiro Nagano and Colonel Motto Nakayama of Japan's 14th Army.

King's group began the trip in two jeeps traveling 150 yards apart, with Major Hurt guiding the way in the first jeep—Colonel Williams had been kept behind by the Japanese—and King and two aides riding in the second vehicle. Although white flags were prominently displayed on both cars, and others were waved constantly by members of the surrender party, they came under repeated attacks by low-flying Japanese planes.

The attacks continued for more than an hour, with King and the others forced to jump out of the vehicles every few hundred yards along the winding road and take cover in ditches or behind trees. Eventually, a Japanese reconnaissance plane showed up, and after its pilot dipped his wings and waved at the Americans, the attackers flew away.

No further hostility or harassment was encountered by King and his party, but by the time they arrived at the designated meeting place, it had taken them two hours to cover a distance of approximately three miles. It was now 11 a.m. on April 9, and the ordeal for the thoroughly shaken and disheveled King was far from over.

At a bridge over the Lamao River, Japanese soldiers with fixed bayonets lined the roadside, but the Americans were allowed to proceed unmolested. A short distance farther on, they were met by the same Japanese soldier who had previously guided Major Hurt to the front lines. He escorted them to a nearby house where General Nagano and Colonel Williams were waiting at an outdoor table. Nagano spoke no English, but he informed the group through an interpreter that General Homma's representative would be there shortly. Moments later, Colonel Nakayama arrived in a shiny, late-model Cadillac sedan.

The meeting began on a less-than-promising note when King rose to greet Nakayama and the latter ignored him while seating himself at the head of the table. For the Americans, it went downhill from there.

"You are General Wainwright?" Nakayama demanded, fixing King with an impassive stare.

"No," King said. "I'm General Edward King, commander of American forces on Bataan."

"Where is Wainwright, and why is he not here?" Nakayama asked.

King replied that he could speak only for his own command on Bataan and not for the commander of all forces in the Philippines. He explained that he had ordered his troops to disarm, that they were no longer capable of fighting, and that he wished to avoid further bloodshed. He asked for an immediate armistice and the cessation of all aerial bombardment. He asked that his troops be allowed to march out of Bataan under their own officers and that his sick and wounded be transported in trucks reserved for this purpose. In return, he promised to deliver his men to any place and at any time dictated by General Homma.

But Nakayama flatly refused even to discuss any terms—much less grant them. He said that Japanese pilots had been assigned missions until noon and that the bombardment would be continued until then. He made it clear that he had no intention of negotiating an end to hostilities unless the terms included the surrender of all U.S. forces in the Philippines.

"It is absolutely impossible for me to consider negotiations in any limited area," he told King. If the Bataan forces wanted their surrender to be accepted, he said, they would have to do so "voluntarily and unconditionally by each individual or each unit." Negotiations for the cessation of hostilities, he declared, had "failed," and King's surrender would be viewed by the Japanese as the act of a single individual, not the surrender of an organized military force.

Finally, King was told that he, Colonel Williams, and the two aides who had accompanied them would be held in custody as a guarantee against any further U.S. resistance. They were, in effect, hostages rather than prisoners of war. Orders for the final disposition of American and Filipino troops would come from General Homma.

At this point, King could see that his position was hopeless and each minute of further delay would only result in the deaths of more of his defenseless troops. Again and again during the futile discussions, he'd asked Nakayama for assurances that his men would be treated as prisoners of war according to provisions established in 1929 at the convention in Geneva, Switzerland, guaranteeing humane treatment for POWs. Officials from forty-three nations, including Japan, had signed the so-called Geneva Convention accords. But the Japanese government had never ratified the accords, and after World War II broke out, its military leaders refused to be bound by them.

Now, as King faced the inevitability of unconditional surrender and laid his pistol on the table—Nakayama had asked for his sword, but King had left it behind in Manila at the start of the war—he repeated his plea one last time.

"Will you treat the prisoners well?" King asked.

"We are not barbarians," Nakayama replied.

The orgy of cold-blooded barbarism that followed would forever disprove that assurance. Over the next two weeks, it would become the epitaph for more than 18,000 Bataan defenders.

As the surrender took full effect on the morning of April 10 and squads of excited, belligerent Japanese infantrymen descended in droves on areas previously held by the Americans, Captain Ralph Hibbs was as leery as any of his comrades of the rampaging interlopers. But as medical officer of the Second Battalion, 31st Infantry, who wore Medical Corps insignia and a Red Cross armband on his shirt, he was accorded considerably more leeway than the average GI.

The usually ebullient Hibbs had been heavy-hearted even before the surrender order came. Within a matter of hours, he'd learned of the deaths of two men for whom he'd developed great affection. Early on April 8, Major Lloyd Moffit, Hibbs's former battalion commander, had been trying desperately to rally about 100 stragglers to form a defensive line when he was killed instantly by shrapnel from a Japanese bomb. And a day or two earlier, Captain George Williams, one of the five original Whiffenpoof Boys, had suffered a similar fate when a Japanese dive-bomber planted a 500-pound bomb squarely on top of his motorcycle.

"I hadn't seen George since our Fiesta Pavillion dinner the night before the war started," Hibbs remembered. "He was the first of our Whiffenpoof Boys to be killed. I choked at the thought of the news reaching [his family]. I couldn't stop swallowing."

Now the shooting was supposedly over, but as Hibbs witnessed the wanton cruelty of many of the Japanese soldiers, he realized that the killing hadn't stopped. If anything, it was increasing, but now it was taking on an even more terrifying dimension.

"The message to discard anything 'made in Japan' [was] spread rapidly by the 'bamboo wireless,'" Hibbs said. "In [the Japanese] mind, possession of such an article meant you'd killed a Jap to get it. . . . We witnessed a GI being knocked down, then stood up and prodded with bayonets, and finally driven into the woods. Suddenly, a shot rang out—the penalty for wearing a 'made in Japan' watch.

"Several of the Nips peered into the GIs' mouths. I couldn't figure out why until I saw a Jap knock a GI senseless and extract a tooth with a gold filling."

When Hibbs was accosted by a hostile-looking group of Japanese, he saluted smartly and was allowed to continue on his way. "My Red Cross armband was prominently displayed," he recalled. "No one called my bluff, [but] increasing atrocities by the Japs hurried our decision to move the [battalion] medical detachment inside the confines of Hospital No. 1."

That evening, Hibbs, accompanied by Corporal Paul Decker, who had been the captain's personal aide and constant companion for the past three months, and another medic, slipped down a trail toward Mariveles. They passed thousands of milling American troops and heard occasional shots, possibly signifying that other unlucky dogfaces had been caught with "made in Japan" contraband.

The next morning, April 11, they saw a long column of prisoners forming, then starting to move north under the watchful eyes of bayonet-wielding Japanese guards. Not knowing what else to do, Hibbs and the two medics joined them.

"Rifle shots rang out frequently to finish a fallen prisoner," Hibbs recalled. "We continued up the road three or four kilometers to . . . a narrow, twisting section [leading] up a hill in dense jungle. The nature and fate of this march was soon quite obvious. We had seen enough. It was a march of death. We decided to get out quickly."

Fortunately, this stretch of road, known as the "Zig-Zag," provided an excellent opportunity to slip unnoticed into the jungle, which was only a few feet away. Hibbs, Decker, and the other medics were able to escape by ducking into the undergrowth almost instantly, then crouching there, holding their breath with pounding hearts and waiting for an outcry and rifle shots from the guards. Instead they heard only the crunching sound of marching feet fading away into the distance.

By what Hibbs called "sheer luck and a sprinkling of front-line savvy," he and the two medics were able to sneak unnoticed back to Hospital No. 1 and join a small handful of American military personnel who remained on Bataan but managed to avoid the Death March. They would successfully "lose" themselves there, mingling with hospital medical staffers whom the Japanese allowed to remain at the hospital to care for hundreds of sick or wounded Americans—yet without any assigned duties of their own—from April 11 until June 24, 1942.

"The Nips never stationed troops at the hospital or demanded a head count," Hibbs said. "My luck was holding."

For most of the surrendered American troops, however, luck had run out. None of the captives knew what to expect from their captors, and, like Hibbs, the majority were gripped with apprehension as they awaited their first close-up encounters with the victorious Japanese. Many felt relief when they weren't executed immediately, but it soon became clear that they weren't blessed with Hibbs's temporary good fortune.

On the morning of April 10, Captain Marion "Manny" Lawton, a member of the same 31st Infantry as Hibbs, stood in a group of about 250 milling prisoners in an assembly area beside the East Road. Lawton was as nervous as the others about what lay ahead, but he tried to sound a positive note as he shared his last two cans of food with several other men and listened to the apprehension in their voices.

"What do you think they'll do to us?" one soldier asked a buddy.

"Be prepared to be lined up and shot," the other replied.

"Well, there's no use working up a lather over what might happen," Lawton told them. "We'll just have to try to take what comes."

A few moments later, Lawton spotted Colonel Jack Erwin, his regimental CO, in the crowd. As he edged his way closer to Erwin, he noticed the pain and worry etched on the older officer's face.

"What do you think we can expect, Colonel?" Lawton asked.

Erwin didn't mince words. "You can anticipate the very worst, Lawton," he said. "It's going to be tough. These Japs are running around like crazy men. They're excitable and unreasonable under stress. Who knows what they'll do? It's very obvious that they want to get us out of the way and move their troops in for the invasion of Corregidor."

Erwin was carrying a barracks bag filled to capacity with personal items, and when Lawton tried to pick up the bag, it felt as if it weighed at least forty pounds. He set the bag down again and pointedly suggested that Erwin, who was twice Lawton's age, sick with malaria, and hollow-eyed with exhaustion, consider lightening his load.

"Oh no," Erwin protested. "I may need these things."

Just then, a convoy of trucks sped past, heading south. The trucks were filled with Japanese soldiers, who yelled derisively at the prisoners and flailed out with bamboo poles, striking several Americans across their heads and backs and sending the group along the roadside scrambling to get out of the way. Some were trampled underfoot in the rush.

"It was humiliating," Lawton would recall much later, "and there was no chance of fighting back."

But this was only one small example of what lay ahead for the prisoners that day—and for hundreds of days to come.

It was hot and humid, and the air was choked with dust as ragged lines of American and Filipino soldiers—most of them reeling from at least one major illness, compounded by near-starvation and/or unhealed wounds—were herded by their Japanese guards onto the East Road leading north from Mariveles. Thus began one of the most gruesome episodes in the annals of warfare, a marathon of savagery and suffering remembered by a dwindling minority of present-day Americans as the Bataan Death March.

Rather than one long, unbroken procession of prisoners, the march was divided into groups of several hundred men each, formed into columns of four and separated by a distance of a few hundred yards. Each group was guarded by a detachment of eight to ten Japanese soldiers, who were relieved by a fresh set of guards at three-hour intervals. Other types of traffic were heavy, with the marchers sharing the road with large parties of Japanese troops in trucks, on horseback, and afoot, as well as tanks and other heavy equipment.

The first large contingents of marchers set out from Mariveles, then proceeded almost due east to the village of Cabçaben, with additional groups joining the procession at assembly points along the way. From Cabcaben, the march headed north through the towns of Lamao, Limay, Orion, Pilar, and Balanga. After Orani, it would leave the Bataan Peninsula, veer briefly west to the village of Dinalupihan, then turn back northeast to Lubao and Guaqua.

At the town of San Fernando, the prisoners would be crammed into freight cars for a rail trip to Capas, followed by a final six-mile walk to Camp O'Donnell, an unfinished Philippine Army training camp that would serve as their first prison compound. None of the marchers knew their destination, and it was just as well. Had they foreseen what awaited them at Camp O'Donnell, many probably would have chosen death on the march.

As guards brandished fixed bayonets and shouted "Speedo! Speedo!" at them, each group of POWs would be force-marched for a week or more over a distance of about seventy miles in oppressive heat with almost no food, water, or rest. Those who faltered or fell out of line because of untreated illness, injury, or exhaustion were slaughtered where they lay. Countless others were selected at the whim of their captors to become victims in the most vicious imaginable forms of blood-sport amusement.

Because of the mass confusion in which the fighting ended and the mass killings that took place along the route of the march, no exact count is available of the total number of prisoners who began trudging north from southern Bataan. Estimates run as high as 78,000, but in all probability the figure was closer to 70,000. Regardless of which number is more accurate, fewer than 52,000 would reach their destination alive.

Colonel Jack Erwin would be among the first American officers to succumb to the rigors of the march.

By mid-afternoon, under a broiling sun and still weighted down with his heavy load, Erwin was disoriented and drenched with sweat. To Captain Lawton, who attempted to stay close by, it was obvious that Erwin was weakening and beginning to fall behind.

"I pleaded with him to throw the bag away," Lawton said. "He only mumbled, 'I will need these things.'"

The colonel steadily lost ground on the other marchers, until, by 3:30 PM, he'd drifted so far to the rear that Lawton was no longer able to keep him in sight. At the tail end of the column, delirious from illness and thirst, Erwin was scolded and slapped around by the guards, one of whom poked him with a bayonet hard enough to draw blood.

"Finally," said Lawton, who learned of Erwin's fate a short time later, "the impatient and merciless guard pushed him to the side of the road, pressed the rifle to his back, and pulled the trigger."

Roughly each 100 yards of ground covered would cost the life of one of the approximately 11,800 American servicemen who started the march, but fatalities among the 58,000-plus Filipino troops in the march would total many times that number. The East Road would literally be paved with dead bodies after the surviving marchers had passed.

Captain John Coleman, former commander of the 27th Materiel Squadron, had this recollection of one portion of the route: "I stepped on what looked like a piece of khaki cloth [and} I slipped back as if in mud. It was human flesh that we were walking on. We could smell decayed human flesh all along the road, where men had been killed [and] their bodies left where they had fallen. The columns of tanks, trucks, and cavalry horses had run over them, pulverizing their bones into pulp."

To his extreme distress, PFC Blair Robinett of C Company, 803rd Engineers, actually witnessed this horrific "paving" process taking place when a sick American soldier wobbled out into the road as a line of Japanese tanks approached.

"One of these Jap soldiers . . . grabbed this sick guy by the arm and guided him to the middle of the road," said Robinett. "Then he just flipped him out across the road. The guy hit the cobblestone about five feet in front of a tank, and the tank pulled on across him. Well, it killed him quick. There must have been ten tanks in that column, and every one of them came up there right across the body. When the last tank left, there was no way you could tell there'd ever been a man there. But his uniform was embedded in the cobblestone. The man disappeared, but his uniform . . . had become part of the ground."

The methodical, yet almost casual, extermination process employed by the Japanese was also carried out by shootings, beheadings, throat cuttings, stabbings, disembowelments, and fatal beatings with clubs or rifle butts. Numerous victims were buried alive as they cried weakly for help and struggled to free themselves from shallow graves.

Any prisoner who fell or was unable to keep pace with the others faced immediate execution, and anyone who tried to help a straggler was subject to the same fate. In many other instances, however, Japanese soldiers seemed to select their victims at random and for no particular reason, then make a macabre diversion of killing them and mutilating their bodies.

"They marched us down the road in a column of fours," recalled Sergeant Louis Read of the 31st Infantry, who was hampered by an assortment of painful wounds, "and I learned early on to get over to the far edge of the road if I wanted to stay out of trouble. Japs would ride by on horseback and crack the guys nearest to them with their rifle butts.

"Many of the men I saw killed died because they couldn't keep up, but in one case, a squirrelly-looking Jap officer pulled this guy right in front of me out of line and turned him over to a group of soldiers. The guy had Signal Corps piping on his cap, and he was tall and good-looking with a small black mustache. I didn't see him do anything to offend any of these Japs, but they took him across the road and tied him to a tree and used him for bayonet practice. They didn't seem to be in much of a hurry, and it took them a while to kill him. After they'd jabbed him to death, they threw his body under a clump of bushes. Then they sauntered off like it was no big deal. I also saw several guys beheaded. The Japs would a lot rather bayonet you or chop your head off than shoot you."

Enemy truck drivers appeared to enjoy driving over the live bodies of fallen prisoners, and Japanese on horseback or in passing vehicles on the traffic-clogged highway amused themselves by lashing out with bamboo poles and rifle butts at helpless prisoners on the roadsides. Others struck with swords or bayonets at stumbling lines of POWs, inflicting multiple and sometimes fatal wounds. For no discernible reason, groups of prisoners were made to sit in the blazing sun for hours without shade, helmets, or water. Many of those who asked for a drink or voiced the slightest complaint were slain on the spot.

Hundreds of prisoners also died of festering battle wounds or rampant disease, compounded by their captors' calculated refusal to allow them food, water, sleep, or medical treatment. Tens of thousands of others would succumb to the after-effects of Japanese brutality on the march after reaching the primitive internment facilities at Camp O'Donnell in Luzon's Tarlac Province.

In the beginning, some of the Japanese enlisted men were tentative toward their captives. Usually, their first acts when confronting surrendering Americans was to snatch away the prisoners' rings, watches, fountain pens, money, cigarettes, and any other items of value, but physical mistreatment was applied mainly when prisoners resisted. As the less aggressive Japanese witnessed examples set by their angrier, more brutish comrades, however, violence and bloodshed became routine. On the Death March, they would escalate into a homicidal frenzy.

When shouted orders that none of the POWs could understand weren't instantly obeyed—and often even if they were—the prisoners received kicks, punches, clubbings, nonfatal bayonet jabs, and other "milder" forms of punishment. But instant death for a minor offense was never out of the question, depending on the mood of the nearest guard. Even some Japanese officers seemed to find perverse pleasure in the deadly games.

* * *

How well—or how poorly—an individual prisoner fared depended to a great extent on his position in the march. Those on the inside of the column were exposed to greater danger than those on the outside and nearest the shoulder of the road, and by some accounts, the POW groups who began the march early on were subject to less harassment than later groups. The disposition of the guards in a prisoner's immediate vicinity was also a factor—as vicious as many of them were, not all were brutes, and some showed genuine compassion.

A POW who was among comrades he knew well and could depend upon for help also had a much better chance of living through the march than one surrounded by strangers.

"A fellow I'd been in the first grade with back in Brainerd, Minnesota, had such a bad case of malaria that he lost his sense of direction and could hardly walk," recalled Sergeant Ken Porwoll of the 194th Tank Battalion. "The Japs told him, 'You walk or you die!' We helped keep him moving forward for three days, and when he got too weak to go on, we helped him crawl into a culvert. He hid there for two days until he got some strength back, and he made it through the march."

Marchers who had learned to deal with hardships and physical stress early in life were sometimes able to use those bitter experiences to their advantage. "I had a bad case of malaria the whole march," said Sergeant Henry Stanley, formerly of the 454th Ordnance Company, "but I think I survived because of the way I was raised. My father died when I was a year old, and I worked hard on the family farm from the time I was old enough to walk right up to the time I joined the Army."

Sometimes an unexpected bit of good fortune became the difference between long-term survival and an early doom. Such was the case with Captain Bill Adair, an Alabama native who had commanded an infantry battalion in the Philippine Army's 21st Division and was later assigned to General Wainwright's Bataan headquarters.

"On the first morning of the march, I jumped in the back of a pickup truck along with a couple of other American officers," Adair remembered. "The Japs later stopped us and took the truck and made us walk. But before that, I was fortunate enough to find two large boxes, one of food and one of quinine.

"I think one reason I was treated so well was because I had the quinine and I was wearing my captain's bars, and the Japs thought I was a doctor. I had no symptoms of malaria, and, in fact, I was one of the few that never caught it, so I gave the quinine away to sick men a bottle at a time, but I kept the food to share with men around me, and the Japs made no effort to take it away from me. I was naive as hell at that point, and I figured everything was going to be okay. I had no inkling that they were going to start killing us in wholesale lots."

Captain John Coleman's situation, meanwhile, was totally opposite from Adair's and full of potentially fatal disadvantages. Coleman, who'd been serving as executive officer of the Air Corps Infantry's First Battalion when the fighting ended, was burning with fever from malaria and had no access to quinine. He was also hobbling along with the aid of a crude walking stick because of a shrapnel wound in his left leg that he feared was infected. Worse yet, he started the march on a totally empty stomach, not having had a single morsel of food in more than four days. But worst of all, he incurred the wrath of a Japanese guard before he'd gone more than a few yards.

"When we walked across the road and started toward Manila, I noticed a supply sergeant who had been at Nichols Field lying face-down with a hole in the back of his head," Coleman recalled. "I took his blanket roll and covered him with it, [while] the Jap guard was yelling at me, trying to make me hurry."

The guard stopped short of shooting or bayoneting Coleman, but as the column plodded on through the stifling road dust and 100-degree heat, the American officer grew steadily weaker. He didn't recognize any of the men in his immediate group, but he could tell that they were trying to walk slowly enough for him to keep pace, and some of them helped him when he started to sag.

The only pause in the march came when some of the higher-ranking prisoners were taken to a tent to be questioned by Japanese officers. During his interrogation, Coleman refused to give any information other than his name, rank, and serial number, as Geneva Convention regulations specified, and the questioning officer struck him twice in the head, bloodying his face and knocking him out cold.

As he was being dragged outside by two Japanese soldiers, Coleman regained consciousness in time to hear his assailant shout, "You wait outside! You are going to talk!"

Coleman managed to escape by hiding among a different group of POWs and finding a water spigot where he could wash the telltale bloodstains off his head, but he was left with a splitting headache from the blows he'd received, and the shrapnel wound in his leg was also causing him intense pain.

"When morning came, we were lined up facing the sun with an open field in front of us and a grove of trees to our backs," Coleman recalled. "We knew we were going to get the sun treatment. The guards wanted as many of us to die as possible under these conditions."

Coleman survived the hours spent in the blistering sun, but by the next morning, he was too weak to walk unaided. He probably would have been killed that day if not for the help of a captain from the 31st Infantry, who let Coleman hold onto his belt as they walked and gave him water and a wet towel for the wounds on his head.

"I would drop down on my knees to rest," Coleman remembered, "and he would get me by the hair of my head when we were to move up, and say, 'Let's go! It's just a little farther.'

"We passed an artesian well with lots of cold water squirting out, about 100 feet from the road. A few of the men from the front of the column started running out to get water for their canteens. The front guard shot three of them before they stopped running, and there were already seven or eight bodies lying around the well."

When the march resumed the next day, Coleman thought he could feel death closing in on him, and he didn't see how he could possibly keep going. Two men tried to carry him, but his legs simply wouldn't work. Fearing that his helpers would be killed because of him, Coleman pulled away and told them to leave him. Then he fell to his knees on the gravel and saw a guard running toward him with a fixed bayonet.

"I felt the grinding of bones and a streak of fire in my right side, and I passed out," Coleman remembered. "Then I had a dream or a vision . . . I saw my wife, Ethel, in tears, saying, 'Don't leave me with these children.' Then my daughter, Lennie Lou, who was ten years old when I left the States, appeared in a light blue dress, with her hair done up in pigtails. Tears like dewdrops were running down her cheeks. She said, 'Daddy, don't leave me.' Then my son appeared. He had his two front teeth out, just as I had left him (he was six years old), and in an excited tone, he said, 'Daddy, don't leave us.' I could see them from the waist up, and they seemed very close to me."

Several hours later, Coleman awoke in terrible pain and found himself lying between two corpses. One was a Catholic chaplain with his rosary beads still around his neck; the other was a soldier. Both were stiff and cold, and Coleman realized that he, too, had been left for dead.

Somehow, he found the strength to crawl to a water well about a hundred yards away. He drank all the water he could hold, filled his canteen, and washed his face, hands, and feet. The shrapnel wound in his leg had bled into his shoe and dried, and it smelled "like a decayed animal." Bloody bubbles came out of the bayonet wound in his side, and he wondered if the blade had punctured his lung. As well as he could remember, it had now been nine days since he had last eaten anything.

But by some mysterious quirk of fate, he was still alive.

On the fourth day of the march, Corporal Lester Tenney of Company B, 192nd Tank Battalion, a National Guard outfit from Illinois, was walking along with two buddies when a Japanese officer came galloping up the road on horseback. Suddenly, without warning, the unthinkable happened.

"He was waving his samurai sword from side to side, apparently trying to cut off the head of anyone he could," Tenney recalled "I was on the outside of the column when he rode past, and although I ducked the main thrust of the sword, the end of the blade hit my left shoulder, missing my head and neck by inches. It left a large gash that had to have stitches if I were to continue on this march and continue living."

Fortunately, a nearby medic was able to sew up the wound hurriedly with ordinary thread, and Tenney's two friends carried him for the next two miles to keep him from falling out of line, thus saving him from certain death.

The very next day, Tenney witnessed what he described as "one of the most sadistic and inhumane incidents" of the entire march. "One of the men had a very bad case of malaria and had barely made it to the rest area. He was burning up with fever and severely disoriented. When ordered to stand up, he could not do it. Without a moment's hesitation, the guard hit him over the head with the butt of his gun . . . then called for two nearby prisoners to start digging a hole to bury the fallen prisoner. . . . [W]hen the hole was about a foot deep, the guard ordered the two men to place the sick man in the hole and bury him alive. The two men shook their heads; they could not do that.

"Once again without warning . . . the guard shot the bigger of the two prisoners. He then pulled two more men from the line and ordered them to dig another hole to bury the murdered man. . . . They dug the second hole, placed the two bodies in the holes, and threw dirt over them. The first man, still alive, started screaming as the dirt was thrown on him."

Tenney would survive to return home to his native Chicago, but within seven months, both of the friends who had been instrumental in saving his life during his personal ordeal that day would be dead.

The countless acts of bloodlust and deliberate savagery committed by the Japanese during and after the Death March are impossible to rationalize, much less justify. Yet several strong, underlying factors apparently served as triggers for these acts and may help to clarify why they occurred with such sickening regularity.

Hatred for Americans and other Westerners had been deeply instilled in Japanese soldiers as part of their military indoctrination, and their fury toward Bataan's defenders, in particular, had been whipped to fever pitch by the severe losses they'd suffered during three months of fierce combat. Nowhere else in Asia or the Pacific had the Imperial Japanese Army encountered such tenacious resistance or incurred such heavy casualties.

As historian Gerald Astor noted, "Resentment toward those whose bullets, grenades, and shells had killed friends was understandable and expectable. But racism also influenced [Japanese] behavior. Their knowledge of the United States, much of it drawn from Hollywood's gangster movies . . . coupled with propaganda, persuaded them [that] Americans were crude, thuggish people bent on the destruction of the Japanese way of life."

In addition, the Japanese warrior's code of Bushido taught the soldiers who lived under it to hold in utter contempt any foe who surrendered rather than fight to the death. Since the Filipinos and Americans on Bataan had, in fact, surrendered, they became objects of total scorn—considered worthless, without honor, and undeserving of humane treatment.

Besides the highly emotional factors involved, there were also practical—if equally callous—motivations for reducing the number of prisoners. General Homma and his staff had expected no more than 30,000 to 40,000 American and Filipino troops to surrender. But now they were confronted by up to twice that many POW mouths to feed, and there wasn't nearly enough food to go around.

"After the Russo-Japanese War, Japan tried to assume the role of a world power, but she expended so much of her resources on building up a massive war machine that her economy went to pot," explained Colonel John Olson, who helped shape the Philippine Scouts into one of the world's elite combat forces and later authored several books on the Philippine campaign and its aftermath.

"Japan never had enough of any of the most vital resources for a nation at war. She was short of oil, steel, rubber, and even food," Olson said. "This is what made her covet the western colonial possessions in the Far East so intensely. Japanese soldiers never had enough to eat, and after the fall of Bataan, the Japanese commanders were faced with all these American and Filipino troops who were even hungrier than their own men. Given a choice of feeding their defeated enemies or killing them off by the thousands, they chose the latter. It wasn't hatred that motivated them so much as greed."

Few Americans who survived the Death March did so without finding deep within themselves a source of strength that they'd never known was there. The source might vary widely from man to man, but many were able to use it as a successful psychological tool for survival.

"Memories and hate—that's what kept me going," said Sergeant

J. S. Gray, late of the 27th Bomb Group. "After you saw them shoot the first American soldier who fell out of the line of march, your disposition changed. You became a man who hated every Japanese walking. When you would see a Japanese snatch a Filipino baby out of its mother's arms and throw it up and catch it on his bayonet, you felt like killing the whole bunch of them. It made you want to live long enough to dance on their graves."

Consequently, any opportunity to exact revenge against their Japanese tormentors could have a tremendously energizing effect on the prisoners. Sergeant Sidney Stewart, an Army medic, was still carrying a small kit of medicinal supplies on his belt when a Japanese guard ripped it loose and dumped its contents on the ground, inadvertently creating just such an opportunity.

"Grunting, he stooped forward and picked up a bottle of sodium amytal, a potent sleeping medicine," Stewart recalled. "Then he uncorked the bottle and poured the contents out into his hand."

"Are they good?" the guard asked in Japanese.

"Yes, they are very good," replied Stewart, who had picked up a smattering of Japanese from enemy troops captured in the fighting.

As Stewart watched, the guard gulped down a large handful of the pills, then moved along to shake down the next man in line, unaware that he'd consumed a lethal dose of sodium amytal—as many as twenty tablets by Stewart's estimate.

"I felt a small triumph," Stewart said. "I knew he would live only a few minutes. He wouldn't vomit because [the pills] would act as a sedative. Slowly, he would fall asleep and die."

When Stewart told a group of buddies from his medical unit a short time later how he'd "gotten one of the bastards," they could hardly conceal their glee.

"Oh, God," exclaimed one friend, "if only we could give it to them all!"

"We laughed at that," Stewart said, "and it helped."

For Private Leon Beck, an Oklahoman who served in the 31st Infantry's Antitank Company, the key to survival could be summed up in two words: "willpower" and "escape."

"I was mentally to the point where I thought I was going to die,"

Beck recalled, "but I also knew, come hell or high water, I wasn't going to die a captive. Up till then, I kept going, as sick and weak as I was, out of sheer will power. There wasn't any magic formula other than willpower."

Beck had recently joined a new group of POWs and had heard scuttlebutt to the effect that anyone with escape on his mind would have to act before the march reached the rail junction at San Fernando, where prisoners would be loaded aboard trains.

"In this new group, I couldn't get anyone to go with me," he said, "so when I got to the town of Guaqua [the last settlement south of San Fernando] . . . they all helped me watch the guards, and I took off. I said, 'Dear Lord, if you don't let my feet get stuck in the swamp, I'll keep pickin' 'em up and puttin' 'em down.' It was all rice crops and fish ponds around me, and I kept moving through a swamp, getting farther and farther away from the column."

Private Beck's personal miracle began that night. The Death March guards had seen the last of him, but before the end of the war, the Japanese would hear far more than they wanted from Beck and the band of guerrillas he joined.

Mental images of home and family, such as the ones that had pulled Captain Coleman back from the brink of death, also came to the rescue of many other prisoners, and so did a firm belief in God.

"I inherited a strong faith from my mother, who was a very religious lady," recalled Private Charles Baum, who had served with the 19th Bomb Group. "She never seemed to lose her temper or get angry. When the Japs started roughing me up and trying to make me scream—they really liked to do that—I could tune it all out by imagining my mother's calm voice, telling me, 'It's all right, son. It's going to be all right.'"

As much as they despised Americans, many Japanese soldiers reserved their harshest treatment for the Filipinos—both military personnel and civilians. "The Japanese considered themselves a superior ethnic strain," wrote historian Gerald Astor, "and treated the subjugated Filipinos, along with the Chinese, Polynesians, Koreans, and other Asians, as inferior."

For sympathetic Filipino civilians who lined the road as the march passed through native barrios, efforts to offer food, water, or other aid to POWs often brought swift retribution. Likewise, the slightest show of resistance toward the demands of the conquerors could mean instant death.

Sergeant Clem Kathman of the 200th Coast Artillery learned through firsthand observation how quickly a seemingly minor disagreement could turn shockingly fatal when a Japanese guard stopped a young Filipino family at the roadside and forced them to wait while a military convoy passed by. What followed, in Kathman's words, was "one of the most brutal and sadistic acts that one human can impose on another."

> The mother, obviously pregnant and carrying a small baby in her arms, was trailing along behind the husband when it became evident that there was some sort of confrontation. The Jap was patting down the man and came up with something the Filipino was reluctant to give up. When the man reached toward the soldier, the Jap stepped back, raised his rifle, and bayoneted the Filipino in the gut. Our ears were immediately filled with the screams of the wife as she dropped the baby to the ground and fell prostrate across her husband's body. The Jap guard raised his rifle again and drove the bayonet between the woman's shoulder blades. Then, withdrawing the blade, he casually pocketed something and joined his comrades at the rear of the convoy.
>
> We were too stunned to do anything. We stood dumbfounded, hardly able to believe what we'd just seen. It was like a bad dream. Yet there they were, the two bodies thrashing in the last throes of death and a helpless baby crying in the blood of its own mother and father.

The tableau of horrors went on and on, defying the senses and threatening the sanity of those forced to watch. It included scenes almost too awful for seventeen-year-old Private Glenn Frazier of the 31st Infantry's 75th Ordnance Company to comprehend.

The hot-tempered youngster from south Alabama had joined the Army to escape the wrath of a local bar owner whose establishment Frazier had wrecked while roaring through it on a motorcycle. But he would have much preferred to face the owner's shotgun than confront the surrealistic visual torment that erupted before him as the marchers entered a small Filipino village.

"A Jap was in the village and brought a woman and a girl, who was about nine years old, out in the road at gunpoint," Frazier recounted in his memoir, *Hell's Guest*. "The woman was pregnant. The Jap cut her throat in front of her child; then he cut her stomach open as we passed. We could see her unborn child half out of her stomach. It was a gruesome sight and almost made me sick. The Jap told the girl to go back to the village. When she got to the edge of the road, he shot her in the back."

Frazier had to restrain his best friend, Private Gerald Block, from trying to kill the Japanese soldier with his bare hands. "Look," Frazier told him, "we have to make the best of this because we no longer have the power to change any of these things. This is a battle, and we are fighting to save our lives."

Over the next day or two, a fierce will to survive kept Frazier's feet moving forward when the rest of his body wanted to collapse. Later, he thought of the Japanese he had killed during the fighting, and as they blatantly murdered the marchers around him, he rationalized that it was "their time now." But toward the end of the march, as he grew steadily weaker, he tried to make his mind go totally blank. Only then could he continue to stumble forward.

"I told myself to forget about the hunger, forget about the thirst, forget about the pain, forget about the killing, and push on step by step," he remembered. "Just let my body become as numb as possible. Don't think. Don't feel. Just keep moving."

After drinking all the water he could hold and splashing more of it on his face and shirt, Captain John Coleman, who had all but given himself up for dead just hours earlier, felt better than he could remember feeling in days. He knew he'd come perilously close to death, but now he felt strong enough to make his way slowly down the road to a small native barrio about a half-mile away in hopes of finding food—even a dog or cat that he could kill and eat. Raw or cooked, it didn't matter.

Instead, just as he reached the village about sundown and started around the corner of a building, he stumbled headlong into four Japanese soldiers with bayonets at the ready. For once, however, the guards who apprehended him weren't impatient to kill.

"I didn't try to run," Coleman remembered. "I put my hands up over my head. . . . One of them put his finger on my bloody shirt, then looked at the blood that stuck on his finger. I pulled up my shirt to show them the bayonet wound. One of them pointed to the tip of his bayonet, and I nodded my head."

Two of the Japanese motioned Coleman to go down the road, and then both went with him. "They were very reasonable, letting me set my own pace," Coleman said, "which was very slow."

About ten o'clock that night—Coleman thought the date was April 15, but he wasn't sure—they reached the town of Lubao, and the soldiers led Coleman to a large barbed-wire enclosure where several hundred POWs were being held. The Japanese officer in charge of the compound was also reasonable. After noticing the blood on Coleman's shirt, he allowed the wounded man to sit and rest instead of placing him on a work detail.

"I slept on my right side that night, thinking it would stop the bleeding and help the blood to clot, [and] I felt better the next day," Coleman said. "I was still weak, but I didn't have such a bad headache. It was pretty cloudy that morning and not as hot as it had been. It was a relief to know that we couldn't be given the sun treatment as long as it was cloudy."

The streets of the town were lined with elderly civilians and a few small children, who stared silently as the marchers filed past. The Filipinos' faces were drawn with sorrow, and many had tears running down their cheeks.

"I noticed an elderly lady . . . who was holding out an egg to anyone who would come out and get it," Coleman said. "The guards wouldn't let the civilians get near us . . . [but] when I got about even with her, I ran out and she gave me the egg. The guard at the front of the column looked back and saw me. . . . He aimed his rifle at me just as I entered the ranks."

As Coleman ducked desperately from one side of the column to the other with the guard chasing after him, he stooped down and cracked the egg on the pavement. Then he swallowed it in one gulp. At first, the egg refused to stay down, and he had to swallow it a second time to keep it in his stomach.

"I threw the eggshell over my shoulder, and it hit [the guard's] helmet," Coleman said. "When he saw what it was, he stopped chasing me."

Although he scarcely tasted it, Coleman had just had his first mouthful of food in thirteen days, by his calculation.

The compassion displayed by Filipino civilians in town after town through which the march passed—always at great risk to themselves—not only prevented hundreds of prisoners from collapsing from starvation but also inspired them to keep pressing on.

Sergeant Sidney Stewart also held vivid memories of the harrowing trip through Lubao. The prisoners in Stewart's group had been walking for eight days with, at most, only a few handfuls of rice to sustain them.

"The Filipinos stood at the open windows of their homes and threw food to us," he recalled. "A scramble started among the prisoners. I watched them through a haze, wondering how they had the strength to fight. The guards screamed in frenzy, stamping and grinding the food under their feet and beating a man if he picked up a piece of it.

"My eyes burned with the sun and sweat and dust," Stewart said, "but when I looked at the compassion and pity on the faces of the Filipinos, I became more determined."

I will go on, he thought. *I'll live to see these bastards die.*

Prisoners who expected a measure of relief when they reached the railroad at San Fernando found instead only crushing disappointment and a new ordeal that was, in some respects, worse than the one they'd just endured.

Many of the men arrived in San Fernando at the end of another long day's march, then spent their one night in the town in either a barbed wire bullpen or a cockfight arena with a bare dirt floor and crude wooden bleachers at one end. Conditions were equally horrific at both.

"When I pulled into the bullpen, it was full of people," recalled PFC Robert Brown, once of the 17th Pursuit Squadron. "It was night. There was a lot of dust, dirt, filth on the ground. Everybody had dysentery. There were no toilets. It was absolutely horrible. I just fell down in the dirt and slept, but there wasn't much sleeping because people were going crazy. My God, they were screaming and going nuts. . . . It was like being in a cage with animals. I don't know how else to describe it."

From these "accommodations," the prisoners were herded through the streets to the railroad station, past crowds of local residents, many of whom risked severe punishment by flashing "V for victory" signs at the POWs or trying to toss food to them.

"San Fernando was the largest town through which we had marched," said Captain Manny Lawton. "It appeared that the Japanese intended to display us as physical proof that they were the conquering, superior race. Our humiliation was designed to warn the civilian populace that Nippon now ruled supreme. . . . Instead of cheering their new masters, the bewildered witnesses shed unhidden tears of sympathy."

To Sergeant Louis Read of the 31st Infantry, one of the civilians offered a gift that he'd never forget. "As I was about to climb into the boxcar, a Filipino woman handed me a banana leaf folded over with cooked rice inside," he recalled. "This was like manna from heaven, since I hadn't eaten anything in a week, except for a couple of wild turnips I'd pulled out of the ground. The woman risked her life to do that for me. If a guard had seen her, he probably would have bayoneted her on the spot."

"Shortly after noon, all that could walk were lined up outside the barbed wire and marched a few blocks to the railroad," said Corporal Hubert Gater of the 200th Coast Artillery. "There was a train and a few boxcars. . . . Our spirits rose. We were going to ride instead of more marching. In a few minutes, we all wished we'd continued to march."

The narrow gauge boxcars, Gater and his comrades soon discovered, had been sitting in the tropical sun with their doors tightly shut, and when the doors were opened, the heat struck the men like a blast from a furnace. The boxcars were also very small by American standards—just thirty-three feet long, eight feet wide, and seven feet high. They were known as "40-and-8s," meaning that they were intended to accommodate no more than forty humans or eight horses.

"Figuring two square feet per person, fifty men could have sat pushed together," said Manny Lawton. "The Japs crowded nearly three times that number into each boxcar and closed the doors. . . . There was no fresh air, and the sun's rays bearing down against the steel sides intensified the heat. Many of the prisoners fainted. Some died."

Frequent stops along the way made the twenty-five-mile trip from San Fernando to the town of Capas take two hours or more, and the loaded boxcars often sat at the San Fernando station for an additional hour before they moved an inch. For the men inside, the misery seemed interminable.

"Men [were] fainting with no place to fall," said Gater. "Those with dysentery had no control of themselves. As the car swayed, the urine, sweat, and vomit rolled three inches deep back and forth, around and in our shoes."

Decades later, Sergeant Nicholas Fryziuk of Company B, 192nd Tank Battalion, still seethed with fury as he recounted the agony inside the boxcars: "When they closed the doors, it was like suffocating. It was hotter than a son of a bitch. . . . A lot of guys were in bad shape. I wiggled as best I could and got by the goddamn door and forced it open a little.

"Some guys said, 'The Japs are going to shoot us.'

"'Fuck 'em!' I said. 'Let 'em shoot me!'"

The air that blew into the boxcar through the open door was hot, but the stifling prisoners gulped it in like cold spring water. The guards made no effort to restrain them or reclose the door.

After the agonizing ride to Capas, the boxcars were unloaded, and the men who were still able to walk dragged or carried their dead or unconscious comrades outside.

During a brief rest, the POWs were counted, then lined up in columns of two and marched down a dirt road to begin the six-mile trek to Camp O'Donnell. Before they moved out, some were actually allowed to accept gifts of food from Filipino civilians, who were waiting at the railroad station to greet them. Along the road toward the camp, the Filipinos had erected crude signs that warned the marchers to throw away any Japanese money or souvenirs still in their possession.

By the time the last groups of prisoners reached this final leg of their journey, the Bataan Death March had continued for almost two weeks. Each contingent of prisoners had averaged spending a week or more traveling the total of about ninety-one miles from the starting point to the finish line. They had traveled under more hellish conditions than any of them could have envisioned in their worst nightmares a few months earlier.

But a deeper, darker, more enduring nightmare lay ahead at O'Donnell, a place that Corporal Gater would later describe—with haunting accuracy—as "one big graveyard."

9

The Rock—"A Shining Example"

Beginning on the morning of April 10, 1942, the tadpole-shaped fortress island of Corregidor—known to every American soldier, sailor, and Marine who served there as the Rock—stood alone against the Japanese juggernaut that had consumed Bataan.

Slightly more than two miles away, where the infamous Death March was taking shape, Japanese troops on Bataan were busily moving seventy-five of the same powerful artillery pieces that had smashed the American-Filipino lines on the peninsula a few days earlier. Now they were being repositioned to bear on Corregidor from what amounted to point-blank range.

For many of the estimated 2,000 men who had escaped from Bataan as triumphant enemy troops moved in to claim their prisoners, Corregidor had long been a symbol of security and relative surcease from the rigors of front-line warfare. Almost to a man, the escapees believed that merely reaching the island alive gave them a ticket to a more comfortable, less hazardous existence than the one they'd known for months on Bataan.

Although the Rock had been subjected since mid-December to daily air raids and intermittent artillery fire from the Cavite shore and other points around Manila Bay, its belowground facilities and reinforced-concrete fortifications remained basically unscathed. Its garrison still received two reasonably balanced meals per day instead of the few handfuls of wormy rice—and sometimes nothing at all—that had been standard fare on Bataan. The Corregidor troops were also sheltered from the elements and the clouds of mosquitoes that infested the jungles of Bataan. They had access to laundry facilities, showers, and clean drinking water instead of living in filth, rags, and pollution, and they didn't have to worry about being bayoneted in their sleep by Japanese infiltrators.

The escapees knew nothing, of course, about the Death March they'd narrowly avoided, but even so, they expected their lives on Corregidor to be infinitely more "normal" than the ones they'd left behind.

Former B-17 crewmember Ed Whitcomb's reaction, as he arrived in Malinta Tunnel after reaching the island in a small boat moments ahead of a flight of enemy bombers, was fairly typical.

"Inside the tunnel, we greeted friends we hadn't seen for a long time and found some other people who'd made their way over from Bataan during the night just past," Whitcomb recalled. "We also found many officers and enlisted men in freshly washed and starched uniforms, living as comfortably as if the war had never caused them the slightest inconvenience. Malinta Tunnel was very clean, and we felt it would be a comfortable place to stay while we waited for reinforcements. We congratulated ourselves on successfully reaching this haven of security."

Whitcomb and his fellow Bataan escapees, Lieutenants Jim Dey and John Renka, were further bolstered when they were told by a senior Air Corps colonel that submarines were en route to Corregidor to pick up surviving U.S. flight crew members and take them to Australia, where they would shortly be flying again.

"This was great news," Whitcomb said. "It meant we'd soon be away from this one-sided war where we were always on the receiving end of the bombs."

But as Whitcomb and his fellow Bataan refugees quickly learned, any such assumptions were tragically premature. Corregidor's laterals were already overcrowded with supply, service, and headquarters troops, as well as Filipino civilians, and most newcomers were billeted outside and assigned to beach defense. By dusk that first evening, Whitcomb found himself in charge of an antique, wooden-wheeled 75-millimeter gun, manned by an all-Filipino crew and situated on a desolate corner of the island's south coast called Monkey Point.

"I slept on the ground beside my gun position that night," he recalled, "but I felt more as if I were sleeping on a powder keg that was about to blow up."

Whitcomb's feelings were prophetic. In a sense, he *was* sleeping on a powder keg. Within a few days, Corregidor would become the most hellish five square miles on the face of the earth—a place that would make Whitcomb's experiences on Bataan "seem like a Sunday School picnic."

Although they were equally glad to be there instead of on Bataan, Marines Karl King and Ike Williams, both toughened by weeks of front-line combat, failed to share Whitcomb's rosy projections about life on the Rock. They had no illusions about what was coming and what their role in it would be.

They were immediately assigned to their former outfit, L Company, Third Battalion, Fourth Marines, and sent to the rocky beach near Battery Point on the island's north coast to set up and man a .50-caliber machine gun position facing Bataan.

There were a few minor problems, however. First, they had to locate a gun and transport it themselves, then take all necessary steps to protect and conceal their position. "That afternoon, we found a Navy supply dump that had an air-cooled .50, salvaged from a disabled PBY flying boat," King recalled. "A two-wheel cart hauled the gun back to the company area, along with several boxes of ammo and the metal links for belting the ammunition. Looking for a place to set up our gun pit, we spotted a small earthen formation about sixty feet up the side of a cliff, [and] we dug in."

On April 12, after some fifteen trips up and down the steep cliff by King and Williams to get the gun and ammo where they needed to be—and at least that many hours of rigorous labor—the gun position was fully equipped, camouflaged, and ready for action. It became part of a complex beach-defense system that included a second .50-caliber machine gun on their right flank, with a field of fire that overlapped their own, and a pair of .30-caliber guns between the two .50s. A trench connected the various emplacements, and a concrete bunker near its center provided protection from enemy artillery fire and air raids. A road connecting a large storage tunnel for ammunition to the gun positions ran around the face of the cliff.

The approximately 1,500 soldiers, sailors, and Marines whose job was defending Corregidor's north beach did a commendable job of preparing for the Japanese amphibious landings that they knew were coming. But they were thinly spread over three and a half miles of rock and sand, and most of their hastily constructed gun pits offered only minimal protection against concentrated bombing and heavy artillery attacks.

"Enemy artillery spotters in observation balloons on Bataan had a clear view of the defensive positions," said King. "Japanese 240-millimeter howitzers, firing from Cavite and Bataan with high-angle trajectories, could drop rounds into every deep ravine and concrete gun emplacement [on Corregidor]." By mid-April, these advantages had enabled enemy planes and ordnance to knock out an increasing number of Corregidor's antiaircraft batteries—of which the island had far too few to begin with.

On the night of April 14, a thirty-six-inch searchlight was wheeled into position near the King-Williams gun pit and turned on to test its effectiveness in spotting Japanese invasion barges. None was in sight at the moment—most, in fact, had been left at the enemy's major Luzon landing site on Lingayan Gulf and the smaller sites on the west coast of Bataan—but the searchlight drew instant attention from Japanese batteries on the peninsula.

"Jap gunners must have had their hands on the firing lanyards waiting for the searchlight to come on," said King. "It was on for all of thirty seconds before an artillery barrage . . . swept our position, snuffing out the light with a direct hit."

Dodging shell bursts, King and Williams hurried down the cliffside trail in response to the cries of wounded men. They had made two trips to carry the wounded to the protection of the ammo tunnel when a Navy corpsman grabbed King by the arm.

"Is that your blood on your pants leg, or is it from one of the wounded?" the corpsman asked.

At that moment, King felt a sharp pain and saw a piece of shrapnel lodged in his right leg. The medic removed the fragment and treated the wound, and King returned to his gun. (He was promoted to corporal the next day and awarded a Purple Heart, but the record of the promotion and decoration would be lost in the holocaust that followed, and neither would become official until six years later.)

The shelling that night was but a small foretaste of what was to come. Over the next three weeks, King recalled, "Life on Corregidor could be compared to sitting in the middle of a bull's eye during rapid-fire target practice."

The attacks steadily increased in intensity until April 29, when General Homma's army celebrated Emperor Hirohito's birthday by launching the most awesome fireworks display yet seen in the Philippines. It would continue day and night without letup for six days. When it finally subsided, any resemblance to the impregnable citadel that Corregidor had once represented had vanished in a cauldron of fire, smoke, dust, and death.

As fate would have it, one of General Wainwright's final chances to evacuate some of the Army nurses, female civilians, older officers, and a few key military personnel from the closing trap on Corregidor occurred on the same day that the enemy began his all-out avalanche of air and artillery attacks.

Two U.S. Navy seaplanes had been dispatched from Australia by General MacArthur to handle the evacuations. After a flight from Mindanao, they were scheduled to land at about 11 PM on April 29 in a sheltered area near the wreckage of Corregidor's south docks and off the low-lying section of the island known as Bottomside. A minesweeper had cleared a path through the minefield surrounding the island and planted two lighted underwater buoys to guide the planes in. By that hour of the night, the shelling had tailed off considerably, and most of the rounds still falling were hitting along the opposite north shore, but dozens of fires from that day's bombardment still blazed across the island.

Between them, the PBYs could accommodate only fifty passengers, and except for a lucky few who had been handpicked by MacArthur, the rest would be chosen by Wainwright with the help of Captain Maude Davison, commander of the Army nursing unit.

Twenty of the seats aboard the planes went to the MacArthur appointees, along with a half-dozen senior officers whose health would have made their survival doubtful in prison camp, and two or three civilian women. The remaining thirty places were filled from the 150-member nursing corps, meaning that only one of every five nurses would be allowed to go. Some of those not selected reacted with understandable bitterness, and at least one who *was* selected, forty-eight-year-old Lieutenant Josephine Nesbit, the unit's deputy commander, flatly refused to accept a seat.

"I want to stay," she said simply.

Filled with a mixture of relief and regret at being one of the chosen, Lieutenant Juanita Redmond remarked that she "felt like a deserter" as she took her place among the evacuees waiting to board a small boat to take them out to one of the idling seaplanes. At the last moment, she turned impulsively to General Wainwright, threw her arms around him, and kissed him.

"Oh thank you, General," she exclaimed.

"We stood there and watched the seaplanes roar and take off and prayed they wouldn't be hit," Wainwright later recalled. "They sailed right off the water beautifully, pulled out over the side of Cavite beyond the range of the anti-aircraft guns, and were enveloped in the night. Then we turned and walked back to our jobs."

Only one of the two planes would make it safely to Australia. The other PBY would strike a submerged object as it landed on Lake Lanao on Mindanao, causing irreparable damage and stranding its twenty-five passengers, including about a dozen nurses, all of whom would end up as prisoners of the Japanese.

Only a handful of others were able to leave Corregidor by air—via two-seater "puddle-jumper" planes—before the surrender. They included Associated Press correspondents Clark Lee and Dean Schedler and Frank Hewlett of United Press, who had been instrumental in nicknaming the Battling Bastards of Bataan.

In their farewell meeting, Hewlett, whom Wainwright characterized as "an especially close friend," told the general: "Skinny, I hate to go off and leave you here, but I'll see to it at home that they know what you're doing."

Although Wainwright would have no way of knowing it until after the war, Hewlett was as good as his word.

Over the six days from April 29 through May 5, life deteriorated into sheer bedlam for the 12,000 American military personnel on Corregidor as the enemy's ceaseless bombing and shelling ate away at the elaborate infrastructure that had previously kept life bearable in Malinta Tunnel and its laterals.

The island's main electrical generating plant, located in the valley called Bottomside, had been severely damaged in a bombing raid in mid-March that cut its power production to a fraction of its original capacity. After that, a patched-up set of diesel generators had to produce most of the power for the tunnels, including the hospital laterals—where more than 1,000 sick and wounded now lay—and the bone-rattling enemy attacks frequently plunged them into total darkness. One small diesel engine was available as a backup power source for the hospital, but medics were routinely called upon to hold flashlights when the operating room lost power as surgery was being performed.

Adequate supplies of fresh water were also endangered by the air and artillery bombardments. "We built three emergency wooden water tanks on the side of Malinta Hill to take care of the tunnel and the hospital whenever the main water system suffered a hit on a central conduit," said Wainwright. "One of these tanks was destroyed by a shell, adding to our discomfort."

In its last days, Corregidor's communications system was totally shredded by Japanese explosives. Batteries and beach-defense units were connected by underground telephone cables, but they weren't buried deeply enough to survive bomb and shell blasts that left the island more pockmarked by craters than the surface of the moon. "[The phone lines] were constantly being rooted out and broken by the shells," said Wainwright, "and we didn't have enough equipment to replace the broken strands." This meant that all messages had to be delivered by runners, who courted suicide as they raced through open areas with shells and bombs exploding around them every few seconds.

No final tally exists of the number of bombs and artillery rounds that struck the Rock during its final days of life as a U.S. military outpost. It seems likely, however, that it was battered and blasted by more tons of high explosives than any other spot of its size on planet Earth had ever endured in a similar period. It was the target of more than 300 full-scale Japanese air raids, many of which lasted for hours and were repeated from dawn to nightfall for days. Simultaneously, the island was struck by hundreds of thousands of heavy artillery rounds, including up to 16,000 on a single day.

Early on the morning of May 2, at the start of a typical combined enemy air-artillery bombardment, two of Wainwright's staff officers decided to count the number of explosions. They determined that at least a dozen bombs and shells averaged hitting the island every minute for five straight hours—a total of 3,600 rounds armed with an estimated 1.8 million pounds of explosives. After that, they quit counting.

The last opportunity for anyone to leave Corregidor before its fall came on the night of May 3, when the U.S. submarine *Spearfish* slipped through the Japanese blockade to pay a final visit. Wainwright had arranged for the sub to stop on its way back to Australia for a fresh load of torpedoes to pick up important military records and as many as twenty-five passengers.

Wainwright's chief of staff, General Lewis Beebe, had high hopes that the USFIP commander himself would be among those passengers. Beebe had sent a message to MacArthur's headquarters the previous day urging that Wainwright be evacuated. The message read in part:

> I am sending this because General Wainwright believes he should go down with the ship. However, I do not believe that he should be permitted to fall into the hands of the Japs. His experience and knowledge of Jap tactics are too valuable to the government to be lost. . . . I do know from various conversa-

> tions that he expects to remain here to the end and surrender himself with the troops if the necessity arises. Since he is a soldier, he will move only if he is ordered to do so. It is my fixed belief that he should be ordered to move with such members of his staff as can be accommodated, in the near future.

Beebe and other staff officers argued, with considerable logic, that if Wainwright could reach the relative safety of Mindanao and set up a new headquarters there, the surrender of all U.S. forces in the Philippines could be avoided if and when Corregidor fell. If either Beebe or General George Moore of Wainwright's staff were designated as commander on Corregidor, they theorized, the surrender could be limited to the fortified islands of Manila Bay.

The reply from MacArthur's chief of staff, General Sutherland, was both chilly and negative. It seemed to suggest that MacArthur was still smarting over Washington's decision to place Wainwright in overall command of U.S. forces in the Philippines.

"General Wainwright was assigned to his command by the War Department," Sutherland said, "and General MacArthur has no—repeat no—authority to relieve him therefrom."

Wainwright was quick to let MacArthur know that Beebe had acted on his own volition, that the message had been "prepared without my knowledge or consent," and that, although Wainwright had known in advance that it was being sent, he had "neither authorized nor prohibited its dispatch."

In the same transmission, Wainwright included a grim assessment of conditions on Corregidor: "Situation here is fast becoming desperate. . . . The island is practically denuded of vegetation and trees, leaving no cover, and all structures are leveled to the ground. Communications and utilities are almost impossible of maintenance. Casualties since April 9 approximate 600."

When the *Spearfish* surfaced that night, there was no further mention by Beebe or anyone else of Wainwright leaving. A handful of staff officers were sent aboard, some for health reasons, others to carry out specific assignments on reaching the States.

Wainwright selected Colonel Pete Irwin, his assistant chief of staff, to serve as his personal emissary to General Marshall in Washington. Irwin was suffering from ulcers, and Wainwright feared that he wouldn't survive long in prison camp, but the general also trusted Irwin to deliver a roster of the Corregidor garrison and other important documents to Marshall and to take Wainwright's favorite pistol home to the general's son, a captain in the Merchant Marine.

The last thirteen available spaces on the sub went to women—one Navy wife, one Navy nurse, and eleven Army nurses. But one who was high on Wainwright's list of evacuees but who refused to go was Captain Gladys "Ann" Mealor, the Corregidor hospital's chief nurse.

"I couldn't see how anybody could walk off and leave all those wounded people," she said. "I had enough faith in that old tunnel that I could make it if the Japs came in."

Wainwright was deeply touched by Mealor's decision. "I considered—and still consider—this a truly great act of patriotism," he said later. "She knew as well as I that she was signing her captivity warrant."

Lieutenant Ruth Straub, whose fiancé, Army pilot Glen Adler, had been fatally wounded on December 10 by a Japanese bomb, accepted her spot on the submarine with mixed emotions. "I was thrilled, but I felt like a heel," she wrote in her diary. "What of all those left behind? Would they get away?"

The answer was no, they would not. When the conning tower of the *Spearfish* slipped beneath the surface of the bay, Corregidor's last physical link with the outside world was broken, and there was no hope of restoring it.

Fifty-four Army nurses, twenty-six Filipino nurses, and twenty-one civilian female hospital staffers would still be tending their patients when Japanese troops entered Malinta Tunnel.

Three nights later, safe in Melbourne, the evacuees would receive the news that Corregidor had fallen.

On May 4, the day after the *Spearfish* departed, the Japanese stepped up their artillery bombardment to the point that there was virtually no pause between the explosions. Wainwright described it as "a continuous drum-fire of bursting shells." In a physical sense, much of the shelling was overkill, since there were few permanent facilities left to destroy on the island's surface. But casualties increased among the beach defenders, and the incessant pounding took a heavy toll on morale, even among men who were physically safe below ground.

"The troops began to crack," wrote Colonel John R. Vance, a staff officer in Wainwright's headquarters. "Almost everyone was overwhelmed by the psychosis of doom." Some men left their assigned positions to look for hiding places in caves and crevices. Scattered incidents of self-inflicted gunshot wounds and even several suicides were reported.

Two days earlier, on the afternoon of May 2, a saturation barrage by Japanese gunners had finally found the central magazine supplying the giant mortars of Battery Geary near the island's southern coast. The 1,600 powder charges stored there, weighing a total of nearly 50,000 pounds, had all blown up at once, shaking the entire island and hurling ten-ton mortar barrels up to 150 yards. One six-ton section of concrete from the magazine's top landed more than a half-mile away. Twenty-seven soldiers died in the blast, and dozens of others were injured.

By this time, the pattern of enemy shell fire had changed, with more of the high-explosive rounds falling on the "tail" at the east end of the island and along a depression called James Ravine, which served as a path for men and supplies between the beaches and the high ground known as Topside. From this, Wainwright deduced that these areas were probable sites for enemy amphibious landings that were, in all probability, only hours away.

Meanwhile, life in the tunnel grew steadily more unbearable. Thousands of civilian Filipino laborers, who had been forced from their homes on the island, flocked into the tunnel seeking refuge, creating a massive problem. "They relieved themselves where they stood," said Colonel Vance. "For food, they were issued canned goods, and the empty and dirty containers were added to the human filth on the pavement. Dirty clothing was discarded on the spot. Several dead lay on stretchers at the end of the hospital section, awaiting a lull in the bombardment for burial."

It was a lull that refused to come. From dawn until long after dark, the shells continued to fall, and Japanese planes made leisurely, uncontested bombing runs. Every antiaircraft weapon on the island had been destroyed, and only a few machine guns were left to challenge the raiders from below. Lights in the tunnel failed frequently for up to half an hour at a time. Dwindling water supplies brought a halt to all bathing and tight restrictions on drinking water. Corregidor's quartermaster reported that food supplies would be exhausted before the end of May. Outside, a thick pall of dust and smoke obscured the entire eastern end of the island.

From Washington, General Marshall asked Wainwright for a "very frank estimate" of the situation on Corregidor, and Wainwright gave it to him: "In my opinion, the enemy is capable of making an assault on Corregidor at any time. The success or failure of such an assault will depend entirely on steadfastness of beach defense troops. With morale at present level, I estimate that we have something less than an even chance to beat off an assault."

From Melbourne, MacArthur transmitted an even more dismal assessment to Marshall: "You must be prepared for the collapse shortly of the harbor defenses in Manila Bay. . . . The occupation of Bataan definitely condemned these fortresses, and enemy guns of large caliber located there are rapidly destroying our fixed fortifications. . . . It is apparent to me . . . that morale is rapidly sinking, and the end is clearly in sight."

Marine PFC Roy Hays didn't have to read MacArthur's message to realize that time was running out for Corregidor. Everyone in the contingent of Marines, U.S. Army troops, and Philippine Scouts defending the beaches at Corregidor's extreme eastern tip had known for days that their struggle to hold the Rock was almost over. The tantalizing rumors about reinforcements being only days away had been pounded to dust by the Japanese bombers and artillery.

But now, late on the night of May 5, nothing drove home the truth with greater finality than the sight unfolding before Hays's eyes. Out of the darkness, multiple Japanese landing barges were approaching the beach at North Point. After days of around-the-clock artillery barrages and bombing raids, Japanese amphibious assault troops were about to land on Corregidor.

1

A relaxed atmosphere prevailed in late 1940 at Fort McKinley, just outside of Manila, where General Jonathan Wainwright posed in his dress whites before a dinner party celebrating his arrival from the States. With the general is Captain John Olson of the 57th Infantry, who helped shape the Philippine Scouts (below) into an elite fighting force.

2

3

Prewar Manila was a favorite duty station for many young U.S. servicemen. Lieutenant Ed Whitcomb, shown climbing into the cockpit of an Army Air Corps trainer, arrived in fall 1941 as navigator of a B-17 heavy bomber. Many others couldn't wait for legal enlistment age. Private Joe Alexander (below, left), later certified as the youngest POW of World War II, was only fourteen when his grandmother signed him into the Army, and Private Otis H. "Karl" King (right) finagled his way into the Marines at fifteen.

4

5

Generals Douglas MacArthur and Wainwright, top military commanders in the Philippines, strove to have their mostly Filipino forces ready for war by April 1942, but were unprepared when the Japanese struck four months earlier.

6

7

8

Lieutenant Edwin Ramsey of the 26th Cavalry Regiment and his former polo pony, Bryn Awryn, led the world's last mounted cavalry charge during the fight for Bataan. After the American surrender, Ramsey rose to the rank of lieutenant colonel (right) by leading one of the Philippines' largest and most active guerrilla forces.

9

On Christmas Eve, 1941, MacArthur declared Manila—"the Pearl of the Orient"—an open city in hopes of sparing it from total destruction. But Japanese bombs had already been falling for more than two weeks, touching off massive fires across the Philippine capital. Hours after MacArthur's declaration, Japanese tanks rumbled unopposed along Manila's picturesque Dewey Boulevard.

10

11

After their retreat into Bataan in early January 1942, U.S. forces set up a series of defensive lines across the peninsula and held the Japanese at bay with weapons such as this 37-millimeter antitank gun (top) and 30-caliber machine guns (below). As members of the 31st Infantry, the only all-American ground unit in the Philippines, Corporal Louis Read (right) and other tenacious troops wreaked havoc on the Japanese.

12

13

14

After a valiant three-and-a-half-month defense of Bataan, General Edward King—acting against orders from Wainwright—surrendered his starving, disease-ridden, 70,000-man force (above). King acted with grave misgivings but agreed to Japanese terms after an enemy officer assured him, "We are not barbarians." A wounded GI (below) was among the first POWs to be led by Japanese guards to an assembly point for the Death March.

15

16

With prisoners lined up four abreast, the Death March began near the port of Mariveles (above), with prisoners forced to travel on foot with almost no food or water for about sixty-five miles. During so-called "rest breaks" (below), marchers were often made to sit for extended periods unprotected from the blazing sun and temperatures above 100 degrees.

17

18

The level of severity with which POWs were treated on the march depended largely on the mood of Japanese guards and officers at any given moment. When a Japanese photographer demanded a "photo op" in which Americans appeared to be surrendering (above), marchers were ordered to raise their hands. Meanwhile, other marchers were forced to travel with their hands tied behind their backs (below).

19

20

In the crush and chaos of the Death March (above), hundreds of Americans and thousands of Filipinos died of hunger, dehydration, disease, calculated brutality, and cold-blooded murder. One who came perilously close to death but somehow survived was Captain John Coleman, commander of the 27th Materiel Squadron, who went without food for thirteen days, during which he was bayoneted by a guard and severely beaten.

21

22

There was no relief from the POWs' torment when they reached Camp O'Donnell at the end of the Death March. Up to 300 sick, wounded, and starving prisoners died each day during the weeks they were confined at the camp. Their surviving comrades were forced to carry their bodies to mass graves in long processions past the unfinished nipa shacks that passed for barracks.

23

24

25

Lieutenant Colonel William E. Dyess (left) flew dozens of missions against the Japanese as leader of a squadron of P-40s. But his most heroic act came after he escaped from a POW camp in 1943 and reached the States, where he alerted the public for the first time to the horrors of the Death March. Captain Ralph Hibbs (right) a 31st Infantry medical officer, miraculously avoided the Death March and Camp O'Donnell but was the last POW led to freedom at Cabanatuan during the famed 1945 raid by Army Rangers.

26

Sergeant Clem Kathman of the 200th Coast Artillery witnessed countless Death March atrocities at close range. The worst was the wanton slaughter of an entire family of civilian Filipinos—a husband, pregnant wife, and small child—by a Japanese guard.

27

Corregidor's Malinta Tunnel (above) housed the headquarters of U.S. Army Forces in the Far East (USAFFE), from which MacArthur and later Wainwright directed the defense of Bataan. But on May 7, 1942, less than a month after Bataan fell, Corregidor's defenders were also forced to raise a white flag (below) at the main entrance to the tunnel. This marked the end to organized American resistance in the Philippines.

28

29

Of the 1,619 POWs who set out from Manila for Japan aboard the *Oryoku Maru* (above), only about 425 lived to reach their destination. The rest died in attacks by U.S. planes or succumbed to starvation and maltreatment. Sergeant Cletis Overton (right) was fortunate when his "hell ship," the *Shinyo Maru*, was sunk; he managed to escape and reach the States long before the end of the war. The *Hokusen Maru* (below), on which Corporal Louis Read sailed to Formosa, reached port intact after several narrow escapes from prowling U.S. submarines. However, some 21,000 U.S. and Allied troops lost their lives on the hell ships.

30

31

32

General MacArthur fulfilled his "I shall return" pledge, as he and his staff officers waded ashore on Leyte in October 1944. Three months later, American forces landed on Luzon and drove toward Manila. As the troops advanced, a group of newly freed Army nurses celebrated while boarding a truck to leave their prison compound.

33

34

POWs rescued from Cabanatuan in a surprise raid by Army Rangers relaxed in a cart used to transport them to safety. After three and a half years as a Japanese prisoner, an emaciated General Wainwright smiled broadly for the camera in his first photo after his release.

35

36 

 37

Sergeant J. S. Gray, who fought with the Air Corps Infantry on Bataan, is shown soon after his enlistment in 1940 (above, left) and as he looked in 1945 on release from three-plus years in prison camps. During captivity, Gray and other POWs each risked their lives to keep and hide one of the stars from an American flag they were forced to destroy. After the war they made a new flag, using red, white, and blue cloth from parachutes carrying relief supplies, and attached the stars. Their flag is now displayed at the National Museum of the Pacific War in Fredericksburg, Texas.

38 

"God, how many of 'em you reckon there are?" whispered Hays's buddy Tommy, who was manning the machine gun next to him.

"A lot more than there are of us," Hays replied. "But there'll be a whole lot less of 'em pretty soon."

Hays had been a Marine since July 1940, when he and his kid brother had left home in Mount Vernon, Illinois, to join the Corps together. He'd served an eleven-month hitch on Guam, then been sent to Shanghai to protect American interests. Late the previous November, when his Fourth Marine Regiment was ordered to evacuate China, Hays had fleetingly hoped to make it back to the States, but the Philippines was as far as he got before the war caught up with him. The last he'd heard, his kid brother was home on leave—lucky stiff—and now Hays was stuck in the toughest spot of his life.

"Hold your fire, men," a sergeant shouted as he ran past. "Everybody get ready, but don't open up till I give the order."

Spread out around Hays's position were five dozen American and Filipino defenders, each of them armed with *something*. Hays and Tommy had the only two machine guns—water-cooled .30-caliber refugees from World War I—but several other guys had Browning automatic rifles (BARs). Others had regular rifles, mainly bolt-action 1903 model Springfields or old British Enfields. Still others had only pistols.

Hays kept looking for the sergeant and listening for his order to fire until he saw the closest barges bump against the beach.

"Christ, if we don't hit 'em now, they'll be right on top of us," he told his ammo handler. Then he turned and yelled down the line: "Fire! Open fire!"

"I truly believe we killed every Jap on the beach," Hays would confide some sixty-eight years later. "I don't think any of them got ashore alive. At first light, we saw eight landing barges bobbing in the surf, and there was no sign of life on any of them."

According to best estimates, all but 800 of the first wave of 2,000 Japanese invaders died before they reached dry land, either from bullet wounds or drowning.

"The Marines were slaughtering the Japanese invaders," wrote historian Duane Schultz. "There was no other word for the strength and fearlessness of their defense. The sea ran red with blood. A Japanese observer said that it was a 'spectacle that confounded the imagination, surpassing in grim horror anything we had ever seen before.'"

It was among the Fourth Marines' finest hours, but it wasn't enough to halt the invasion.

Unnoticed by the defenders in the predawn darkness of May 6, the enemy had managed to land three tanks—one of them a captured American M-3—on Corregidor's north beach. But when the tanks attempted to leave the beach and move inland to support the Japanese infantry, they were blocked by steep cliffs and temporarily left behind by the advancing troops.

At about 4:30 that morning, Fourth Marines commander Colonel Sam Howard committed his last organized reserves—the 500 Marines, sailors, and soldiers of his Fourth Battalion, commanded by Major Francis H. Williams—to the battle for the beaches. As dawn broke an hour and a half later, however, the Japanese were able to reinforce their beachhead with 900 fresh troops of General Homma's 61st Infantry, accompanied by several light artillery pieces. This second amphibious force had originally been scheduled to come ashore some three hours earlier, but the loss of so many boats in the initial landing had caused a serious delay.

Soon after this second landing, the enemy tanks began a cautious advance along a circuitous route that bypassed the cliffs and enabled them to leave the beach and penetrate several hundred yards in the direction of Malinta Hill. As the morning wore on, their progress was slow but persistent—and their presence was still unknown to the beach defenders.

It was after 9 AM when Marine PFC Silas Barnes, crouching in a gun pit a few hundred yards west of Roy Hays's position, spotted the enemy tanks. At first, he blinked and shook his head, thinking he was seeing things. After an all-night vigil, his own shootout with the Japanese invaders, and a long string of days with little food, less sleep, and constant enemy shelling, hallucinations seemed perfectly logical. It was only when Barnes saw the bright flashes from the tanks' cannons that he knew they were the real thing. Then his whole body went tense.

"Sweet Jesus," he muttered to the Army private crouched in the hole behind him. "There's Jap tanks moving along the beach. Three of 'em about 800 yards away. They're blazing away at our positions, and it looks like they're headed for Malinta Tunnel."

The Army private frowned and scrambled up beside Barnes to see where he was pointing. "Oh shit, this isn't good," he said. "What do you think we ought to do?"

Barnes—a shifty, hard-punching lightweight nicknamed "Mr. Tiger" by boxing fans in the Fourth Marine Regiment—had spent most of his waking hours for the past few weeks huddled behind the venerable .30-caliber Browning machine gun where he squatted now. Sometimes, he'd slept on the beach, but for the most part, his home had been this camouflaged recess gouged into an outcropping of solid rock jutting over Manila Bay some fifteen feet above Corregidor's northern coast.

The gun emplacement was accessible only by climbing a twelve-foot rope, but it afforded an excellent view along the beach to the west as well as exceptional protection for the two men who manned it. These factors had allowed it to be one of only two machine gun positions for hundreds of yards in both directions to survive around-the-clock enemy fire over the past few days.

The first time Barnes had passed Corregidor on his way from Manila to Bataan, the island had sparkled in the morning sun like a brilliant green emerald. Now it was a pulverized, denuded wasteland from which every leaf and blade of grass had long since been blasted or burned away by tens of thousands of enemy artillery shells and countless tons of Japanese bombs.

Barnes knew that barges filled with Japanese assault troops had landed on this same north beach under cover of darkness at about ten the night before. He'd used his machine gun to riddle and sink one of the first barges to reach shore, killing or wounding most of the men aboard it. But Barnes had never expected to see enemy tanks so near the north entrance to Malinta Tunnel, and its subterranean labyrinth of military headquarters, supply depots, fuel storage areas, and medical facilities.

Consequently, the young Marine from Lexington, Missouri, didn't know how to answer his Army comrade's question, and there was no one else available to offer any guidance. Like all other Corregidor defenders assigned to isolated gun emplacements along the beach during this final phase of the struggle for the island, the two of them had no way of contacting anyone beyond shouting distance. The field phones were all dead as were most of the runners who had tried to carry messages through the melee on the beaches. All Barnes and his comrade knew was that they'd been ordered to hold their position come hell or high water.

"Well, we could shoot at the bastards, I guess," Barnes said, tightening his finger on the trigger of the machine gun.

"But we can't do anything against tanks with a .30-caliber," the Army guy protested.

"No, but they've got some infantry with them," Barnes said, "and we might even be able to hit some of 'em if we get lucky."

His comrade shrugged. "We can give it a try."

Barnes sighted along the barrel of the weapon and fired a series of short bursts. But after only about thirty rounds, the gun fell silent.

"C'mon, feed me another belt," Barnes told the Army private.

"I can't," he said. "We're all out. We hauled 6,000 rounds of ammo up here yesterday evening, but we haven't got a damn bit left."

They stared at each other for a long moment.

"Then we'd better go look for some," Barnes said. "You go inland and west toward Denver Battery. I'll head back toward Monkey Point. We'll try to meet back here as soon as we can."

Barnes led the way up the rope. On the ledge above the gun pit, they shook hands and turned in opposite directions. The Army private had a rusty '03 Springfield with seven rounds. Barnes had only a .45 automatic with two clips of ammunition.

They never saw each other again.

Deep in the laterals housing the headquarters of U.S. Forces in the Philippines, Wainwright had also been alerted to the presence of Japanese tanks near Malinta Tunnel. The tanks were merely the latest piece of bad news in an endlessly expanding mosaic of disaster.

The bodies of dead Americans and Filipinos were piling up in the laterals outside the hospital section, awaiting burial until the bombing and shelling slackened—if they ever did. Countless other corpses and wounded men now littered the beaches and ravines along the north side of the island, but no one could get close enough to retrieve them.

Under the constant bombardment, the lights in the tunnels had failed several times within the past few hours, plunging everything into total darkness. The supply of drinking water was almost exhausted, and headquarters had lost touch with every outpost beyond the tunnels. By early on May 6, the entire tadpole tail at Corregidor's far eastern end, where PFC Hays and his comrades had repelled one of the Japanese landings the night before, had vanished behind a thick veil of smoke and dust.

All but one or two of Corregidor's coastal artillery batteries had now been silenced, eliminating the garrison's ability to strike back against the enemy's big guns on Bataan. Most of the island's mortars and beach-defense weapons had also been destroyed. Along the length of the north shore facing Bataan, only a handful of deeply entrenched machine gun emplacements still survived. Everything else had been obliterated.

Wainwright had already ordered what few remaining reserves he had to reinforce the Marines and other ground troops now slowly being driven west toward Malinta Hill in savage hand-to-hand fighting. That done, he'd scrawled a terse message to General Marshall 10,000 miles away in Washington:

> Landing attack on Corregidor in progress. Enemy landed North Point. Further details as situation develops.

At about four o'clock that morning, Wainwright had received a stirring message from President Franklin D. Roosevelt himself:

> During recent weeks, we have been following with growing admiration the day-by-day accounts of your heroic stand against the mounting intensity of bombardment by enemy planes and heavy siege guns.
>
> In spite of all the handicaps of complete isolation, lack of food and ammunition, you have given the world a shining ex-

> ample of patriotic fortitude and self-sacrifice. . . . The calm determination of your personal leadership in a desperate situation sets a standard of duty for our soldiers throughout the world.

Wainwright deeply appreciated his commander-in-chief's sentiments, but the tone of the message made it clear that Corregidor and its defenders were being consigned to their fate.

Because of the communications breakdown on the Rock, Wainwright couldn't know how much punishment had been dished out by his men against the Japanese assault force. In their final showdown with the Japanese, they had shown an incredible ability to stand and fight with rifles, machine guns, and bayonets. The Japanese had already suffered 2,100 casualties in the fighting on the beaches, including more than 900 killed, and some sources have estimated total Japanese losses for May 5–6 at 4,000 dead and wounded.

Wainwright also had no knowledge of the deep despair into which General Homma, his Japanese counterpart, had fallen on learning of the heavy toll among his first wave of invaders. Homma doubted that he had enough available landing barges to send in sufficient reinforcements. He feared that his whole amphibious force—now critically short of ammunition—would be wiped out, and he envisioned himself being sent home to Japan in disgrace. "My God," he muttered to a staff officer, "I have failed miserably on the assault."

But despite the sketchy information at his disposal, Wainwright *did* know that Corregidor's defenders had also suffered staggering losses. Most of the Americans who had met the Japanese in hand-to-hand fighting along the north beaches were now dead or wounded. Colonel Sam Howard of the Fourth Marines had already committed his last small group of reinforcements, so there were no combat troops left to send. And now—as if to confirm the finality of the situation—came the news that the Japanese had put tanks ashore and that three of them were grinding their way toward the main entrance to Malinta Tunnel.

Wainwright's decimated forces had not a single weapon capable of slowing down—much less stopping—a tank. With nothing more powerful than rifles, a few light machine guns, and moldy 1918 vintage hand grenades, more than half of which were duds, they were utterly helpless against Japanese armor.

A chilling image flashed through Wainwright's mind. He could envision the resulting bloodbath if the tanks should get inside Malinta Tunnel and fire their 75-millimeter cannons along its length, where scores of nurses were treating more than 1,000 sick and wounded men and vast quantities of munitions and gasoline were stored.

In that instant, the general knew that, regardless of the consequences, he couldn't allow this to happen.

PFC Barnes had searched for more than an hour for machine gun ammo, but his efforts had proved fruitless. He hadn't seen even one other live American in his wanderings—much less any rounds for his machine gun—as he made his way cautiously back toward the gun pit where the useless .30-caliber still sat. He passed through a no-man's-land of shell holes, hoping to spot some friendly troops who might know more than he did about what was happening.

Instead, he stumbled into a four-man Japanese patrol.

Barnes hit the deck and drew his .45 as the enemy soldiers ran toward him, shouting at each other and brandishing Arisaka rifles with fixed bayonets. He fired two or three shots and thought he saw one of the Japanese stumble while two others scurried away. The fourth one charged directly at Barnes with his bayonet lowered.

Barnes fired twice more, but both shots missed the onrushing soldier, and when he squeezed the trigger of the .45 again, there was only silence. Realizing the clip in the pistol butt was empty, Barnes fumbled at his belt for the other clip. But before he could grasp it, the tip of his assailant's bayonet was only inches away.

Barnes pulled himself to his knees and raised both arms, trying to fend off the blow he knew was coming. But the Japanese soldier was a split second too fast for him. The bayonet slipped past Barnes's upraised arms and sliced through his rib cage high on the right side of his chest.

An electrifying jolt of pain flashed through Barnes, and he saw his own bright red blood staining the bayonet's blade as the soldier withdrew it and aimed a second thrust at him.

Somehow Barnes got to his feet. With blood streaming down his side and his head spinning, he sprang backward a step or two. As he did, he heard a small voice whispering inside his ear.

This son of a bitch thinks he's gonna kill you, but he doesn't know he's messing with Mr. Tiger, the toughest 132-pounder in the whole damn Pacific. And maybe—just maybe—you've got enough left to take him with you.

With a nimble desperation that amazed Barnes himself, he sidestepped the bayonet's next thrust, catching the rifle with both hands and ripping it from his off-balance attacker's grasp. He smashed the rifle butt into the invader's face, knocking him to the ground.

Then he drove the length of the bayonet squarely through the man's throat.

The Japanese made faint gagging, gurgling sounds as blood spewed from his ruptured carotid artery. His body writhed spasmodically for a few seconds, then lay still.

Barnes dropped the rifle and staggered across the beach toward the water, clutching the hole in his chest as tightly as he could grip it with his left hand.

Maybe I'll be safer in the water, he thought. *Maybe the other Japs won't see me there. Maybe the saltwater will help my wound. On the other hand, though, maybe I'll drown . . .*

At 10 AM, word reached Wainwright from Colonel Howard that the Japanese were landing more tanks and driving steadily west against dogged but failing resistance toward Malinta Hill and the massive tunnel underlying it.

Afterward, Wainwright paced the floor of his subterranean command center for several minutes. Finally, he picked up the phone and summoned General Beebe, his chief of staff, and General Moore, commander of the Manila Bay harbor defenses, to his headquarters.

"We can't hold out much longer," Wainwright told them. "Maybe we could last through this day, but the end must certainly come tonight. It would be better to clear up the situation now, in daylight. What do you think?"

"I think we should send a flag of truce through the lines right now," Beebe said.

"There should be no delay," Moore added.

Wainwright sighed. "Tell the Nips we'll cease firing at noon," he said.

After Beebe and Moore left to broadcast a previously prepared surrender message to the Japanese and send runners to spread the word of the cease-fire to Corregidor's garrison, Wainwright scribbled a final message to President Roosevelt and handed it to his radio operator:

> It is with broken heart and head bowed in sadness, but not in shame, that I report to Your Excellency that I must go today to arrange terms for the surrender of the fortified islands of Manila Bay. . . .
>
> There is a limit of human endurance, and that limit has long since been passed. Without prospect of relief, I feel it is my duty . . . to end this useless effusion of blood and human sacrifice. . . .
>
> With profound regret and with continued pride in my gallant troops, I go to meet the Japanese commander. Goodbye, Mr. President.

Wainwright sent a similar message to MacArthur in Australia, and there would be a handful of other communications that morning between members of the garrison on Corregidor and the outside world. Captain Ken Hoeffel, commander of all remaining Navy forces in the Philippines, dutifully informed the Navy Department that all military equipment was being destroyed and all remaining ships sunk. Lieutenant Commander Melvyn McCoy, a Navy communications officer, wrote out a terse message on a scrap of paper, gave it to his radio operator, and told him to send it to Radio Honolulu without code.

"Going off air now," it said. "Goodbye and good luck."

Corporal Irving Strobing, an Army radio operator from Brooklyn, was the last member of Corregidor's garrison to tap out a message. It was aimed at anyone listening: "Tell Joe [Strobing's brother], wherever he is, to give 'em hell for us. My love to you all. God bless you and keep you. Sign my name, and tell mother how you heard from me. Stand by."

After that, there was only silence from the Rock.

* * *

By 11:30 AM, the Fourth Marines' attempt at a counterattack outside Malinta Tunnel had ended in bloody defeat, and the Americans' fragile line had fallen apart as the defenders tried vainly to withdraw to a series of concrete trenches on Malinta Hill for a final stand. Japanese artillery made the areas surrounding the main tunnel entrance a murderous no-man's-land, and the marauding Japanese tanks began methodically chewing to ribbons the remaining clusters of beach defenders.

"Men made their way to the rear in small groups and began to fill the concrete trenches at Malinta Hill," wrote Marine historian J. Michael Miller. "The Japanese guns swept the area from the hill to Battery Denver and then back again several times. In thirty minutes, only 150 men were left to hold the line."

Aggressively pursuing the American retreat, the Japanese infantry moved to within 300 yards of the defenders' positions, and the enemy tanks drove around the Americans' right flank. At that point, Major Williams, the Fourth Battalion commander, could see that the situation was hopeless. He reported to his CO, Colonel Howard, that his men could no longer hold, and Howard broke the news that General Wainwright had ordered a surrender at noon.

A moment later, Howard buried his face in his hands and wept. "My God," he groaned, "and I have to be the first Marine officer ever to surrender a whole regiment!"

Marine PFC Ernest J. Bales, a native Kansan who'd come to the Philippines in late 1940 straight out of boot camp, learned of the surrender when a runner managed to reach his position in James Ravine, where he was assigned to one of four .30-caliber machine guns. At the moment, Bales was huddled with six other Marines and soldiers in a trench only a few dozen yards from the water's edge. All of them were waiting for something—but not this.

"We're throwing in the towel," the runner said, gasping for breath. "You're supposed to destroy all weapons."

For a long moment, Bales could only stare at the runner in

stunned silence. "It was really hard to take," he recalled. "Was this what we'd spent all these damned days and nights dodging bombs for? I couldn't believe it."

"Who the hell says so?" demanded one of the other men in the trench, pointing his pistol at the soldier who'd delivered the message.

"It's straight from Wainwright," the runner said. "It's on the level."

"I honestly think this guy might've shot the runner," Bales would recall many years later, "if some of the others hadn't grabbed his arm and wrestled the gun away."

PFC Ben Lohman of the Second Battalion, Fourth Marines, did as he was told when the surrender order came, destroying the Browning automatic rifle he'd inherited when the regular BAR man in his squad had been struck down by shrapnel from a 500-pound bomb. But Lohman soon regretted his action because the Japanese gave no indication of honoring the so-called cease-fire. Instead, they kept right on shooting.

"We had plenty of ammo for the BARs," he recalled. "There were boxes of it lying out in the open along the beach, and I was carrying two bandoleers and an ammo belt filled with rounds. The main landings were more than a mile away, but I could see the Jap barges coming in, and I'd had a chance to fire on some of them with the BAR. Once I'd wrecked it, though, it was useless."

Lohman and his mates huddled low in their hand-dug gun pits while enemy artillery rounds poured in with no discernible letup from the direction of Mariveles.

"We didn't know what the hell was going on," he said. "If the fighting was over, the Japs didn't seem to have gotten the word. I'd say they had us by the ass, and they knew it and didn't care. But I'll also say this for the bastards: They were tough fighters, and they had no mercy for their enemies."

After a lengthy wait, Lohman and his group received word to proceed to Malinta Tunnel. "We picked up what few belongings we had," he said, "and marched toward the Japanese, not having any idea what to expect."

* * *

The confusion surrounding the end of hostilities on Corregidor stemmed from two causes. One was Japanese determination to use the surrender to close out the Philippines campaign once and for all by ending the U.S. military presence throughout the archipelago. The other was a last-gasp attempt by General Wainwright to avoid exactly that.

Wainwright had devoted considerable thought and effort to setting forth details of the proposed surrender in a simple, straightforward manner, and he and his staff had high hopes that it would go smoothly. Beginning at 11 AM on May 6, the surrender message was broadcast three times over a period of an hour and a half, in both English and Japanese, over the *Voice of Freedom* transmitter in the tunnel.

The radio broadcasts referred only to the four fortified islands in Manila Bay—Corregidor (known officially as Fort Mills), Fort Drum, Fort Frank, and Fort Hughes. By using such an explicit reference, Wainwright hoped to spare U.S. forces commanded by General William Sharp in the Mindanao–Visayan Islands area far to the south from being included in the surrender. To that end, he had officially released Sharp a few days earlier from the USFIP command and instructed him to report directly to MacArthur in the future. It was a major gamble, and Wainwright knew it, but if the Japanese accepted this limitation, it would free some 25,000 American and Filipino troops to keep fighting in the Philippines after Corregidor fell.

Nearly two hours passed with no response from the Japanese, but around 1 PM, the Americans detected a noticeable decline in the shelling outside, and Wainwright recruited young Marine Captain Golland L. Clark to go in search of a senior Japanese officer to relay the surrender message in writing. Another hour went by before Clark returned wearing a grim expression and bearing discouraging news.

"He won't come to see you, General," Clark said. "He insists that you go and meet him."

When Wainwright and five of his staff officers ventured forth under a flag of truce, they were stopped by the first Japanese officer they encountered, a wiry young lieutenant "reeking with arrogance," as Wainwright later put it.

"He identified himself as Lieutenant Uramura," the general recalled, "and before I had a chance to speak, he barked in English: 'We will not accept your surrender unless it includes all American and Filipino troops in the whole archipelago!'"

This marked the beginning of a long evening of fear, frustration, and fury for Wainwright and his staff.

Like General Edward King's earlier attempts to limit the Bataan cease-fire to his own command, Wainwright's initial effort to surrender only the fortified islands of Manila Bay, rather than all U.S. forces in the Philippines, was met by a series of angry rebuffs. Meanwhile, Japanese shelling, bombing, and ground attacks continued that afternoon against a mostly disarmed and virtually helpless Corregidor garrison.

Wainwright barked back at Uramura that he had no intention of negotiating with a mere lieutenant, and in due time, Colonel Motto Nakayama—the same non–English-speaking officer who had taken General King's surrender four weeks earlier—arrived on the scene. With Uramura serving as an interpreter, Wainwright told Nakayama that he was authorized to surrender only the four fortified islands. This sent Nakayama into a rage.

When Nakayama repeated that no surrender would be accepted if it didn't include all U.S. forces in the Philippines, Wainwright reacted with his own flash of anger.

"In that case," he said, "I will deal only with General Homma and with no one of less rank. I want an appointment with him."

After a brief interval of hostile silence, Nakayama agreed to take Wainwright to Homma's headquarters at Cabcaben on Bataan.

Accompanied by General Beebe and four other staff officers, Wainwright arrived at Cabcaben at 4 PM aboard a Japanese boat, but Homma made a point of showing the Americans who was in charge by keeping them waiting for two hours before summoning them to his headquarters.

Meanwhile, Japanese forces amplified the demand for total American capitulation in the Philippines by sending waves of bombers across the length of Corregidor. Flying from east to west, they blanketed the tortured island with scores of new explosions, enveloping it in billowing clouds of smoke while the American surrender party watched from Bataan.

Fortunately perhaps, Wainwright and his party couldn't see the even more menacing ground action unfolding on Corregidor. Immediately after the bombing raid ended, Japanese tanks smashed through the last U.S. defenses to reach the east entrance of Malinta Tunnel. Then they lined up a few yards from the entrance with their guns pointing down the length of the tunnel.

Eight Japanese soldiers, clad in asbestos suits and armed with flamethrowers, also deployed across the entrance, aiming the nozzles of their weapons into the tunnel. To anyone who witnessed these actions, the message they conveyed was crystal clear: If the surrender wasn't consummated to the Imperial Japanese Army's satisfaction, wholesale slaughter would quickly ensue.

At about 6 PM—seven hours after the first broadcast of the surrender message—Wainwright's party was driven to a small white house near the beach, which served as Japanese headquarters on Bataan, and commanded to sit on the porch. Then they were ordered to line up on the lawn to be photographed by Japanese cameramen. Finally, after another hour's wait, Homma arrived in a shiny Cadillac, sporting a chestful of medals and an ornate sword and accompanied by three resplendently dressed aides.

After the Japanese party was seated, Wainwright handed Homma a signed surrender document, which Homma passed to his interpreter to read. When the interpreter finished, Homma glanced at Wainwright, then spoke sharply to the interpreter.

"General Homma replies that no surrender will be considered unless it includes all United States and Philippine troops in the Philippine Islands," the interpreter said.

Through the interpreter, Wainwright and Homma argued back and forth for several minutes, until Homma terminated the argument with this threat: "Hostilities against the fortified islands will be continued unless the Japanese surrender terms are accepted!"

Then he stalked out of the house, followed by his aides.

"I was desperately cornered," Wainwright recalled in his memoirs. "My troops on Corregidor were almost completely disarmed, as well as wholly isolated from the outside world." There were 11,000 of them, including about 1,000 wounded and almost 100 nurses—and Wainwright knew that the blood of them all would be on his hands unless he yielded to the Japanese demands.

"That was it," he wrote years later. "The last hope vanished from my mind."

Even after Wainwright agreed to surrender all U.S. forces in the Philippines, Homma refused further conversation and drove away in his Cadillac. Wainwright was forced to return to Corregidor, where he typed up and signed a new surrender document that complied fully with Japanese terms. Then, since Homma was no longer available, he submitted the document to Colonel Gempachi Sato, commander of the Japanese invasion forces.

It was after midnight when, as Wainwright put it, "the terrible deed was done" and he was taken under guard to the west entrance of the tunnel. As he passed, hundreds of his surrendered troops stood in downcast groups along the way. Many of them waved or reached out for Wainwright's hand. Others patted him on the shoulder, repeating the same reassurances again and again.

"It's all right, General," they said. "You did your best."

PFC Edward D. Reamer of Battery B, 60th Coast Artillery, was standing near the tunnel entrance and within thirty or forty feet of Wainwright as the general passed.

"I could see tears on Wainwright's cheeks," Reamer recalled, "and you couldn't look in any direction outside the tunnel without seeing a dead body. One guy was holding a tommy gun with half his head blown off. Those guys fought right up to the tunnel, right up to the headquarters."

Tears were still streaming down Wainwright's face when he reached the lateral housing the headquarters of General Moore, who had commanded the harbor defenses in Manila Bay. He explained to Moore what had happened, and Moore tried to assure him that he'd taken the only conceivable course open to him.

"But I feel I've taken a dreadful step," Wainwright said brokenly.

* * *

On hearing the news of Corregidor's surrender, General MacArthur issued a brief statement from his headquarters in Melbourne:

> Corregidor needs no comment from me. It has sounded its own story at the mouth of its guns. It has scrolled its own epitaph on enemy tablets, but through the bloody haze of its last reverberating shots, I shall always seem to see the vision of its grim, gaunt, and ghostly men.

On May 7, 1942, almost five months to the day since the first Japanese attacks, all organized American resistance in the Philippines officially ended.

A longer, deadlier, and unbelievably more horrific struggle for survival loomed ahead.

10

O'Donnell and Other Horrors

Death March survivors expecting even a slight respite from their torment when the march ended at Camp O'Donnell would find a crushing—and frequently fatal—disappointment awaiting them.

Of the total of approximately 9,000 Americans and 42,000 Filipinos who reached O'Donnell alive, almost all were emaciated from hunger, dehydrated from thirst, suffering from wounds and/or tropical diseases, and exhausted to the point of collapse. The drastically debilitated condition in which most of the Bataan prisoners arrived at the camp is demonstrated by figures compiled by Captain John Olson, who served as personnel adjutant of the American Group at O'Donnell.

As of April 8, the day before Bataan surrendered, figures turned up by Olson showed an appalling total of 24,000 men—about one of every three members of the U.S. Luzon Force—hospitalized with wounds, serious illness, or both. Of these, about 10,000 were patients in Hospitals No. 1 and 2, with another 14,000 being treated in field hospitals or military aid stations. Two days later, without any chance to recover or regain strength, these "scarecrows," as Olson called them, were thrust into the Death March. Most of those in the worst condition died or were killed along the route, but thousands of others arrived at the camp so close to death that only a miracle could have saved them.

"These men's terrible condition on arrival at O'Donnell was the chief factor in a death toll that ran as high as 250 per day during their first six or seven weeks of confinement," said Olson, who was among the first contingent of prisoners to reach the camp on April 14, 1942, just five days after the surrender. During the period of roughly seven weeks between that date and early June 1942, when the remaining Americans were moved to other camps, 1,565 of their comrades and an estimated 20,000 Filipinos would die there of untreated illness, starvation, physical abuse, and cold-blooded murder. After the Americans left, an additional 6,000 Filipinos would perish at O'Donnell.

"If the Japanese kept any records of what went on during these grim months," Olson said, "they were destroyed or have never been revealed."

Four decades after the war, based on his own experiences and extensive research, Olson would write and publish *O'Donnell: Andersonville of the Pacific*, a book comparing the Japanese camp to the infamous Civil War prison in Georgia where thousands of Union soldiers died of hunger and disease. As this is written, Olson is recognized as the foremost living authority on the "death factory" at O'Donnell.

As he concluded in the epilogue of his book: "Though what happened to the Americans was reprehensible, the studied extermination of the Filipinos, whom the Japanese had ostensibly come to free from the 'tyrannical oppression' of the imperialist Americans, is utterly inexplicable.

"The majority of those who were most intimately involved in this useless slaughter were made to pay with their lives [in war crimes trials following the war], but the numbers who did were miniscule compared to the thousands they were responsible for destroying."

As it existed in the spring of 1942, O'Donnell was fifty sun-scorched acres of weeds and desolation, dotted by dilapidated nipa and bamboo huts mounted on stilts and encircled by six strands of barbed wire. Bamboo watchtowers stood at the corners of two separate compounds, one for American prisoners and one for Filipinos.

The camp was near the small town of O'Donnell, scene of a fight between the U.S. 25th Infantry and Philippine insurgents around 1900, in which 105 insurgents were captured and numerous weapons seized. Some forty years later, as part of the Greater Fort Stotsenburg Military Reservation, Camp O'Donnell had been designated as a training facility for recruits of the Philippine Army's 71st Division. Several battalions of infantry troops arrived there in the fall of 1941, but the camp was still unfinished when war broke out, and the Japanese had done virtually nothing to prepare it as a detention center for POWs. The roofs of some of the buildings had been blown away by high winds, leaving the site littered with debris.

The camp lay astride the main road from the town of Capas, with its smaller southern sector occupied by the American prisoners and its larger northern sector by Filipinos. When the POWs arrived, the entire water supply for about 9,000 Americans consisted of a single artesian well, a temperamental electric pump, and three slow-dribbling spigots, only two of which were usually operative. Men driven mad by thirst fought each other like animals at these spigots for a sip of water. Some prisoners waited in line for up to twenty hours to fill their canteens, and more than a few died before they were able to quench their thirst.

"Well water was so scarce that it could be used for drinking only, and one was fortunate to get a full canteen a day," Colonel James V. Collier, who had served as G-3 operations officer of the Luzon Force, noted in his diary. "Water for cooking was carried in five-gallon gasoline tins from a small stream about 1,000 yards away. This stream was infested with the dread amoebic dysentery germ, and to drink the water unboiled was practically a death sentence."

For the first fifteen days or so of the camp's operation, not a drop of water was allotted for bathing, shaving, washing hair or clothes, or even brushing teeth, and anyone caught attempting any of these activities was subject to execution on the spot. The water supply situation improved to some degree later on, but obtaining a full canteen continued to be an onerous, exhaustive task for as long as O'Donnell remained in use.

The ramshackle huts that passed as barracks were devoid of bunks or other furnishings and had only holes in the walls to serve as windows. Each was intended to house a maximum of sixteen men, but if all prisoners were to find any type of shelter at the camp, forty or more POWs would have to crowd themselves into every hut, and those who wouldn't fit would be forced to sleep on the ground outside.

The "welcoming committee" waiting inside O'Donnell's main gate consisted of squads of Japanese soldiers brandishing clubs and rifle butts to pummel and prod the stumbling prisoners onto a grassless parade ground in front of the camp headquarters. They seemed to single out the weakest, sickest POWs for the harshest treatment.

"Because I was limping as I entered the camp, the guards began hitting me with their rifle butts," recalled Corporal Lester Tenney of the 192nd Tank Battalion. "One of the guards . . . had taken his military belt off and was swinging it wildly toward me. The belt ripped into my back and across my buttocks, and I felt blood gushing down my back and legs. Then, with a mighty snap, his belt caught me squarely in the face. The shock of the blow and the stinging pain so clouded my mind that I almost tore after the guard in retaliation. Luckily, I caught myself before I did anything foolish."

Next came a shakedown by the guards in which the prisoners were ordered to dump out on the ground any personal items that they'd managed to retain during the march. These included not only possessions of potential value but also blankets, extra clothing, and anything that could have been used for bedding.

Any item identifiable as Japanese in origin represented a death sentence for the POW who possessed it because the guards considered it evidence that it had been taken from a dead Japanese soldier. Likewise, for less obvious reasons, anyone having one of the "surrender certificates" that had been dropped in Filipino territory by Japanese planes was also urgently advised to get rid of it by swallowing it or poking it into his rectum.

"As I started to place all my items in front of me," said Corporal Tenney, "I noticed one of the surrender certificates fall to the ground. I was panic-stricken. . . . I took four or five deep breaths, surreptitiously put the paper into my mouth, and chewed it as fast as I could. After two or three chews and a mighty gulp, I managed to swallow the incriminating document."

Nearby, one of Tenney's buddies was hustled away and shot after a guard found a Japanese coin among his possessions. According to Tenney, the man had been given the coin earlier by a Japanese soldier in exchange for some cigarettes, and such untimely generosity now cost the American his life.

The "welcoming address" by the camp commandant, Captain Yoshio Tsuneyoshi, was a rambling, vitriolic harangue that no prisoner who heard it was ever likely to forget. It was repeated any number of times, with slight variations, as each new batch of about 2,000 prisoners arrived, and in each performance, the commandant worked himself into a towering anti-American rage while an interpreter translated his gibbering into pidgin English.

John Olson described Tsuneyoshi's diatribe quite accurately as a "God-damn-you speech." It was accompanied by howling curses, wild fist shaking, and showers of spittle while semi-comatose prisoners were forced to stand at attention in the blazing sun. It went on for at least an hour, but to its audiences it seemed to last forever.

Described by historian Gerald Astor as "an overage caricature of a Japanese soldier," Tsuneyoshi's appearance might have been laughable in another context. He was short, squatty, and bowlegged, dressed in baggy shorts, tall riding boots with spurs, a white sport shirt draped with medals, and a sword that hung to his ankles. He screamed epithets through his buckteeth until he was red-faced, hoarse, and out of breath. Many of his listeners mouthed silent curses at him, but none of them ever cracked a smile.

"You are the enemies of Nippon," he shouted, "and we fight a righteous war against you. You have been our enemies for a hundred years, and we shall fight you for a hundred years more, until our grandsons and great-grandsons have fought you, and we will win! You are not honorable prisoners of war. You are captives, and you will be treated as captives. You are ours, and we will do to you whatever we want to do. You have no rights! You have no honor, and you should have no hope! All Americans will be driven out of Asia, but you will never go home again. You will pay for the rest of your lives for the way Japanese people have been treated by piggish Americans.

You are cowards who are lower than dogs, and you will find that your dead comrades are the lucky ones!"

He warned the prisoners of the severe consequences they would face for the slightest infraction of camp rules. Every American was required, on pain of death, to salute and bow to any Japanese soldier he encountered. Those who disobeyed this rule would be punished or killed, depending on what the Japanese soldier decided at the time. Prisoners who ventured within four or five feet of the barbed wire fence would be shot instantly.

"You need not expect to be protected by the so-called Geneva Convention agreement on the treatment of prisoners of war," Tsuneyoshi warned. "This agreement was never ratified by Japan, and therefore you can be treated any way a Japanese soldier wants to treat you. If you fail to obey any order from a Japanese soldier, or to bow and salute—even to a private—you will be severely punished. Geneva Convention cannot protect you here. The Imperial Japanese Army makes its own rules, and nothing can protect you here!"

While the men around him clenched their teeth, squeezed their eyelids shut, or clung to comrades next to them to keep from falling, Sergeant Cletis Overton of the 27th Bomb Group endured the commandant's "hollerin' and carryin' on" with no visible change of expression. "This guy didn't deserve any reaction from us, and he wasn't about to get any from me," Overton said decades later. "He was crazy as a dadburn loon."

General Edward King, the officer who had surrendered Bataan, had preceded most of the other prisoners to O'Donnell and had been ordered by Tsuneyoshi to serve as "commander" of the American POWs. This meant that he was responsible for explaining camp rules and seeing that they were obeyed. Conversely, however, Tsuneyoshi refused to meet directly with either King or his Filipino counterpart. Instead, he would present his edicts and demands to one of their representatives to be passed along to the responsible party.

The perceived "dishonor" of surrendering the largest U.S. military force in history continued to weigh heavily on King, who bore an oppressive load of guilt over his own actions and the blatant Japanese disregard of prisoner rights under international law. He felt certain that if he ever made it back to the States, he would face a court-martial—and possibly a prison term—for defying the no-surrender order from General Wainwright, and he felt a need to express his feelings personally to the arriving groups of Americans.

"You men remember this," he told them. "I surrendered you; you didn't surrender. I'm the one responsible for that, and the blame and disgrace are mine, not yours, so let me carry them. You've suffered far too much as it is. All I ask is that you obey the orders of the Japanese so that you don't bring further pain on yourselves."

Because many of the POWs were little more than walking skeletons when they reached O'Donnell, thousands of them were to lose their fragile grip on life in the immediate aftermath of the march. No one among the prisoners had either the stamina or the stomach to make an accurate count of the dead, but most estimates place the average figure at between fifty and seventy new American corpses per day. The bodies were stacked like cordwood under the buildings until they could be hauled away to mass graves by POW burial details.

One area in the American sector of the camp was designated as a "hospital" and staffed by military doctors and medics brought to O'Donnell from Bataan. These medics had virtually no medicine, no equipment, and no means of sterilizing anything, but they did their best to relieve suffering and save lives. Most of their "patients" were too far gone to help, anyway.

"Our medics held daily sick call, but only sympathy was dispensed," wrote Captain Manny Lawton of the 31st Infantry. "Perhaps there was some mental relief in being able to talk to a doctor [but] with no beds, no drugs or equipment, the so-called hospital wasn't much more than a morgue."

Hospital patients were housed in two separate buildings. One was for those who were given some chance of recovery. The other was known as the "Zero Ward," and it was for the obviously dying.

"The latter was a miserable, depressing, hopeless place," said Lawton, who was fortunate to be a patient in the other building.

"In it, men lay in their own filth, being too weak and indifferent to struggle to the outdoor latrine. . . . There was neither hope for life nor fear of death left in them."

When he first got to O'Donnell, Sergeant Louis Read was pleased to be reacquainted with dozens of friends and acquaintances who had served with him in the 31st Infantry. But by the time Read observed his twenty-second birthday on April 30, 1942, many of those former comrades were dead, and others were hovering at the brink of death.

"I celebrated my birthday with a mess kit half full of lugao, a kind of rice gruel that was mostly water," he recalled. "It was about the only thing we ever had to eat there, but I was plenty glad to get it. People were dropping like flies by that time. Bodies were stacked in a shed to the ceiling waiting for burial, and large green blowflies were in abundance."

The deceased included two close buddies of Read's, one of whom had conspired to escape with him during the chaos prior to the Death March, then accompanied him most of the way from Bataan to O'Donnell.

"A couple of times," Read remembered, "guys I knew really well developed a headache about two in the afternoon, and by ten o'clock that night they were dead. Soon, practically everyone I knew was dead."

The 31st Infantry had begun the war with about 2,500 enlisted men and officers, and Read heard later that 819 men from the regiment died during the first six weeks at O'Donnell.

"I decided if I stayed there, I was going to die, too," he said, "so after Corregidor fell and the Japs started calling for volunteers for work details outside the camp, I signed up. I thought, 'God, nothing could be worse than O'Donnell.' I was wrong."

Read's work party was taken back to Bataan on trucks to salvage artillery shells left behind in abandoned U.S. ammunition dumps. The rainy season had now set in, and the prisoners were forced to work up to twelve hours a day in the tropical downpours, then sleep outside on the ground with only a blanket for cover. The food was mostly rice, just as it was at O'Donnell, with a little fish thrown in. After about a week of this, several men developed pneumonia, and an epidemic of hepatitis—commonly known at the time as "yellow jaundice"—also swept through the work detail.

"We walked around looking like a bunch of canary-colored zombies," Read recalled. "I'd already contracted malaria on this trip, and I got so weak and in such a daze from the chills and fever that I couldn't even climb onto a truck without help. So many of us were so sick that the Japs decided to terminate the detail and take us back to prison camp."

Another work detail took Sergeant Henry Stanley back to Clark Field, where he'd once been assigned to load bombs on B-17s, but unlike Louis Read, Stanley never had reason to regret the work party.

"Fortunately for me, I was only at O'Donnell from April 15 until May 6," Stanley recalled. "I got out by jumping on a truck and volunteering for a job I didn't know anything about, and it turned out to be a lifesaver. Otherwise, I don't think I would've ever lived to leave O'Donnell. The job of rebuilding Clark for the Japs to use wasn't all that bad—at least we had plenty of water—and I stayed there until September 1944, when they shipped me to Japan."

Only a small minority of prisoners at O'Donnell were considered strong enough for outside work details. But any POWs who were still ambulatory were routinely assigned to one of three types of closely guarded work groups within the camp itself. One group was assigned to gather wood for cooking fires, another to fetch barrels of nonpotable water from a stream three-quarters of a mile away, and another to bury the daily quota of dead.

"The burial detail didn't have to walk as far as the wood or water detail, [so] those who were the least able to walk were used most of the time to dig graves and bury the dead," said Captain John Coleman, who had been appointed executive officer of the Air Corps Regiment POWs. "A man might be on the burial detail one day and be buried the next day himself. . . . [T]here were never less than fifty to die every day."

According to Coleman, more men died from dysentery than any other cause at O'Donnell. Some men managed to ease their symptoms by eating the charcoal from burned wood, but their starved condition often left them too weak to fight off any type of disease. The "wet" form of beriberi, which caused hundreds of men's bodies and limbs to swell to grotesque proportions, could be quickly relieved with even small amounts of B vitamins, but the prisoners' diet of almost nothing but rice contained scarcely a trace of these nutrients.

As the rainy season descended, the dead had to be weighted down to keep them from floating out of the graves during a downpour. Usually, at least ten men were buried in each common, unmarked grave, many of them identified only as "unknown" because the Japanese had taken their dog tags as souvenirs. Most were buried naked to allow their clothes to be recycled. No funeral services of any kind were allowed by the Japanese.

"I was put on the burial detail at O'Donnell, and I think it was the hardest thing I ever had to do in my life," recalled Sergeant J. S. Gray of the 27th Bomb Group. "Hour after hour, we would carry the bodies out and just push them into a hole, and it was so sad to know that those young men we were burying had tried so hard to make it, but then they'd just given up. Some of them weren't dead yet, and once in a while, one would cry out and beg us not to dump him in the hole, but when you had a Jap bayonet against your head or stomach, you'd go ahead and drop the body. If you didn't, you'd just become another body in that same hole. Even now, sixty years later, I have nightmares where I see and hear those poor souls begging me not to throw them in."

Among Captain John Coleman's most depressing jobs was checking the regimental roll each morning. "The condition of these once-healthy and proud soldiers was pathetic," he recalled. "Not a single one of them was well. They weighed from 80 to 120 pounds. . . . Many couldn't wear their shoes because of swelling in their feet and legs. Many were too sick to get to the formation for roll call, and I would have to go with the first sergeant to find them. They would be under the old buildings or in a hole without any covering to keep them warm at night."

In the Filipino compound to the west of the American camp, Coleman observed conditions that were far worse. "Their death rate ran from 300 to 400 a day," he said. "They would file by . . . our camp carrying their dead from about nine o'clock to eleven o'clock in the morning. Their corpses were carried by two Filipinos . . . [on] litters made of bamboo poles with a blanket tied on them."

Lieutenant Sam Grashio, formerly a pilot in the 21st Pursuit Squadron, described a typical day at O'Donnell in these terms: "We were awakened at about 6 AM by the bugler, if we hadn't already been roused by the maniacal yelling of the Japanese taking early-morning bayonet practice. Then we went to the mess hall for breakfast. This always consisted of about half a mess kit of lugao, a soupy form of rice. Many men simply ate their meager breakfast, then lay down again and slept most of the day, a habit that became increasingly prevalent as we grew weaker from lack of food. The main activity of everyone in camp who wasn't dead or wishing himself dead was trying to get more food. If someone was sick and about to die, others stayed close to him . . . [in] hope of getting his rice ration."

The quest for water was perhaps even more urgent and consuming. The supply problem that had plagued the prisoners from the time they arrived never really improved. Most still had access only to a single spigot, from which water flowed at a trickle at best. At times, even when there were no mechanical problems, the Japanese simply turned off the water, for reasons the prisoners never understood.

The repeated scenes of torment, anguish, and death that surrounded him triggered vague plans of escape in Corporal Les Tenney's mind. But given his fragile state of health—he was told by a doctor who had a thermometer that he was running a temperature of 102 degrees from malaria and was still nursing wounds that made walking difficult—the plans seemed next to impossible to carry out. Meanwhile, he received no encouragement from his close friends, Lew Brittan and Bob Martin.

"Les, you don't have a snowball's chance in hell in those unfamiliar jungles," Brittan warned, "not knowing the language or which way to turn once you're out there."

But rumors were circulating that a system of prisoner numbering would soon be activated to prevent escapes. Tenney had first begun to hear the rumors soon after arriving at O'Donnell, and they convinced him that if he intended to test his luck, he needed to do so before such a system went into effect.

"One of the doctors had told me that some of the men sent out on work details were placed in groups of ten and told that if any of them escaped, the remaining members of that group would be beheaded," Tenney said. "No person or group inside Camp O'Donnell had been given a number at this time, but the doctor expected such a numbering system would be implemented any day."

But until that happened, Tenney reasoned, the Japanese would have no way of knowing whether a prisoner was missing or not, and even if they suspected an escape attempt, no other POW was likely to be punished for it.

With this in mind, Tenney grew steadily more determined to make a solitary break for freedom at the first opportunity—and that opportunity came on only his sixth day at O'Donnell, when he was sent out on a water detail.

"I was in luck that morning," he recalled. "Only one guard was assigned to look after the twenty-five men who had volunteered for the detail. . . . Because of the number of men . . . the guard decided that we would make three round trips to the creek. My waiting paid off. It was starting to get dark as the last trip began. . . . Everyone was tired, including the guard."

With darkness falling, Tenney slipped unnoticed into the surrounding jungle and hid in some tall grass. When the guard ordered the men to start the long trek back to camp with their five-gallon cans of water, no one missed Tenney, and he watched excitedly as the detail trudged off into the night.

After waiting in motionless silence for what seemed at least an hour, he started to stand up. At that instant, he felt a strong hand clamp down on his shoulder, and a cold panic flooded over him.

"I broke out in a sweat," he said. "My heart pounded like a triphammer, and nausea filled my throat."

"Don't worry," he heard a gruff voice say behind him. "I'm an American. I've been watching you for the past hour. I'm going to help you get some medical attention and some food. Come with me."

Tenney turned to see a massive, bearded man of about thirty, dressed in old U.S. Army fatigues and a ragged cap, staring back at him. Slowly, it dawned on Tenney that he was face-to-face with the first American guerrilla he'd ever encountered.

"My name's Ray," the man said.

Over the next hour or so, they walked a long way in silence—through a mango grove, a pineapple field, and a herd of wild carabao—until they came to a well-camouflaged bivouac area, where Ray opened his knapsack and took out two cans of Spam and a bottle of what looked like wine. It even tasted like wine, Tenney soon discovered.

A few minutes later, with a broad smile on his face, he stretched out on the grass and fell into a deep sleep.

For the next two weeks, Tenney traveled and fought with Ray's guerrilla band, participating in five skirmishes with the Japanese, all of them won handily by the guerrillas. One mission was a highly successful attack against an enemy convoy in which more than a dozen Japanese were killed and a large amount of crucial supplies seized—accomplishments that filled Tenney with fierce satisfaction.

But the guerrillas' successes brought swift and savage retribution from the Japanese against residents of a Filipino barrio, where Tenney witnessed atrocities that were almost too horrific to describe carried out against helpless civilians.

"As we approached the barrio, we heard women screaming and the sound of rifle fire," Tenney recalled. "We took cover at the top of a ridge and looked down at the village. We were aghast at what we saw."

Tied to the supporting legs of several nipa huts were young Filipino women whose clothes had been torn off. As the guerrillas watched, Japanese soldiers beat the women viciously with bamboo sticks loaded with sand and gravel until their bodies were covered with blood. Meanwhile, other soldiers shoved short lengths of bamboo containing fused explosive charges into the women's vaginas.

"Just as I was about to turn my face away," said Tenney, "I saw a few of the soldiers light the fuses. . . . Within twenty seconds, I heard the explosions. God, what a horrible sight! The women were blown apart, and their huts were reduced to rubble."

"That was for not answering our questions about guerrilla activities in your village," the loud voice of an interpreter announced. "Next time, we will eliminate the whole barrio."

The following night, each member of the five-man guerrilla band was given shelter in a separate hut in the village. At about 1 AM, Tenney awoke to find a bayonet piercing his leg and its owner standing over him, screaming curses in Japanese.

"The simple instructions my guerrilla friends had given me quickly came to mind," Tenney remembered. " 'If captured, show military respect. Give name, rank, and serial number. Say you are not and never were a guerrilla . . . you have no idea where any other Americans are . . . you have been in the jungle for months because your outfit got split up.' I quickly applied everything I was taught. I stood at rigid military attention . . . and said, 'My military number is 20-600-429.' "

Tenney was silenced with a blow across his face from the scabbard of a Japanese officer's sword, leaving a five-inch gash on his right cheek.

Thus began four days of unrelenting torture and interrogation in which Tenney was struck repeatedly in the face with rifle butts that broke his nose, knocked out several teeth, and brought blood gushing from a dozen wounds. He was hung on a stretching rack for a day and a half, first by his thumbs, then by his testicles. Frustrated when he still refused to admit anything, his tormentors shoved slivers of bamboo under his fingernails and set them on fire.

And through it all, the semiconscious prisoner continued to moan over and over again, "I don't know anything. If I did, I'd tell you. I don't know. I don't know."

Finally, they gave up. They threw him into the bed of a truck, drove him back to O'Donnell, and dumped him on the ground near the front gate. As the truck roared away in a cloud of dust, the hazy semblance of a thought formed in Tenney's tortured brain: *At least I'm alive. Not alive and well, but alive.*

* * *

On June 2, the slightly more than 7,000 surviving American prisoners at O'Donnell were told they would soon be moved to three recently opened prison camps near the Luzon town of Cabanatuan, located on the Pampanga River forty miles north of Fort Stotsenburg. O'Donnell's much larger Filipino population, however, would be left behind at the "Andersonville of the Pacific" for several more months, and thousands more would die or be killed before the camp was eventually shut down.

One of many O'Donnell survivors who were stunned by the level of Japanese brutality toward the Filipinos was Colonel Irvin Alexander, former quartermaster at Stotsenburg who later commanded an infantry regiment on Bataan. After the war, he recounted his experiences as a POW in a memoir entitled *Surviving Bataan and Beyond.*

"The object of Japan being to develop the Philippines into a vassal state, it was difficult to understand why the Japanese were so openly contemptuous, cruel, and arbitrary in their treatment of the Filipinos," Alexander wrote. "The Nips made no attempt to conceal that they considered Filipino soldiers to be the scum of the earth, unworthy of any respect or consideration."

One possible explanation may be that, unlike the Americans, who would be held as prisoners for the duration of the war, the captured Filipino soldiers would soon be released into the general population. With this in mind, the Japanese may have made a concerted effort to wipe out as many as possible of those who had actively taken up arms against them before these releases occurred.

Other American POWs also being sent to Cabanatuan at this time included former members of the Corregidor garrison, many of whom had been confined for almost three weeks after their surrender in a large enclosed area on Monkey Point known as the 92nd Garage. The area had originally been a seaplane base, but more recently it had been taken over by the 92nd Coast Artillery and used as a motor pool.

"Our holding pen consisted of two big hangars used as warehouses and a big concrete seaplane ramp some three acres in size and ringed with enemy .30-caliber machine guns," recalled Seaman First Class Paul Edward Perry, a former crewman of the sub tender *Canopus*, who was among 16,000 captives eventually confined at the 92nd Garage.

(Most of the high-ranking officers from Corregidor, including General Wainwright, fourteen other generals, and 106 colonels, were moved on June 9, 1942, to a separate prison camp for senior officers in Luzon's Tarlac Province. They would remain there until August 12, when they would be among the first American prisoners placed aboard prison ships and transported to Formosa, Japan, or Korea to serve as slave labor.)

Because the Corregidor garrison had been spared both the rigors of the Death March and the septic torment of O'Donnell, most prisoners from the Rock arrived at Cabanatuan in much better physical shape than those from Bataan. But overall conditions at the 92nd Garage were about as bad as those at O'Donnell—and possibly even worse in some respects. The most favorable difference was that the POWs at the 92nd Garage were held there for only about a third as long as those Americans held at O'Donnell. Consequently, far fewer died.

Immediately after the surrender, in the words of Marine PFC Karl King, "More than 11,000 walking wounded, sick and battle-weary men of Corregidor were herded like cattle into the site of the 92nd Garage, a flat area [shaped] like the bottom of a three-sided bowl [with] the fourth side . . . open to the water on the south shore." Heavily armed Japanese guards patrolled the upper rim of the "bowl" and showed no hesitancy about shooting to kill.

The destruction of all surface structures in the area by enemy bombs and shells had left it littered with wreckage and totally devoid of shade from the blistering tropical sun. From blankets and bits of debris, the more able-bodied prisoners constructed crude shelters to provide small amounts of shade, with the result resembling a vast shantytown.

"It took two days for the Japanese to provide food for the prisoners, [and] the meager rations consisted of two meals a day of a rice-barley mixture," King recalled. "Drinking water came from a single spigot near the entrance to the area, where a garage had once stood." Just as it was at O'Donnell, the prisoners had to wait in long lines to fill canteens or other containers.

With only open-air slit trenches to serve as latrines, black clouds of flies descended on the area, and dysentery, diarrhea, and other diseases quickly became rampant. One favorable difference from O'Donnell, however, was that POWs were allowed, under close guard, to bathe and wash their clothes in the seawater at the south end of the area. Groups of prisoners, watched by one or more Japanese guards, were also allowed to leave the area on various types of work and foraging details.

Marine PFC Silas "Mr. Tiger" Barnes was still nursing a festering chest wound from a Japanese bayonet when Corregidor's conquerors booted him out of the hospital and into the 92nd Garage on May 15. He'd managed to reach the hospital on the day the Rock fell by hiding aboard an abandoned Japanese landing barge for several hours, then slipping past another enemy patrol into the Navy Radio Tunnel.

"I was blank for a long time after I first got treatment for the wound," he recalled. "The first thing I saw when I woke up in the hospital was a bunch of dead guys being carried out."

After being herded and prodded into the 92nd, Barnes worried that he might be among the next batch of dead hauled away, but he had the good fortune to make contact with a Navy corpsman, who redressed his wound and "stuffed it full of sulfa drugs."

"After he bandaged it, he told me, 'Don't take this dressing off for any reason. You leave it on there till it rots off,'" Barnes recalled. "I did exactly as he told me, and I think that's the only reason I survived. It took three or four months for all the scar tissue to burn off, but there was no permanent damage to my heart or lung. I was lucky."

"I don't think I can stand this infernal place another day," former B-17 navigator Ed Whitcomb muttered to his friend, Marine Lieutenant William Harris. "We've got to figure a way to get out of here."

The pair had been confined in the 92nd Garage area for more

than two weeks, and since striking up a friendship they'd done little but talk about escape. Harris favored making a break at night by climbing a nearby ridge to reach the beach. But Whitcomb had seen enemy machine guns on that ridge, and he convinced Harris that their best chance was to slip away from a daytime work detail, hide until dark, then swim across the north channel of Manila Bay to Bataan.

"I've swum that route before, coming in the opposite direction," Whitcomb said. "It's only two or three miles. We can make it easily."

At about 2 PM on May 22, the two young officers joined about sixty other men on a firewood-gathering detail. As time passed, the men gradually scattered out over a wide area, picking up anything they could find of potential value along with the plentiful wood fragments that littered the island. The group was watched over by a single Japanese guard, and Whitcomb and Harris found it easy enough to slip away while the guard's attention was elsewhere.

"Over this way!" Harris directed in a loud whisper. "I know a place where we can take cover till dark."

Moments later, the two of them were crouching in a four-by-ten-foot underground room that had been dug weeks before by Harris and his fellow beach-defense Marines. In one corner of the pit, they found several bottles in which they stashed Filipino and American currency and a few other valuables.

When it was fully dark, they took off their shoes, socks, and shirts and lowered themselves into the water. There was no sign of life along the shoreline for as far as they could see in either direction.

"How're you doing?" Harris asked.

"Great," Whitcomb replied. "The way I feel, I could swim all night."

They did exactly that, through a thunderstorm that blew them dangerously off course and landed them back on Corregidor after hours of hard swimming, followed by a brush with what they feared were sharks but turned out to be only small fish.

As dawn broke over the bay, they stumbled onto a deserted stretch of the Bataan shore, dragged themselves into a clump of bushes, and fell into a deep sleep.

"When we awoke," Whitcomb would recall many years later, "the sun was low in the western sky. We'd slept almost the whole day, but at least for the time being, we were free!"

In his exuberance, he almost laughed at the irony of the situation. *First I escaped from Bataan to Corregidor*, he thought. *Now I've escaped from Corregidor right back to Bataan!*

Had Whitcomb and Harris waited a mere forty-eight hours longer, their escape efforts would have been too late. By May 24, the 92nd Garage area was virtually vacant. Most Corregidor prisoners had been loaded aboard a Japanese freighter, transported across the bay to Manila, and marched six miles along Dewey Boulevard to the old Spanish-built prison of Bilibid. There they would be held for three or four days before being marched to a railway station and packed into cattle cars for the ninety-mile trip to Cabanatuan.

The main camp at Cabanatuan was located on about 100 acres in a rich valley with a striking backdrop of the Sierra Madre mountains. It had once been the site of a U.S. Department of Agriculture station and had later become a training facility for Philippine Army conscripts. It was now surrounded by eight-foot barbed wire barriers, overlooked by guard towers with machine guns and spotlights. Yet it appeared to many arriving Americans as a cleaner, more civilized place than O'Donnell—"less malignant," as historian Gerald Astor described it.

First impressions can be deceiving, however. After a few days, most of the Americans who spent time in both O'Donnell and Cabanatuan found it difficult to detect any major differences between the two.

"The barracks were in wretched condition when the inmates moved in," said Astor. "[R]oofs leaked, plumbing facilities and electricity did not exist, the water supply was inadequate, and no provision had been made for the treatment of the sick and injured. . . . Deaths in the first months at Cabanatuan equaled those at O'Donnell."

According to Captain Manny Lawton of the 31st Infantry, finding the hospital at Cabanatuan was easy. "I could have found it by scent," he recalled. "As I approached the fence, the odors of death and human waste pervaded the air. . . . Like its counterpart at O'Donnell, it housed unrecognizable, unwashed skeletons of formerly proud soldiers awaiting death." Lawton estimated that the average number of deaths per day during the first weeks at Cabanatuan held steady at twenty-five to thirty.

"The hospital compound was more of an isolation area than a place of treatment and cure," Lawton said. "Food and drugs were the solution to most of the health problems [but] both were in extremely short supply. Of the more than 2,500 who died at Cabanatuan from June to November, most could have survived at U.S. Army or Navy hospitals."

At Cabanatuan, Captain John Coleman was again asked by his friend and former CO, Colonel Bill Maverick, to take charge of one of the barracks where about ninety men were quartered. But in this case, the barracks housed a sick bay, and Coleman was, in his own words, "stunned beyond description" when he reached the building and looked inside.

"[The men were] lying on the ground in the dirt, naked and unconscious. They were skin and bones. . . . Their hair and beards were a tangled mess, soiled by their own excretion. Their mouths hung open, and their eyes were half closed. They all looked like dead men."

Coleman called his assignment "the worst detail I had ever been asked to serve on," and he went back to talk to Maverick about the men's condition and the possibility of getting them food and treatment.

"He knew they were beyond help," Coleman said. "He'd tried to get help from the Japanese, but they wouldn't help in any way. All of the ninety men were dead within four days."

Even for relatively healthy POWs, the problem of obtaining water was critical. "I would appoint a detail from our barracks to take ten canteens and stand in line at the water faucet until they could fill them," Coleman recalled. "Sometimes it would take five or six hours to get the water. . . . Most of the time, it would be eleven or twelve o'clock at night before they could get back."

Like many of his former comrades in arms, Sergeant Cletis Overton of the 27th Bomb Group realized soon after reaching Cabanatuan that he had a blossoming case of potentially fatal dysentery.

"Flies and their eggs were everywhere, and so was dysentery, but up to this point, I'd managed to keep from getting it," Overton recalled some sixty-eight years later. "I knew it could be a death sentence if it got worse, but I got lucky."

One day, as Overton was walking outside his barracks, he spotted something on the ground under the building—something that didn't seem to belong there. "As I got closer, I could tell it was little pills of some kind, so I crawled under the building and started picking them up. When I finished, I had twenty-eight sulfathiazole tablets in my hands. It was almost too good to be true because sulfathiazole was a sure cure for dysentery."

After taking four of the tablets daily for several days, Overton's dysentery symptoms vanished. "I never found out whose pills they were or how they'd gotten there," he said. "Maybe they'd been stashed there by a corpsman, or maybe somebody had spilled them and they'd fallen through the cracks in the floor, but I never felt an ounce of guilt about keeping them. They were like a gift from God. They probably saved my life."

Thousands of other Cabanatuan prisoners didn't share Overton's good fortune, as the terse entries in a diary kept by Colonel Calvin G. Jackson, a young Army doctor from Kenton, Ohio, clearly reveal. He frequently closed his entries with the number of deaths recorded that day. A few examples:

> June 11, 1942—[M]y building is full of patients, all in bad condition. Guess there is no surgical department as we have nothing to work with. . . . Water still shut off. Five hundred new patients came in (1,500 in hospital area). The barracks are crowded, hideous mess! Their looks are unbelievable and sickening. These young men look like old, old men. Swollen faces, hands, legs. Little clothing, rags. One boy fell dead in the road in front of the hospital. . . . New guards came, very strict. Had to get rid of our beds and sleep on floor. Nip orders. They are putting more barbed wire around us . . . 25 deaths today.
>
> June 26, 1942—6 Americans and 2 Filipinos were caught

> outside barbed wire fence. They were beaten and tied to a post all day with no food or water. . . . They were then marched through our hospital area. There were 16 Jap soldiers with rifles and three with shovels behind them. They were marched through a fence to a rice paddy with a big ant hill in it. One grave was already dug. There was water in the grave. . . . They were blindfolded. Four Japs in firing squad. Two to aim at head and two to aim at neck. . . . Five were shot in other camp for trying to escape. All members had been warned what would happen if they tried to escape. 19 [starvation/disease-related] deaths today.
>
> June 28, 1942—More diphtheria and malaria coming in. Still no medicine. . . . Used last of my toothpaste, so I'll be brushing with toilet soap. It isn't too bad. 25 deaths.
>
> July 19, 1942—Rained hard during night. . . . Coolish, too. Pity patients with no clothes or blankets. . . . Latrines are overflowing. I hope all maggots are drowned . . . 36 deaths.

The Japanese administrators at Cabanatuan were well organized, highly efficient, and totally devoid of mercy, as demonstrated by their method of combating escape attempts by assigning all prisoners to "blood-brother" groups of ten men each.

Under the direction of the camp commander, Lieutenant Colonel Masao Mori, whom the prisoners nicknamed "Blood," the guards had refined and perfected the numbering system originated at O'Donnell, and it worked simply and effectively: Every prisoner was given a number, and each was assigned to a specific ten-man "shooting squad."

At any hour of the day or night, Japanese guards could hold a "tenko" or roll call in which all ten-man groups were required to fall out for inspection. If any member of a group was found to be missing, the other nine faced immediate execution—in the most painful and prolonged manner possible. If the culprit himself were caught, his punishment usually involved being tied to a post, beaten with ropes, clubs, and rifle butts, jabbed with bayonets, and otherwise tortured for several days, then made to dig his own grave before being shot or beheaded while his fellow prisoners were forced to watch.

"A lieutenant colonel and a Navy lieutenant . . . tried to escape one night," recalled Captain Coleman. "They were caught trying to get under the barbed wire fence. . . . The Jap guards would throw them against the ground and whip them with ropes until they got up. . . . The next morning, they were tied to the gatepost at the entrance of the compound. Every hour or so, a guard would come by and hit them with a board that looked to be a two-by-two. The Navy lieutenant had his left eyeball dangling from its socket down on his cheek. Their heads were bloody all over."

With their hands bound behind them, the two men were tied to the back end of a truck by ropes around their necks and made to run behind it down the road toward the burial ground, Coleman said. When one of the men fell, the truck would stop long enough for him to be pulled back to his feet; then it would surge forward again. Finally, when the lieutenant colonel was unable to stand, a Japanese officer drew his sword and beheaded him.

"They threw his head and body into the back of the truck and drove on out of sight," Coleman said. "In about thirty minutes, we heard a shot fired . . . [and] later we heard dogs fighting where we thought they had buried the two officers."

As the weeks dragged by, the situation at Cabanatuan moderated somewhat. A major catalyst for this positive change was a decision by the Japanese to put Marine Lieutenant Colonel Curtis T. Beecher, a highly competent combat veteran of World War I, in charge of the inmate population. Within a matter of days, far-reaching changes were instituted.

As historians Michael and Elizabeth Norman observed: "He ordered the sprawling camp cleaned up, organized the men, lobbied his Japanese overseers for more medicine, supplies, and food, and the monthly death rate dropped from several hundred to a handful. In 1943, the camp census averaged between 3,000 and 4,000 men. And everyone, including the officers, worked."

In this atmosphere, many prisoners who had lost all interest in personal hygiene and appearance began to regain it. "Most of us from Bataan hadn't shaved or had a haircut since before the surrender," said Sergeant Clem Kathman of the 200th Coast Artillery. "But as soon as a pair of clippers became available, I had my first haircut and shave. After that, we kept our heads and faces clipped as close as possible. It was easier to keep clean and more hygienic."

Beginning on September 5, 1942, when the first forced labor group of 500 Americans embarked from Manila aboard the Japanese freighter *Nagaru Maru*, Cabanatuan began serving as a major staging point for large groups of POWs being shipped to Japan and Formosa to work in Japanese heavy industry. Although this was a blatant violation of international law, one result was a gradual but steady decline in the camp's inmate population.

An active underground smuggling operation, organized by two American women—widows of soldiers who had died at Cabanatuan—began bribing guards to help them spirit sizable quantities of food, medicine, and money into the camp. These supplies markedly diminished the daily death toll and improved the overall level of health among the POWs. The mere introduction of modest amounts of protein into inmate diets could produce striking health improvements within as little as two or three days.

Beginning in December 1942, the Japanese initiated a Cabanatuan farming program on 300 acres of arable land, where up to 2,000 prisoners cultivated such crops as rice, corn, beans, cucumbers, radishes, eggplant, carrots, and okra. Although forbidden to bring seeds back to camp, many prisoners did so anyway to grow their own small gardens, thus adding further to the available food supply.

"Many of the more able-bodied men were assigned to farm work," recalled Sergeant Clem Kathman, "and we produced some tremendous crops. Okra plants grew to more than six feet tall with pods ten to twelve inches long, and cucumbers grew up to eighteen inches. After the farm started producing, more and more fresh veggies started showing up in the men's mess kits."

Shortly before Christmas 1942, officials of the International Red Cross were finally admitted to the camp, and the first Red Cross packages were distributed to the prisoners. They contained such delicacies as Spam, potted meat, corned beef, chocolate bars, jam, cheese, coffee, dried milk, and raisins.

"Coming at Christmas like they did, the Red Cross boxes were a psychological boost for all the prisoners," said Kathman. "With the aid of the Red Cross food, the death rate started to drop pretty drastically."

January 18, 1943, was a red-letter day for the POWs at Cabanatuan. It was the first twenty-four-hour period since the opening of the camp seven months earlier in which not a single American prisoner died.

"We had a big celebration," recalled Sergeant Forrest Knox of the 192nd Tank Battalion. "We'd finally broken it. [The death rate] was down to what you'd consider a standstill. Now the medics would fight for those that were sick."

After losing himself for two and a half months among the staff of Hospital No. 1 on Bataan—thereby miraculously avoiding both the Death March and the deadliest periods of captivity at O'Donnell and Cabanatuan—the long-delayed moment of reckoning finally arrived for Captain Ralph Hibbs on June 24, 1942.

A convoy of Japanese trucks appeared at the Bataan hospital that morning, and all patients were loaded aboard them for the trip into Manila. Hibbs and the four former 31st Infantry medics who had remained with him at the hospital after slipping out of the ranks of the Death March also became passengers on the trucks. Their destination was the old stone-walled prison of Bilibid, which had housed the worst civilian criminals in the Philippines for more than sixty years before it had fallen into disuse in the 1930s.

It was a singularly unappealing destination, yet to some degree, Hibbs's phenomenal luck was still holding—particularly in comparison to that of Colonel James Duckworth, the Hospital No. 1 commander, and his cadre of physicians, surgeons, and medics. Instead of accompanying their patients to Bilibid, Duckworth and his entire staff would be shipped the following day to the hell hole of O'Donnell, where they would try, with virtually no medicine or medical equipment, to stem the horrendous death toll there.

Despite its age and run-down condition, Bilibid was at least a traditional prison with such amenities as flush toilets, an ample supply of fresh water, some minimal furnishings, windows, and solid walls and floors while O'Donnell and Cabanatuan had none of these. It was also within the heart of the city of Manila, where potential contact with and assistance from the outside world was close at hand, rather than in the remote wasteland of central Luzon.

Although many uncertainties loomed ahead, Hibbs was actually glad to be leaving Bataan at long last. As he would later express it, "This disease-ridden, infested, smelly piece of mountainous jungle and burial ground had been a place of suffering, starvation, and fear of unlimited proportions. The bleak hopelessness was well left behind." The future, he reasoned, would simply have to take care of itself.

Always observant and sharp-witted, Hibbs noticed early on that the Japanese had made no effort to conduct an accurate count of the American prisoners boarding the trucks. When the convoy reached a small barrio near the midway point of the eighty-mile trip, Hibbs had no difficulty getting off his truck, filling his canteen from a spigot at an artesian well, and wandering more or less freely about the immediate area.

When two Filipinos approached him and offered him food, he accepted it gratefully but thought nothing of it. Moments later, however, with no guards in sight, the pair motioned for him to follow them behind a building, where one of them whispered excitedly: "Come with us, and we'll help you escape into the hills."

Sorely tempted, Hibbs weighed the offer for a long moment with his heart pounding in his ears. Then he shook his head, turned resolutely back toward the truck, and climbed aboard, checking to see that all the men around him had received a drink of water.

Over the months and years ahead, when he felt the pangs of slow starvation gnawing at his gut, saw his legs and ankles swell with edema and beriberi, and felt his tongue and mouth turn raw and cracked with pellagra, he would have many opportunities to reflect on his decision.

Bilibid prison covered a seventeen-acre quadrangle on the north bank of the Pasig River in central Manila. Its stone, stucco, and concrete design was circular with long cell blocks and dormitories extending outward from a central rotunda like spokes on a wheel.

One section of the compound was used as temporary housing for groups of prisoners en route from one forced labor project in the Philippines to another, so there was a more or less continuous stream of arriving and departing POWs. Another, smaller section contained maximum security cells for hardcase prisoners with disciplinary problems, and a third section served as offices and quarters for the guards.

But approximately half of the prison served as the largest POW hospital in the archipelago, and in this case—unlike the so-called hospitals at O'Donnell and Cabanatuan—it was a place where actual healing occurred, rather than a mortuary-in-waiting. It still lacked many of the components that most hospitals considered necessities, but its patients had a far better chance of leaving it alive than those in any other POW medical facility in the islands.

It hadn't always been that way. When the Bilibid hospital was opened shortly after the surrender, it was staffed by a group of U.S. Army doctors who had almost nothing to work with, and patients were left to languish and die in the same Zero Ward environment found in the outlying prison camps.

But in early July 1942, a large U.S. Navy medical team—including twenty-six physicians and surgeons, eleven dentists, and 165 other skilled personnel—was brought in by the Japanese, and a far-reaching series of positive changes began. The team was headed by Commander Lea B. "Pappy" Sartin, who described what he inherited at Bilibid as "a filthy, degrading hell hole" and who launched a massive repair and cleanup program.

Sartin's second in command and chief of surgery was Lieutenant Commander Thomas Hayes, a career officer from Virginia's Tidewater region who had served as chief surgeon to the Fourth Marines on Corregidor. When the Rock fell, he had his staff gather up every available medicine bottle, roll of bandages, and surgical instrument they could carry, and these salvaged supplies enabled the Bilibid hospital to function as a true medical center.

Hayes's first entry in his notebook upon arriving at Bilibid was anything but encouraging, however. "A walk thru the length of the wards, each holding about eighty cadaverous animals that once were men, is one of the most desperate, heartrending sights conceivable."

The Navy medics set up wards, treatment rooms, and an operating room, as well as living quarters for the staff, and a percentage of those "cadaverous animals" began showing signs of recovery. The Japanese immediately took notice and began depositing the spent and broken relics of dozens of work details at Bilidid—not always to die as in the past, but sometimes with the idea that the Navy medical team could somehow restore the POWs' ability to perform additional man-killing labor.

Captain Ralph Hibbs had been at Bilibid only a few days when four Japanese trucks arrived, loaded with remnants of one especially brutal work detail. Suffering from multiple diseases himself, Hibbs was nonetheless stunned at their condition as he helped them unload.

"Most were beaten, emaciated, and as sick a group of men as I had ever seen," he recalled. "Originally, there had been about 125 Americans who had gone down to Batangas [Province] to work on roads. Less than thirty survived the three-month ordeal. . . . A real but unsuccessful effort was made to help the men [but] most of the thirty . . . never did recover—they just faded away."

When Hibbs received a message that a patient in the dysentery ward wanted to see him, he was surprised to find his friend, Lieutenant George McClellan, a onetime P-40 pilot and one of the Whiffenpoof Boys, whom Hibbs hadn't seen since the party at the Manila Hotel on the night of December 7.

"He would drift in and out of consciousness and stare at me blankly," said Hibbs. I scrounged a few vitamin and morphine tablets from my Navy pals and stuck them in his mouth. . . . I helped him with his meals, begging him to swallow."

Despite all these efforts, McClellan lasted only three or four days. "He went rapidly downhill and died in my arms," Hibbs said. "And now there were only three Whiffenpoof Boys."

McClellan was one of many patients who were too far gone when they reached Bilibid for even the dedicated Navy medical team to save.

Not long after McClellan's death, Hibbs had a much more uplifting encounter with Rev. Theodore Butienbruch, a Catholic priest whom he remembered affectionately from prewar days as "Father Ted." What Butienbruch told him made Hibbs's heart leap with excitement.

"Pilar asked me to come and visit you," the priest whispered. "In January, she had heard you were killed. She's been cycling outside the north wall of the prison every day between 2 and 2:30 PM in hopes of seeing you."

Hibbs was struck almost speechless when he realized that the courageous Filipina beauty whom he hadn't seen since the previous December—and often doubted that he'd ever see again—had been riding her bike just outside the window of his third floor quarters.

Then the priest handed him a note from Pilar along with a wad of Japanese occupation currency. "I'm anxious to see you," the note read, "so we can establish contact and I can send you money, food, and medicine. Love, Petie."

The next afternoon, Hibbs waited nervously, pacing back and forth in front of his window as 2 PM arrived. He thought about how shabby he must look. He was forty pounds lighter than the last time Pilar had seen him, and his clothes consisted of a dirty sleeveless shirt and ragged khaki shorts.

I must be the most unromantic figure on earth, he thought grimly.

A lengthy procession of strangers passed on bicycles before he saw Pilar, but he recognized her instantly. She was only about 100 feet away, pedaling parallel to the prison wall and wearing a large floppy hat. At the next corner, she turned and disappeared without any gesture of recognition or even a glance toward him. But fifteen minutes later, she rode by a second time, following the same route, and he soon spotted her again, standing on the porch of a house a half-block away with several other young women. He saw her clearly, and he knew that she could see him, too, because she made short, waving gestures in his direction.

"I felt warm inside," he said, "and my morale soared. Then she was gone."

Later, as he stared out the window toward where he'd last seen her, aftershocks of worry and fear pounded him like physical blows.

My God, what a terrible risk she's taking, getting mixed up in this mess! he thought. *My God, how brave she is!*

11

Hell Ships—Voyages to Oblivion

Soon after the Japanese victory on Bataan, officials at the Imperial War Ministry in Tokyo met to consider how to turn what initially appeared to be a huge liability into an economic asset.

The Japanese military was now the custodian of more than 190,000 American and Allied prisoners captured during its march across the southwestern Pacific. What to do with those prisoners was a problem of vast proportions because, even confined to the most primitive prison compounds and surviving on the barest subsistence rations, the POWs represented a massive drain on Japan's thinly stretched resources.

As demonstrated by their callous brutality, many Japanese soldiers held little feeling beyond disdain for American POWs. They believed the prisoners had dishonored themselves by surrendering in the first place and were thus unworthy of compassion. They were viewed merely as a troublesome nuisance to be stamped out whenever possible in such extermination exercises as the Death March and the death camps.

But beginning in the fall of 1942, cooler, more opportunistic heads prevailed in Tokyo, where War Minister Hideki Tojo and his bureaucrats came up with a practical way to make the POWs pay dividends for Nippon. They realized that, rather than useless chattel, their American captives actually represented a major economic asset in the form of forced labor, not only for the Imperial Army but for Japan's entire industrial apparatus.

Since a few days after their surrender, relatively healthy American POWs had been pressed into service on a variety of work details in the Philippines. But with virtually all able-bodied Japanese males now serving in the armed forces, the nation was increasingly desperate for workers to fill quotas in heavy industrial and agricultural production all across Japan's expanding empire. Infusions of new manpower to fill jobs in factories, foundries, mines, steel mills, smelters, shipyards, railroad freight terminals, heavy construction, rice plantations, produce farms, and other enterprises, both in Japan proper and Formosa, Korea, and Manchuria, were vital to sustain the Japanese economy.

Since Japan had never ratified the Geneva Convention accords, the War Ministry decided, her use of POWs as industrial and agricultural slaves was unrestricted. To facilitate this decision, more than 500 labor camps were set up in Japan proper and her captive territories, and their commanders were ordered by Tojo not to allow the prisoners "to remain idle for even a single day."

In the Philippines, Camp Cabanatuan was designated as the central staging point for groups of prisoners bound for a life of industrial servitude. Bilibid prison in Manila would provide the project's primary feeder hospital, charged with getting debilitated, diseased POWs sufficiently back on their feet to be loaded aboard ships and sent north and west as laborers for Japan. A percentage would undoubtedly die along the way, but those who did wouldn't have been productive workers anyway.

Cabanatuan also became one of the first camps to specialize in producing farm crops to feed Japanese troops on Luzon. But the largest agricultural project in the Philippines was to be located at the Davao Penal Colony (DAPECOL for short), a former Philippine federal prison on the archipelago's large southernmost island of Mindanao.

The first group of 1,000 Americans to be interned at Davao arrived on October 22, 1942, and was made up entirely of survivors of the Mindanao Force who had been confined to smaller camps on the island for about five months. Composed mainly of three Philippine Army infantry divisions led by American officers, the Mindanao Force had been commanded by Brigadier General William F. Sharp, who had been forced to surrender in early May along with General Wainwright's garrison at Corregidor.

A second group of 1,000 Americans reached Davao on November 6, after traveling from Cabanatuan to Bilibid prison in Manila by boxcar, then from Manila to Mindanao aboard a Japanese troopship, and finally by truck to DAPECOL.

"The group that arrived ahead of us were in much better shape than we were," recalled Sergeant Cletis Overton, a member of that second group. "The Japanese had let them keep their personal items, fed them pretty well, and treated them somewhat humanely. Most were still of normal weight, and they couldn't believe what they saw coming into Davao when we got there. We were one sorry-looking bunch."

When he reached Davao, Overton was suffering from scurvy, a disease caused by a lack of vitamin C in which the skin inside the mouth peels off and many victims lose their teeth. Meanwhile, the "wet" beriberi that Overton had endured for weeks abruptly transformed into the "dry" variety. The swelling in his feet and legs subsided, only to be replaced by a fierce, bone-deep burning in his feet and toes, which continues to affect him nearly seventy years later.

To his captors, the diseases didn't matter. Overton was sent into the fields with the rest of the prisoners, all of whom had their shoes confiscated by the Japanese—yet another effort to prevent escapes. In addition, the prison compound was surrounded by a massive barbed wire enclosure, and beyond the wire were miles of swamps and impenetrable jungle. The Japanese considered DAPECOL virtually escape-proof, but American determination and ingenuity would eventually prove them wrong.

The area under cultivation covered 100,000 acres (1,000 hectares), about two-thirds of which was planted in rice. The rest produced vast quantities of black beans, Chinese cabbage, hot peppers, okra, onions, pumpkins, radishes, and other vegetables. The POWs had frequent opportunities to steal small quantities of food to supplement their regular rations.

Overton would spend the rest of his confinement at Davao wading barefooted through muddy fields and rice paddies and enduring frequent and painful beatings by Japanese guards. Americans attempting to escape the penal colony were summarily beheaded, and their severed heads displayed as a warning to other prisoners.

"One morning, all POWs in the camp were called outside and

ordered to sit on a large concrete slab," recalled Overton's 27th Bomb Group buddy, Sergeant J. S. Gray. "We sat there a long time, until our legs were blistered by the sun. Finally a Jap officer came out leading three soldiers carrying long poles. On top of each pole was the head of an American POW, and the officer announced that they'd been caught trying to escape. The Japs turned it into a party and parade that lasted for hours, while a lot of the prisoners got sick and threw up. I've never seen a more horrible sight."

Nevertheless, Gray, Overton, and the other men selected to remain at Davao as farm laborers were more fortunate, at least for the time being, than those immediately assigned to industrial work groups bound for Japan. The food rations at Davao were ample, compared to those at O'Donnell and Cabanatuan, although they still consisted mostly of rice, with small amounts of fish and sometimes carabao meat mixed in. Lemons grew plentifully in the area, and the Japanese allowed Overton to pick and eat a few occasionally, which helped relieve his scurvy.

"There was even some medicine available," Overton recalled, "and although the latrines were still open pits, they were enclosed and had good seats, and there was plenty of water from shallow wells for drinking and bathing. The Japs actually issued me a toothbrush and some bad-tasting tooth powder, and I was able to brush my teeth for the first time since I was captured."

For men forced aboard the "hell ships," however—and Gray's and Overton's turns would eventually come—such small amenities would quickly become forgotten parts of another world.

Overton and Gray had been at Davao only a few weeks when their group of POWs was approached by a young Japanese officer carrying a large American flag.

"This flag must be destroyed," the officer said in perfect English, "but as a courtesy, I want to give you the opportunity to destroy it properly, as your country's rules specify."

When the officer left, the Americans took the flag back to their barracks, where they unfolded it and ran their fingers over it reverently. When it was spread out, it measured about four feet by six feet.

"Oh, man," somebody said. "Why can't we just keep it?"

But most of the men realized that the flag was too big to keep hidden and that there would be serious repercussions if they should be caught with it. After a lengthy discussion, one man offered a suggestion. "Why can't we cut out the forty-eight stars and keep them? We can divide them up, so that forty-eight guys will have just one star apiece to take care of."

At first, Gray was dubious about the whole idea. "We knew if we ever got caught hiding those stars, we might all be killed by the Japanese," he recalled many years later. "But dividing them up so that each man just had one star to take care of did seem to make the most sense. So one POW who had an old hacksaw blade cut them apart and forty-eight guys took one star apiece. They hid them in their G-strings or in their mess kits, sometimes with food on top, and every time we moved to some other camp, we had to divide them up all over again. I still don't know how we did it, but we carried those stars until August 18, 1945, when we found out the war was over."

They would carry them all the way to Toyama, Japan, where they would end the war as slave laborers in a steel mill.

On that day of celebration, using material from parachutes dropped by American B-29s and a needle made from a piece of barbed wire, the POWs reassembled the stars on a new Old Glory and hoisted it above their abandoned camp.

Today, those stars and their flag are proudly displayed at the National Museum of the Pacific War in Fredericksburg, Texas.

Falling under General Sharp's command at the time of his surrender were several hundred former Army Air Corps personnel. Although they weren't technically part of the Mindanao Force, they'd taken refuge at Del Monte Field on Mindanao shortly after the debacles at Clark and Nichols Fields in early December 1941 had left them without functioning bases on Luzon. The original plan had been to send the air personnel on to Australia at the earliest opportunity, but that opportunity had never come.

Most of General Sharp's forces obeyed the surrender order transmitted by General Wainwright on May 10, after Colonel Jesse

Traywick, a personal emissary from Wainwright, was flown to Mindanao by the Japanese to explain that all U.S. forces in the Philippines were included in the surrender. But word was slow in reaching some isolated units in hidden mountain camps, including elements of Brigadier General Guy O. Fort's 81st Philippine Division, and the surrender wasn't fully consummated until the end of May.

(A short time later, in retaliation for the fact that many 81st Division troops melted into the mountains to carry on guerrilla warfare after the surrender, General Fort was executed by the Japanese.)

Among the displaced air personnel left stranded on Mindanao was fifteen-year-old PFC Joe Alexander (Trejo) of the 440th Ordnance Aviation Squadron—later officially confirmed as the youngest person ever to serve in the U.S. Army Air Corps. Now, therefore, Alexander also had the dubious distinction of being the youngest American POW in the Philippines.

"There were Japanese troops all over Mindanao, but we weren't in any real danger at the time we got the surrender order," Alexander recalled, "and the Japs didn't treat us that bad at first. They split us up into groups and took us to various small camps. There weren't any barbed-wire fences, and they fed us pretty well. I'd say they were rough but not mean. We weren't mistreated until later, but then they really made up for it."

Alexander never saw the inside of DAPECOL. After about three months in one of the small temporary camps, he and 500 of his fellow prisoners were told they were about to be shipped to Japan. They had no idea what they'd be expected to do there once they arrived, but the prospect of the voyage touched off panic in young Joe's heart.

"I was so scared that I broke down," he recalled. "The thought of being taken into the heart of an enemy country just terrified me and a lot of other guys, too. We didn't know what the hell was going to happen to us. We thought we might never see America again."

The first leg of the men's voyage was to Bilibid prison, where they were quartered for a week before being marched to Pier 7 on the Manila waterfront and loaded aboard a decrepit vessel named the *Toro Maru*. That was when the hell began.

"From that moment on, they treated us like animals," Alexander said. "They herded 1,100 of us aboard ship like a bunch of cattle and then packed us into the hold so tightly that nobody could sit or lie down. There was hardly even standing room. We were literally like sardines in there. The only toilet facilities were a couple of five-gallon buckets that kept getting turned over in the chaos as guys tried to move around. The stench was overpowering, and it was like there was no air to breathe because the Japs refused to open the hatches. It was unbearably hot. I know it had to have gotten up to at least 120 degrees in that hold."

The trip to Japan would take forty-five days, and conditions for Alexander and subsequent fellow travelers aboard the hell ships would only get worse—infinitely worse.

Ironically, there was nothing particularly hellish about the voyage made by Marine PFCs Karl King and Ike Williams in September 1942 aboard a rusty Japanese freighter named the *Lima Maru*. Even King and Williams freely admitted as much.

"I believe the *Lima Maru* was among the first Jap freighters used to transport POWs out of the Philippines," King would write many years later. "This opinion was based on the knowledge that the American officers on board were all colonels and generals. . . . [T]his voyage . . . was like a tourist trip on an ocean cruise liner compared to the ill-fated 'hell ships' that followed."

Just as they had in various prison camps in the Philippines, the POWs continued to get their daily ration of rice balls and soup, and on the fourth day out the guards opened the hatches and allowed half the men at a time to go on deck. The ship's crew had rigged an open structure on the leeward side of the ship that served as a sanitary latrine, and a place was also provided where prisoners could have saltwater baths.

"We were even allowed to fill our canteens with fresh water," said King. "The on-deck privileges occurred nearly every day and made the nights more bearable below decks. The Jap troops were housed somewhere aft of the superstructure. I think the senior American officers occupied cabins below decks."

On November 26, Thanksgiving Day, the POWs from the Philippines—286 of the 300 who had begun the trip survived to finish it—arrived in Yokohama, Japan. They were marched through an icy fog to a dismal gray building framed by barbed wire. Through cracks in the exterior wall of the warehouselike structure, the men could see the gray light from outside. There were no windows.

For King and Williams, this was where their version of hell—two long years of it—would begin.

Even during their first year or so, the hell ship voyages usually represented long days of misery and torment for American POWs, and there were inevitable fatalities from disease, starvation, stress, and brutality, resulting in numerous burials at sea. Yet the death toll was markedly lower than those of the Death March, O'Donnell, and Cabanatuan—Joe Alexander estimated that only about thirty of his 1,100 shipmates died en route to Japan—and the risk of POWs being killed by air raids or undersea torpedo attacks by their own comrades was slight at first.

But beginning with the Battle of the Coral Sea in early May 1942, where U.S. Navy forces foiled an attempted Japanese invasion of Australia, thereby halting enemy territorial expansion for the first time in the war, the balance of power in the Pacific began a dramatic shift. After the decisive Battle of Midway a month later, in which four enemy carriers were sunk, the Japanese fleet basically went into defensive posture, and American naval and air forces increasingly assumed the role of aggressors. On August 7, 1942, the First Marine Division landed on Guadalcanal in the Solomon Islands, and from that point on, the Americans were on the offensive permanently, on both land and sea.

Captain John Coleman, formerly of the 27th Materiel Squadron and the Air Corps Infantry, was actually encouraged when he received word in early November 1942 that he and 1,500 other American prisoners at Cabanatuan would be among the first large POW contingents to be shipped to Japan.

"I thought surely we would get better treatment and more food if we were in the Japanese homeland," Coleman recalled. "I didn't believe that the Japanese people would sanction the kind of treatment we were being subjected to if they knew about it."

As preparations for the voyage began, Coleman noticed several signs that supported his optimism. He and the other prisoners were assembled at a ballpark, where each of them was issued a new blue-denim jumper and trousers to replace the rags and loincloths they were wearing. Then, on the morning of November 6, the POWs traveled by rail to Manila, where a Filipino band surreptitiously played "God Bless America" as they marched to Pier 7. ("The band leader could have been executed for this if the Japanese had known what he was playing," Coleman noted.)

The ship awaiting the Americans was the first indication that everything wasn't so rosy, after all. It was called the *Nagato Maru*, and it had been sold to Japan as scrap by the United States in 1935. Its most recent passengers had been horses, as Coleman, a native Texan, could tell by the smell in the hold. It was cramped, stuffy, and unbearably hot. As an added cause for worry, the Japanese promptly took away all the prisoners' life belts—and Coleman had noticed that the ship carried exactly four lifeboats for the 3,000 passengers and crew.

Once under way, however, conditions aboard the *Nagato Maru* weren't all that bad. At 10 AM, the prisoners were served a breakfast of rice and soybean soup, followed by a lunch of rice and fish at 3 PM and another small meal later. Groups of sixty men were allowed on deck at one time, and six of them at a time were permitted to smoke. Sometimes the Japanese guards would even supply a few cigarettes to the POWs. An air funnel was installed to help combat the heat and seasickness in the hold.

One evening midway through the voyage, as Coleman was taking the empty rice buckets from dinner back to the galley, he was jarred by a loud explosion, which touched off frantic activity among the crew as guards tried to hurry the POWs back belowdecks. The sound was identified by the guards as an exploding torpedo from a U.S. submarine, and Coleman heard depth charges being dropped by the lone destroyer accompanying the twelve-ship convoy. It took about two hours for conditions to return to normal.

On November 25, after several Americans had died in the hold and been buried at sea, but without further surprises from the U.S. Navy, the *Nagato Maru* docked at Moji, Japan, where each POW received a small box of food containing cheese, a small fish, pickled radishes, a slice of orange, a roll of kelp, and, of course, some rice.

"It looks as if we're going to be fed well during our stay in Japan," Coleman later remembered telling himself.

Similar thoughts crossed the mind of PFC Joe Alexander when he disembarked from the *Toro Maru* after forty-five days at sea and got his first look at the Japanese seaport city of Kawasaki.

"They hadn't fed us anything but hardtack during the whole voyage," recalled the youngest American POW, "but when they put us on a train to take us to our camp, they gave each of us a really nice box lunch, and we all thought, 'Man, we've got it made!' Turned out it was the last decent meal we had in Japan."

Assigned to jobs in a steel mill that produced structural components for ships, Alexander and 500 fellow prisoners were forced to work from dawn to dusk seven days a week. Regardless of a prisoner's physical condition, there was no such thing as "sick time." In fact, a prisoner's only reward for fulfilling his quota of work was to have more work piled on him.

"Our only meal each day was a cup of maize—the stuff we use for chicken feed in the States," Alexander recalled. "We marched to work before daylight, and we'd pick up orange peels or whatever else we could find on the streets that was remotely edible. We'd scrounge in trash cans along the way, but if they caught us doing it, they'd beat the hell out of us for 'stealing.'

"Many times, at the end of a long day, the guards would make us stand at attention all night outside in the cold, and they'd threaten to kill us because of something one of us had said or done. Usually, we had no idea what it was. Then, in the morning, they'd march us to work with nothing to eat. This would go on for two or three days before they'd feed us or let us rest."

Thus, even in those earliest days of industrial slavery, any hopeful expectations by the POWs inevitably gave way to bitter reality. But Americans who made hell ship voyages to Japan only a few months later—and were fortunate enough to reach their destinations alive—would gladly have traded places with Alexander, Coleman, and their shipmates. At least those early voyagers didn't have to dodge American bombs, torpedoes, and .50-caliber machine gun bullets along the way.

By February 1943, Guadalcanal was finally secured by U.S. forces, and America's Pacific offensive turned its attention to New Georgia, New Britain, New Guinea, and other targets.

In early 1944, with U.S. air and naval superiority in the Pacific growing more apparent by the hour, swarms of American submarines converged on the most traveled shipping lanes connecting the Philippines, Japan, and Formosa. Flocks of U.S. dive-bombers from the aircraft carriers of Admiral William F. Halsey's Third Fleet were also appearing with increased regularity. By that July, it was clear that General MacArthur would soon make good on his promise to return to the Philippines, and this realization sent the Japanese high command into a frenzy of activity where the American prisoners still remaining in the archipelago were concerned.

"In a desperate effort to get the American prisoners to Japan before they could be liberated," wrote historian Donald Knox, "the Japanese were forced to take extreme measures. Without a sufficient number of available freighters, the Japanese authorities tried to make do with what they had . . . [and] too many prisoners were put on too few ships."

The Japanese also made no effort to mark the vessels carrying American POWs so that they could be identified as prison ships by prowling U.S. submarines and aircraft—as international law required. The result was a catastrophe of epic proportions for the POWs aboard one hell ship, the *Arisan Maru*, the sinking of which caused the deaths of more American prisoners than had died at Camp O'Donnell.

The unmarked ship went down in the South China Sea at about 5 PM on October 24, 1944. About 1,800 Americans were aboard, most of them officers, when it was struck amidships by a torpedo believed to have been fired by the U.S. submarine *Shark II*, which was also sunk in the day's action with the loss of all eighty-seven hands. (Another American sub, the *Snook*, was also in the area that day and is credited by some sources with the hit on the *Arisan Maru*.)

The Japanese quickly evacuated their own people from the stricken vessel, but afterward they cut the rope ladders leading out of the holds where the prisoners were confined. The POWs were able to repair the ladders, however, and most are believed to have gotten off the ship before it sank. The Japanese survivors were picked up by the *Arisan Maru*'s destroyer escorts. But when the POWs swam toward the destroyers, they were beaten away with poles, according to William Bowen, whose father, Army Captain William E. Bowen of Tawas City, Michigan, was among the victims. Only eight of the 1,800 POWs are known to have survived.

Despite a series of close calls, the ship on which Sergeant Louis Read, late of the 31st Infantry, sailed from Manila's Pier 5 for Hong Kong in September 1944 fared far better than the *Arisan Maru*.

"For reasons that became obvious," Read noted, "we came to know this ship as the *Benjo Maru*—benjo being the Japanese term for toilet or latrine—but its real name, I discovered many years later, was the *Hokusen Maru*. About 1,200 prisoners were put aboard the ship, and I was among about 600 who were directed down an iron ladder into what had once been a coal storage hold. The other half were put into some stables on the other end of the ship."

Among the POWs were some 200 British and Dutch prisoners who had survived the sinking of another prison ship by American planes as it was en route from Malaya to Japan. The *Hokusen Maru* was part of a convoy of fifteen merchant ships and a pair of "crummy-looking" destroyer escorts bound first for Formosa, then to Japan.

It was stifling hot in the coal bin, and the prisoners weren't given any water for several days. A residue of about a foot of powdered and chunky coal covered the floor with deeper mounds in the corners and along the sides of the hold.

"It didn't matter much about the coal," said Read. "We were packed in so tightly that it was impossible to move, much less see the floor. We could only stand there, pressed against one another until enough of us died off to leave more room—which didn't take long."

The convoy headed warily up the coast of Luzon, sticking close to the land and apparently keenly aware of imminent danger. On the second day out, it was attacked, with devastating effect, by an unknown number of American submarines.

"People on deck saw several ships sunk and torpedo wakes narrowly missing our ship," Read recalled. "One torpedo headed directly for us but dived under the ship and came up on the other side. It was the practice of the Japs to lash timbers over the top of the hold when they were under attack so prisoners couldn't escape if the ship were sunk. At night, we could hear the pinging sound of sonar on the hull of our ship. We were all scared, and a few people went stark, raving mad."

The stress level in the holds remained at near-unbearable levels for several days, according to Read's former 31st Infantry buddy, Corporal Paul Kerchum, with whom Read had been reunited aboard the ship.

"We got chased all over the South China Sea by those U.S. submarines," Kerchum recalled. "We managed to hang onto our sanity by taking turns reading out loud from a book that Read had. It was the complete works of William Shakespeare. I guess there's nothing like a little culture when you're shin-deep in coal dust and human waste and expecting to be blown out of the water at any second."

Just as the submarine attacks were intensifying, an October typhoon blew up in the China Sea, and the *Hokusen Maru* suddenly changed course and headed for Hong Kong. It arrived there on October 11, in time for the Americans to see bombers from the U.S. 14th Air Force striking at shipping in the crowded harbor.

"We were hit but not sunk or seriously damaged," said Read. "We stayed in port for eleven days before sailing out again at midnight under full blackout in the dark of the moon. The bodies of our dead were stacked on deck since they weren't allowed to be dumped in the bay. But once we were back in the China Sea, all the bodies went overboard.

"We arrived at Takao, Formosa, on October 25, but we weren't allowed to leave the ship until two weeks later. When we finally went ashore, I stooped down and literally kissed the ground. That was how glad I was to be on dry land again."

Although none of the prisoners knew it at the time, their arrival on Formosa came just five days after General MacArthur had waded ashore on the island of Leyte—as grinding newsreel cameras recorded the moment for posterity—to make good on the promise he'd made two and a half years earlier.

"People of the Philippines, I have returned," he said. "By the grace of Almighty God, our forces stand again on Philippine soil—soil consecrated in the blood of our two peoples. . . . The hour of your redemption is here."

Four or five hours earlier that same day, October 20, 1944, assault troops of the U.S. Sixth Army, commanded by Lieutenant General Walter Krueger, had stormed ashore on Leyte in strength. MacArthur would get the worldwide headlines, but the 200,000-plus dogfaces of the First Cavalry Division and the Seventh, 24th, 32nd, 77th, and 96th Infantry Divisions would get the fighting.

Luzon would be next.

Sergeant Cletis Overton had survived the Death March, two and a half years in various prison camps, prolonged starvation, a conglomeration of tropical diseases, endless days of backbreaking labor, and countless beatings by Japanese guards. He'd watched his friends and fellow soldiers wither and die from illness and abuse. But nothing he'd yet faced was as daunting and demoralizing as the scene before him as he descended an iron ladder into the hold of a cargo ship identified only by the number "38" on its bow.

The date was August 20, 1944, and Overton was among 600 American POWs forced into the steamy, stinking bowels of the ship with no idea when they would ever see the outside world again. There were bales of straw scattered around the hold, but the space was too crowded with panicky, shouting prisoners for anyone to sit down. A handful of officers tried to calm the men, but when the Japanese slammed down the hatch covers and plunged the hold into sweaty darkness, the noise level rose like an ominous wind. The ship swayed and vibrated as it got under way and gained speed, and the men were thrown hard against each other and the bulkheads. For Overton and his shipmates, the days "down on the farm" at the Davao Penal Colony were history now, and a bleak unknown loomed ahead.

"They had battened down the hatches, and we tore off through some rough water," recalled PFC Victor Mapes, formerly of the 14th Bombardment Squadron. "That old boat was pitching and rolling, and we were thrown every which way. After a few hours, some of the men started passing out from the heat; others were yelling for the last rites. Everyone was screaming and yelling. Finally, the Japanese opened up the hatch, pointed machine guns at us, showed us hand grenades, and told us to keep quiet. Then they closed the hatches again."

After a day or two, the ship stopped to pick up another 150 men and pile them in on top of the other 600. Toilet facilities for 750 prisoners, many suffering with dysentery, consisted, as usual, of two five-gallon buckets. But by now, it was impossible to move so most men merely relieved themselves where they stood.

After an unexplained ten-day stop, the prisoners were herded onto the deck and hosed down with seawater. Then they were marched across a wooden walkway to a Japanese freighter tied up adjacent to them. It was named the *Shinyo Maru*, and its hold was every bit as foul and forbidding as the one they'd just vacated.

"There was no fresh air, and the heat was stifling," said Overton. "There were the same five-gallon buckets for toilets and the same lack of room to sit down, but my buddy, Charles Watson, and I worked out a system where one stood or squatted and the other sat between his legs."

On the afternoon of September 7, the U.S. submarine *Paddle* sighted a convoy of eight Japanese ships near Sindangan Point on Mindanao. Shortly before 5 PM, the sub fired multiple torpedoes at two of the ships. One, an oil tanker named the *Eiyo Maru*, was left blazing like a giant torch. The other was the *Shinyo Maru*, where Cletis Overton heard an ear-splitting explosion, followed by a flash of light, then another explosion. He found himself in rushing, waist-deep water and surrounded by a sea of screaming humanity. His friend, Watson, was nowhere in sight.

"I just knew it was my time to go," he recalled. "I thought there just wasn't any way I was going to live through this. I hated it because my parents and my girlfriend would never know what happened to me. But I kept trying to get out of the hold, and I asked the Lord to help me. I promised to put Him first in my life if I ever got back home, and I kept that promise."

Somehow, Overton got out of the ship and away from the deadly suction he knew it would create as it sank. He paddled hard and suddenly found himself among three other Americans, and the four of them managed to put together a crude raft out of floating debris. They found a first-aid kit and several Japanese canteens filled with weak tea. A wooden box floated by filled with cans of pork and beans and bars of soap.

Hey, maybe we're going to be all right, Overton thought.

The same couldn't be said for the 688 American POWs who died that afternoon, many of whom were shot by Japanese guards as they struggled to get out of the *Shinyo Maru*'s hold or while they were helpless in the water.

Overton looked behind him in time to see the rear half of his ship sticking straight up out of the sea, its props turning in the air and its horn blowing forlornly. Then it slid straight down and vanished.

Two and a half miles to the south, he could see the green hills of Sindangan Point. Nearby he heard machine guns firing and he ducked under the water and stayed submerged as long as he could. When he resurfaced, the firing had stopped. The raft with the precious supplies was gone, but he ran into one of the three men he'd encountered earlier.

The man was a better swimmer than Overton, but he wasn't optimistic about their chances of making it to land. "They may be waiting to shoot us if we do get there," he warned.

"Maybe so," Overton said, "but I'm not giving up. I'll make it somehow."

And he did. He never knew what happened to the other man.

Miraculously, once Overton reached shore, he found himself in secure territory controlled by Filipino guerrillas. They helped him and eighty other American POWs make contact with the U.S. submarine *Narwhal*, which took the entire group aboard and spirited them to an American base in New Guinea. From there, they were flown to Brisbane, Australia, where they boarded a U.S. Liberty ship for the States.

On November 6, 1944, Overton arrived at Pier 7 in San Francisco exactly three years and five days after he'd sailed from there for the Philippines. A few days later, after a cross-country train trip, he received a promotion, a Purple Heart, an audience with Army Chief of Staff General George C. Marshall, and a ninety-day furlough. For the young soldier from Malvern, Arkansas, the war was over.

For Captain Manny Lawton, once an officer in the 31st Infantry, the bedlam, hysteria, and sheer lunacy aboard the converted passenger liner *Oryoku Maru* started on the afternoon of December 13, 1944, while the ship was still tied up at Pier 7 in Manila harbor.

Earlier, before the POWs were hustled aboard, Lawton had surveyed the big vessel, and the thought had crossed his mind that there was ample space in its first- and second-class cabins for the entire group of prisoners. If that was what the Japanese had in mind, he thought, this would be the first time in the captive Americans' forced travels that they'd been treated so considerately.

It soon became obvious, however, that their captors planned no such niceties for the prisoners. The ship's upper decks would be occupied by Japanese family groups, members of the business and diplomatic communities now desperately seeking to get out of the Philippines before a U.S. invasion of Luzon that was expected within days. Two months earlier, the U.S. Third and Seventh Fleets had soundly defeated the Imperial Japanese Navy in the Battles of Leyte Gulf, paving the way for MacArthur's much publicized return to the Philippines. Favored Japanese civilians were now embarking on the same type of mass exodus that had occurred among American dependents in the fall of 1941.

The POWs traveling on the same ship with the Japanese civilians would be relegated to a starkly different world from the other passengers. For the balance of the trip, the Americans' home would be two sweltering holds in the bowels of the *Oryoku Maru*. In these ovenlike quarters, according to shipping records obtained after the war, 1,619 POWs would be confined in airless, pitch-black, standing-room-only chaos, struggling for breath, sanity, and life itself.

More than 800 prisoners were crammed into each of two spaces estimated by Lawton to contain no more than 4,000 square feet. In that amount of room, he calculated, 250 men might have been able to lie down simultaneously, but as it was, there was no room even to sit. Most of the POWs were officers, ranging in rank from Army lieutenant colonels and Navy commanders to second lieutenants and ensigns. But in this sweltering cauldron, where bulkheads facing the western sun were too hot to touch, rank was meaningless. Only survival mattered.

At least fifty prisoners would die that night, but the toll might have been much higher if not for Commander Francis Bridget, former leader of the Naval Battalion on Bataan, who took control of the situation and convinced the Japanese to allow men dying of asphyxiation to be taken out of the hold for fresh air.

"Mr. Wada," Bridget shouted up to a sadistic Japanese interpreter on the deck above, "the lack of oxygen is killing men down here. We'll all die if you don't do something immediately. Let us put the worst cases on deck for a while."

Grudgingly, and after consulting with a lieutenant, the interpreter surprised the POWs by agreeing to Bridget's request. "Bring four at a time," he instructed. "Any who attempt to escape will be shot."

It was late afternoon when Japanese guards removed the hatch cover, and a shaft of sunlight pierced the total darkness of the hold. With it came welcome whiffs of oxygen.

"Pass the unconscious men toward the center of the hold," Bridget ordered, "so that they can be moved topside."

The calm authority in Bridget's voice restored a semblance of order and cooperation among the POWs. The bodies of men near death from oxygen deprivation—most of them older officers—were handed forward, and the worst cases were eased upward to the hatch opening and the deck. A few minutes in the fresh air revived them sufficiently to walk back down the ladder to the hold under their own power so that four others could take their places.

"Not only did this save the lives of some who surely would have died," Lawton observed, "but it also served to make Wada and [the Japanese lieutenant on deck] aware of what was happening below."

Shortly before dark, buckets of rice-and-seaweed soup were lowered to the prisoners. But those nearest the food got large portions while many others got nothing, and much was spilled and lost. After full darkness descended, the POWs might as well have been blind. It was impossible to see anything. Fights erupted. Angry shouts, tortured screams, and maniacal rantings echoed off the walls of the holds.

"Get this bastard away from me! He's trying to kill me!"

"Don't touch me, you son of a bitch!"

"Somebody's clawing at me. Oh, God, he's cut me!"

"I need air! Give me water!"

"Let us out of here, goddamn you!"

"That first night . . . there was madness," Lawton would recall much later. "Claustrophobia and total darkness created a terrible, terrible feeling. There was the heat. The desperate need for air. . . . There was thirst. Many of the men, those that had gotten some water, gulped it right down. . . . When all the liquid was gone, men became desperate. They went mad. They drank urine. Some turned vampire. They tried to drink the blood of the sick men who couldn't resist."

PFC Lee Davis, formerly of the 30th Bombardment Squadron, experienced the madness and mayhem at close range, then found himself inexorably swept up in it.

"That night, it was like being in the Black Hole of Calcutta," Davis said. "The men went literally mad. I saw Americans scrape sweat off the steel sides of the ship and try to drink it. One person near me cut another person's throat and was holding his canteen so he could catch the blood. . . . I was told later that I went out of my head. I was screaming and cursing the Japanese. Men around me told me if I didn't shut up, they'd kill me. I didn't listen to them. I didn't know what I was doing. Somebody knocked me unconscious."

Most of the dead succumbed to heat prostration or suffocation, but an undetermined number of others were bled to death in their sleep by men transformed by thirst and panic into blood-sucking animals. Others were beaten to death in self-defense by their would-be victims.

In the midst of this ongoing horror, one of the small group of friends and fellow Army medics with whom Sergeant Sidney Stewart had managed to stay since the surrender finally succumbed to the combined effects of disease, thirst, starvation, and lack of air. To keep the dead man from being trampled underfoot, another friend stood on the body as Stewart slumped nearby, hovering on the verge of unconsciousness until a third comrade shook him awake.

"You have to be careful," the friend warned. "Don't let anyone touch you that you don't know, and don't let anyone get too close to you. Men are killing each other around us. Listen!"

Stewart heard terrifying sounds in the darkness—sounds of men choking each other and grappling frantically, hoarse curses, and muffled screams. Then he caught a vague glimpse of an unfamiliar body on the floor a few feet away. The man's throat had been cut, and someone was drinking his blood.

"Terror ate into my soul," Stewart would later recall. "If I lost consciousness again, anything could happen. . . . I began to pray."

As daylight returned the next morning, Navy Corpsman Estel Myers, a native Kentuckian who'd grown up in the shadow of the Churchill Downs racetrack, looked anxiously at his two closest buddies, fellow Corpsman Leonard Tarpy and a man Myers knew only as "Tex."

Myers was relieved to see that both were still alive, although their skin was as wrinkled as if they'd spent the entire night immersed in water. Then he noticed that his own skin was shriveled and prunelike as well.

"Must be the humidity from all of us sweating and breathing in such a cramped space," Myers said, feeling his breath coming in shallow gasps. The others nodded listlessly, watching as other men licked condensation from a bulkhead like dogs lapping at a puddle.

As the light improved, Commander Bridget ordered the dead collected and their bodies placed directly below the hatch for removal. In one case, two men hauled out the body of a third from a congested corner of the hold and carefully laid it down. A few moments later, after being exposed to oxygen from the open hatch, the "dead man" regained consciousness and crawled slowly away.

No water rations were issued that morning, but around 7 AM, buckets of rice with some fish mixed in were lowered. Before the men finished scooping up the mixture and wolfing it down from mess kits and bare hands, they heard Japanese sailors yelling from the deck above, following by the staccato rattle of the ship's machine guns.

Suddenly, an ear-splitting blast echoed through the *Oryoku Maru*, followed by another. And another.

"My God!" someone screamed. "We're being attacked by our own planes!"

The bombing raid lasted about twenty-five minutes, and the toll among the Japanese sailors and civilians caught in the open was so heavy that blood dribbled down through cracks in the deck onto prisoners in the hold below. Several dozen POWs were hit by stray bullets from strafing American planes, which returned at intervals until mid-afternoon, but most of those belowdecks were unhurt.

The ill-tempered interpreter Wada called out in desperation for American medical personnel to come up on deck to help treat the Japanese wounded. When an American doctor asked, in return, for supplies to treat injured POWs, Wada angrily refused. Then, in a fit of rage, he turned on the medical team he had just asked for help and ordered Japanese guards to beat them with clubs and rifle butts.

"Americans are sinking Japanese ships!" he railed.

The *Oryoku Maru* was left limping along at a speed of dead-slow with gaping holes in her side and a broken rudder. From her deck, Corpsman Myers and other Americans could see a second Japanese ship blazing furiously in the distance. The rest of the convoy had disappeared.

After the final air attack of the day, the crippled *Oryoku Maru* managed to reach Subic Bay and was run aground off Olongapo Point, just north of Bataan and only a few hundred yards from the onetime site of the Olongapo Naval Station. Her voyage had ended barely twenty-one hours after it began and only about 200 miles, as the crow flies, from its point of origin in Manila harbor.

Evacuation of the approximately 2,000 Japanese passengers, crewmen, and military personnel aboard the *Oryoku Maru* lasted for the rest of the day and far into the night. Several hundred had been killed or wounded in the bombing and strafing attacks, and American doctors were again summoned on deck to treat the injured Japanese.

In the holds below, meanwhile, only a few dirty rags were available to bandage the wounds of injured POWs.

As darkness approached for a second night, the Americans in the holds faced another outbreak of violence, insanity, and bloodshed. "Though the air was better, it was still hot," Lawton noted, "and there were still men with deranged minds roaming around. Also, there was hunger and thirst, for no meal had been served since the evening before. Additionally, there were corpses among us—victims of thirst, murder, and the air raid."

Fortunately, there would be no recurrence of the mass insanity of the previous night. Army Major Houston P. Houser, a muscular West Pointer from Georgia, assumed the role of security officer and recruited four husky enlisted men to help him enforce order. When identifiable troublemakers were confined to one corner and kept under close guard, violent outbursts were reduced to a minimum.

Early the next morning, the prisoners again heard the drone of approaching aircraft engines, and the Japanese frantically rushed some of the POWs onto the deck in hopes that they'd be seen by the returning American pilots.

With the *Oryoku Maru* lying dead in the water and all her deck guns destroyed by the previous raids, it was clear that the U.S. planes would make short work of the defenseless ship unless the pilots could be warned.

"Clad only in G-strings, several officers raced up the steps and ran across the deck, waving their arms," recalled Captain Lawton. "Seeing the white bodies . . . the pilots pulled out of their dives, circled, and dipped their wings in recognition. . . . After several passes, the pilots . . . turned and headed south. We cheered and gave thanks to God."

The prisoners' initial relief was soon replaced by fear of what plans the Japanese might now have in store for them. After twenty months of the harshest imaginable treatment by their captors, they were conditioned to expect the worst. A day earlier, the interpreter Wada had threatened to have the guards fire into the holds if disturbances among the POWs continued. Now he was enraged by the deaths of so many Japanese at the hands of American pilots, and many prisoners worried that he and the officers on deck might carry out a mass execution.

But when Wada finally addressed the prisoners, his tone was surprisingly mild. "Prisoners will disembark immediately," he said. "Commander Bridget will come on deck for instructions."

When Bridget returned, he told the prisoners to remove all their clothes and shoes and swim ashore carrying them. No one was to leave the ship from the starboard side, and anyone who did so or who otherwise strayed from the group would be shot.

"They mean what they say," Bridget cautioned the men. "Machine guns are set up on the beach. It looks like it's about three hundred yards to shore. Let's get moving."

Merely being allowed to climb out of the fetid holds into sunlight and fresh air boosted the prisoners' spirits. So did the opportunity to have the filth and slime of the holds washed away by the cool waters of Subic Bay, and the realization that American warplanes were now striking back at the Japanese buoyed them still further. Even in their weakened, debilitated condition, some men were so excited by these prospects that they jumped thirty feet from the deck of the *Oryoku Maru* without thinking of the consequences. Some drowned, and many others had to be rescued by fellow POWs.

Once ashore and under the sights of Japanese machine gunners who fired occasional warning bursts to steer them toward their destination, the Americans found themselves on a 100-foot square of concrete, enclosed by a fifteen-foot wire fence. From the white lines still visible on the concrete, some could identify this impromptu holding pen as a onetime tennis court at the Olongapo Naval Station. Most of the men were either completely naked or clad only in improvised G-strings, and their next realization was that there wasn't a solitary speck of shade on the concrete slab to protect them from the blistering tropical sun.

With Commander Bridget already suffering several minor wounds from the air attacks and further weakened by the long swim to shore, two surviving officers of the Fourth Marines stepped forward to assume key leadership roles in keeping the men under control in their new place of confinement.

One was rugged, gray-haired Colonel Curtis Beecher from Chicago, who had previously helped maintain order in the forward hold and who now took charge of the situation ashore with the help of Major Reginald "Bull" Rigley. They attempted to take roll—a virtually impossible task—and then organized the men into rows so that those in need of medical help could get what treatment was available.

During this process, Marine Sergeant Harold "Gunner" Ferrell appeared carrying another Marine, Warrant Officer John H. Rice, who was unconscious and barely breathing.

"I had to haul Johnny ashore or he would've drowned," Ferrell told one of the doctors tending to sick and injured men. "He needs help, Doc. He's in a bad way."

The doctor leaned over Rice for a moment, checked the man's pulse, then shook his head. "Nice try, Gunner, but you may as well just lay the poor bastard down. He's dying, and there's not a damned thing we can do for him."

Ferrell nodded. Then he eased himself to a sitting position, still cradling Rice in his arms. "Okay, Doc," he said, "but if you don't mind, I guess I'll just hold him a while longer."

For the next six days, the 1,300 American survivors of the *Oryoku Maru* endured the shadeless, shelterless torment of the tennis court, their bodies alternately blistered and burned lobster-red by the relentless sun and chilled by the nighttime cold. Their only food was two tablespoons per day per man of uncooked rice.

Numerous surgeries were performed during this time by American doctors without medicine, anesthesia, antiseptics, surgical instruments, or bandages. Undergoing one of the more serious operations was a young Marine corporal whose arm had been mangled by bomb fragments that left the broken bone protruding from a mass of exposed muscles and tendons.

Lieutenant Colonel Jack Schwartz, assisted by Lieutenant Colonel James Sullivan, cauterized a razor blade to serve as a scalpel, and two strong men held the Marine down while the gangrenous limb was cut away. The patient screamed lustily but made no effort to stop the doctors from their work. He lived for five days, but on

December 20, during the prisoners' last few hours on the tennis court, he died.

A short time later, a convoy of nineteen trucks arrived to transport the prisoners to the town of San Fernando in Pampanga Province, where one ghastly chapter of the Death March had played itself out some two and a half years earlier. The trucks made frequent stops beneath protective trees when the drivers heard American planes approaching.

After three days and nights in San Fernando, where the POWs were quartered in a provincial jail and an old movie theater, they were marched to the railroad station. A battered steam engine and a line of small boxcars—the same 40-and-8 type that had carried many of these same men toward the nightmare of Camp O'Donnell in April 1942—stood waiting.

"Are we going back to Camp O'Donnell?" asked Lieutenant Colonel Harold Johnson nervously.

"No," the interpreter Wada told him coldly. "You are going to Japan."

There were two new hell ships waiting for the prisoners. The larger of the two bore the name *Enoura Maru*, and the smaller was called *Brazil Maru*. They were among an aggregation of six rusty freighters lying in the harbor of the port city of San Fernando, La Union, on Lingayen Gulf (roughly 100 miles from the inland Luzon town of San Fernando, Pampanga, where the Americans had boarded the train), and the Japanese seemed in an even greater rush than usual to get them loaded and under way.

None of the 1,305 surviving prisoners had any way of knowing that only three weeks after the *Enoura Maru* and the *Brazil Maru* sailed, a liberating U.S. invasion force would land at Lingayen Gulf. Most scarcely realized that Christmas had just passed, and even those who did had no reason to celebrate. They'd been quartered for two days and nights without food or shelter on a barren, windswept beach facing the South China Sea.

But now, after the long delay, their captors suddenly were in one hellacious hurry to embark, and the captain of the *Enoura Maru* was noticeably nervous and agitated. Prisoners were still climbing aboard the ship from the loading barge when he weighed anchor and pulled away from the dock. At least one man fell, or was pushed, to his death during the loading process. His death brought to 314 the number of Americans who had died since boarding the *Oryoku Maru* on December 13.

On the morning of January 9, as the *Enoura Maru* lay at anchor and tied to another freighter in the harbor at Takao, Formosa, the POWs were awakened by the now familiar drone of approaching aircraft. Captain Lawton and his close friend, Captain Henry Leitner, scrambled to the narrow bow of the ship and huddled there, holding their breath.

"Suddenly, there was a . . . deafening explosion as the bomb hit the deck near the port side rail," Lawton recalled. "Hunks of metal, large and small, ripped through the air and ricocheted off the steel walls. Agonized screams of the crushed and wounded rent the air."

Lawton and Leitner suffered only slight wounds, but hundreds of mangled bodies were strewn everywhere in the hold, and at first it looked to Lawton as if almost everyone had been killed. Scores of critically injured men were trapped under massive steel girders and fallen timbers. It took three days before the wreckage was cleared sufficiently to remove the dead.

Among the POWs who had started the voyage on the *Oryoku Maru*, only 930 were still alive, and many of them were sick or wounded. Within thirty-one days, 652 Americans had died, but the Japanese were determined to get those who were still breathing to Japan. By January 13, the survivors had been loaded aboard the *Brazil Maru*, and at sundown that evening, the smaller ship sailed out of Takao harbor into the East China Sea among a convoy of a half-dozen other freighters.

By then, the weather had turned bitterly cold, and the decks of the *Brazil Maru* were coated with thick sheets of ice. Under these conditions, many of the weakened, debilitated prisoners began falling victim to pneumonia. Among them was Navy Commander Francis Bridget, whose inspired leadership had saved—or at least extended—the lives of hundreds of men. Gripped by a raging fever, Bridget died quietly during the last week of January. Lawton's buddy, Captain Leitner, succumbed a few days after going ashore.

The POW food ration remained at half a canteen cup per day of a mixture of rice and barley. Water continued to be doled out at the rate of four teaspoons per man per day, and dehydration became an even more severe problem than hunger. To capitalize on the situation, the guards put out the word that any prisoner still in possession of a gold ring could trade it for a cupful of water.

On January 30, the *Brazil Maru* docked at the port of Moji, on the north coast of Japan's southernmost home island of Kyushu. The last roll call aboard the ship revealed a total of about 425 living prisoners. The corpses of three-fourths of the Americans who had left Manila on the *Oryoku Maru* on December 13 now lay somewhere on the ocean floor between Lingayen Gulf and Moji. By Captain Lawton's calculation, 161 more POWs would die within the next thirty days after reaching their assigned prison camps, leaving only 264 living prisoners out of the original 1,619.

Some lists compiled over the nearly seven decades since the hell ships sailed show a total of more than 200 vessels that allegedly took part in this mass and merciless transfer of American and Allied prisoners. Some of the names on these lists, however, are obvious duplications, and the exact number of ships involved will probably never be determined.

In his book *Death on the Hellships*, author Gregory F. Michno claimed that a total of more than 126,000 American, Australian, British, and Dutch POWs were transported in this way and that about 21,000 Allied and American prisoners died in the process, most of them at the hands of "friendly" submarines. In addition to those cases cited previously in this chapter, at least two other documented hell ship sinkings should be mentioned:

The *Montevideo Maru* was sunk by torpedoes from the U.S. submarine *Sturgeon* on July 1, 1942, off the coast of Leyte with the loss of 1,053 Australian POWs and civilians.

The *Junyo Maru* was sunk on September 18, 1944, by the British submarine *Tradewind* while en route from Java to Sumatra in what ranked at the time as the world's worst maritime disaster. A total of 5,620 passengers were killed, including 1,420 Dutch, British, Australian, and American POWs and 4,200 Javanese slave laborers.

12

Escape—The Ultimate Revenge

At some point during his captivity, almost every American prisoner in the Philippines considered the possibility of escape, and perhaps as many as one in every dozen or so probably engaged in some degree of planning for an escape. But converting plans into realities was a daunting task, one that became infinitely more so after the Japanese organized the POWs into ten-man shooting squads and made it clear that every member of the group faced torture and execution if any of them attempted to escape.

The interlude immediately after the fall of Bataan and Corregidor—and before the organization of the shooting squads—unquestionably offered early escapees a greater chance of success than those who tried later. Once the men were confined to prison camps with barbed wire barriers and watchtowers equipped with spotlights and machine guns, the odds of remaining alive and free for more than a few hours—or a few minutes—plunged dramatically.

On the other hand, the Death March, brutal as it was, represented a golden opportunity for escape, especially for Filipino soldiers who were familiar with the countryside and had friends or family along the route. With this type of assistance close at hand, an undetermined number of native captives were able to melt temporarily into the civilian population, then join guerrilla groups operating in remote areas.

Most Americans who contemplated escape did so with the vague hope of locating a sufficiently seaworthy boat to get out of the Philippines entirely and somehow make their way to Australia or China. It was a next to impossible goal that few ever managed even to attempt, much less achieve. But for a few score Americans, escape meant much more than merely freeing themselves from Japanese savagery by leaving the Philippines. Along with thousands of captured Filipino soldiers, these men yearned to keep fighting, to strike back at their captors and torturers. The most accessible route toward this goal was to locate and offer their services to the massive guerrilla movement that mushroomed across the Philippines in mid-1942.

"With the help of friends who distracted the guards, I was able to slip away from the Death March before we reached Camp O'Donnell," recalled Private Menandro "Andy" Parazo of the 26th Cavalry, Philippine Scouts. "Later, I joined the guerrillas led by Colonel Claude Thorp, along with two of my brothers and my sister. I was recaptured once, but I escaped again."

Thorp, a onetime cavalry officer at Fort Stotsenburg, became a legendary figure in the jungles of northeastern Luzon after the fall of Bataan. Along with a handful of other trusted officers, Thorp had been handpicked by General MacArthur to organize guerrilla resistance in that area, and his efforts were highly productive in the beginning.

At its peak, the Luzon Guerrilla Force led by Thorp is believed to have numbered up to 30,000 Filipino fighters under the well-organized leadership of American officers. Among those leaders were two battle-hardened veterans of the 26th Cavalry—Captain Joe Barker and Lieutenant Ed Ramsey—who had agreed with a simple handshake on the day Bataan fell to stick together and do whatever they could to resist capture.

After several frantic weeks of dodging Japanese patrols and working their way north from Bataan with the help of friendly Filipinos, Ramsey and Barker first learned the grisly details of the Death March from a Filipino farmer who gave them shelter and food.

"I saw it with my own eyes," the farmer told them. "When a man collapsed, he was immediately shot. Others who stopped to drink from filthy roadside puddles were also killed, as were civilians who tried to help the prisoners. Now the people are enraged. Small resistance groups are forming in the countryside, and I can take you to one of them in the mountains above the village of Dinalupihan."

When the farmer left, Barker turned to Ramsey. "Do you think this resistance group can help us?" he asked.

"It looks like it's the only thing we've got going for us right now," Ramsey replied.

The next day, the farmer and several friends guided Ramsey and Barker to the village, where they were greeted by three Filipinos and—much to their surprise—a young American, who identified himself as Corporal John Boone, formerly of the 31st Infantry.

Like Barker and Ramsey, Boone had chosen not to surrender, but after meeting Colonel Thorp, he'd decided to remain on Luzon as part of Thorp's guerrilla movement, rather than try to escape from the Philippines.

"It's strictly voluntary," Boone said, "but Thorp is authorized to enlist any Filipinos and Americans who want to join into a guerrilla force that will carry on the war behind Jap lines."

"Where is he now?" Barker asked.

"He has a camp in the hills above Fort Stotsenburg," Boone told him. "The Japs control the lowlands and the roads, so everything's done from the hills."

After several days, Thorp sent a messenger to the village to invite Barker and Ramsey to visit him at his mountain headquarters. By that time, both Americans had made up their minds to do something they'd never contemplated a few weeks earlier.

The idea of joining the Luzon guerrillas and carrying on the fight against the Japanese had been the furthest thing from Ramsey's mind on the day when he and Barker had found themselves cut off from the rest of their tattered regiment as the American defense of Bataan fell apart around them.

When the two young officers had shaken hands and promised to stick together, the whole idea had been to find a way to get to Australia and rejoin traditional American forces. Now, however, that goal was beyond their reach, and it had been preempted by another—to wreak as much havoc as possible on the conquering Japanese.

"As an American soldier, the war had been over for me since the surrender of Bataan, and my duty now was to escape," Ramsey would write years later. "Yet . . . I began to reflect that perhaps I still owed the Filipino people something. The war . . . was not over for them. I might escape, but they could not."

After discussing it with Barker, Ramsey was certain that his former captain felt the same. "It's settled then?" Barker asked.

"It's settled," Ramsey replied. "We're volunteering for the guerrillas."

Barker and Ramsey were placed in charge of one of four major segments of Thorp's guerrilla force. Their main assignments were to cultivate the support of local civilian leaders, recruit and train new blood for the resistance, gather intelligence for MacArthur's forces in Australia, build an arsenal of weapons, and commit covert acts of sabotage against the Japanese. They were not, however, to engage the enemy in direct combat except in situations where the odds were strongly in the guerrillas' favor, and they were to be scrupulously careful to avoid any acts that would bring harsh retaliation against Filipino civilians.

In the fall of 1942, Barker was sent to Manila to organize new guerrilla cadres while Ramsey remained in the hills of Luzon, struggling to make a complete recovery from lingering cases of malaria and dysentery and still considered too weak for extensive travel.

The new year of 1943 brought stepped-up efforts by the Japanese to crush the resistance movement on Luzon. Raids on guerrilla camps and villages known to be sympathetic to the guerrillas increased in frequency, as did wholesale torture of suspected sympathizers. Prices were placed on the heads of all guerrilla leaders, resulting in the capture and death of Captain Ralph McGuire, one of Colonel Thorp's four unit commanders.

During the first two weeks of January 1943, a rash of disastrous reports filtered back to Ramsey from Manila: Thorp had been captured by the Japanese secret police, the dread Kempeitai, and was being held at Fort Santiago in the city. Then, on January 13, came the news that Barker himself had been captured in a raid. After days of continuous torture, during which Thorp's eyes were torn from his head, and he was paraded—blind and more dead than alive—through the streets of Manila, both were executed.

"I was now the sole commander of the Luzon Guerrilla Force," Ramsey recalled, "and one of the few American guerrilla commanders still at large in Luzon. Meanwhile, the price on my head had been doubled, to a quarter-million pesos, some $100,000."

For his own security, Ramsey felt it necessary to move farther north into even more remote areas. A reliable report that Ramsey had been elevated to the rank of major by order of General MacArthur was small consolation. The only real consolation would be when MacArthur fulfilled his promise to return to the Philippines at the head of a powerful American army.

Ramsey seriously doubted that he'd ever live to see it.

While the guerrilla organization built by Colonel Thorp may well have been the largest and strongest on Luzon between mid-1942 and early 1943, it was far from the only one. At least two or three other large, American-led groups also became active during this period. One was led by Second Lieutenant Robert Lapham, a twenty-five-year-old Army infantry officer, who had been authorized as early as mid-February 1942 to slip through Japanese lines into the Zambales Mountains to begin organizing resistance groups. By that summer, the group known as "Lapham's Raiders" was believed to include about 13,000 guerrillas.

Other, less predictable guerrilla organizations included a militant force of communist "Huk" insurgents, who now fought the Japanese as fiercely as they had once fought the Americans and the Philippine government. The Huks were tenacious fighters, but their motives and actions couldn't always be trusted by the U.S.-led resistance groups with whom they were sometimes loosely affiliated.

Private Leon Beck, late of the 31st Infantry's Antitank Company, and PFC Blair Robinett, formerly of Company C, 803rd Engineers, hadn't known each other at the time they'd staged separate escapes from the Death March a few hours apart. But they soon became well acquainted as members of a Luzon resistance force known as the USAFFE Guerrillas, commanded by Colonel Gyles

Merrill, another old U.S. Cavalry officer who had fought Pancho Villa on the Mexican border before World War I.

Like Colonel Thorp and Lieutenant Lapham, Merrill supposedly operated under direct orders from General MacArthur, and as senior officer among the American escapees in Pampanga Province he sought to consolidate a number of smaller guerrilla groups under his jurisdiction. His first assignment to Private Beck was to meet with the leaders of these groups and relay Merrill's orders that they should report to him.

"I wouldn't say it was a dangerous mission," Beck later recalled, "but it was easier for him to send a private than all those captains I was hanging around with. I was also picked because of my height. I was small like the Filipinos . . . I blended in, didn't tower over them. Lastly, I was willing to go. I needed something to do."

The officers who came down out of the mountains in response to Merrill's summons, along with those already aligned with Merrill, were assigned to take charge of guerrilla "squadrons" in specific sectors of the province.

"We rearmed ourselves by going back down into Bataan," Beck recalled. "We'd go over the battle areas picking up weapons or scavenging parts to make new ones. . . . That's how we got started."

Beck and Robinett first met each other in early 1943 when both were forced into hiding during a sweep of the area by Japanese patrols, and they quickly discovered that they were kindred spirits—as well as occasional antagonists.

According to Robinett, the main thing that MacArthur wanted from Merrill's force was information on Japanese strengths and troop movements in Pampanga. "He'd been ordered to offer only passive resistance to the Japs because of retaliation possibilities," Robinett said.

Neither Robinett nor Beck was interested in passive resistance, however. Their sole aim was to strike at the Japanese as hard as possible. Thus, when Merrill moved his operation far up into the mountains, they stayed in the lowlands and became "freelance" fighters with other guerrilla groups—including the communist Huks.

As Robinett bluntly summed it up, "The major difference between the USAFFE Guerrillas and the Huk guerrillas is that the Huks fought the Japs and the USAFFE Guerrillas didn't. To me, fighting was what it was all about. Hell, all I wanted to do was maintain civilian anger against the Japanese. . . . I wanted retaliation."

Beck embraced similar sentiments, but the pair stayed together only when it suited their purposes of the moment. At other times, they struck out in opposite directions, doing their fighting for different guerrilla groups and sometimes even operating alone.

"During the next six or seven months, I kept running into Blair," Beck recalled. "[But] the time came when I just had to re-establish my own independence, and going off by myself was the only way I had of doing it. You could go off strictly by yourself or go join some other guerrilla unit and operate with them for a while."

In many respects, the life of an American guerrilla in the Philippines bore similarities to that of a hired gun in the Old West. It was a high-risk life of constant stress, raw nerves, and sudden danger in which even hot-tempered friends sometimes came close to killing each other. Beck and Robinett both remembered an incident—one that started as a joke—when they came perilously close to shooting one another before their guerrilla comrades interceded.

"They jumped on us and pulled us apart," Beck recalled, "but I couldn't stop thinking about it. I thought I couldn't let that big devil run over me . . . so I went ahead and hid behind a bush. When Blair came riding up, I stepped out and challenged him again. Everybody piled all over us again. They wouldn't let us settle it. I was so mad by then that . . . I left and went out on my own. The next day I ran across some chickens . . . [and] decided I'd have them for dinner. I pulled out my pistol, and the first two rounds misfired. If I'd had the fight with Blair, he'd have killed me deader than hell. Blair and I laugh about it now, but it wasn't funny then."

For the most part, the two sometimes friends continued to spend more time fighting the Japanese than each other. But in August 1944, they finally separated for good with Beck leaving Pampanga Province and returning to the Zambales Mountains and Robinett remaining in Pampanga with a band of Huks.

About a month later—on September 21, 1944—Beck was a close-up eyewitness to the first air strike by U.S. Navy planes against Japanese targets on Luzon.

"Needless to say, I was quite exhilarated," he said. "For the first time in two and a half years, I began to see that there might really be a light at the end of the tunnel."

If not for the freakish twists and turns of fate, onetime B-17 navigator Ed Whitcomb and his Marine buddy Lieutenant Bill Harris might also have spent the rest of the war as guerrilla fighters on Luzon following their swimming escape from Corregidor on the night of May 22, 1942.

As it happened, Harris would, in fact, do a turn in the Philippine resistance movement. But in Whitcomb's case, fate and the future had something stunningly different in store.

When they awoke from an exhausted sleep on the afternoon following their all-night swim, the fugitives knew only that they were a few dozen yards inland from the east coast of Bataan and not far from the remains of Cabcaben Field, where Whitcomb had spent considerable time before the surrender.

Alert for Japanese patrols, they began making their way north and west with only the sketchiest idea of what to do next. They'd agreed earlier that their first objective would be to reach Subic Bay some seventeen miles away and try to find a boat there, but a greater and more immediate need was to find food. Dusk was rapidly approaching, and both men were weak from hunger. More than thirty hours had passed since they'd last eaten.

"I think I remember a little shack not far from here where an old Filipino lived with his family," Whitcomb said. "If we can find it, and if he's still there, maybe he'll give us something to eat."

Although his family was sick with malaria, the old Filipino did, indeed, provide the fugitives with an ample supply of rice as well as a bolo knife for hacking their way through the jungle. After that, though, food became incredibly scarce, and they subsisted on wild cashews, green bananas, and swarms of ants to keep from starving. On the positive side, they were able to salvage weapons, ammo, and supplies from a couple of abandoned Philippine Army camps. They managed to escape unscathed from their only brush with a Japanese patrol but were forced to leave behind a freshly butchered horse they had just killed.

At Moron, site of the 26th Cavalry's gallant last charge, they encountered a small boy who offered to take them to his home. There they feasted on wild pork, honey, rice, and papayas, but they also received some disheartening news.

"There are no boats," the boy's father told them. "The Japanese have confiscated all boats that they could use and destroyed the rest. All the boats are gone, but if you stay, we will find a place for you to live and give you plenty of food. The Japanese are everywhere, and they will catch you unless you hide."

"No, we can't stay," Whitcomb told him. "We have to go on to Subic Bay. Maybe we can find a boat there."

On the morning of June 6, they arrived at Subic Bay. It had taken them two weeks to cover the seventeen miles from Cabcaben. Two days later, they bought a tiny native *banco* fishing boat with a sail and outriggers for 30 pesos, but realizing that they had no chance to make it to Australia or China in such a flimsy craft, they decided to head back south toward Manila Bay.

Almost immediately, they encountered rough seas, and on the third day, a large wave slammed their boat against the shore, snapping off one of its outriggers and putting it out of commission. After a fifteen-mile cross-country hike, they were welcomed by the first of a succession of Filipino groups, each of which showered them with food and urged them to stay. They also encountered two other American escapees—Marines named Reid Carlos Chamberlain and "Army" Armstrong—who were living the good life on a 5,000-acre plantation owned by a wealthy Filipino while waiting for a seaworthy boat to be prepared for them.

It was late July when the boat was finally ready, but the finished product was well worth the wait. It was a sleek, twenty-four-foot outrigger sailing craft equipped with a stove and firewood, a fifty-five-gallon drum of water, vast quantities of food and quinine, a flashlight, and native sailing suits to help conceal the four Americans' identity.

As the Filipino fishermen had repeatedly warned, however, this was not the right season of the year for successful sailing, especially for escapees on the run. During the daytime, the winds blew steadily, but they tended to die away to nothing at night. After five nights at sea, the boat had covered less than twenty-five miles.

"At this rate," groused Harris, "it'll take us twenty-five years to get to Australia."

Impatient to keep moving, Harris and the other two Marines began urging sailing in the daytime to take full advantage of the winds. But Whitcomb was convinced that this was far too risky, and the disagreement quickly developed into a crisis.

"I'm sure not for this daytime sailing," Whitcomb said. "Not with these Jap patrol planes coming over every day and Jap patrol boats working up and down the coast all the time."

A vote was taken on daytime sailing, and Whitcomb found himself a minority of one. "Okay," he said bitterly, "you can outvote me, but you can't force me to go. I don't think you've got the nerve to sail off and leave me, and if you do, I don't think you'll get very far."

In retrospect, Whitcomb would recall much later, "I guess I gave them little choice but to call my bluff"—which was precisely what they did.

Early the next morning, Harris came to the Filipino house where Whitcomb was staying to make a final plea for Whitcomb to change his mind. "Please think it over, Ed," he urged. "We've come a long way together. Let's not split up now."

"If you sail away today," Whitcomb told him, "we *are* splitting up because I'm not willing to take a risk that isn't necessary."

"Well, we're going," Harris said, shrugging in resignation. He stuck out his hand, and Whitcomb grabbed it and shook it. A few minutes later, after Harris, Chamberlain, and Armstrong had sailed away, Whitcomb went back to bed and slept most of the day.

He had never felt more alone in his life, but his determination to reach Australia and rejoin the war was as strong as ever.

By late February 1943, the heady days when Lieutenants Sam Grashio and Ed Dyess of the 21st Pursuit Squadron had zoomed low in their P-40s to strafe the Japanese beachhead at Lingayen Gulf were only a faded memory from another life.

Since early childhood in Spokane, Washington, Samuel Charles Grashio, son of an Italian immigrant, had been something of a paradox—a deeply religious altar boy on Sundays and a wiry kid who never ducked a fight any other time. Only average in the classroom, he was a gifted natural athlete who excelled as an amateur boxer and quarterbacked his high school football team to three straight championships.

An addiction to action led Grashio to enroll in a federal flight training program in 1938, and after earning his pilot's license in 1940, he completed two Army Air Corps cadet programs and was assigned to the 21st Pursuit Squadron commanded by Lieutenant William Edwin Dyess, a lanky young officer from the plains of West Texas who harbored a lust for adventure at least as strong as Grashio's. Dyess was barely two years older than his twenty-three-year-old squadron mate, but in Grashio's own words, "He was like a father to me at first. Then . . . he was like a pal."

From the initial attack on Clark Field on December 8, 1941, until there were no P-40s left to fly, they'd flown together almost constantly, and with every mission their friendship had deepened. Then they'd endured the agonies of the Death March, Camp O'Donnell, Cabanatuan, and finally the torturous trip to Davao Penal Colony aboard a decrepit hulk named the *Erie Maru*—and always together.

They'd been prisoners of war for close to a year now, and since early the previous November, the two former aerial daredevils had been spending long, arduous days as captive rice farmers slogging through the knee-deep mud of DAPECOL. Their long nights were consumed with dreams of escape, but in the harsh reality of daylight the dreams inevitably faded. In fact, the longer and more intensely they struggled to come up with a plan, the more impossible the whole idea seemed.

As Grashio put it, "It was one thing to decide to escape, quite another to determine when, where, and how."

The problems confronting them seemed to stretch into infinity—an endless series of riddles and imponderables. Yet they and the other eight Americans who shared their would-be conspiracy refused to give up. Over the late winter, they continued to collect a crazy-quilt assortment of ingredients that they hoped would somehow produce a recipe for freedom:

A compass . . . a wristwatch . . . a homemade sextant . . . a yellowed copy of *Ripley's Believe It or Not!* . . . tools from an engineer's drawing set . . . a quart bottle of stolen quinine tablets . . . a book on astronomy . . . a navigational table of nearby seas . . . a well-stocked first-aid kit . . . a hand-drawn map of the DAPECOL area . . . matches swiped from the Japanese kitchen . . . socks stuffed with grains of rice . . .

And so on.

Participants in the plot represented a broad cross section of American military personnel stationed in the Philippines at the time the war had broken out.

In addition to Dyess and Grashio, the Army Air Corps was represented by Lieutenant Leo Boelens, a onetime Wyoming farm boy who had developed into a skilled aeronautical engineer.

Lieutenant Commander Melvyn McCoy, a former radio matériel officer at Cavite, represented the U.S. Navy and had actively recruited three other co-conspirators for the mission—Army Major Steve Mellnik, a USAFFE staff officer on Corregidor, and two tough, enterprising Army enlisted men, Paul Marshall and Robert Spielman.

The Marine Corps contingent was headed by First Lieutenant Austin "Shifty" Shofner, a former football star at the University of Tennessee and protégé of legendary coach Robert Neyland, a West Point graduate, and onetime aide to General MacArthur. It also included Lieutenant Jack Hawkins, an Annapolis graduate who'd chosen dry-land service over shipboard life, and Lieutenant Mike Dobervich, Hawkins's best buddy from their Shanghai days with the Fourth Marines.

Despite their many similarities—mental and physical toughness, proven leadership abilities, and a positive attitude that rejected the idea that escape from DAPECOL was impossible—each man brought a set of highly specialized skills and talents to the task at hand.

In mid-March, Grashio—described by Hawkins as "the most steadfastly enthusiastic member of our little conspiracy"—recruited two more-than-willing Filipino inmates as guides for the escapees. Both were serving life sentences in DAPECOL for murder, but Grashio was convinced that they would make valuable, trustworthy additions to the group.

Benigno "Ben" de la Cruz, who admitted to "accidentally" killing another young man in a fight over a girl when he was a teenager, spoke fluent English, Tagalog, Visayan, and several other Filipino dialects, and he was also trained in first-aid and pharmacy. Just as importantly, he was intimately familiar with the dense jungle and supposedly impenetrable swamp through which the escapees would have to travel.

The other guide—without whom de la Cruz said he wouldn't go—was Victorio "Victor" Jumarong, who was shorter, older, and quieter than Ben. He was also illiterate and spoke almost no English. He'd been convicted of killing two men, one in a fencing match with bolo knives. His major assets, in addition to his skills with a bolo, were that he was strong as an ox and well acquainted with the menacing territory that lay between the POWs and freedom.

It had been decided well in advance that "E-Day," as Shofner had designated it, would have to fall on a Sunday, the only day of the week when armed Japanese guards didn't accompany the POW details into the work areas beyond the main compound.

The idea was to act as if it were any other Sunday, and the prisoners were on their way to a routine work assignment. The ten Americans—all members of the same shooting squad—would march as casually as possible through several gates and past a half-dozen sentry posts with their vital gear and supplies hidden on their persons.

Dyess had already run a similar gauntlet a week earlier when he'd packed a bull cart frequently used to haul tools and work gear with telltale essentials of the escape—large amounts of food, medicine, and equipment gathered over many weeks. He'd pushed the cart across the breadth of DAPECOL to a plower's shack beyond the main compound, where the others had helped him hide the supplies. If a sentry had stopped him to examine the cart, it would have meant certain death.

On E-Day—April 4, 1943—as Dyess and the others followed the same route, the guards at each checkpoint took a count of the prisoners and conducted an inspection. The two Filipino guides, being civilian inmates and under less rigid restrictions than the POWs, would rendezvous later with the Americans outside the compound.

"There was plenty of chance for a slip," Dyess recalled later. "Even a cursory examination of our persons would've disclosed enough contraband to have lost all of us our heads. It seemed to me that I clanked when I walked."

Dyess remembered that as the POWs approached the one main road they had to cross to reach the dense, protective foliage a short distance beyond, his heart was pounding so hard that it "seemed to be beating my brains out." When they crossed the road one at a time, they passed within a few feet of the guard's machine gun, but he scarcely seemed to notice them.

"When we were all across," Dyess recalled, "I thought to myself: *The Old Man is with us today. What we're having is more than luck—a lot more than luck.*"

This motley, haggard ten-man aggregation may have been among the unlikeliest groups imaginable to stage the first successful mass escape in the history of Davao Penal Colony. But on that bright, clear Sunday morning—just five days short of the first anniversary of the fall of Bataan—that's exactly what they did.

During the bleak period after Bill Harris and his two Marine friends had sailed away and left Ed Whitcomb to his own devices, the onetime B-17 navigator stayed close to the coastal Filipino village where he'd taken refuge. He had comfortable lodging and plenty of food there, and the natives remained as friendly as ever—too friendly. They were unanimous in their zeal to convince Whitcomb to forget about trying to reach Australia and stay in their village for the duration of the war.

Meanwhile, Whitcomb had heard tantalizing rumors about two American miners who were supposedly living in another small town about fifteen kilometers down the coast. "I was tired of arguing with the villagers," he recalled, "so one night I just picked up my knapsack, told my host I was leaving, and started walking to see if I could locate these Americans."

Although he was first told that the miners had moved farther down the coast, Whitcomb found them with little difficulty, still in the village. The younger of the pair, a tall blond in his late twenties, introduced himself as Ralph Conrad from Oakland, California. The other, who appeared to be in his mid-thirties, identified himself as Frank Bacon from El Paso, Texas.

"Are you military?" Whitcomb asked.

"No, we're civilian mining engineers from Baguio," Conrad said.

"We've been dodging the Japs for the past eight months," said Bacon. "We've just finished getting a boat ready to sail to Australia."

Whitcomb's heart leaped in his chest at this news. He could hardly believe his good fortune. "That's just where I'm hoping to head," he said. "I was traveling with three Marines, but we had a disagreement, and they took our boat and left."

"Well, our boat's plenty big," Conrad said, "and you're welcome to come with us if you want. We've got everything ready but the sail, and it may take a couple more days before we shove off."

This time, there was no dispute about sailing during the daylight hours. Both Conrad and Bacon readily agreed that they should travel only after dark, and on the second night after Whitcomb's arrival, they launched their boat from a point about fifteen miles east of the town of Batangas and set a course eastward across Tayabas Bay with a stout northwest wind at their backs.

Whitcomb could never recall feeling more exhilarated as the boat gained speed and the outriggers knifed through the waves. Conrad and Bacon were similarly lighthearted as one manned the tiller and the other sang and told stories. The next morning, after sailing completely across the bay, they put into shore near the town of Agdagnan.

But their euphoria was to be short-lived. By early afternoon that day, a group of armed Filipinos, led by the pro-Japanese mayor and chief of police of Agdagnan, had taken the Americans into custody and locked them up in the town jail.

"I'm going to turn you over to the Japanese, whether you like it or not," the mayor told them, pushing a paper toward the Americans through the bars. "It will be to your benefit if you sign this paper stating that you have turned yourselves in voluntarily. The Japanese are very nice people, and they will take good care of you."

Whitcomb trembled inwardly as Bacon and Conrad signed the paper and tried to explain that they were civilian miners traveling from Baguio to Australia. As the sheet of paper was handed to Whitcomb, he was seized by a cold wave of panic. He dared not sign his real name for fear it would link him to the U.S. military, but what name *could* he sign?

"Numerous times over the past few days, I remembered Frank and Ralph mentioning the name 'Johnson,'" Whitcomb would later recall. "But I'd never heard them mention a first name to go with it, so I did the only thing I could think to do under the circumstances. I signed the name 'Robert Johnson' to the paper and handed it back."

It was an act of sheer desperation, one that Whitcomb would have cause to regret hundreds of times in coming months. In assuming the identity of a nonexistent American civilian, he was exposing himself to countless hours of confinement, interrogation, threats, beatings, and torture by the Japanese.

Yet, now that the die was cast, there was no turning back. If he ever gave in and admitted that there was no such person as Robert Johnson, Whitcomb knew he would be signing his own death warrant.

Within a few days, Whitcomb found himself spending long hours in an interrogation room at historic Fort Santiago overlooking Manila Bay, which the Japanese were utilizing as a maximum security prison for suspected guerrillas, spies, saboteurs, and fugitive U.S. military personnel.

"Tell me the names of the Filipinos who helped you," demanded the snake-eyed Japanese officer interrogating Whitcomb. It was at least the twentieth time the question had been repeated.

"I don't know," Whitcomb said. "I called all of them 'Joe,' and they called me 'Joe.' I never knew any of their names."

"You must tell the truth," an interpreter warned Whitcomb, as he had numerous times before. "If you tell the truth, it is very good for you. You will be sent to the civilian internment center at Santo Tomas University to live comfortably with your friends. If you do not tell the truth, you will be killed."

Ancient Fort Santiago, built by the Spanish in the 1500s, had long been associated with torture, savagery, and death, and the Japanese had made full use of its prison facilities. Its lowest levels of cells lay below sea level at high tide, and countless prisoners had been purposely drowned in them. Hundreds of others were held in the dank darkness of cramped, filthy cells where they were forbidden to speak, except during intervals when they were taken out for interrogation and systematic torture.

The campus of Santo Tomas University in Manila's old Walled City, the oldest chartered university in Asia, was only a few hundred yards from Fort Santiago, but its atmosphere and living conditions were a world removed from the horrors of the prison.

Santo Tomas had been converted by the Japanese into a comfortable internment camp for some 3,500 foreign-born civilians. Here, many families lived together in small houses they had constructed from materials brought in from the outside. Others resided in separate, well-equipped dormitories for men and women. All were allowed to move freely about the university grounds and participate in various social activities. They were never threatened or harassed by the Japanese, and they were served two or three nutritious meals each day. Best of all, they held out hope that they would soon be repatriated to their home countries as part of an exchange program with the Japanese.

Since arriving at Fort Santiago, Whitcomb had had only a few fleeting chances to talk to Frank Bacon and Ralph Conrad, the two American mining engineers with whom he'd been arrested. Bacon and Conrad were confined to different cells, so Whitcomb had been unable to glean more than a few scant scraps of information about the family, professional history, and personal background that he was desperately trying to claim as his own.

Meanwhile, the Japanese continued to interrogate Whitcomb day after day in sessions ranging from two to six hours, each of which invariably began with the same warning from the interpreter, followed by the same series of questions:

"What your name?"

"Robert Fred Johnson."

"What your father's name?"

"Fred Johnson."

"Your mother's name?

"Betty Johnson."

"When you come to Philippine Islands?"

"In July 1941."

"How you come to Philippine Islands?"

"On a Swedish freighter."

"Why you come to Philippine Islands?"

"To work with my father in the mines."

Whitcomb did his best to keep his answers uniform, but after so long, it all became a blur, and sometimes he couldn't be sure if he was succeeding. But now that the snake-eyed Japanese officer altered his approach and began demanding the names of Filipinos who had helped Whitcomb and others avoid capture, it was easier to keep repeating the same answer: "I don't know. I don't know."

The persistent denials infuriated the Japanese officer, and he became steadily more abusive. Soon Whitcomb's nonanswers triggered a flurry of slaps across his face and a series of kicks in his side.

"You tell names of Filipinos!" the officer shouted.

"I don't know," Whitcomb muttered again, knowing that even if he gave his questioner a name as fictitious as the one he was using himself, it could set off an investigation resulting in the brutal deaths of innocent people.

Whitcomb watched in disbelief as the officer turned furiously toward the wall, and the interpreter handed him a length of cast iron pipe leaning there.

Surely, he's not going to hit me with that! Whitcomb thought. *Surely, he's only trying to scare me!*

"You think of names!" the officer ordered. "Now!"

"I . . . I don't know," Whitcomb whispered.

The officer swung the pipe, striking Whitcomb across the back with a blow that made his entire body go numb. Then the officer pounded him repeatedly with the pipe between his shoulders and hips until Whitcomb sank to the floor, writhing in pain. When he tried to stand, he felt as if several bones were broken in his back and left arm.

"I've told you everything I can," he moaned. "There's nothing more I can say. If I've told you a single lie, go ahead and shoot me!"

Following another, less violent interrogation a day or two later—and through a sheer quirk of fate—Whitcomb was taken, apparently by mistake, to the cell where Ralph Conrad was being held. There, before the mistake was discovered, Whitcomb was able to obtain crucial information from Conrad about the mine where the fictitious Robert Johnson had supposedly worked as well as important background on the real-life Fred Johnson, who was now back in the States. Conrad also slipped him a crude, hand-drawn map showing the layout of the Filipino village near the mine.

Not long afterward, Whitcomb's blood ran cold when he, Conrad, and Bacon were ordered from their cells simultaneously. For a moment, he was certain that they were about to be executed, but it soon became clear that they were merely to be questioned again separately. One at a time, they were led into an interrogation room, but now there was one important difference. For the first time since his imprisonment, Whitcomb believed he had sufficient information to make his story jibe with the other two men's.

When the interviews were over and the three Americans stood anxiously in the hallway outside the interrogation rooms, waiting to see what their fate might be, they heard a stunning announcement by the same Japanese officer who had dealt Whitcomb so much recent misery: "Ralpho Conrado, Franco Bacon, and Roberto Johnson will be taken this day from Fort Santiago to the civilian internment facility at Santo Tomas University."

With sudden relief flooding through him, Lieutenant Edgar D. Whitcomb, U.S. Army Air Corps, alias Robert Fred Johnson, imaginary miner, could almost feel the jaws of hell slamming shut—empty—behind him.

Many obstacles and challenges to his hopes for freedom still lay ahead, but as the stone-faced Japanese officer turned and marched away, Whitcomb sensed for the first time that the worst was over.

By early 1944, former cavalryman Edwin Ramsey had become the officer in charge of the east central Luzon Guerrilla Force, estimated by some sources to have claimed 45,000 members at its peak. But in building this organization, Ramsey had learned that many of the local and regional guerrilla leaders who nominally aligned themselves with him actually held allegiance to no one but themselves.

That January, Ramsey and his second-in-command, Pat Gatson, had set out on a trip to the island of Mindoro, where they hoped to cement closer relations with various resistance groups there. Among the key figures with whom they met on this excursion was Major Ramon M. Ruffy, a former Philippine constabulary officer whose guerrilla force held sway over a large portion of Mindoro.

"I was impressed with Ruffy's camp," Ramsey later recalled. "It was large and well organized, with a kind of permanence I didn't usually associate with guerrilla forces. Rows of well-built thatch-and-nipa barracks stood on streets edged in stone, and there was even a parade ground."

It became obvious that Ruffy's group was in close contact with American military leaders in Australia. Near the end of Ramsey's ten-day visit on Mindoro, Ruffy informed him quietly of a radio message from Panay, the next large island to the south, concerning the imminent arrival of a U.S. submarine on southern Mindoro to bring money and supplies for the guerrillas.

"The sub can take you out," Ruffy confided to Ramsey, "but you'll have to leave at once to get down there in time."

Ramsey was jolted—and intrigued—by this news. He'd never seriously expected such an opportunity to rejoin the main U.S. war effort, and the prospect was tempting. But it took him only seconds to realize that he couldn't go. "I had too much invested in Luzon to walk away," he said. "For better or worse, I was the leader, and I had no idea whether there was anyone to replace me."

"Tell them 'no thanks,'" he told Ruffy.

Ramsey's purpose on this trip, as always, was to build support for General MacArthur's impending return. He'd also come to take possession of an invaluable shortwave radio to enhance his ability to communicate with U.S. headquarters in Australia, only to discover that the Americans who were to deliver the radio had been ambushed by a Japanese patrol. At about the same time he learned of the ambush, Ramsey's cohort Gatson disappeared and was never seen again.

Except for the news about the sub, the only piece of positive information that Ramsey encountered on the Mindoro trip came in the form of a written radio message handed to him by Ruffy just before Ramsey left the guerrilla camp. It was short and to the point:

> *Request that you return to Luzon and command of your resistance forces.*
>
> (signed) *MacArthur*

To Ramsey, the terse note from the supreme commander of U.S. forces in the Pacific could mean only one thing—MacArthur's return to the Philippines was coming soon.

When it happened, every resistance group in the archipelago would have to be ready to mount an all-out offensive against the Japanese. And the responsibility for organizing that offensive in east central Luzon—the almost certain site for an American invasion of the island—would rest squarely on the shoulders of Edwin Ramsey.

As he lay awake that night in a desolate shack south of Manila Bay, he thought of the submarine mentioned by Major Ruffy, where space had been reserved to take Ramsey to Australia. *Will there ever be another chance for me like that?* he asked himself. *Or will I end up like Joe Barker and Colonel Thorp and Pat Gatson and all the rest?*

There was no answer except for the wind-driven rain pounding against the nipa roof.

Among natives of the Davao Gulf region of Mindanao, legend had it that the vast swamp stretching north from the Davao Penal Colony harbored an inexplicable life of its own. It was inhabited, they said, by physical demons too monstrous for the human mind to contemplate and possessed by evil spirits capable of driving the strongest men insane.

After four days and nights struggling through its slimy, slowly rising water, attacked by swarms of leeches, and flailed bloody by massive stands of razor-sharp cogon grass that constantly blocked their way, the ten American escapees from DAPECOL had no reason to doubt the legend.

Although their reactions varied from man to man, all ten were breaking down physically and mentally and hovering perilously near the point of giving up.

Melvyn McCoy, the Navy officer who manned the compass and tried to keep them on course toward a railroad sketched on a makeshift map, now estimated that they were traveling at an abysmal pace of less than fifty yards per hour. Worse yet, McCoy was beset by chills and nausea, signaling the onset of a malaria or a dysentery attack. He battled the urge to sit down in the water and stay there.

Pilot Ed Dyess, normally among the most stalwart of the group, was staggering noticeably and on the point of abandoning his gear to the swamp when he was restrained by Marine Mike Dobervich.

In a state of semi-delirium after a shift of hacking at the ubiquitous cogon grass with a bolo knife, Sam Grashio was ready to collapse from exhaustion. "Tell McCoy to go on without me," he mumbled to Steve Mellnik, his partner.

Mellnik was equally hopeless—so much so that he announced his intention to turn around and start back toward DAPECOL until he was deterred by an angry yell from Shifty Shofner: "No, you are not!"

"We were all visibly frightened over our circumstances," said Shofner's fellow Marine, Jack Hawkins. "Things looked really bad. . . . The swamp was proving to be an enemy more deadly than the Japanese."

Maybe the legends are true, thought Mellnik. *Even if the swamp didn't kill you, it would drive you mad.*

Sick as he was, McCoy eventually managed to inject some rationality into the situation. "Look at the map," he said. "It shows we're only two or three miles from the railroad. If we keep on that compass course, we're bound to get out tomorrow or the next day at the latest."

After agreeing to stop early for the night, the escapees were stunned—yet somehow reassured—by a sudden sequence of events that was about to signal a dramatic change in their luck.

First came an outburst of explosions—a mix of rifle shots, machine gun fire, even mortar blasts—that seemed to come from a point no more than a mile or two away. To the experienced ears of the escapees, some of the weapons involved were clearly Japanese, others just as clearly American.

"That's a Nip burp gun," someone said.

"And that's a BAR," said Shofner.

Suddenly, a fiery red glow filled the sky, suggesting that the mortar shells had set one or more houses ablaze in a nearby barrio. As the glow intensified, the small-arms fire began to ebb, and Hawkins grabbed the compass. The needle pointed due north toward the glow and the gunfire.

"That way is out," said Dobervich. "Japs or no Japs."

After nightfall, while everyone was still tense and unable to sleep, Dyess suggested that his friend, former choirboy Grashio, recite a prayer for the men, and he did. It was one the nuns had taught him at school in Spokane.

"[O]h most gracious Virgin Mary, never was it known that anyone who fled to your protection or sought your intercession was left unaided. . . . To you I come, before you I stand, sinful and sorrowful. Oh, mother of the word incarnate . . . in your mercy and kindness, hear and answer me. Amen."

When he finished, the calming effect of the prayer seemed to change the atmosphere in the swamp. As Dyess put it, "I felt easier and more optimistic than I had since the start of the escape."

Grashio sensed that a miracle had occurred. "I felt now that God would save us," he said.

One of the first things they noticed the next day was that the water level of the swamp was steadily receding. Soon, it was barely ankle-deep, and they were splashing easily through it. By early afternoon, the swamp was behind them.

A short time later, they came upon the site of the firefight of the previous evening, but there were no Japanese in sight. They also found the railroad and a Filipino village where they were welcomed with food and chants of "Brave American soldiers! Brave American soldiers!"

They were congregated around a well, washing away the filth of the swamp, when they were confronted by a large, burly Filipino with two .45 Colt revolvers and double bandoleers of ammo across his barrel chest, who drew his pistols and demanded to know who they were.

When they convinced him that they were American escapees, a broad smile spread across the big Filipino's face. "I am Sergeant Casiano de Juan of the Mindanao guerrillas," he said, spreading his arms as if to embrace all of them at once. "We are happy to see Americans!"

A moment later, at de Juan's signal, several dozen other Filipinos emerged from the jungle armed with weapons ranging from BARs and old bolt-action rifles to homemade shotguns, bolos, Japanese swords, spears, and even bows and arrows.

These men were the ones who had ambushed the Japanese on the railroad, triggering the firefight of the night before, de Juan explained. "My men killed ten Japs there," he said proudly. "They [the Japanese] fired their machine gun and the small cannon [mortar] but hit nothing. They fought only a few minutes, and then they tied their dead on poles like pigs and ran away."

Although the escapees were still a long way from safety and their ultimate goal of getting back to the States, they could tell that their luck had turned, that their prayers had been answered.

In mid-July 1944, Major Ed Ramsey received orders by shortwave radio from MacArthur to initiate an all-out offensive of sabotage against the Japanese—a clear indication that an American invasion was no more than weeks away.

The centerpiece of Ramsey's response was one of the most spectacular explosions ever seen in Manila. At about 1 AM on July 16, a munitions expert named Wally Roeder set off a massive series of blasts that lasted through much of the rest of the night, destroying the main Japanese fuel oil storage depot in the city, sending flames hundreds of feet into the sky, and sinking a 10,000-ton Japanese tanker.

Ramsey was elated as he radioed MacArthur with news of the destruction, but even as he did so, his body was wracked with the most excruciating pain he'd yet experienced. The guerrilla leader had been stricken with repeated bouts of disease and infection since taking charge of the Luzon resistance, and now he was threatened by a grave new malady—acute appendicitis.

"You must be operated on immediately," said the Filipino doctor who examined Ramsey. "Otherwise, you'll die."

Because Ramsey was deemed too weak for chloroform, and there was no spinal anesthetic available, the emergency surgery was performed with only a bottle of rum to numb the patient.

On the eighth day after the surgery, although weakened by loss of blood, malnutrition, and an ongoing case of dysentery, Ramsey resumed his command duties. "I couldn't afford a convalescence," he said. "An invasion was coming, and I had to be ready for it. I sent communiqués to all my unit commanders to be on alert and stand by for emergency orders."

Meanwhile, Ramsey's message to MacArthur was simply this: The main strength of Japanese General Tomoyuki Yamashita's forces was concentrated on Luzon. Leyte was a much more favorable target for the initial U.S. invasion. Obviously, MacArthur had taken this information to heart when he waded ashore on Leyte on October 20.

By the time the invasion of Luzon occurred on January 9, 1945, Ramsey's hilltop headquarters had been discovered by the Japanese and was under relentless attack by enemy mortars and infantry.

"Tell MacArthur we may be closing up shop here," Ramsey told his radio operator before abandoning his camp and fleeing with the precious radio.

"Unleash maximum violence against the enemy," MacArthur's

headquarters had replied, even as the 280,000 troops of General Walter Krueger's Sixth Army poured ashore at Lingayen Gulf onto the same Luzon invasion beaches used by the Japanese in December 1941.

Facing the Americans were some 275,000 well-dug-in Japanese troops, who enjoyed the advantage of years of preparation for the defense of Luzon. "Behind [the Japanese], however," Ramsey noted, "were our guerrillas—over 40,000 of them—armed with every kind of weapon from machine guns to swords."

Other guerrilla units also joined the Sixth Army as it rolled south. "In every village," said Ramsey, "the American officers were greeted by organized . . . regiments that formally attached themselves to the Sixth Army . . . and they eagerly volunteered to [lead] the advance."

On January 31, Ramsey received his final message as a guerrilla leader from MacArthur: "All Luzon guerrilla forces will now pass under the control of Sixth Army, commanded by Lieutenant General Walter Krueger. You are directed to report to General Krueger for instructions."

"After three years as a guerrilla behind Japanese lines," Ramsey later recalled, "I was formally back in the war and once again an officer in the United States Army."

Private J. D. Merritt, a self-confessed brawler from rural Michigan who served with the 27th Bomb Group at Nielsen Field and in the Air Corps Infantry on Bataan, never made a serious effort to escape when he became a POW. He was having too much fun killing enemy guards and civilian Japanese bullies on their own turf.

After seeing troops of Japan's 65th Brigade, which had been badly mauled by American forces, slaughter hundreds of surrendered and helpless Filipino soldiers—hacking them to death with sabers and bayonets—Merritt developed an intense hatred of his captors. When he narrowly escaped being sent to Camp O'Donnell and was instead assigned as a slave-labor stevedore on the Manila docks, he spent most of his waking hours plotting and carrying out violent revenge against his captors.

Among his first victims were a group of recently arrived rear-echelon troops assigned to guard duty on the docks. "These 'newbies' all wanted to know where they could go swimming," Merritt recalled, "so I directed them to a shark-infested area where food scraps and other garbage were dumped."

He was rewarded by watching at least three or four of the guards torn to pieces by the sharks and several others severely injured.

Later, when Merritt was assigned to operate a winch to load cargo aboard ships, he caused a series of fatal "accidents" that claimed dozens more Japanese victims over a period of months. "I never got in any serious trouble," he said, "partly because the Japs had such low regard for human life, and partly because failures in the steam lines that operated the winches were so commonplace. Sabotage by winch was a great success and would become our number one way of destroying certain major assets for waging war."

As Merritt readily admitted, sheer luck also played a role in his ability to continue his killing spree. After he was sent to Japan aboard a hellship to work in a coal mine, one of his targets was a huge, vicious guard named Fukuka, who delighted in beating POWs unmercifully for minor offenses.

Although Merritt was hobbled by an injured leg, and the only weapon at his disposal was a sharpened stick used to help him pick his way through deep snow to a latrine, he lured the guard into a empty tunnel of the mine by screaming insults at him.

"Eat shit, you fat bastard!" Merritt yelled. "You gross, stinking pig!"

When the enraged Fukuda lunged at him, Merritt drove the sharpened point of his stick up the guard's nose and straight into his brain.

"I watched the man-mountain cradle his head in his hands and . . . slowly sink to his knees," Merritt wrote in a memoir published in 2010 titled *Adapt or Die*. "Then . . . he slowly rolled over, stone-cold dead."

As Merritt hurriedly tried to cover the body with gravel, an earth-shaking explosion rumbled through the mine shaft, and timbers and boulders began falling all around him. He narrowly escaped death by crawling under a nearby rail car, but the cave-in conveniently buried the guard's body.

"All evidence of his untimely 'accident' was totally obliterated,"

Merritt wrote, "and I shouted, 'Thank you, Lord, for granting me another miracle!'"

More than sixty-eight years later, Merritt declined to speculate on the total number of deaths he was able to cause as a POW. "After the first hundred or so," he said, "I quit counting."

13

A Race Between Freedom and Death

By late 1943, the tides of war were steadily and inexorably turning against Japan. Her dreams of permanent military, economic, and cultural dominance over East Asia were crumbling into dust. One by one, her conquered territories were being wrested away, and her limited resources—from fuel for her ships and planes to food for the bellies of her troops—were near exhaustion. The inevitable end of the conflict she had started at Pearl Harbor two years earlier grew more apparent with every passing week.

In view of this, it would seem that the callous arrogance with which rampaging Japanese soldiers had butchered innocent civilians and helpless prisoners in the early days of the war would have been tempered to some extent by harsh reality. Many of Tokyo's legions were now ravaged by illness and near starvation themselves. Thousands were trapped by an omnipresent U.S. Navy on remote islands with no hope of reinforcement or resupply, and thousands more were in retreat.

Yet the slaughter of American and Allied prisoners continued, either out of mindless desperation or in the belief that the fewer American captives lived to survive the war, the easier it would be to conceal their fate.

One particularly blatant example of such premeditated mass murder occurred on the night of October 7, 1943, on a beach at Wake Island, where the first pitched battle between Japanese and American troops had taken place during a sixteen-day siege in December 1941.

More than 1,200 civilian American construction workers had been marooned on Wake when the war broke out. Many had fought side by side with U.S. Marines and Navy Bluejackets in defense of the tiny atoll, then become part of the only group of U.S. POWs to be confined for a longer period by the Japanese than those from Bataan. The vast majority of these workers, however, had been shipped to Japan and China as slave laborers, and on the night in question, only ninety-six remained on Wake.

After dark that evening, three platoons of Japanese soldiers, directed by Lieutenant Torashi Ito and following orders issued by Admiral Shigematsu Sakaibara, the Japanese commander on Wake, were positioned with machine guns and rifles behind a single long line of bound and blindfolded prisoners.

"Go ahead as ordered," Ito told the executioners, and they opened fire, not stopping until they were convinced that all their victims were dead. The bullet-riddled bodies were then buried in a mass grave. (One prisoner somehow escaped death but was later captured and executed.)

Under questioning by members of the postwar military tribunal that eventually sentenced him to death, Sakaibara at first denied any knowledge of what had happened to the Americans. But he finally testified that he'd ordered the massacre because his own men were starving, and the American civilians were consuming food that was vital to the survival of his isolated garrison.

A motivation that seems equally likely, however, was retribution for intensive attacks on Wake during the forty-eight hours preceding the executions. During this time, carrier-based U.S. planes blistered Wake with 340 tons of bombs, and U.S. ships pounded Japanese positions with 3,200 5- and 8-inch artillery rounds. All civilian POWs had been in shelters during the attacks, and none had been injured.

The American public wouldn't learn about the wholesale murders on Wake until the war was over and Sakaibara was on trial—and conceivably, the bloodbath might never have been discovered if not for the diligence of American war crimes investigators.

Even more amazing, considering the massive death toll involved, is that it took the U.S. civilian population nearly two years to learn about the thousands of blatant atrocities committed during the Bataan

Death March and at Camp O'Donnell. And perhaps most incredible yet is the fact that, if not for the escapees from Davao Penal Colony who reached the United States in late 1943 determined to see the facts made public, it might have taken much longer for the truth to come out.

A major contributor to the delay in releasing such important information to the public was fear at the highest levels of the U.S. government. Federal officials were concerned—with good cause—that a tidal wave of outrage would engulf the American public. But they also feared bloody Japanese reprisals against the thousands of American POWs still at the mercy of their captors.

No veteran of Bataan or Corregidor had a longer—or more tension-packed—trip home to America than Lieutenant Ed Whitcomb, aka Robert Johnson. As the only impostor among the hundreds of American civilians in the Philippines hoping for repatriation, Whitcomb lived in constant fear for months that his true identity as a U.S. military officer would be discovered.

His incredible around-the-world journey began in the early fall of 1943 at the civilian internment center at Santo Tomas University in Manila, then took him to a similar facility in Shanghai, then to Hong Kong, and—discouragingly—back to the Philippines. On the next leg, after stops at Saigon and Singapore, the route stretched through the straits between Java and Sumatra, then across the Indian Ocean to the Portuguese colony of Goa on the west coast of India.

"At Goa, we met the Swedish ship *Gripsholm*, which had brought Japanese civilians from the United States," he recalled. "There, without ceremony, but with much exaltation, we exchanged ships with the passengers from the *Gripsholm*."

Going aboard the luxuriously appointed Swedish liner was, in Whitcomb's words, "like stepping into heaven. It represented freedom and everything we'd dreamed of for so long. It was a neutral ship, and for all intents and purposes, we were free from the domination of the Japanese."

In mid-October, the *Gripsholm* sailed from Goa to Port Elizabeth, South Africa, then across the South Atlantic to Rio de Janeiro. Finally, on the gray morning of December 9, 1943—nearly three months after his journey began—Whitcomb awoke in New York harbor within sight of the Statue of Liberty.

As thoughts of going home to the small town of Hayden, Indiana, and being reunited with his parents, his brother, and his sisters tugged at Whitcomb's mind, a fellow passenger rushed up to him.

"Hey, Bob, somebody's looking for you," the man said.

Seconds later, Whitcomb found himself face-to-face with a well-dressed stranger. "Are you Robert Johnson?" he asked, looking Whitcomb straight in the eye.

"Yes, sir," Whitcomb responded.

"Are you also Edgar D. Whitcomb?" the stranger demanded in a low tone, flashing an FBI badge.

Stunned, Whitcomb could only nod.

Once they were off the ship and in a taxi bound for Grand Central Station, the FBI agent broke some bitter news to Whitcomb. There would be no Indiana homecoming for him, at least not anytime soon.

"You're to proceed directly to Washington, D.C., and report to this address," the agent said, handing Whitcomb a slip of paper. "But you're not to make any attempt to contact any of your friends or anyone you've ever known before, and under no circumstances are you to talk to anyone about your experiences."

The next day, Whitcomb found himself deep in the bowels of the Pentagon, being interrogated by a fat colonel of military intelligence. The colonel's questions had a decidedly unfriendly tone, and they continued hour after hour.

"Well," said the colonel finally, "it seems that about the only thing left for you to do is to be interned for the duration of the war. If it ever became known to the Japanese that an American Air Corps officer was repatriated on a civilian exchange ship, it might be impossible to negotiate any more exchanges of civilians. I've talked with some of the other intelligence officers about your case, and it's been suggested that you be put up in a hotel where you'll continue to live under the name of Robert Fred Johnson. You would, of course, not be able to contact your family or any of your friends until the end of the war."

The colonel's suggested solution to the problem left Whitcomb wide-eyed with disbelief.

"The idea was too fantastic for me to comprehend," he would recall years later. "I thought it would've been better for Bill [Harris] and me to have accepted the Filipinos' offer to take care of us until the Americans came back to the Philippines. For that matter, I wouldn't have been any worse off back in the internment camp in Shanghai. I was starting to feel like a man without a country."

Whitcomb tried desperately to explain to the colonel that the Japanese had no record of his real name. At the 92nd Garage on Corregidor, he'd been assigned the number 0-200, but his name had never been recorded by his captors. In all the other places where he'd been interned—Fort Santiago, Santo Tomas University, and the Chapei camp in Shanghai—he'd used the name Robert Fred Johnson. The Japanese had no record that Lieutenant Edgar D. Whitcomb had ever been their prisoner.

It all seemed so simple, but the colonel refused to understand. Every day for the next two weeks, Whitcomb was placed in an empty room in the Pentagon with only a desk, a chair, and a typewriter and told to write the complete details of his experiences, from the initial attack on Clark Field to his arrival in Washington.

It was like being a prisoner all over again, but at least this time there was no iron pipe.

In early July 1943, former P-40 squadron leader Ed Dyess was among the first of the Davao Penal Colony escapees to be spirited out of the Philippines en route to the United States by way of Australia. As a survivor of the Bataan Death March, Dyess had been handed the special mission of relating to a still unaware American public exactly what had happened during the march, in the charnel house of Camp O'Donnell's Zero Ward, and during other wholesale atrocities committed by the Japanese against American POWs. Dyess's "travel arrangements" were courtesy of the captain and crew of the U.S. submarine *Trout* and a vast Mindanao guerrilla force led by "General" Wendell Fertig, a former Army Corps of Engineers officer who had appointed himself its commander.

It was only now, nearly a year and a half after the fall of Bataan, that high government officials in Washington—including President Roosevelt—would learn the full extent of Japanese brutality against American captives.

Dyess had been personally designated by General MacArthur to reveal the horrific details of the Death March and other Japanese crimes against humanity. But until FDR himself determined the right moment to release this bombshell to the public, the president decreed that it remain one of the war's most closely guarded secrets.

At this point, government censorship played an integral role in the nation's war strategy, and in many quarters, the subject of Bataan, in particular, was considered one to avoid. As historian John Lukacs put it, "The news of Bataan's surrender had been devastating when finally delivered in full, deflating detail in the spring of 1942. A funereal gloom had shrouded the country as newspapers, radio, and newsreels revealed that approximately 36,000 U.S. troops were believed to have been surrendered . . . [in] the largest and most ignominious [defeat] in U.S. military history."

In the view of some Washington leaders, this news had triggered the first serious public doubts about the Europe First strategy embraced by the Roosevelt administration. Carried to extremes, some officials believed, the reaction to the Death March could undermine public support of the entire war effort. The War Department's Office of Censorship had warned America's media to lay off stories about atrocities, and had, in fact, forbidden publication of photos of American soldiers killed in action. But now, growing rumors of the unspeakable horrors committed on Bataan threatened to inflame the controversy.

At the center of this maelstrom was Ed Dyess, recently promoted to the rank of lieutenant colonel, who had given a fourteen-page deposition to officials at the Pentagon as what Dyess considered an inseparable part of the assignment handed him by General MacArthur. It was a document studded with hair-raising revelations about Japanese brutality on Bataan as well as deep insights into the young officer's own tortured emotions.

During his stint as a Japanese prisoner, Dyess had become a legendary figure back in the States. Beginning in July 1942, while Dyess was still suffering from disease and starvation at Cabanatuan, a series of major articles about his prowess as a P-40 pilot had appeared in the *New York Times*. Now many magazines and newspapers were bidding for the publishing rights to the entire Dyess saga. But Dyess himself was most favorably impressed with *Chicago Tribune* assistant managing editor Don Maxwell and reporter Charles Leavelle, both of whom had visited Dyess while he was convalescing from exhaustion in a West Virginia hospital.

"The thing I must do—the thing I'm going to do—is to tell the American people what the Japs have done and are doing to their sons and husbands and brothers out in the Philippines," Dyess told the *Tribune* representatives. "I'm going to tell my story through the medium that will get it to the most people most effectively."

The *Tribune* offered $21,000 for first publication rights to what would soon become known coast to coast as "The Dyess Story," and although money wasn't a major consideration for Dyess, the audience of up to 14 million readers promised by the *Tribune* prompted the young officer to sit up in bed and stick out his right hand to Maxwell and Leavelle.

"It's a deal," he said.

Before the story would see the light of day, however, official Washington—and the White House itself—would step in to suppress it.

As Roosevelt confided to Secretary of War Henry Stimson and Navy Secretary Frank Knox in a letter dated September 9, 1943: "I agree with your opinion that any publication of Japanese atrocities at this time might complicate the present and future missions of the *Gripsholm* and increase the mistreatment of prisoners now in Japanese hands. I request, therefore, that you take effective measures to prevent the publication or circulation of any stories emanating from escaped prisoners until I have authorized a release."

Leavelle received clearance from Washington to conduct interviews for a series of articles based on Dyess's personal experiences and observations as a Bataan POW, to be published in the *Tribune* at an unspecified future date. But when Brigadier General Alexander Surles, chief of the War Department's Bureau of Public Relations, came to confer with Dyess, Leavelle, and Maxwell, he refused even to read the five chapters of "The Dyess Story" that they tried to submit for his approval. A blanket ban had been placed on all atrocity stories, he informed them, so it would be pointless for him to read the material.

Tragically, Ed Dyess wouldn't live to see his story made public. On December 22, 1943, he was killed in a plane crash while taking off on a test flight in one of the Army's new P-38 fighters. It was more than a month later—and only after intervention by the Joint Chiefs of Staff—that the government's gag order on atrocity stories was finally lifted.

On Sunday, January 28, 1944, the first installment of the "The Dyess Story" appeared on page one of the *Chicago Tribune* and ran simultaneously in a hundred associated newspapers. Other major media outlets satisfied themselves by featuring the atrocity reports by Dyess and fellow escapees Commander Melvyn McCoy and Lieutenant Colonel Steve Mellnik under such blaring headlines as "5,200 AMERICANS, MANY MORE FILIPINOS DIE OF STARVATION, TORTURE AFTER BATAAN" (*New York Times*). The Associated Press called the revelations "a horror story scarcely paralleled in the annals of modern war."

The exposé struck the American people and their elected leaders with tornadic force and launched a national tidal wave of fury and outrage.

"Let the Japanese know in plain and no uncertain terms that we're going to hold them responsible for this nasty, damnable, despicable business," said New York congressman Sol Bloom, chairman of the House Foreign Affairs Committee.

"May this great ship be an avenger to the barbarians who wantonly slaughtered the heroes of Bataan," intoned Senator Harry S. Truman as he presided over the christening and launching of the battleship *Missouri* at the Brooklyn Navy Yard.

"The Japanese have violated not only the principles of international law," added British foreign secretary Anthony Eden, "but all canons of decent, civilized conduct."

By some accounts, the revelations of Dyess and his fellow escapees aroused the American nation like nothing since Pearl Harbor. But a haunting question remained, and no one in the United States could reliably predict the answer. Now that the truth was out, would it serve to deter Japanese barbarism in the future? Or would it encourage the Japanese to hold fast to their belief that international law was whatever they wanted it to be in any given situation—and to hell with the consequences?

After spending two seemingly endless weeks gravitating between nights in a lonely room at Washington's Lafayette Hotel and days in an equally lonely office at the Pentagon, Lieutenant Ed Whitcomb could only wonder if his status as a nonperson would ever end.

By this point in the fall of 1943, the B-17 navigator had virtually abandoned any thought of getting back into action with the Army Air Corps, and he would gladly have settled for a train ticket home to Indiana and a reunion with his family—who still had no knowledge of his return to the States.

When he was summoned to yet another interview with the now familiar colonel of Army intelligence, Whitcomb reported to the designated room with little hope of escaping the limbo in which he floundered. Instead, he was handed a stunning surprise.

"It's been decided that you should be returned to active duty in the Air Corps under your real name," the colonel informed him. "You'll be given a couple of weeks leave to visit your family. Then you'll report to the Army Air Corps Redistribution Center in Miami for reassignment."

Whitcomb could hardly believe his ears. "That's great!" he said. "Does that mean I can call my family now?"

"Sure, any time," the colonel replied. "But there's one thing I can't impress on you too strongly. You're not, under any circumstances, ever to leave the continental limits of the United States or enter the Asiatic Theater of Operations for the duration of the war. If you try it, you'll find yourself facing a court-martial."

An hour later, Lieutenant Edgar D. Whitcomb had been reborn. He was dressed in a brand-new uniform with second lieutenant's bars on his shoulders and a pair of silver wings on his chest. He was also headed, as fast as his legs would carry him, for his hotel room to call his mother and tell her the news: He was safe in the United States, on his way home, and no longer missing in action!

As Whitcomb would recall triumphantly years later, "Robert Fred Johnson, who had occupied my body for a year and a half in a world of fantasy, had disappeared from the face of the earth."

When General Walter Krueger's Sixth Army landed at Lingayan Gulf on January 9, 1945, American military brass realized that they were entering a crucial period of maximum danger for the POWs still being held at the Cabanatuan prison compound about thirty-five miles inland from the U.S. beachhead.

From virtually every guerrilla unit and resistance organization on Luzon came the same urgent warnings by radio and messenger: The 500-plus remaining American captives at Cabanatuan—many of them already near death from disease, starvation, and abuse—would be executed immediately by their Japanese guards at the first sign that U.S. forces were approaching the compound.

The high-risk task of preventing this massacre and freeing the POWs was assigned to an assault team of 107 U.S. Army Rangers and thirteen members of the Alamo Scouts, an elite commando group specializing in infiltration tactics. Under the command of Lieutenant Colonel Henry Mucci, a thirty-three-year-old West Pointer, the Americans would be supported by 220 or so Filipino guerrillas familiar with the territory—bringing the total U.S. assault force to about 325 men.

Opposing them, once they reached the Cabanatuan stockade, would be an estimated 250 heavily armed guards, and as the rescuers made their way across the miles of enemy-infested territory to reach the prison camp, unknown numbers of Japanese combat troops could be expected to stand in their way. Then there was the trip back over the same perilous route to escort the sick, emaciated, exhausted POWs to safety. It was a mission that would test the nerve and skill of even the most battle-savvy Rangers.

"We've got to hit the Japs tonight," Colonel Mucci warned his troops on the morning of January 30, 1945, as they crept to within a rifle shot's distance of the prison compound. "Intelligence says there are 9,000 Japs in this region, so we can't stay right in the center of all this Jap activity indefinitely without being discovered."

Meanwhile, inside the Cabanatuan stockade, the tension was equally high. "All of us were fearful," recalled Texas-born PFC Cecil Easley. "From clandestine radio sets hidden in the camp, we knew that General MacArthur's troops had landed at Lingayen Gulf, but most POWs felt the Japanese would embark on a murderous rampage . . . as our forces grew closer."

By January 1945, the phenomenal run of good fortune that had followed Captain Ralph Hibbs for months after the fall of Bataan had vanished like a puff of smoke. That much seemed apparent from the fact that the young former medical officer in the 31st Infantry now found himself among the last 511 American prisoners still being held at Cabanatuan, where a peak inmate population of 12,000 had once been incarcerated.

As recently as the previous autumn, Cabanatuan had still housed some 6,500 POWs, but between October and December, three large groups of prisoners, numbering about 2,000 each, had been evacuated for transfer by hell ships to work sites in Japan and elsewhere. The majority had been drowned or killed in attacks by U.S. planes or submarines before they reached their destinations. (Hibbs would later learn that his friend Bill Tooley, the fourth member of the Whiffenpoof Boys, had drowned after the attack on the *Oryoku Maru*, leaving Hibbs as the group's sole survivor. The fifth Whiffenpoof, Captain Dwight T. Hunkins, is listed among eighty-seven members of his H Company, 31st Infantry, who died in captivity, but the details of his death are unknown.)

After the transfers, the only POWs remaining in camp were, in Hibbs's words, "500 of the sickest and most maimed patients, carefully selected by the Japs . . . a sorry lot, many minus legs and arms." They included every patient in the tuberculosis ward overseen by Hibbs, a primary reason that, when the camp's medical contingent was cut by more than two-thirds in late 1944, he was one of just ten staff members selected to stay.

Soon afterward, even the regular detachment of guards disappeared, to be replaced by itinerant cadres of unfamiliar Japanese soldiers, who, it was theorized, would have even less compunction about machine-gunning and bayoneting helpless captives than the guards they replaced.

From the way his luck had been running, Hibbs considered his selection to remain at Cabanatuan tantamount to a death sentence, and the sound of friendly artillery fire in the distance only increased the tension within the stockade.

"We were entirely defenseless," he recalled. "Any wild, undisciplined Jap outfit could wipe us out for kicks or for the emperor. . . . Our options were zilch. We waited with grim smiles on our faces."

But at precisely 7:45 PM on January 30, Hibbs would discover that his "misfortune" in remaining at Cabanatuan was actually the luckiest break of his entire life.

The first volleys of small-arms rounds erupted at the south gate of the compound. Seconds later, rapid bursts from automatic weapons echoed from the direction of the main guard house. Then the entire perimeter of the camp exploded with gunfire.

"My God, they're finally going to kill us!" one of the POWs screamed. But it became clear almost instantly that it wasn't the Japanese doing the shooting. In the pale glow of the setting sun, Hibbs saw the lifeless bodies of both Japanese sentries topple over the railings of the watchtowers by the main gate. The sight sent a thrill racing through him.

"It must be a guerrilla raid!" he shouted.

Suddenly, a series of ear-splitting blasts shook the compound, and the prisoners saw several Japanese tanks that had arrived that afternoon transformed into balls of fire by rockets from American bazookas. Within seconds, dozens of running figures appeared, darting through the compound in all directions. At first, many of the POWs thought the green-clad figures were Japanese, but then the figures started to yell.

"We're Americans! You're all free! Everybody head for the main gate!"

"By golly, they *are* Americans!" shouted Sergeant Abie Abraham, a career NCO who had served in the 31st Infantry on Bataan. "It's true! They've come!"

As Abraham dragged a critically ill POW from beneath one of the barracks buildings and led him toward the front gate over the bodies of dead Japanese, he saw an American Ranger waving him on.

"We've got orders to bring out every damned man," the Ranger told him. "We're gonna bring them all out even if we have to carry every man on our backs. That's our instructions."

Meanwhile, amid the shambles of his TB ward, Hibbs stared incredulously at the figure nearest him. "What the hell's going on?" he demanded. "Where did you come from?"

"We're Army Rangers," the heavily armed soldier said. "General Krueger's boys. Now get the hell out of here."

"But my men can't even walk," Hibbs protested.

"The rest of the prisoners have been carried out," the Ranger said. "You're the last damn one. Now get going!"

To emphasize the urgency of the situation, the Ranger picked Hibbs up bodily with one hand, turned him downhill, and gave him a persuasive nudge in the backside with his foot. Hibbs paused momentarily to glance back into the ward, but he found it totally vacant, just as the Ranger had said.

My God, he thought, *how did they do this?*

As he stumbled toward the main road, he heard another Ranger yell a warning at him: "Hurry, a Jap column's approaching our roadblock! You're the last man."

Hibbs glanced over his shoulder at orange flashes from enemy rifles on a knoll behind him, met by a withering counterfire from the Rangers. Bright yellow streaks marked the paths of rockets from American bazookas.

As he stumbled over the body of a dead Japanese soldier, Hibbs caught a glimpse of Cabanatuan's headquarters building being consumed by flames. The sight warmed his heart.

Nearby, Ranger Captain Bob Prince checked his watch. It was 8:13 PM—barely twenty-eight minutes since the Rangers had opened fire in their initial assault. Only a handful of Americans had been hit, but the Japanese garrison of 250 soldiers had been wiped out virtually to a man, and the freed POWs were being carried or escorted northward with all possible speed toward the Pampanga River.

Prince fired a red flare into the sky, signaling the Rangers and Alamo Scouts to withdraw from the area. Off in the distance to the east, he could hear constant gunfire from where Captain Juan Pajota's 150-man Filipino guerrilla force was holding pursuing Japanese troops at bay. Meanwhile, a mile or two to the west, a similar guerrilla force under Captain Eduardo Joson was manning the other half of a V-shaped roadblock to shield the Rangers' and POWs' retreat.

By 8:45 PM, only an hour after the assault on the stockade had begun, Captain Prince and the rear of the American column were at the south bank of the Pampanga, where the Rangers began the task of carrying or guiding the prisoners across the shallow stream. Waiting on the opposite bank were twenty-six two-wheeled, carabao-drawn carts, whose job was to transport the POWs to safety across miles of enemy territory. The carts and draft animals had been collected from virtually every Filipino farmer in a ten-mile radius.

Within a half-hour, the river crossings were completed, and Prince was able to fire a second red flare, signaling Captains Joson and Pajota to withdraw their guerrillas from the roadblocks and alerting the Alamo Scouts to assume their position as a rear guard.

Meanwhile, high above, a squadron of eleven P-61 "Black Widow" night fighters searched for any evidence of enemy troop movements that might attempt to block the American withdrawal. At about 9 PM, one of the planes spotted a convoy of five troop-filled Japanese trucks and a tank moving toward the retreating column from about two miles away. Within minutes, all six vehicles were left burning, with their human cargo either dead or scattered in confusion along the roadside.

It was early the next afternoon, following a seventeen-hour trek through hostile territory and still nearly five miles from American lines, when the bone-weary caravan was met by a convoy of U.S. Army trucks, ambulances, armored cars, and troop carriers, escorted by a company of infantry and protected by an umbrella of friendly aircraft.

Exuberant Filipino civilians, alerted by the "bamboo telegraph," descended in droves on the dusty roadside to celebrate the rescue mission's success and offer gifts of food to the newly liberated prisoners. Some POWs sat in a daze while others laughed, cried, munched hamburgers brought by the trucks, and jabbered excitedly to each other while exhausted Rangers stretched out on the ground and fell asleep.

"If this is a dream," muttered one emaciated survivor of Cabanatuan, "then don't wake me up."

Deeply saddened by the death from wounds of a fellow medical officer just as the journey to safety was ending, Captain Ralph Hibbs was overcome with emotion at his first sight of an American flag fluttering from the turret of one of the arriving tanks.

"My heart stopped," he recalled. "What a sight, blurred through my teary eyes. My chin came up. This produced an exhilaration I hadn't experienced in three years. I was free!"

From General MacArthur's headquarters came this official communiqué summing up the mission:

> Five hundred and thirteen prisoners [actually 511] were freed by a force of 121 Rangers and 286 Filipino guerrillas. Two of the prisoners died from heart attacks in the course of the rescue. The Japanese guard of 73 men and 150 other Japanese soldiers were killed in the camp. In the action at the camp proper, two Rangers were killed and two wounded. Our total losses were 27 killed and two wounded. Jap losses were at least 532 dead and 12 tanks destroyed. . . . Nothing in this entire campaign has given me so much personal satisfaction.

After reaching safety, Dr. Hibbs was quickly promoted to the rank of major, but the exhilaration he had felt on realizing that he was finally a free man was short-lived.

During the second week of February, advancing American forces heard ominous rumors describing the vicious fighting within the embattled city of Manila. As U.S. troops battered their way into the heart of the Philippine capital, dug-in Japanese resisted them block by block and house to house. According to reports, the main fighting was centered on the south side of Manila between Dewey and Taft Boulevards and in the Intramuros, the old Walled City.

As Hibbs well knew, the home of Pilar Campos and her family was at 1462 Taft Boulevard, almost in the center of the battle zone, and every rumor that reached the rear area where Hibbs was stationed flooded him with a new wave of dread. Artillery from both sides was pounding that area around the clock, causing tens of thousands of civilian casualties, and Japanese troops were taking a last measure of vengeance against helpless Filipinos trapped between the two armies.

On February 12, as the fighting in the city had begun to ebb somewhat, Hibbs saw two skinny, barefoot Filipinos armed with bolo knives approaching the hut where he was quartered, and he heard them calling his name.

"I'm Major Hibbs," he said from the doorway. "Do you want me?"

The two men lowered their heads apologetically and in unison. Then one of them spoke softly and hesitantly in good English. "Sir," he said, "we have bad news."

Hibbs froze where he stood, sensing what the man was about to say.

"Pilar has . . . been killed," the Filipino said in a barely audible voice. "Friends sent us here after hearing of your release. They . . . wanted you to know."

"Oh, God, no!" Hibbs said in a choking gasp, slumping on jellylike knees to a sitting position on the steps of his hut.

Please, not her, he thought as tears gushed onto his cheeks and images of Pilar flashed through his mind. He saw her face close to his on a moonlit night in another world. He saw her standing at attention and facing the American flag at retreat at Fort McKinley. He saw her riding her bike past Bilibid prison, then slipping close to its walls to deliver money and medicine to him. He saw her smiling and heard her singing, "I'll be with you in apple blossom time . . ."

"Do you know what happened?" he finally managed to ask.

The two did their best to explain. Japanese soldiers had been going door-to-door through the neighborhood, shooting and bayoneting people in their homes, they said. By the time they pounded on the front door of the Campos mansion, Pilar had let more than a hundred frightened, fleeing civilians into the house. She opened the door a few inches, leaving the security chain attached, and told the Japanese soldiers that she wanted to speak to their commanding officer. Instead, they shot her through the door, hitting her in the stomach. Then they rushed the door and broke it down. They dragged her onto the front lawn, and as she knelt there bleeding, one soldier lunged at her and drove his bayonet into her chest.

While Pilar lay mortally wounded, the men added, her mother was gunned down inside the Campos home, along with dozens of other civilians, by Japanese firing automatic weapons. After completing the massacre, the soldiers then doused the house with gasoline and set it ablaze.

Hibbs learned for the first time how Pilar's brother, Tony, had been seized as a suspected American sympathizer by the dreaded Kampeitei in January 1942, strung up by his feet from a column at the Spanish Club, and left there to die. A few days earlier, Pilar's father, an international banker and president of the Bank of the Philippines, had suffered a fatal heart attack, induced by Japanese threats and harassment.

The hundreds of bodies littering the streets and yards along Taft Boulevard in the wake of the Japanese retreat had been collected later by American troops of the Sixth Army and buried in mass, unmarked graves gouged out by bulldozers. In one of them—no one could be certain which—were the bodies of Pilar and her mother.

With a stifling feeling of remorse and recrimination, Hibbs remembered Pilar telling him how she'd gone to his apartment and taken his footlocker to her home for safekeeping. If the Japanese had found the locker and seen his name and military rank stenciled on it, he knew that the Campos house and its occupants might well have been marked for death even before the rampaging Japanese soldiers broke in.

"I was demolished," Hibbs recalled years later, still deeply shaken. "A never to be filled void was born in my life. Guilt overcame me. I was the one in uniform. The end should have been mine, not hers. Somewhere our love was buried—but not my memories."

In many of the slave labor camps in Japan proper and her occupied territories, the POWs may have been in as grave danger of mass execution as the war neared its end as were the civilians in Manila or the skin-and-bones "zombies" at Cabanatuan.

"The Japs told us we'd all be killed if the United States invaded Japan," recalled PFC John Oliver, formerly of the 19th Bomb Group, who traveled by hell ship to the industrial city of Kawasaki to work, first in a steel mill, then unloading ships at the docks, then in a copper smelter.

"We prayed for a miracle, and God sent us two—one at Hiroshima and another at Nagasaki," Oliver said, referring to the atomic bombs that destroyed those Japanese cities.

After the war, Oliver managed to obtain a copy of a now declassified death order issued to Japanese security forces on Taiwan and dated August 1, 1944. The document describes in detail how the "final disposition" of the POW population was to be carried out.

"Whether they [POWs] are destroyed individually or in groups," it reads, "or however it is done, with mass bombing, poisonous smoke, poisons, drowning, decapitation, or what, dispose of them as the situation dictates.

"In any case, it is the aim not to allow the escape of a single one, to annihilate them all, and not to leave any traces."

No surviving American POW was more acutely aware of how close these and similar execution orders came to being put into effect than Sergeant Louis Read, late of the 31st Infantry. After being hospitalized for several weeks with an acute bout of amoebic dysentery, Read returned in the late summer of 1945 to his slave labor job at the Mitsubishi-owned Hosokura mine in northern Japan, where he found tension hanging heavy in the air.

"Each night, there was a total blackout in the camp, the town, and the smelter nearby," Read recalled. "We could hear huge formations of airplanes flying over in the direction of Tokyo every night. There were so many that it seemed to take an hour or more for all of them to go over."

At about this same time, the camp's Japanese commander called the prisoners together and stunned them with the news that all POWs would be executed if the Americans invaded the mainland of Japan. Then, almost in the same breath, he informed them that an execution date had already been set.

"The time of the invasion appears imminent," he said solemnly, "and therefore the date of your execution has been set for August 29."

The date in question was still about four weeks away, but only a day or two later a platoon of hard-eyed Japanese soldiers marched into the compound and proceeded to set up a line of machine guns. Said Read:

> Needless to say, our morale wasn't helped by this information or the sight of troops with machine guns. In the meantime, work continued unabated in the mine, although, admittedly, we didn't get much done.

On August 16, we were marched to work unusually early in the morning, and about noon, we were all ordered outside for a roll call. This was totally unheard of, and we were afraid they'd moved up the execution date, which was still two weeks away. As we marched through town, we saw women office workers standing in the streets crying. It turned out that they'd just heard the emperor's announcement on the radio that Japan had surrendered.

It seemed too good to be true, and we didn't believe it at first. But we noticed that the planes had quit coming over every night, and the lights were back on in the town. After a day or two, all the Japanese guards and the commandant disappeared. Only a few civilian Mitsubishi flunkies were left, and they told us the war was over.

As he looked back on that incredible time some sixty-eight years later, Read was still shaking his head in disbelief.

"I can't help wondering sometimes," he mused, "what would've happened if August 29 had gotten there before the emperor made his surrender announcement."

Ironically, as mass bombing raids intensified against Japan's major industrial centers, more American POWs were fatally wounded in attacks by planes flown by their own countrymen than were intentionally killed by the Japanese.

"In late July [1945], we took a bad bombing," recalled Staff Sergeant James Cavanaugh, who had served in the 28th Bombardment Squadron and was also at Kawasaki. "The bombers really turned our camp over. They came in first with incendiary bombs. Then they hit us with the heavy stuff. . . . We lost twenty-five Americans. It was so close to the end of the war [and] we felt so bad. The shelter where . . . eleven Japs were hiding also took a direct hit. Killed all of them. The one guard who was with us was the only one left. When he learned what had happened to his buddies, he went haywire. He put a bayonet on his rifle and began to wildly stab at us. He cut quite a few men. . . . Most of the men who escaped being killed that night were badly beaten by the Japs."

Such uncontrolled anger on the part of Japanese guards who acted on impulse, rather than orders, played a role in an unknown number of fatal beatings, stabbings, or shootings of American prisoners during this climactic period. PFC Andrew Aquila, formerly of the 192nd Tank Battalion and an inmate at Fukuoka Camp No. 3 at Tobata, Japan, was an eyewitness to one particular incident.

"One guy in our barracks made a wager with someone in another barracks of a half-ration of rice that a raid would take place at a certain time," Aquila recalled. "When he won the wager, he went over to the barracks to collect. . . . On his way back, a Jap guard caught him. He explained what he was doing . . . [but] the guard beat hell out of this guy. When he came into the barracks, he was bleeding badly around the head. . . . They wouldn't permit him to stay in the hospital but returned him instead to work. Finally, when he got worse, he was permitted to go to the hospital. No more than two weeks before we were liberated, he died."

The rage among the Japanese at seeing their own country coming under increasingly lethal attacks was also felt at Camp 17 at Fukuoka, where 1,500 slave laborers in a nearby coal mine were housed. After a particularly bloody strafing run, in which U.S. planes struck only the Japanese guards' section of the camp while merely dipping their wings as they passed over the POWs' side without firing a shot, the guards took vicious retribution.

"They cut our food ration in half that day and hit more of us than ever before," said Corporal Les Tenney, who had served in the 192nd Tank Battalion, "and we knew why. We got the message: the Allies were winning the war, and time would soon tell the story of how the rising sun fell."

When Tenney was cruelly beaten that night for a minor breach of rules, he took the punishment unflinchingly and with pride.

Their time's coming, he told himself. *Maybe not today, but soon—real soon.*

On the morning of August 6, 1945, Tenney's prophecy began coming true. As the prisoners reported for work as usual, they noticed a sudden, marked change in the demeanor of the civilian employees in the mine, and the guards were noticeably nervous. A friendly civilian approached Tenney and muttered, "Many Japanese killed by big bomb."

Tenney dared not crack a smile, but he laughed inside.

Three mornings later, on August 9, as the POWs began their routine hike to the mine, they looked to the southeast, toward the city of Nagasaki thirty-five miles away, and saw a peculiarly shaped cloud floating in the air with a long stem trailing at its base.

"Not in a million years could we have dreamed of a weapon like the atomic bomb and the destruction it caused," Tenney recalled. "As far as Camp 17 was concerned, there is no doubt that dropping this devastating bomb saved our lives, as well as the lives of millions of our Allies and our enemy, the Japanese."

The full realization of freedom came on August 15. When the POWs reported to the mines, no one was working, and they were told that it was "rest time." At noon that day, the cook filled the prisoners' food boxes to overflowing, and the soup—usually nothing but warm water—was filled with vegetables. Later, each prisoner was handed a full Red Cross food box, rather than one that had already been ransacked of its most desirable contents.

After a sumptuous lunch, Tenney strolled out onto the parade ground to accept a challenge from his fellow inmates. Instead of saluting or bowing when he encountered a guard, as had always been required in the past on penalty of a beating or worse, he simply waved his hand and said, "Hello."

The guard smiled, bowed, and replied in English, "Hello."

"I knew then it was all over," said Tenney.

On the morning after the first atomic bomb incinerated Hiroshima, the 350-plus prisoners assigned to work at a brick kiln and on the docks at the small Japanese port of Tsuraga were taken by trucks to a nearby rice field instead of to their regular jobs. There, covered by four Japanese machine guns positioned at each corner of the field, they were issued picks and shovels and ordered to begin digging their own graves.

"We were trying to keep each other calmed down," recalled Private Glenn Frazier, formerly of the 31st Infantry. "The guard in charge told us that all POWs were to be killed if and when any Allied forces landed on the Japanese mainland. . . . He also warned us against trying to escape. . . . I thought that if they were going to wait to kill me until I got my own grave dug, I'd be the slowest grave digger on record."

Frazier's fellow prisoners apparently felt the same because, by noon, most of the graves were only a few inches deep, and none was anywhere near completion. At that point, the diggers were told to reboard the trucks and return to their camp, but they were ordered to leave their tools behind to finish their digging later.

Back at the camp, each POW teamed up with two others to make a team of three, according to Frazier. "[W]hen we knew they were going to shoot us," he explained, "we would all break loose with our picks and shovels, running as fast as we could to take down a machine gun in hopes of killing some of the Japs. . . . This way, maybe some of us could survive."

By the third day of digging, the graves were growing dangerously deep, but a raid by a single American B-29 brought the digging to what turned out to be a permanent halt.

All the POWs were out in the open as the plane approached, and Frazier vividly remembered how it headed directly toward them at first. "There was nowhere to go," he said, "so we just lay flat on the ground and braced for the bomb that we knew would probably hit us."

Fortunately, the 2,000-pound bomb struck a large industrial building directly across the street from the camp instead, raining dust and debris down on the relieved POWs but leaving them unharmed. They were told later that more than 400 workers in the building were killed.

"The interpreter came the next morning to tell us that the Japanese emperor was going to speak to the nation [about the end of the war]," said Frazier, "and in the meantime, the bombing would stop."

What the infuriated prisoners wanted more than anything at this point, in Frazier's words, was to "grab the guards . . . bring them to the brick kiln, put them in the large oven, and burn them to death. But no such luck; they were all gone."

When the end came, Sergeant J. S. Gray, late of the 27th Bomb Group, was working in a steel mill at Yokkaichi, Japan, and he watched in awe as American B-29s flew over his camp and began dropping parachutes with canisters of food, clothing, and medicine attached. As gratified as Gray was to see these supplies, he was even more excited when he noticed that all the parachutes were colored red, white, and blue.

My God, he thought, *we've got all the necessary colors to make an American flag out of that chute material and sew all those stars on it that we've been hiding from the Japs ever since Cabanatuan!*

Several POWs commandeered a Japanese sewing machine, and others began stripping thread from the parachutes. When the sewing machine's only needle broke during the project, Gray managed to construct two other needles out of barbed wire to finish assembling the flag. Then the forty-eight individual stars—concealed and carried by prisoners for thousands of miles at the constant risk of their lives—were attached.

"The guys finished sewing the stars on by hand," Gray recalled, "and when the flag was completed, we pulled down that 'flaming asshole' rag and raised Old Glory to the top of the camp flagpole. It was one of the most beautiful sights I've ever seen—and a moment I'll never forget. When the flag caught the breeze and unfurled, there wasn't a dry eye in the compound, I can tell you that."

Now the shoe was on the other foot, and it was the turn of the defeated Japanese to wonder whether their American conquerors would treat them with the same deadly lack of compassion that they had shown toward their American captives.

On the morning of August 16, at an agricultural camp near the Korean port city of Inchon, Lieutenant Colonel Jack Schwartz, a former 31st Infantry medical officer, noticed that a young Japanese doctor who was assisting Schwartz in the camp infirmary seemed terribly fearful and depressed.

"Something's bothering you, lieutenant," Schwartz finally said. "What is it? Can I help?"

Tears ran down the young lieutenant's face as he replied. "I fear for my safety, sir," he said. "We have lost the war, and now the Americans will come in and kill me. I have done nothing wrong. I was only serving my country. Now I must die for that."

Schwartz shook his head. Despite all he'd endured over the past three years at the hands of the Japanese—or perhaps because of it—he felt a surge of sympathy for the young lieutenant. "You need not fear for your life," he assured the other man. "Americans don't act like that. I'll speak up for you. You've been kind and helpful to me and to all the prisoners."

The Japanese officer seemed relieved to hear this, but his words were heavy with awe and sorrow as he continued: "The Americans have a new bomb with enough power to destroy a whole city at once. One explosion wiped out Hiroshima with its 250,000 people."

At two o'clock that afternoon, the entire camp population was instructed to assemble to hear a statement from the camp commandant, an elderly Japanese colonel, who seemed deeply troubled and subdued. As the colonel read his message, an interpreter repeated the words in English:

> The war has ended. His Imperial Majesty, the Emperor, has ordered that all hostilities cease. I am to surrender this garrison to the senior American officer present. My duty now is to protect you from outside harm, not to guard you. All arms and supplies will be turned over to you. It is suggested that, for your own safety, you do not leave the compound until American forces come in. However, if you desire to go into the city, I request that you stop by headquarters and allow me to send a soldier with you for your protection.

When the announcement was finished, Captain Manny Lawton of the 31st Infantry watched as the colonel bowed and handed his sword to Colonel Curtis Beecher of the Fourth Marines, the senior U.S. officer present.

"It was high drama," Lawton recalled, "the moment we had dreamed of for so long—a time to shout and be merry. And yet there was only stillness and quiet. Our long captivity was over."

Two days later, early on August 18, at the obscure Manchurian prison camp where General Jonathan Wainwright had been held since the previous March, he and other high-ranking POWs stood silently as the Japanese camp commandant read a statement that none of his audience could understand. Finally, on a signal from the commandant, an interpreter rose, cleared his throat, and began reading the same statement in English.

"By order of the Emperor," he said, "the war has now been amicably terminated . . ."

For a few seconds, Wainwright and his fellow prisoners frowned and glanced querulously at one another. Then they erupted into sudden, uncontrollable fits of laughter. The sound swelled into a roar that drowned out the interpreter's words while the prisoners embraced, punched the air with their fists, and pounded each other on the back.

"There was no stopping the laughter," Wainwright would later recall. "It came up in me, and in the others, with an irresistible force—something born of a combination of our relief, the look on the Jap's face, the blind preposterousness of his beginning, the release from years of tension, [and] the utter, utter joy of having survived to see this blessed day."

On September 2, 1945—the day the Japanese signed the surrender documents aboard the battleship *Missouri* in Tokyo Bay—Colonel Calvin Jackson, a medical officer who had served with the 31st Infantry, remained confined in a POW camp at the town of Ashio in the mountains north of Tokyo. Before retiring to his bunk that evening, Jackson made the following entry in the diary he'd kept since his induction into the Army in February 1941: "A Nip told me our intended fate had [the] U.S. made a landing on Japan, and then [the] Nip C.O. told us at dinner time that we were all to be taken to [the] factory, congregated, and dynamite thrown in on us. (What a nice ending from our humane host.)"

But in the final analysis, despite such murderous intentions and his own painful ordeal at the hands of the Japanese, Jackson was able to feel compassion for some of his former enemies.

"I still think our camp commander is a gentleman and treated us well," he noted in his diary, "especially since we killed his mother, father, sister (all his family) in a burning of Tokyo."

* * *

For Army Air Corps Private Joseph Alexander (Joe Trejo), his release from prison camp in Kawasaki, Japan, came exactly two days after his nineteenth birthday. America's youngest POW of World War II had been a captive of the Japanese for nearly one-fifth of his life.

"When we woke up that morning, all the guards were gone," he recalled. "We didn't know how to act, and we ran around cheering, hugging each other, and crying. We broke into the storehouse where they kept the food. Some of the guys were thirsty for revenge, and they talked about going into the city and killing any Japanese they saw, but they didn't."

Alexander weighed eighty-five pounds and was covered with lice. He was also covered with scars from innumerable beatings. "I was a very accomplished thief, especially of food, but sometimes I got caught," he said. "But when the B-29s came over and started dropping fifty-five-gallon drums of food, none of us had to steal anymore."

Despite the joy and exuberance that came with freedom, Alexander would suffer serious and lasting ill effects from his captivity. He would spend nearly two years in stateside military hospitals receiving treatment for a long list of physical ailments associated with malnutrition, untreated diseases, and constant abuse. But posttraumatic stress and the invisible psychological injuries left in its wake would prove even more resistant to therapy.

"For years after the war, I used to wake up screaming at night," he said. "Once in a while I still do. Some wounds never heal completely."

14

New Lives, Old Scars

A few of those who survived the cataclysm in the Philippines had the incredible good fortune of an early return to home, hearth, and loved ones—a handful of them well before the end of the war.

On November 6, 1944, while fierce fighting still raged in both the Pacific and Europe, the Liberty ship *Monterey* docked at Pier 7 in San Francisco with native Arkansan **Cletis Overton** aboard, along with several dozen other former POWs who had lived through the sinking of the *Shinyo Maru*.

"I remember it was the same day that President Franklin Roosevelt was elected to his fourth term and exactly three years and five days since I'd sailed for Manila from that same pier," Overton would recall more than six decades later. "I also remember passing by Alcatraz, the famous prison, on our way to Angel Island. They put us up in military facilities for a day or two, and then most of us boarded a train for Washington, D.C."

In the nation's capital, they were quizzed extensively by Army intelligence officers concerning Japanese atrocities but otherwise treated as celebrities. They met with Secretary of War Henry Stimson and Army Chief of Staff General George Marshall in their private offices.

"General Marshall wanted to know if any of us wanted a discharge, but none of us held up our hands," Overton remembered. "At that point, none of us knew *what* we wanted, except to go home. Then he asked if we wanted a furlough, and every hand in the room went up.

"'Will thirty days be enough?' Marshall asked, and no hands were raised. 'What about sixty days?' he asked, and again there were no hands. 'Well, then,' he said, 'I guess we'll just have to give you ninety days.' At that, everybody applauded."

On November 11, during a layover in Chicago en route to Washington, Overton sent a telegram to his parents to tell them he was headed home to Arkansas. He also wired the parents of Maxine Cox, the young Army nurse from his hometown of Malvern who had been so often in his thoughts over the past three years.

"Will see you soon," the second telegram said. "Notify Max. Hope she still waits."

She did. On the afternoon of November 28, 1944, with only Maxine's sister, Ila Rhea Crispino (whose husband, Arthur, was serving in Europe), and Overton's close friend, Reece Stiles, as witnesses, Cletis and Maxine were married in Malvern. Then they spent several days honeymooning in the resort town of Hot Springs, twenty-five miles away.

On August 2, 1945—four days before Hiroshima was destroyed by an atomic bomb—Overton was discharged from the Army. Approximately seven weeks later, his and Maxine's first son, Charles, was born.

Despite lifelong health problems and a 70 percent disability related to his long, abusive captivity, Overton fathered four children, earned a bachelor's degree in agriculture from the University of Arkansas, became a devout Christian and a deacon in his church, and remained married to Maxine for more than sixty years, until her death in 2005.

"There was a time," he said recently, "when you could've given me a machine gun and marched those Japanese guards of mine down a gangplank, and I would've felt good just sitting there mowing them down. I don't feel that way anymore. I've gotten over that."

As this is written, Overton lives in an almost new house with his second wife, Adrienne, in the town of 8,000 where he was born ninety-two years ago, and he thoroughly enjoys his status as one of its most celebrated citizens.

* * *

Edgar D. Whitcomb's homecoming was among the earliest on record for a Philippines POW—preceding Cletis Overton's by almost a full year—and in contrast to Overton's subdued Arkansas welcome, Whitcomb's arrival in tiny Hayden, Indiana, was marked by jubilant crowds and raucous merrymaking.

It was December 20, 1943, when Whitcomb walked through his parents' front door and touched off the biggest Christmas celebration his village of 200 had ever experienced.

"Neighbors and friends flocked in from miles around to see the fellow who'd escaped from the Japs," he recalled. "A big Christmas tree was decorated brightly with stacks of packages around it, and in the kitchen was a turkey almost too big for the roasting pan and the biggest ham I'd ever seen. . . . It seemed as if I'd just stepped through the pearly gates into heaven."

But as joyous as the occasion was, the gift that Whitcomb wanted most was the chance to fly again against the enemy in an American bomber, and that gift couldn't be found in Hayden. In pursuit of it, Whitcomb would leave his hometown again in a few days, bound for the Army Air Corps Redistribution Center in Miami, where he hoped to resume his life as a flying officer.

"While I was at home enjoying myself and all the good things of life," he recalled, "I knew that my old friends were still suffering and dying in Japanese prison camps. The more I thought about them, the more I wanted to get back in the air and try to do something to help win the war."

Six weeks later, Whitcomb found himself assigned for a refresher course at the navigation school he'd attended in 1941 at Coral Gables, Florida, and reunited with his old instructor, Colonel Charles Lunn. He also made contact with the parents of the young Marine officer with whom he'd escaped from Corregidor and told them as much as he could about what might have happened to their son.

Whitcomb discovered, too, that all his old classmates at the navigation school were now at least majors in the Army Air Forces while Whitcomb was still a lowly second lieutenant.

Ted Boselli, one of Whitcomb's friends from the 19th Bomb

Group, was now assigned to President Roosevelt's personal crew as navigator of the *Sacred Cow*, FDR's private plane. When Boselli invited Whitcomb along on a flight to Washington to pick up Eleanor Roosevelt and take her to South America, Whitcomb found himself sitting across from the first lady. They struck up a lengthy conversation, during which Whitcomb told her about some of his experiences but cautioned her that they were top secret and not for publication.

Several days later, however, he was surprised to see himself and his ordeal prominently mentioned—although he wasn't identified by name—in Mrs. Roosevelt's syndicated newspaper column, "My Day."

"I had a chance to talk with . . . a young navigator who had been on a bomber plane in the Philippines," she wrote. "He was missing for two years, and as he told his story, I kept thinking of what his family must have gone through . . ."

Whitcomb never knew whether Mrs. Roosevelt's oblique references to him and his experiences had anything to do with a series of orders he began receiving soon afterward. The first order merely assigned him to a new station in Delaware and included a cryptic note that "This officer has escaped from enemy territory . . . and is not to be returned overseas."

A short time later, the first order was superseded by a second that lifted—without explanation—the restriction on overseas duty and authorized Ed to "make operational trips to theaters outside the continental United States, other than the Asiatic Theater."

Within hours of receiving the order, Whitcomb, now a captain, was on a C-54 transport flying across the Atlantic. It was the first of scores of trips he would make to points in Europe and North Africa to deliver cargos ranging from aircraft engines to USO troops—but it wasn't the combat duty that Ed intensely craved.

Then, in April 1945, he was summoned to his headquarters and handed a third set of orders. He could scarcely believe his eyes as he read it: "Captain Edgar D. Whitcomb . . . is relieved of [his present] duty and assignment, and is assigned to the Far East Air Force, Leyte, Philippine Islands, for recommended duty with the Fifth Bomber Command."

In early May, Whitcomb once again flew out over San Francisco Bay and headed west across the Pacific. This time, he was aboard one of hundreds of U.S. military aircraft that flew that same route each day. As his plane approached Leyte, Ed looked down on endless rows of American battleships, carriers, cruisers, destroyers, and transports stretching out as far as he could see in all directions.

"The armed might amassed by the United States to carry the war in the Pacific to a successful conclusion was beyond all comprehension," he recalled. "When we finally landed at Clark Field, it seemed that all my dreams had come true."

Whitcomb had been with his squadron of B-25 medium bombers for only a couple of days when he was called to his first briefing for a mission. "Our target for tomorrow is on Formosa," the briefing officer said. "All squadrons will take off at first light with a full load of bombs."

In the gray dawn of May 11, 1945, Whitcomb's B-25 roared down the runway and into the air, then circled to the right on its way to the Japanese base on Formosa known as Kagitown.

"Below," said Whitcomb, "I could see Subic Bay, where Bill Harris and I had sneaked our sailboat out past Grande Island one dark and stormy night many months ago. The bay was choked with American warships of all descriptions. . . . I felt strong and hopeful."

Some three hours later, the B-25 streaked down over the rooftops of Kagitown at 250 miles per hour, raking the scene below with thousands of rounds from its .50-caliber machine guns and dropping a load of fragmentation bombs that exploded in brilliant flashes as they struck their targets.

Ed Whitcomb had waited more than three years to strike back at the Japanese, but the sensations that raced through him at this moment were worth every minute of the wait.

"The war was going great," he said, "and I was feeling good."

When the war ended slightly more than three months later, Whitcomb concluded his active military career and returned to Indiana to stay, although he remained in the Air Force Reserve for thirty years. In 1958, his memoir, *Escape from Corregidor*, which detailed his wartime experiences, was published and won national acclaim. (The *Seattle Post-Intelligencer* accurately called it "one of the most fantastic stories to come out of World War II.")

After earning a law degree from Indiana University and winning election to several public offices, Whitcomb was elected the 43rd governor of Indiana in 1969, serving a single four-year term. In 1976, he sought nomination for the U.S. Senate in the Republican primary but was defeated by Indianapolis mayor Richard Lugar.

Thereafter, he withdrew from public life and spent much of his time in later years sailing in the Mediterranean and the Atlantic. But after his vessel struck a reef and sank during an attempt to sail around the world in 1995, he retired to a secluded cabin on the banks of the Ohio River near Rome, Indiana, where he observed his ninety-fourth birthday in 2011.

Whitcomb's second book, *On Celestial Wings*, which traces the careers of his 1941 classmates at the Army Air Corps navigation school, was published in 1995, and as this is written he is working on a third book describing his around-the-world sailing adventures.

In September 1945, Whitcomb was able to reestablish contact with **William Harris**, the young Marine officer with whom Ed had escaped from Corregidor and whose father was Major General Field Harris, then commander of all Marine aviation in the United States.

The younger Harris explained in a letter to Whitcomb that he, too, had been captured by the Japanese after spending twenty-nine days fighting monsoons in the China Sea. He was placed in solitary confinement for two months, then moved to an interrogation camp in Ofuna, Japan, where he was beaten repeatedly with a baseball bat and held until January 1945. After being transferred to Tokyo, he survived scores of U.S. air raids and received the unexpected privilege of being present at the surrender ceremonies aboard the battleship *Missouri*.

"I always figured that you'd get back [to the States] one way or another," Harris confided to Whitcomb, "but I never could have dreamed of the way you actually used. My opinion is that your case was the prize put-over on the Japanese."

Harris followed in his father's footsteps by remaining in the Marine Corps, advancing to the rank of lieutenant colonel, and serving in the Korean War as a battalion commander in the First Marine Division. In late January 1951, Whitcomb received the following letter from Harris's mother:

> Dear Ed,
>
> Thought you would like to know about Bill. He is missing in action in Korea. Seems impossible the same thing could happen twice in a lifetime, but it has happened. He went out to Korea in September in command of the Third Battalion, Seventh Regiment. His outfit was way up north of the reservoirs and fought their way out. He got back to Hagaru safely. His dad flew up and saw him there, but coming down the mountain . . . his outfit was doing rear guard duty. Firing started in one company [and] he went back to investigate, and no one ever saw him again. . . . His dad doesn't think there is much chance of his being alive, but of course no one knows. They had such heavy fighting on the reservoirs. He started out with a thousand men and only had 250 when they got back to Hagaru.

Nobody knows for sure if Bill Harris's body was ever found in the barren, frozen wastes of North Korea, but in December 2010, his name was among a list of MIAs whose remains a North Korean general offered to return to the United States under certain conditions. To date, however, nothing has come of this offer.

Harris was posthumously awarded the Navy Cross for "extraordinary heroism" and "inspiring leadership" during a "bold attack" against enemy positions on December 7, 1950. More than sixty years later, Ed Whitcomb still thinks about the friend with whom he swam eight and a half hours to reach Bataan from Corregidor in the spring of 1942.

And he wonders . . .

As one of the rescued POWs from Cabanatuan, **Ralph E. Hibbs, M.D.,** received an express ticket home. His ship docked in San Francisco on the evening of March 12, 1945, as a band played "God Bless America," and after slowly descending the ramp to the ground, Hibbs knelt and solemnly kissed the soil of his homeland. He had never been as glad to reach a destination in his life, but thoughts of **Pilar Campos** still gnawed at his heart and mind.

That night, he phoned his mother and father in Iowa. "You won't have to wait much longer," he assured them. "I'll be home in a couple of days." Then, after a long pause, he added in a breaking voice, "Pilar won't be coming. The Japs killed her."

When the war and Hibbs's five years of service in the Army Medical Corps finally ended, he moved west from his native Iowa to join the staff of the University of Oregon Medical School. Later, along with three other physicians, he established a clinic in Medford, Oregon, and practiced there for thirty-three years until his retirement in 1984, after which he stayed busy with medical missionary work in Honduras, Mexico, and the Philippines.

Hibbs was left with a deep, lasting devotion to the Philippines and its people, inspired in part by memories of the beautiful Manila socialite whom he had loved and lost there. "Pilar was gone, and so were thousands of other friends of our country," he recalled many years later, noting that more than a million Filipinos died in the war. "There should be no cheering on our return [home], I thought, but a sober reflection on those heroes that lie in unmarked graves."

His Asian experience, Hibbs said, left him with a permanent gamut of emotions—from the "panic of danger" and the "despair of captivity" to the "delirium of love" and the "elation of victory"—that could never be erased.

He made his first of many return trips to the Philippines in May 1967—the twenty-fifth anniversary of the fall of Bataan and Corregidor—and it led him to launch a fifteen-year quest to persuade the U.S. government to honor Pilar with a posthumous award for her heroism and lifesaving assistance to American POWs.

In May 1983, the award was presented in Manila to Lulu Abreu, a cousin of Pilar's, by General Charles Getz of the Joint U.S. Military Assistance Group. The citation reads in part:

> The President of the United States, authorized by Act of Congress, has awarded the Certificate of Appreciation to PILAR CAMPOS for her heroic contributions in behalf of American Prisoners of War at Bilibid Prison in Manila and Cabanatuan, Camp #2, the Philippines, during the period of May 1942 to January 1945. At considerable risk to her own life, Miss Campos sneaked past the prison guards to smuggle

> in food, medicine, vitamins, and money. . . . Her help saved dozens, possibly hundreds, of American lives and prevented blindness and permanent disability among the prisoners.

Hibbs and his first wife, Jeanne, to whom he was married for forty years before her death, had four children—Jill Anne, Ralph E. Jr., Stephen Howard, and Jennifer Jeanne.

In 1988, Hibbs's memoir, *Tell MacArthur to Wait*, was published as yet another tribute to Pilar. "The purpose of writing this book was twofold," he explained in the epilogue. "First and foremost was my guilt that Pilar's death lay directly at my doorstep, and my attempt to assuage this feeling. Secondly, I ardently hope that my wife, Jeanne, who died on 17 August 1986, without ever reading it in its final form, and . . . our children would understand their ornery, knot-headed old Dad a little better."

In October 2000, Hibbs died at his home in Medford at age eighty-seven. He was survived by his children and his second wife, Virginia, the widow of novelist Erskine Caldwell, author of the bestsellers *God's Little Acre* and *Tobacco Road*.

On June 16, 1945, almost four years to the day since arriving in the Philippine Islands, **Edwin P. Ramsey** departed for home by plane from Nichols Field in Manila. A day or two earlier, he had been promoted to lieutenant colonel and awarded the Distinguished Service Cross for his "heroism in combat" and tireless leadership in the Philippine resistance movement.

Ramsey was still struggling under the effects of a total physical and psychological breakdown that had hospitalized him for several weeks that spring, and he remained too weak even to carry his single small suitcase to the waiting car outside his headquarters.

He was only twenty-eight, but in three years as a guerrilla, the swashbuckling young officer who had led the world's last mounted cavalry charge on Bataan in early 1942 had withered into a tremulous, skeletal shadow of himself. He had shrunk to ninety-three pounds and was beset by an array of illnesses that left him in precarious health and looking twice his age.

Ramsey's sister, Nadine, a professional pilot and one of only eight American women qualified to fly such top U.S. fighters as the P-38 and P-51, met him at the airport in San Francisco. She told him that she was taking him home to Wichita, Kansas, then stared at him with obvious concern.

"My God, how'd you get so skinny?" she asked.

"It's a long story," he said. "I've got orders to report to Winter General Hospital in Topeka."

"We're going home first," she said, watching him buckle himself into the passenger seat of her small plane with severely shaking hands.

"Does mother know?" he asked.

She nodded. "They called her from Washington a few weeks ago, when you were safe, I guess. You're a big hero, you know."

At the moment, Ramsey didn't feel big or heroic or even safe. When he checked into the hospital two days later, he was diagnosed with malaria, amoebic dysentery, anemia, acute malnutrition, and general nervous collapse. It was only after eleven months of treatment that he recovered sufficiently to resume a somewhat normal life. After leaving the Army, he would travel extensively, receive dozens of honors, be widely sought after as a speaker, and hold a variety of executive positions, including vice president, Far East area, for Hughes Aircraft.

In 1990, Ramsey coauthored, with Stephen J. Rivele, a book entitled *Lieutenant Ramsey's War*, detailing his combat experiences as a cavalryman and guerrilla leader in the Philippines. He dedicated the book to his friend and comrade **Joe Barker** "and to all the other brave men and women of the Philippine resistance who sacrificed their lives in the cause of liberty."

The recipient of numerous awards from the U.S. and Philippine governments and various veterans and service organizations, Ramsey, at age ninety-five, lives in Los Angeles with his wife, Raquel.

Because they were scattered in dozens of prison camps across thousands of square miles of the Far East, and because a large percentage of them were in fragile health, it was mid-September 1945 before the majority of American POWs were able even to begin their long homeward trek across the Pacific.

The U.S. military did its best to speed the evacuation process, but the POWs had to compete for space with tens of thousands of combat troops from Okinawa and other Pacific bases, and it would be well into October before most POWs set foot on American soil. Although a lucky few managed to arrange passage to the States on eastbound aircraft, the journey was usually by ship and included a stopover of several days in Manila, which was now a vast tableau of destruction.

"We passed the old Manila Hotel," recalled **John S. Coleman**, who reached the city on September 21, "and we could see where artillery shells and machine-gun bullets had penetrated the outside walls. . . . it was said the Japanese . . . were chased to the top story before they were killed or surrendered."

Coleman's truck stopped at the old Walled City, where walls that had once been twenty feet thick had been reduced to piles of rubble by bombs and artillery fire.

At the communications center in Manila, Coleman received his first message from his family since being freed. The telegram read: "The children and I are eagerly awaiting news of your liberation. Sunday, September 2, is our seventeenth wedding anniversary. Remember I love you truly. Mrs. John S. Coleman Jr."

It was dusk on the evening of October 8 when Coleman's ship, the transport *Admiral Hughes*, carrying 2,610 ex-POWs, docked in Seattle to a resounding welcome. "Factory whistles blew, battleships anchored there sounded their whistles, and all the fire sirens in Seattle blew for fifteen minutes," Coleman remembered.

But merely reaching the States wasn't a complete homecoming for Coleman, who was still a couple of thousand miles away from his family and his hometown of Wellington in the Texas Panhandle. He and the rest of the freed prisoners in his group spent nine days in a hospital at Fort Lewis, Washington, where they were checked for all types of tropical diseases and received chest X-rays for tuberculosis, which revealed numerous cases of TB among the returnees.

Except for a pain in his right side, Coleman felt in good shape, and he asked to be released and allowed to fly home. But hospital authorities refused and told him that, once he was released, he would have to travel by rail, aboard a hospital coach, to San Antonio, then be admitted to Brooke Army Medical Center for further tests and examination.

At every stop through the Panhandle and West Texas, Coleman was greeted by groups of friends and relatives who had learned he'd be traveling that route. When his train stopped in Childress, south of Wellington, Coleman was met by a huge "welcoming committee" that included virtually his entire family—his wife, Ethel, his son and daughter, his mother, his brother and sister-in-law—as well as many friends.

Still, because of the lingering effects of the brutality he'd experienced as a prisoner, Coleman's ordeal was far from over. He would spend a total of a year and five months in Army hospitals. Before he was finally discharged from the Army on March 11, 1947, he overheard a group of doctors speculating that he might not live more than five years.

But Coleman surprised them. In 1978, his memoir, *Bataan and Beyond*, was published by the university press at his alma mater, Texas A&M. He served for six years (1967–73) as mayor of Wellington and held other positions including president of the local Chamber of Commerce, commander of the Wellington American Legion Post, and president of the local Kiwanis Club.

"He was active in almost every civic, governmental, and veterans organization in Collingsworth County," recalled Coleman's grandson, Richard Sims, now president of the Wellington State Bank.

"Although I shall never forget the years spent in prison camp," Coleman wrote in the epilogue to his book, "time has a way of healing. I was glad to be able to serve my country—still the best in the world—and if called upon, I would gladly serve again."

Coleman died in September 2000 at the age of ninety-eight, surviving his wife, who preceded him in death two years earlier at age ninety—and most likely outliving all the doctors who predicted his imminent demise back in 1947.

For **Louis Read**, who was working in an iron ore mine owned by the Mitsubishi Company and afflicted with amoebic dysentery when the war ended, many of his first encounters with postwar life were full of surprises—not all of them pleasant.

"After the guards left, some of the POWs had gotten hold of a small radio, and we were able to listen to the surrender ceremonies on September 2," Read recalled. "We also picked up some messages from U.S. Sixth Army headquarters, telling us to stay put until they could come and liberate us. The problem was, we waited and waited, and nobody ever came.

"Finally, we decided to go down to the town of Morioka, which was on the main line of the railroad, and we got on a train headed south. We didn't know where we were going, but eventually we came to a large seaport on the east coast of Japan, where we saw some American troops and got off the train."

A short time later, Read found himself aboard the Navy hospital ship *Rescue*, bound for San Francisco. "I was overcome with emotion when we sailed under the Golden Gate Bridge, which I'd last seen four and a half years earlier. I'd eaten so much on the ship that my weight was up to about 150 pounds, but I was mostly bloated because of the dysentery. We were issued a suitcase and a fresh set of clothes and told to pack everything else in the suitcase to be shipped to our home address. Well, I did as I was told, and I never saw any of my stuff again."

At Letterman General Hospital, where he was "punched, tested, diagnosed, and medicated," a large bundle of mail caught up with Read. Some of it dated back several years and conveyed news that was less than reassuring.

"For one thing, I learned that my steady girlfriend had gotten married and now had a child," he said. "And my two younger brothers, who were both in high school when I left, were now back in the States after serving hitches in the Army. One of my brothers, Glenn, had been captured at the Battle of the Bulge and become a German prisoner of war."

Read also discovered that his three and a half years of back pay amounted to a lot less than he'd expected. His aunt, who was his legal guardian when he'd joined the Army, had begun taking about half of his pay as an allotment after Read had been reported missing following the fall of Bataan.

"The Red Cross had told her I was probably dead, so she'd eventually get my back pay anyway," he said, "and they convinced her to apply for the allotment. I later wrote to the allotment office in Philadelphia about it, and they wrote back that I'd authorized the allotment in May 1942, when I was a Japanese POW. That was so ridiculous that I never pursued the matter any further."

Read's postwar luck *did* change for the better after he got home to Texas, however. "I met a girl named Hazel Gilley, and it didn't take me long to fall in love with her," he said.

The couple was married in Dallas on January 5, 1946, with Read's brother Norman, just back from China with the 14th Air Force, as his best man. After earning both a bachelor's degree and an MS from Southern Methodist University, Read accepted a position with the Dallas City Health Department as a biologist-entomologist.

In 1987, to mark the forty-fifth anniversary of the U.S. surrender in the Philippines, the Reads made their only trip back to the islands, exploring many of the places where Louis had served with the 31st Infantry or been held captive during the war. They retraced the original route of the Death March; visited the site of Cabanatuan, where a monument lists the names of more than 3,000 American POWs who died there; and took a lengthy tour of Corregidor, where Louis had, incidentally, "never set foot before."

On March 31, 2011, several months after he was interviewed by the author, Read died at age 90. He was survived by his wife, three grown daughters—Phyllis, Deborah, and Ginny—and several grandchildren. (A son, Phillip, born in 1956, died as a young child from a rare form of cancer.)

"I've been blessed," he said. "We've endured tragedies, but by the grace of God, we've persevered."

When news of the war's end reached the Fusiki prison camp in Japan where **Clemens A. Kathman** had been working as a stevedore since June 1945, the artillery man from New Mexico considered himself to be in reasonably good physical condition, all things considered.

"Sure, I had a few health problems," Kathman recalled some six and a half decades later, "but so did practically every other POW in the camp. As far as I was concerned, I was as fit to work as any of the other guys."

Yet in any American hospital, Kathman wouldn't have been allowed out of bed. One of his "problems" was a blossoming case of tuberculosis that might well have killed him in a year or two if his captivity had lasted that much longer, not to mention a touch of beriberi and frequent bouts of diarrhea. He weighed ninety-seven pounds, roughly half what he'd weighed in December 1941.

But the ailment that most concerned the camp doctor, Captain Sidney Seid, formerly of the 19th Bomb Group, was an abscess in Kathman's groin area that Seid thought could've resulted from a ruptured appendix. It had set off a raging fever and agonizing pain, temporarily paralyzed Kathman's right leg, and refused to respond to treatment until an incision was made and a semipermanent drain installed to carry off a continuous flow of greenish white fluid. That had been more than a year earlier, and the drain was still in place—and still oozing its ugly excretions into a gauze pad.

"Clem, the only reason you're alive today is because you were too damned dumb to die," Seid had told Kathman after the paralysis and fever subsided. "Because of our limited resources here, you'll probably have to keep the drain in place until you get to a stateside hospital where they can do something with that abscess that I can't."

When Kathman eventually reached the hospital ship *Rescue* and was examined by a bevy of Navy physicians, the first medic who saw the drain and incision swallowed hard and shook his head in dismay.

"How long have you been in this condition?" the doctor asked uneasily.

Kathman shrugged. "Oh, a little over a year," he said.

"My God!" the doctor exclaimed. "If I hadn't seen this with my own eyes, I wouldn't believe it!"

An attractive nurse—"the first white woman I'd seen in four years"—asked to see the incision a short time later in order to change the dressing and was shocked almost speechless.

"Man, I thought she'd fall out of her chair," Kathman recalled. "She clucked her tongue a couple of times, then took me to another room, where she rinsed my side with alcohol and taped a bandage over it."

Repeatedly over several days, Kathman was examined by various medical personnel, who poked at his incision, asked him if it hurt, shook their heads, and went away. Finally, he had the good fortune of being taken to Tokyo's largest airport, placed in a bunk aboard a C-54 transport with about two dozen other patients, and flown to a military hospital on Saipan, then on to San Francisco, where he was admitted to Letterman General Hospital.

"All this time, I was feeling fine and eating like pig," Kathman recalled, "and the closer we got to the States, the more I was overwhelmed by a sense of complete relief. It was as though I didn't have a care in the world."

His medical ordeal was far from over, however. He would spend fourteen months undergoing treatment, including several surgeries, before he was finally pronounced cured, released for good, and given his Army discharge.

In July 1947, Kathman moved to Dallas and took a job as a printer at the *Dallas Times Herald*, where he was employed for thirty-five years. The following month, he was married to LaVerne Gensler, a WAC who had worked at an Army hospital in Santa Fe while Kathman was a patient there. Five years later, their son, Clemens Kathman III, was born.

In 1987, after forty-two years of marriage, LaVerne died, and Kathman later married Mary Wilkinson, who succumbed to heart disease just four years after their wedding. Now retired, Kathman lives with his third wife, Margaret Jenkins, in Brenham, Texas, where he recently celebrated his ninety-third birthday.

When his autobiography, *I Was There, Charley*, was published in 2005, Kathman dedicated the book in memory of Captain Seid, the prison camp doctor.

"I owe him my life," he said.

On March 27, 1947, **Otis H. "Karl" King** received an honorable medical discharge from the U.S. Marine Corps after spending a year and a half in various hospitals. He was awarded 80 percent disability because of old injuries and other ongoing health problems related to his forty months as a prisoner of the Japanese.

King had reached the United States by air on September 2, 1945, the day of the Japanese surrender. His trip across the Pacific was expedited because of his gravely debilitated physical condition. While working as a slave laborer in the Tokyo rail yards and on the docks in Yokohama, he lost almost half his prewar body weight, from over 200 pounds to about 118, and was suffering from an assortment of injuries and illnesses that would keep him hospitalized for months.

By the time he returned to his native Texas, the cocky, adventurous youngster who had dropped out of Adamson High School in Dallas and falsified his birth date to join the Marines in 1939 at age fourteen had vanished into the mists of time. He'd been succeeded by a quiet, introspective young man with thinning hair and a slight limp, who appeared older than his twenty-two years—and had every right to.

During this same period in 1946–47, King lost contact with his best buddy and fellow POW, **Isaac C. "Ike" Williams**, who had been at his side almost constantly since their first meeting in China in 1940. "The last I heard from him, he was in a Navy hospital in California," King would recall years later. "After that, I never heard from him again."

Although King had no apparent background in either commercial radio or journalism, he soon found a job as a news reporter-broadcaster for a Fort Worth radio station, which led to a twenty-five-year broadcasting career, during which he covered such major events as the assassination of President John F. Kennedy and the subsequent trial of Jack Ruby, killer of accused JFK assassin Lee Harvey Oswald.

"Karl was the kind of quiet, reserved guy who seemed to look at the world as an observer, rather than as a participant," said veteran Texas journalist and radio-TV personality Alex Burton, a longtime acquaintance who encountered King frequently on assignments. "He'd mention something about the war or being a POW once in a while, but not very often. He had a lot of mechanical aptitude, too, and was the first radio guy I ever saw take a telephone apart and hook a tape recorder to it to transmit a story."

King retired from his broadcast career in 1972 after a stint at radio station KBOX in Dallas, but he demonstrated his dedication to his craft by enrolling at Texas Christian University in Fort Worth in 1980 and earning a bachelor's degree in journalism four years later at age fifty-nine. In 1985, he returned to Manila to receive the Philippine Defense Medal from President Ferdinand Marcos.

King saved most of his recollections and opinions for an autobiographical book titled *Alamo of the Pacific*, which he self-published in 1999. In it, he offered insights based on harsh personal experiences into the brutal world of POWs and its aftereffects.

"At the end of World War II," he wrote, "the condition later described as post-traumatic stress syndrome wasn't in any medical dictionary. Consequently, returning POWs were turned loose on families and friends who couldn't understand . . . or in many cases cope with their trauma and emotions. Often, a former prisoner . . . will break down, unable to share the memories with anyone who couldn't know how it was in those camps."

King died in 2005 at age seventy-nine. His survivors included his wife, Peggy; a daughter, Karen Noah; two grandsons; and a great-granddaughter.

For **Joseph (Trejo) Alexander**, some of his most vivid memories of his first hours in the friendly, civilized surroundings of a U.S. military hospital after three and a half years as a POW are about small, seemingly insignificant things.

"I'll never forget what a pleasure my first hot shower was," he recalled. "It was so much better than being doused every few weeks with a bucket of cold water. And everyone was so nice to us. All the doctors and nurses treated us royally. The mess halls were open twenty-four hours a day, which was great because I was hungry all the time."

After reaching San Francisco, Joe phoned his grandmother to tell her he was alive and homeward bound. "After the surrender on Mindanao, they'd told her I was dead," he said. "She was glad to hear from me."

His next stop was Brooke Army Medical Center in his native San Antonio, where he underwent treatment for about a year. Altogether, he spent nearly two years in Army hospitals before being pronounced fit for active duty.

During this interval, Joe made an incredible discovery. The unfriendly woman whom he'd known since early childhood as his aunt was actually his mother, and her bitterness stemmed from being abandoned by her husband before Joe was born. Once the truth was known, Alexander legally claimed the name of the father he'd never met, had his service records changed accordingly, and Joe Trejo vanished for good.

It was an easy decision for Alexander to reenlist in the U.S. Air Force (which had now succeeded the Army Air Corps), and accept an assignment to the motor pool at Kelly Air Force Base in San Antonio.

"I guess you'd say I found my true home in the Air Force," Joe said recently. "I spent a total of forty years in government service—military and civilian—and most of it was right here in San Antonio."

While stationed at Kelly and even after his retirement in 1981, Alexander had numerous opportunities to hitch rides on Air Force planes headed for the Far East. On one of these trips in July 1998, he met with Yuichi Hatto, who had been what Alexander termed "one of the good guards" at the Omori prison camp in Tokyo in 1943.

Most of Alexander's recollections of his time at Omori were decidedly unpleasant. Three of the guards there were notorious for their cruel treatment of prisoners. One in particular had forced Alexander and his fellow POWs to stand at attention all night, then work in the steel mill all day, and stand at attention again without food or rest a second night. By contrast, Hatto had shown sympathy for the prisoners and treated them humanely.

"I was glad to meet him," Alexander said of the visit. "I'd had bad feelings toward Japanese people in general, but during our meeting all that was blacked out."

One of what Joe considers his greatest honors occurred in May 2000, when he was elected national commander of the American Defenders of Bataan and Corregidor. Another was when he was invited to have breakfast with Presidents George W. Bush and Bill Clinton on Memorial Day 2001.

"On a wall at my old high school, there's a plaque with the names of former students who were killed in World War II," he said with a slight smile. "The name of Joe Trejo is one of them."

But for Joseph Alexander and his wife, Norma, life has been good. They have two grown sons and two grandchildren and still make their home in San Antonio, where America's youngest World War II POW marked his eighty-fourth birthday in 2011.

"Norma's very understanding about the bad dreams I still have sometimes at night," Joe said, "and the fact that I always tear up when I see the American flag waving in the breeze."

For **Jonathan M. Wainwright,** former commanding general of U.S. Forces in the Philippines, the prospect of going home after an absence of nearly five years seemed almost too good to be true. But it was also tinged with remorse and charged with apprehension.

On August 19, 1945, when he was greeted at his prison camp in Manchuria by Major Robert Lamar, the first American officer Wainwright had seen besides his fellow captives since early May 1942, and told that he was a free man, his first question was one that had haunted him daily for years.

"What do the people in the States think of me?" the emaciated general asked hoarsely.

"You're considered a hero there," Lamar said. "Your picture's even in *Time* magazine."

But Wainwright found it hard to accept the other officer's assurances. In his own tortured thoughts, he still felt that his countrymen and fellow officers had every reason to condemn him as a coward and a traitor—even to call for his court-martial—for surrendering his command. He remained doubtful enough to repeat the same question nine days later in Chungking when he met with General Albert Wedemeyer, who had directed the search for Wainwright and other U.S. officers held in Manchuria.

"You're a legitimate hero, General," Wedemeyer told him. "We all admire you here—everyone does."

At Wedemeyer's elegant thirty-room house, where Wainwright was ushered to a private suite and given a new uniform, he was also presented with a picture of his wife, Adele (nicknamed "Kitty"), which had been transmitted by wirephoto, along with a note in her handwriting. "I am very happy today," it read. "Waiting impatiently for your return. We are all well. Best love to you. Kitty H. W."

Wainwright was able to transmit his own photo in reply along with a note: "Kitty darling: My devoted love to you always. Am well and hope to be home soon—to Manila Aug. 30, then to Tokyo."

That same day, Wainwright reported by radio to Army Chief of Staff General Marshall in Washington and received a reply that finally dispelled his doubts about what kind of reception he would receive at home. "I reaffirm the expressions of my last message to you a few hours before the fall of Corregidor," Marshall wrote, "in deepest appreciation of all you did and have done for the honor of the Army."

Wainwright witnessed the Japanese surrender from a seat of honor aboard the battleship *Missouri*, then was flown to Manila for surrender ceremonies in the Philippines. A tiring six-day trip to the States followed with old friends wining and dining him royally and legions of reporters and photographers flocking around him at every stop.

Instead of the rebuke and disdain he had feared from his fellow Americans, Wainwright would be awarded the Medal of Honor, nominated by President Truman for promotion to four-star general, invited to address a joint session of Congress, honored at a tickertape parade through New York City, and showered with adulation by the entire country.

Wainwright also came home a wealthy man. King Features Syndicate offered him $155,000 for the newspaper rights to his story, and Doubleday added a $25,000 advance for the book rights, to be published as *General Wainwright's Story* and written by Bob Considine, one of America's best-known journalists.

He was given a plum assignment as commanding general of the U.S. Fourth Army, headquartered at Fort Sam Houston, Texas, where he was in a key position to pursue such major interests as obtaining awards and decorations for veterans of the Philippines campaign and, especially, recognition for the role of the Philippine Scouts.

But Wainwright never fully overcame the physical problems that grew out of the rigors of prison life. His appearance was strikingly frail, and he had to use a cane for support for the rest of his years. Meanwhile, the pressures of being a sought-after celebrity wherever he went often drained his strength. More stress developed when his wife became ill and had to be hospitalized permanently in Colorado, leaving the general alone in the large house he had bought in San Antonio.

Skinny Wainwright had always been known to his friends as a drinking man, but now he began imbibing more heavily than ever. In his biography of Wainwright, Duane Schultz quoted a friend of the general's who described as "endless" the drinking parties at Wainwright's home after Adele's departure.

"Everybody barged in constantly," the friend added, "sort of a 'hanging on the coattails' syndrome."

It wasn't long until these gatherings came to the attention of General Dwight Eisenhower, who had succeeded General Marshall as Army chief of staff. "He drank too much," a concerned Eisenhower said of Wainwright. "I tried everything. I gave him a high command in Texas. I gave him an aide to look after him, but he wouldn't stop drinking."

Wainwright apparently worried about it, too, and fearing embarrassing himself and the Army he loved, he decided to retire while he could still do so gracefully. At the end of August 1947, at age sixty-four and after forty-five years of continuous military service, he hung up his sword for the last time.

Wainwright knew nothing about business, but a long list of prominent companies were eager to capitalize on his nationwide name recognition and his many influential friends in the military. He was named vice president of a supermarket chain, president of one life insurance company, and board chairman of another.

He had few duties in these capacities other than making an occasional speech and putting in appearances at ceremonial functions, where the inevitable crowds of hero worshippers were always eager to buy him a drink.

Wainwright died on September 2, 1953, three weeks after suffering a stroke and slipping into a coma—and, coincidentally, eight years to the day after he'd witnessed the surrender of the empire of Japan.

"Jonathan Mayhew Wainwright was a soldier of the old U.S. Army," observed *Time* magazine in its obituary. "In an age that produced Army men of many talents—generals who could double as diplomats, orators, and businessmen—'Skinny' Wainwright, a fine horseman, a crack shot, and an all-round good officer, was never anything but a soldier."

Today, nearly half a century after his death, the name **Douglas MacArthur** remains familiar to tens of millions of Americans, and, inevitably, it still evokes strong feelings among the dwindling ranks of World War II and Korean War combat veterans.

In contrast to Jonathan Wainwright, who inherited the quagmire left behind by MacArthur on Bataan and Corregidor, Wainwright's old boss was never noticeably troubled by feelings of regret or self-doubt. He emerged from the war as a military leader of unprecedented power and influence and a hero second only to Dwight Eisenhower in popularity among the American public.

After presiding at the surrender ceremonies aboard the battleship *Missouri*, he became the absolute ruler of Japan—in effect a "substitute emperor"—and by many accounts he did a much better job in this capacity than he'd ever done as a leader of soldiers in battle.

Indeed, despite the many valid criticisms of MacArthur's role in the defense of the Philippines and his later grand strategy for the conduct of the Pacific war, his success in transforming a tyrannical, rapacious, America-hating outlaw regime into a model democracy is unparalleled in political history.

MacArthur biographer William Manchester quoted former U.S. intelligence agent Upton Close (real name Josef Washington Hall), author of *Behind the Face of Japan* and other prominent books on Asian psychology, to help explain how MacArthur was able to accomplish so much in Japan in such a relatively short time.

Prior to its surrender in 1945, Close observed, Japan had been ruled by emotions, rather than a government based on laws. He described the Japanese as a race of people who could "hate tremendously" and "give themselves to the most unspeakable savageries," yet "when the fury passes [become] the most gentle-mannered people in the world."

The Japanese themselves had coined terms to define their own divergent emotions, Manchester noted. "*Zangyaku-sei* is a brutal and savage spirit," he explained. "Weariness of living is *ensei.* The Japanese soldiers who raped Manila were obsessed by *zangyaku-sei*. The country which lay prostrate at MacArthur's feet was in the grip of the most depressing *ensei* in the history of their race."

In his many years of service in the Far East, MacArthur had probably grasped the emotional swings of the Japanese more thoroughly than anyone else in the upper levels of the federal government or the U.S. military, Manchester suggested. Thus, when Treasury Secretary Henry Morgenthau drew up a plan to deliberately punish the Japanese in retribution for the inhumanities they had inflicted during the war, MacArthur rejected the idea.

"If the historian of the future should deem my service worthy of some slight reference," declared the general, "it would be my hope that he mention me not as a commander engaged in campaigns and battles . . . but rather as one whose sacred duty it became, once the guns were silenced, to carry to the land of our vanquished foe the solace and hope and faith of Christian morals."

For MacArthur, the secret to the permanent pacification of Japan lay in revival and conciliation, not punishment. He didn't dethrone Emperor Hirohito or command him to report to U.S. headquarters hat in hand; he allowed the "Divine One" to remain in his palace and pick the proper time for a meeting. He didn't dispatch U.S. troops to disarm Japanese military units; he allowed their own officers to do the job. Sensitive to the obvious fact that millions of Japanese civilians were starving amid the ruins of their country, he demanded that 3.5 million tons of food be shipped from the States to feed them.

MacArthur had never been shy about taking charge of situations and working them to his advantage, and the other major secret to his success was his own imperial personality. When President Truman instructed him to "exercise your authority as you deem proper to carry out your mission," the general turned the occupation of Japan into "a one-man show," in Manchester's words.

"Never before in the history of the United States," added U.S. ambassador to Japan William J. Sebald, "had such enormous and absolute power been placed in the hands of a single individual."

By 1950, MacArthur's influence, along with the ingenuity and industry of the Japanese people, had paved the way for an emerging new Japan. Unfortunately, in June of that same year, a new war would erupt on the Korean Peninsula. It brought out the best—and worst—in MacArthur, and within it lay the seeds of his downfall.

In the spring of 1951, the general's fifty-year Army career ended abruptly and ignominiously when he was relieved of his command by Truman for insubordination and ordered home, where he would remain a lightning rod for controversy even after his death in 1964.

* * *

In May 2010, the nationwide organization of surviving veterans of the Philippines campaign—the American Defenders of Bataan and Corregidor—held its sixty-fourth and final convention in San Antonio and formally disbanded. The few score living members, virtually all of them past the age of ninety, were forced by failing health and mounting years to pass the torch they'd carried for more than six decades to their descendants. Only seventy-three veterans were in attendance at the last convention.

Even as taps sounded for the ADBC, rumors continued to circulate that the Japanese government would extend an invitation for the Philippine veterans to visit Japan and receive a formal state apology for the atrocities committed against them between April 1942 and August 1945. As this is written, however, no such apology has been issued—only a few verbal expressions of regret offered by minor officials—and even if an official apology should be tendered at this point, its acceptance would be doubtful, many veterans say.

"It's a little late now," said **Henry G. Stanley** of Garland, Texas, one of two living members of the 27th Bomb Group's 181-man 54th Ordnance Company. "Most of the boys who were on Bataan are gone now, so it just doesn't make much sense to try to travel that far," Stanley said. "It's a fourteen-hour flight one way, and a lot of us aren't healthy enough to make that kind of trip, even if we wanted to."

Death March survivor and battalion commander in the Philippine Army **Bill Adair** had an even stronger reaction. "To me, the idea of a Japanese apology is nothing but a sick joke," he said. "Why the hell should I accept their apology? I'm not saying anything about the young people in Japan, but as for the ones who treated us worse than dogs, I'll never forgive them."

Over the decades, at least three bills have been introduced in Congress demanding that Japan pay penalties to American POWs forced to work as slave labor, and several federal lawsuits have sought reparations on the prisoners' behalf. But none of these efforts has produced tangible results, primarily because the peace treaty signed in 1951 between Japan and forty-eight adversary nations expressly absolves Japan of financial damages to POWs.

Among today's thinning ranks of Battling Bastards from the 31st Infantry, the 26th Cavalry, the Fourth Marines, the Air Corps Infantry, and other front-line outfits, such symbolic failures and losses are of small concern. These survivors have endured much worse. They've suffered more than the vast majority of younger Americans can begin to comprehend, but sympathy and apologies have never been high on their list of priorities. They prefer to be remembered instead for the stand they made against impossible odds and under impossible conditions.

MacArthur himself would later say of the Philippine garrison he left behind: "No army in history more thoroughly accomplished its mission. Let no man henceforth speak of it other than as a magnificent victory."

Few if any of today's handful of surviving members of that army would agree, however, with such a gross-but-typical overstatement by their onetime commander. They know that what U.S. forces did in the Philippines during the winter and spring of 1941–42 was neither "magnificent" nor a "victory." Their mission was dirty, bloody, disheartening, and ultimately doomed to failure.

Even so, they bought five months of precious time for America's devastated forces in the Pacific to regroup by tying down tens of thousands of Japanese troops that might otherwise have been used to invade Australia. They denied Japan the use of Manila's harbor—the finest in the Pacific—robbing her of a base from which to launch further aggression and disrupting Tokyo's timetable for conquest. And they did this with obsolete weapons and bad ammunition while they were sick, starving, and abandoned.

In interviews and memoirs quoted in these pages, many of those who survived have stated their feelings about what happened to them clearly and repeatedly. And if anyone bothered to ask them, they could sum up those sentiments in a few simple, eloquent words.

"We were surrendered," they still wish to remind their junior fellow citizens seventy years after the fact, "but we were never defeated!"

Sources and Notes

Note: Throughout the narrative, the author frequently presents the thoughts of various protagonists in the form of italicized dialogue or in a simple third-person description of what the individual was thinking at the time. In each case, these are based on (a) information developed during author interviews with the source, (b) oral history interviews in which a surviving veteran recounts what he was thinking at a certain point, or (c) a first-person memoir—either published or unpublished—written by the source.

Chapter 1: A $36-a-Month Paradise

Author interviews with Joseph Alexander, Smith Green, Louis Read, Cletis Overton, Clemens Kathman, Walter Bell, Russell Gill, John Olson, and Edgar Whitcomb help to establish the idyllic scene in Manila as war clouds gathered. The prevailing atmosphere in the Philippine capital is also captured in such autobiographical accounts as Ralph Hibbs's *Tell MacArthur to Wait*, Whitcomb's *Escape from Corregidor*, and Kathman's *I Was There, Charley*. Otis H. "Karl" King's memoir, *Alamo of the Pacific*, provides particularly graphic glimpses of Manila nightlife in the fall of 1941.

The MacArthur Controversy and American Foreign Policy by Richard H. Rovere and Arthur Schlesinger Jr. contains keen insights into the military situation in the pre–World War II Philippines, as does William Manchester's *American Caesar: Douglas MacArthur, 1880–1964*. The Rovere-Schlesinger book takes a highly critical view of General MacArthur's preparations for the defense of the Philippines in the event of war with Japan, while the Manchester biography is generally more charitable toward MacArthur. Each, however, helps to explain the confusion and complexities surrounding War Plan Orange, the long-standing

U.S. strategy for responding to an act of war initiated by Japan in the Pacific. Both sources help to clarify the conflict between War Plan Orange and a newer, competing strategic concept known as Rainbow Five, which became the cornerstone of official Washington's Europe First policy implemented in the months preceding the outbreak of war in the Far East.

Both these studies of MacArthur's role in the prewar Philippines also shed light on the reasons for the American military's physical and psychological lack of readiness to fight a war with Japan. Rovere and Schlesinger, in particular, explore several little known incidents in MacArthur's private life that may have affected his overall performance as the most powerful U.S. military leader in the Far East, as well as his unusual relationship with Philippines president Manuel Quezon.

The unfolding minute-by-minute drama as news of the Japanese attack on Pearl Harbor reached U.S. military radio operators in the Philippines is graphically captured in William Bartsch's *December 8, 1941: MacArthur's Pearl Harbor.*

Historian Duane Schultz's *Hero of Bataan: The Story of General Jonathan M. Wainwright* also contributes insights into America's "days of empire" during the years between the world wars.

PAGE

10 *"He thought I was stealing his publicity"*: This explanation from Eisenhower on his rift with MacArthur is quoted in *The MacArthur Controversy*, but the person to whom Eisenhower made the remark is not identified.

Chapter 2: Paradise Lost

Author interviews with Alexander, Henry H. King, Edward Jackfert, Overton, and Whitcomb provide eyewitness accounts of the Japanese attacks of December 8, 1941, and the confusion and chaos they created. Hibbs's memoir, *Tell MacArthur to Wait*, graphically captures the scene in Manila early that morning as the stunning realities of war were driven home to American troops.

General Lewis H. Brereton's *The Brereton Diaries* was an invaluable source of information in establishing the ominous sequence of events preceding the initial Japanese attack on Clark Field and the destruction of many of the aircraft based there. Other published sources adding important details of the events of December 8 include Donald Knox's *Death March*, John Costello's *Days of Infamy*, William Bartsch's *Doomed at the Start* and *December 8, 1941*, Otis King's *Alamo of the Pacific*, and Sidney Stewart's *Give Us This Day.* Also providing rare behind-the-scenes details is Karl H. Lowe's Internet website history of the 31st Infantry Regiment.

Author interviews with Henry King and Jackfert graphically reveal the naïveté that clouded the thinking of American officers and enlisted men stationed at Clark Field. John S. Coleman's memoir, *Bataan and Beyond*, Otis

King's *Alamo of the Pacific*, and Hibbs's *Tell MacArthur to Wait* vividly describe the scenes as Japanese attacks later that day, following the massive raid at Clark, targeted Nichols Field and the Cavite Naval Base.

General Wainwright's autobiography and Schultz's *Hero of Bataan* provide details of Wainwright's reactions to the first damaging attacks on Fort Stotsenburg and the heavy losses inflicted on the 26th Cavalry and other key units of his North Luzon Force.

PAGE

24 *"So the bastards have hit us":* The descriptions of General Brereton's emotions and reactions on the morning of December 8 are drawn from *The Brereton Diaries.*

26 My God, *he thought:* Hibbs's alarmed reaction to news of the Pearl Harbor attack is described in his memoir.

28 *"The General hasn't responded":* Brereton's angry exchange with General Sutherland is recounted in *The Brereton Diaries* and Bartsch's *December 8, 1941.*

28 *Less than half an hour later:* The experiences and observations of Japanese airmen who helped carry out the raids of December 8 are described in detail in Bartsch's *December 8, 1941.*

Chapter 3: A Black-and-Blue Christmas

Author interviews with Overton, Alexander, Whitcomb, and Robert B. Heer, along with King's *Alamo of the Pacific*, Hibbs's *Tell MacArthur to Wait*, Whitcomb's *Escape from Corregidor*, Coleman's *Bataan and Beyond*, and Kathman's *I Was There, Charley* provide glimpses of personal emotions and the generalized shock and dismay felt by U.S. forces in the days following the first Japanese attacks. Sergeant J. S. Gray's oral history also contributes rare, little-known information about Manila-bound American supply ships carrying unassembled warplanes being diverted to Australia well before the outbreak of hostilities. Schultz's *Hero of Bataan* provides important information on day-to-day military action by Wainwright's forces.

The postwar report on supply problems on Bataan by Captain Harold A. Arnold of the Army's Quartermaster Corps (see Internet website in bibliography) reveals a major cause of the acute food shortage on the peninsula as well as the frustrations felt by personnel who knew about the glut of supplies languishing in dockside Manila warehouses that could have altered the course of the battle for Bataan.

Costello's *Days of Infamy* traces the formation of the Europe First defense policy of the United States and details the agreement between President Roosevelt and British prime minister Winston Churchill that the severity of the Nazi threat required that aid to Britain be given priority. Along with Rovere and Schlesinger's *The MacArthur Controversy*, Manchester's *American Caesar*, and Gerald Astor's *Crisis in the Pacific*, Costello's book also describes the confusion and vacillation on MacArthur's part that largely paralyzed the top U.S. command structure after December 8, delaying the crucial fortification of Bataan. Bartsch's *Doomed at the Start* provides key information on the disintegration of Army Air Corps pursuit squadrons during the last three weeks of 1941.

Sidney Stewart's *Give Us This Day* vividly re-creates his Christmas Eve visit to the posh Manila Hotel and the resignation to what lay ahead by the Americans grimly partying there while awaiting the arrival of Japanese troops. Hibbs's *Tell MacArthur to Wait* captures with equal drama Hibbs's last visit to his Manila apartment and his farewell meeting with Pilar Campos.

PAGE

55 *"MacArthur and [General] Sutherland":* General Bluemel's harsh criticisms of MacArthur are quoted in Astor's *Crisis in the Pacific* and Schultz's *Hero of Bataan.*

56 *"It was not possible to attack":* Wainwright's quote is from Schultz's book.

58 *"In the Tondo district of Manila:* The quotes from Captain Arnold are taken directly from the official quartermaster report issued after the war.

73 What irony, *Kathman thought:* These musings about Christmas are taken from Kathman's memoir, *I Was There, Charley.*

Chapter 4: The Last Bridge to Nowhere

Wainwright's memoir, *General Wainwright's Story*, and *Hero of Bataan*, Schultz's biography of the general, provide in-depth background on the retreat into Bataan and the difficulties involved. These sources are supplemented by Astor's *Crisis in the Pacific*; Louis Read's unpublished memoir, "No Bugles, No Parades"; Coleman's *Bataan and Beyond*; King's *Alamo of the Pacific*; Elizabeth Norman's *We Band of Angels*; Whitcomb's *Escape from Corregidor*; and Hibbs's *Tell MacArthur to Wait.*

Gray's oral history interview; and author interviews with Read, Overton, Kenneth Porwoll, Edwin Ramsey, Whitcomb, and Kathman, along with Ramsey's memoir, *Lieutenant Ramsey's War*, offer dramatic close-up views of the battlefield action.

PAGE

86 *"The Marines got more than their share of glory":* MacArthur's remark is mentioned in both Rovere and Schlesinger's *The MacArthur Controversy* and Otis King's *Alamo of the Pacific.*

88 *The nurses merely laughed:* The thoughts of the nurses bound for Bataan are described in Schultz's *Hero of Bataan.*

Chapter 5: Victory, Retreat, and a Final Charge

Wainwright's memoir, Shultz's biography of Wainwright, Astor's *Crisis in the Pacific*, Hibbs's *Tell MacArthur to Wait*, and Coleman's *Bataan and Beyond* contribute important background on the first weeks of the American defense of Bataan. The detailed accounts of how Lieutenant Colonel Philip Fry's Third Battalion, 57th Regiment, Philippine Scouts scored some of the first major victories against Japanese ground forces are taken from Astor's book. They are augmented by an author interview with John Olson, in which he described the heroic actions of young Lieutenant Alexander "Sandy" Nininger, for which he was posthumously awarded the first Medal of Honor of World War II.

Despite the successes of Fry's troops, as Schultz explains in *Hero of Bataan*, Wainwright had little confidence in the ability of General Parker's II Corps to hold off an all-out assault by enemy forces against the eastern side of the American-Filipino front. But as both Astor and Schultz point out, it was Wainwright's failure to close up the mountainous gap between his own lines on the west and Parker's on the east that nearly resulted in disaster for the defenders.

King's *Alamo of the Pacific* provides details on the contribution made to Bataan's defense by about 200 Marines, even after MacArthur refused to commit the main Marine force at his disposal to the Bataan battle.

The contributions made to Bataan's defense by the crippled but still viable U.S. submarine tender *Canopus* are explained in an author interview with Randall Edwards, a member of the ship's crew who witnessed those contributions firsthand. Other information about the *Canopus*'s role was obtained from Lester Tenney's memoir *My Hitch in Hell* and Tenney's oral history.

Background on the erroneous reports emanating from Washington and passed along by MacArthur that substantial help was on the way for Bataan's defenders was drawn from John Toland's *But Not in Shame*, Schultz's *Hero of Bataan*, and Astor's *Crisis in the Pacific*.

Ramsey's *Lieutenant Ramsey's War* and an author interview with Ramsey provide detailed eyewitness descriptions of the last mounted cavalry charge in history as carried out by the 26th Cavalry at the Bataan village of Moron on January 16, 1942.

PAGE

113 *"You gave up a good defensive position":* The orders and dressing-down administered by Wainwright to General Segundo are quoted in *Lieutenant Ramsey's War.*

113 *"Ramsey, you take the advance guard":* Wainwright's order is quoted verbatim in *Lieutenant Ramsey's War.*

123 *"All the horses are gone":* The exchange between Wheeler and Ramsey is recounted in *Lieutenant Ramsey's War.*

Chapter 6: Abandoning the Battling Bastards

Overviews of the complex actions, bitter fighting, and strategic withdrawals by U.S. forces during the mid portion of the Bataan campaign are drawn from Wainwright's memoirs, Schultz's Wainwright biography, Manchester's MacArthur biography, Astor's *Crisis in the Pacific*, Whitcomb's memoir, and Coleman's *Bataan and Beyond*.

Author interviews with Whitcomb, Overton, Olson, and Henry G. Stanley add personal eyewitness accounts.

Hibbs's memoir, in particular, provides a gripping, close-up look at the hard fighting and heavy casualties suffered by the 31st Infantry Regiment during the readjustment of American lines. His reconstruction of the incident in which Hibbs's frustrated battalion commander, Major Moffit, shoots off his own toe graphically illustrates the level of exhaustion and desperation experienced by the regiment.

While Wainwright's memoir offers excellent overviews of the battles of the points and pockets, it also includes key personal insights on the dangers to which the general was exposed during these actions. King's *Alamo of the Pacific*, meanwhile, includes revealing information on the role played in these battles by the Navy Battalion and, in particular, by the 200 or so Marines who served in the battalion. Recollections of the late Marine Gunner Harold Ferrell, as recorded by his son, Davis Ferrell, add another important dimension to the battlefield action and make it clear that small forces were being sent from Corregidor to help the Bataan defenders hold their ground.

Whitcomb's interviews with the author and memoir, along with Norman's *We Band of Angels*, Astor's *Crisis in the Pacific*, and other published sources, reveal the emotions aroused by persistent rumors that reinforcements for Bataan's garrison were on the way, the inevitable letdown when the rumors proved false, and the crushing realization after MacArthur's evacuation that no help was coming.

Wainwright's memoir contains only a brief reference to his final meeting with MacArthur on Corregidor, but Schultz's *Hero of Bataan* provides a detailed account of that meeting and of MacArthur's surprise announcement that he was being ordered by President Roosevelt to leave the Philippines and go to Australia. Manchester's *American Caesar* provides a full description of MacArthur's departure from Corregidor, and Astor's book also contributes details. Robert Heer's interview with the author and written narrative provides an invaluable eyewitness account of MacArthur's arrival on Mindanao aboard *PT-41*.

PAGE

131 *"God damn it, General"*: Wainwright quotes his orderly, Sergeant Carroll, in his memoir.

133 *"Rations were reduced from sixteen ounces a day"*: Colonel Townsend is quoted on the growing scarcity of food in Astor's *Crisis in the Pacific*.

147 *"The statement 'I shall return' was typical"*: Olson made this comment about MacArthur during his interview with the author.

147 *"But no one condemned MacArthur's flight . . . more caustically"*: General Brougher's condemnation of MacArthur is quoted in Astor's book.

Chapter 7: Chaos on a Collapsing Front

Wainwright's memoir, Schultz's *Hero of Bataan*, Manchester's *American Caesar*, Astor's *Crisis in the Pacific*, and Norman's *We Band of Angels* are among major secondary sources providing a broad framework for the story of Bataan's last-gasp defense against the all-out Japanese offensive in the spring of 1942. Wainwright's writings, in particular, as well as his reflections quoted in Schultz's biography, shed important light on the change in command on Corregidor, the atmosphere on the island, and its key defensive strengths and weaknesses.

But author interviews with Read, Olson, Overton, Ramsey, Kathman, Wayne Carrington, Charlie James, Charles Baum, and Whitcomb—along with memoirs by King, Kathman, Read, Hibbs, Coleman, Ramsey, and Whitcomb—provide searing close-up glimpses of the action over the length and breadth of the disintegrating American front.

PAGE

149 *MacArthur's plan to appoint four separate commanders:* Secretary of War Stimson's derisive comment on MacArthur's plan is quoted in Rovere and Schlesinger's *The MacArthur Controversy and American Foreign Policy.*

167 *At 3 AM on April 9, General Wainwright made:* There is some disagreement among sources as to the exact time of Wainwright's final call to King, as well as about the exact wording of his order to King. In his memoirs, *General Wainwright's Story*, Wainwright himself says: "I last spoke to King at 3 AM April 9. He did not mention surrender. My last order to him was to launch a counterattack at dawn." Historian Duane Schultz, however, sets the time of the call at 11:30 PM on April 8, and he uses the term "offensive" rather than "counterattack."

168 *King's quartermaster, Colonel Irvin Alexander:* General King's comments about his fear of being court-martialed are quoted in Astor's *Crisis in the Pacific.*

Chapter 8: Through One Hell to Another

Details of General King's desperate surrender journey and his humiliating meeting with Colonel Nakayama are drawn primarily from Astor's *Crisis in the Pacific*, Shultz's *Hero of Bataan*, and Michael and Elizabeth M. Norman's *Tears in the Darkness: The Story of the Bataan Death March and Its Aftermath.*

Various versions of these events have been based on recollections by Japanese and American military personnel who witnessed them, but most existing information has been drawn from the handwritten diary of Major Achille C. Tisdelle, an aide to General King, who was present at the surrender. The only known formal statements by King himself were contained in his January 1946 testimony before a war crimes tribunal.

The scenes unfolding among the troops on Bataan as the Japanese took control and the Death March began are graphically captured through memoirs by Coleman, Hibbs, Kathman, and Read. Other published sources including Knox's *Death March*, Sidney Stewart's *Give Us This Day*, Manny Lawton's *Some Survived*, Glenn Frazier's *Hell's Guest*, and Lester Tenney's *My Hitch in Hell* add grisly details.

Author interviews with Bill Adair, Henry Stanley, Ken Porwoll, Baum, Gray, Kathman, Overton, Olson, and Read contribute eyewitness accounts of atrocities and horrors committed against POWs and Filipino civilians.

Chapter 9: The Rock—"A Shining Example"

Wainwright's memoir and Schultz's biography of the general help to re-create the methodical, minute-by-minute destruction that rained down on Corregidor and the sense of impending doom that hung over the Rock and its trapped garrison in early May 1942. Along with Elizabeth Norman's *We Band of Angels*, they also describe the desperate efforts by Wainwright and his officers to arrange last-minute evacuations by seaplanes and submarines of some of the 150 nurses trapped on the island.

Ed Whitcomb's interview with the author and memoir trace his interlude on Corregidor from his initial relief after escaping from Bataan to disillusionment, despair, eventual capture by the Japanese, yet another escape, and a return to the jungles of Luzon in search of a boat capable of reaching Australia.

In similar fashion, Otis King's memoir reveals how he and his buddy Ike Williams also made the long, harrowing swim from Bataan to Corregidor to join hundreds of other Marines in manning defensive positions on the island's north beach.

Author interviews with Marines Roy Hays, Silas Barnes, Ernest Bales, and Ben Lohman provide firsthand accounts of the last-ditch fighting for Corregidor. Information for the segments describing the situation at Wainwright's headquarters and his decision to surrender the island are drawn from Schultz's *Hero of Bataan*, Astor's *Crisis in the Pacific*, and Wainwright's autobiography.

PAGE

219 *A chilling image flashed through Wainwright's mind:* This reference is drawn from a passage in *General Wainwright's Story* in which the general states: "But it was the terror that is vested in a tank that was the deciding factor. I thought of the havoc that even one of these could wreak if it nosed into the tunnel, where lay our helpless wounded and their brave nurses."

Chapter 10: O'Donnell and Other Horrors

A 2010 author interview with John Olson, widely recognized as the foremost living authority on what happened at the O'Donnell POW camp following the Death March in the spring of 1942, forms a major cornerstone for this chapter, as does Olson's self-published book, *O'Donnell: Andersonville of the Pacific.* Most of the figures on fatalities at the camp are based on records kept by Olson as the camp's American adjutant.

Other author interviews with Kathman, Read, Overton, and Stanley, as well as Tenney's oral history, help portray the almost indescribable horrors endured by prisoners at O'Donnell and later at Cabanatuan. Secondary sources providing valuable details include Coleman's *Bataan and Beyond*, Knox's *Death March*, Michael and Elizabeth Norman's *Tears in the Darkness*, Astor's *Crisis in the Pacific*, Tenney's *My Hitch in Hell*, Frazier's *Hell's Guest*, Kathman's *I Was There, Charley*, and Lawton's *Some Survived.*

Lawton's book, Coleman's memoir, Joseph Lajzer's autobiography, *3.6 Years of Hell*, and the diary of medical officer Calvin Jackson also paint graphic pictures of life at the Cabanatuan camp, where prisoners were unable to detect any significant difference from O'Donnell and thousands more died.

Author interviews with Barnes and Whitcomb, plus Tenney's oral history, King's *Alamo of the Pacific*, and Whitcomb's *Escape from Corregidor* re-create the agonies of the temporary stockade on Corregidor known as the 92nd Garage. Hibbs's memoir describes life in the "hellhole" of the Bilibid prison hospital in Manila.

PAGE

257 *My God, what a terrible risk she's taking*: Hibbs's thoughts are taken directly from his memoir, *Tell MacArthur to Wait.*

Chapter 11: Hell Ships—Voyages to Oblivion

Author interviews with Alexander, Gill, Kathman, Olson, Overton, Read, and Stanley paint a firsthand portrait of the conditions aboard the ships carrying American POWs from the Philippines to slave labor jobs in Japan and her conquered territories. Oral history interviews with Gray, Overton, and Tenney, along with Read's unpublished memoir, provide additional insights.

Published sources contributing important eyewitness accounts of the hell ship voyages include the memoirs by Coleman, Frazier, Kathman, Lajzer, Lawton, and Stewart. Knox's *Death March*, Astor's *Crisis in the Pacific*, the Normans' *Tears in the Darkness*, John D. Lukacs's *Escape from Davao*, Toland's *But Not in Shame*, and the diary of Colonel Calvin Jackson provide key additional details. Background on increasingly aggressive U.S. actions in the Pacific during the hell ship period is drawn from Volume 12 of Samuel Eliot Morison's *History of United States Naval Operations in World War II.*

Judith L. Pearson's *Belly of the Beast*, a biographical account of the experiences of her father, POW Estel Myers, offers a unique perspective on the disaster aboard the *Orokyu Maru.* The Internet article "The *Arisan Maru* Tragedy," by William Bowen, provides details of the attack on that hell ship by a U.S. submarine and the massive resulting loss of life.

Gregory F. Michno's *Death on the Hellships* provides the most authoritative statistics on the number of hell ships and the total number of fatalities suffered aboard them. King's *Alamo of the Pacific* also contains key information about the scope—and deadly results—of the hell ship operation. Davis Ferrell's Internet bio of his father, Gunner Ferrell, provides details of the latter's attempts to save a dying Marine.

PAGE

276 *"Get this bastard away from me!"*: This quote and the four that follow represent a composite of exclamations contained in various author interviews and memoirs.

278 *"Americans are sinking Japanese ships!"*: The outburst by Wada is quoted in Tenney's book.

Chapter 12: Escape—The Ultimate Revenge

The author's interview with Edwin Ramsey and Ramsey's memoir, *Lieutenant Ramsey's War*, provide graphic eyewitness accounts of guerrilla activities in the Philippines by the only high-level American guerrilla leader still living. They also offer insightful glimpses into the shadowy lives of such other legendary guerrilla commanders as Claude Thorp, Robert Lapham, Gyles Merrill, and Ramon Ruffy.

Ramsey gives an insider's unique overview of the vast resistance movement that flourished throughout the Philippines from the fall of Bataan in April 1942 through the U.S. invasion of Luzon in early 1945, when he coordinated efforts between his thousands of irregulars and MacArthur's headquarters to aid the invasion force.

The guerrilla activities of Army Privates Leon Beck and Blair Robinett, as recounted in the two Bataan escapees' own words in Knox's *Death March*, add another major dimension to the story of the resistance movement and the assortment of clandestine, often competing, organizations comprising it.

The daring escape from Davao Penal Colony by ten American POWs, their subsequent arrival in the United States, and their revelations of Japanese atrocities in the Death March and prison camps to a stunned U.S. public are described by Ed Dyess, one of the escapees, in his book *The Dyess Story.* Additional details are provided by Lukacs's *Escape from Davao.*

Whitcomb's author interviews and his memoir, *Escape from Corregidor*, focus initially on his and fellow fugitive Bill Harris's efforts to avoid capture and obtain a boat capable of taking them to Australia. Later they follow Whitcomb's attempt to pose as a fictitious civilian, his imprisonment and torture by the Japanese, and his eventual release to an internment camp for civilians awaiting repatriation.

J. D. Merritt's memoir *Adapt or Die* and his author interview describe how he caused many Japanese deaths while a POW.

Chapter 13: A Race Between Freedom and Death

A description of the execution of ninety-six American civilians on Wake Island in October 1943, based on war crimes trial testimony in 1946, appears in the author's 2003 book, *Given Up for Dead: America's Heroic Stand at Wake Island.* The book also lists each of the victims by name.

The final chapter in the long escape saga of Edgar Whitcomb and the unexpected ordeal he faced on his return to the United States is drawn from author interviews with Whitcomb and from his memoir, *Escape from Corregidor.* Details of the censorship difficulties confronting Ed Dyess and the other Davao escapees in trying to make the American public aware of the Bataan Death March and later atrocities are drawn from two principal sources—Dyess's autobiography, *The Dyess Story*, and Lukacs's *Escape from Davao.*

Two other published sources include vital information on the raid by American Rangers and Filipino guerrillas to free the sick, maimed, and starving POWs remaining at Cabanatuan prison camp. Both *Ghost Soldiers: The Epic Account of World War II's Greatest Rescue Mission* by Hampton Sides and *The Great Raid: Rescuing the Doomed Ghosts of Bataan* by William B. Breuer provide minute-by-minute accounts of the high-risk mission.

Lending a unique perspective on the same events is Ralph Hibbs's memoir, *Tell MacArthur to Wait*, which recounts Hibbs's own rescue as the last POW to leave Cabanatuan and his consuming grief a short time later when he learns of the death of Pilar Campos.

Author interviews with John Oliver, Louis Read, and Joe Alexander, along with memoirs by Read, Tenney, Frazier, and Lawton, capture the rampant fear and tension in POW slave labor camps during the war's final days. A copy of the execution order distributed to Japanese security forces on Formosa and provided to the author by Oliver offers convincing proof of Japanese intentions. Gray's oral history interview, Wainwright's memoir, Schultz's *Hero of Bataan*, Knox's *Death March*, and Dr. Calvin Jackson's diary provide additional insights and perspectives.

PAGE

329 *"Whether they [POWs] are destroyed individually or in groups":* This excerpt comes directly from the copy of the execution order provided by Oliver.

334 My God, *he thought,* we've got all the necessary colors: This realization by Gray is recounted in his oral history interview.

336 *"There was no stopping the laughter"*: The quote from Wainwright is taken verbatim from his memoir, *General Wainwright's Story*.

Chapter 14: New Lives, Old Scars

These brief capsules of the postwar lives of the narrative's principal protagonists and other Philippine veterans are drawn from author interviews with Overton, Whitcomb, Ramsey, Alexander, Kathman, and Read as well as the memoirs of Coleman, Hibbs, Ramsey, Read, Whitcomb, Kathman, and King.

Author interviews with Coleman's grandson, Richard Sims, and King's former journalistic colleague, Alex Burton, provide additional information on the later lives of these two deceased veterans of Bataan. Efforts by the author to locate King's widow were unsuccessful.

References to the later years of Wainwright and MacArthur are based on each general's memoir, Manchester's *American Caesar*, and Schultz's *Hero of Bataan*.

Author interviews with Stanley and Adair, prompted by a September 2009 article in the *Dallas Morning News* (from which the original idea for this book sprang), illustrate the ongoing anger and frustration felt toward Japanese officialdom by the American Defenders of Bataan and Corregidor at the time the organization was taken over by their descendants.

PAGE

359 *It wasn't long until these gatherings came to the attention of General Dwight Eisenhower:* General Eisenhower's remarks are quoted in Schultz's book.

360 *Prior to its surrender in 1945, Close observed:* Close's observations are quoted in Manchester's book.

Bibliography

Books

Abraham, Abie. *Ghost of Bataan Speaks.* New York: Vantage, 1971.

Alexander, Irvin. *Surviving Bataan and Beyond.* Mechanicsburg, Pa.: Stackpole, 2005.

Astor, Gerald. *Crisis in the Pacific: The Battles for the Philippine Islands by the Men Who Fought There.* New York: Dell, 1996.

Bartsch, William. *December 8, 1941: MacArthur's Pearl Harbor.* College Station: Texas A&M University Press, 2003.

———. *Doomed at the Start: American Pursuit Pilots in the Philippines, 1941–1942.* College Station: Texas A&M University Press, 1992.

Brawner, Steve, and Melissa Brawner. *The Lord Is Our Shepherd: The Story of Former Prisoner of War Cletis Overton and Maxine Overton.* Little Rock: The Story of Our Lives, 2000.

Brereton, Lewis H. *The Brereton Diaries.* New York: William Morrow, 1946.

Breuer, William B. *The Great Raid: Rescuing the Doomed Ghosts of Bataan.* New York: Hyperion, 2002.

Caidin, Martin. *The Ragged, Rugged Warriors.* New York: E. P. Dutton, 1966.

Coleman, John S., Jr. *Bataan and Beyond: Memories of an American POW.* College Station: Texas A&M University Press, 1978.

Condit, Kenneth W., and Edwin T. Turnbladh. *Hold High the Torch: A History of the Fourth Marines.* Washington, D.C.: Historical Branch, U.S. Marine Corps, 1960.

Costello, John. *Days of Infamy: MacArthur, Roosevelt, Churchill—The Shocking Truth Revealed: How Their Secret Deals and Strategic Blunders Caused Disasters at Pearl Harbor and the Philippines.* New York: Pocket Books, 1994.

Daws, Gavan. *Prisoners of the Japanese: POWs of World War II in the Pacific.* New York: William Morrow, 1994.

Dyess, William E. *Bataan Death March: A Survivor's Account.* Lincoln, Neb.: Bison, 2002.

———. *The Dyess Story.* New York: G. P. Putnam's Sons, 1944.

Ferrell, Robert H., editor. *The Eisenhower Diaries.* New York: W. W. Norton, 1981.

Frazier, Glenn D. *Hell's Guest.* Springfield, Mo.: RoJon, 2007.

Hibbs, Ralph Emerson. *Tell MacArthur to Wait.* Medford, Ore.: Giraffe, 1998.

Hitchcock, Pat. *Forty Months in Hell.* Jackson, Tenn.: Page, 1996.

Jackson, Calvin G. *Diary of Col. Calvin G. Jackson, M.D.* Ada: Ohio Northern University Press, 1992.

Kathman, Clemens A. *I Was There, Charley.* Bloomington, Ind.: AuthorHouse, 2005.

Keith, Billy. *Days of Anguish, Days of Hope.* London: Hodder & Stoughton, 1973.

King, Otis H. *Alamo of the Pacific: The Story of the Famed "China Marines" on Bataan and Corregidor and What They Did to the Enemy as POWs.* Fort Worth: O. H. Karl King, 1999.

Knox, Donald. *Death March: The Survivors of Bataan.* New York: Harcourt Brace Jovanovich, 1981.

Lajzer, Joseph D. *3.6 Years of Hell in Japanese Prisoner of War Camps, 1942–1945.* San Antonio: Watercress, 2002.

Lawton, Manny. *Some Survived: An Eyewitness Account of the Bataan Death March and the Men Who Lived Through It.* Chapel Hill: Algonquin, 2004.

Lukacs, John D. *Escape from Davao: The Forgotten Story of the Most Daring Prison Break of the Pacific War.* New York: Simon & Schuster, 2010.

MacArthur, Douglas. *Reminiscences.* New York: McGraw-Hill, 1964.

Manchester, William. *American Caesar: Douglas MacArthur, 1880–1964.* Boston: Little, Brown, 1978.

McGee, John H. *Rice and Salt: A History of the Defense and Occupation of Mindanao in World War II.* San Antonio: Naylor, 1962.

Merritt, J. D. *Adapt or Die.* Cape Coral, Fla.: J. D. Merritt, 2010.

Michno, Gregory F. *Death on the Hellships: Prisoners at Sea in the Pacific War.* London: Pen & Sword, 2001.

Morison, Samuel Eliot. *History of United States Naval Operations in World War II,* Vol. III: *The Rising Sun in the Pacific, 1931–April 1942.* Boston: Little, Brown, 1948.

———. *History of United States Naval Operations in World War II,* Vol. XII: *Leyte: June 1944–January 1945.* Boston: Little, Brown, 1956.

Morton, Louis. *U.S. Army in World War II: The War in the Pacific: The Fall of the Philippines.* Washington, D.C.: Center of Military History, U.S. Army, 1989.

Norman, Elizabeth M. *We Band of Angels: The Untold Story of American Nurses Trapped on Bataan by the Japanese.* New York: Random House, 1999.

Norman, Michael, and Elizabeth M. Norman. *Tears in the Darkness: The Story of the Bataan Death March and Its Aftermath.* New York: Farrar, Straus & Giroux, 2009.

Olson, John. *O'Donnell: Andersonville of The Pacific.* San Antonio: John Olson, 1985.

Pearson, Judith L. *Belly of the Beast: A POW's Inspiring True Story of Faith, Courage, and Survival Aboard the Infamous WWII Japanese Hell Ship* Oryoku Maru. New York: New American Library, 2001.

Petak, Joseph A. *Never Plan Tomorrow.* Fullerton, Calif.: Aquataur, 1991.

Ramsey, Edwin Price, and Stephen J. Rivele. *Lieutenant Ramsey's War.* New York: Knightsbridge, 1990.

Rovere, Richard H., and Arthur Schlesinger Jr. *The MacArthur Controversy and American Foreign Policy.* New York: Farrar, Straus & Giroux, 1965.

Schultz, Duane. *Hero of Bataan: The Story of General Jonathan M. Wainwright.* New York: St. Martin's, 1981.

Sides, Hampton. *Ghost Soldiers: The Epic Account of World War II's Greatest Rescue Mission.* New York: Anchor, 2002.

Stewart, Sidney. *Give Us This Day.* New York: W. W. Norton, 1957.

Tenney, Lester I. *My Hitch in Hell: The Bataan Death March.* Washington: Brasseys, 1995.

Toland, John. *But Not in Shame: The Six Months After Pearl Harbor.* New York: Random House, 1961.

Wainwright, Jonathan M. *General Wainwright's Story: The Account of Four Years of Humiliation, Surrender, Defeat and Captivity.* Garden City: Doubleday, 1946.

Whitcomb, Edgar D. *Escape from Corregidor.* Chicago: Henry Regnery, 1958.

Whitney, Courtney. *MacArthur: His Rendezvous with History.* New York: Alfred A. Knopf, 1956.

Williams, Ted R. *The Return of the Rogues: A Marine Unit's Fight for Life and Freedom.* Self-published, 2004.

Articles

Bowen, William. "The Arisan Maru Tragedy." Internet article.

Boyle, Hal. "Marines Will Not Forget 'Demon Doctor.'" Undated Associated Press dispatch.

Case, Homer. "War Damage to Corregidor." *Coast Artillery Journal*, May–June 1947.

Chan, Sewell. "WWII Memorial Bill Signed." *Washington Post*, May 29, 2001.

Farwell, Scott. "Veterans Say No Thanks to Apology." *Dallas Morning News*, September 13, 2009.

Fattig, Paul. "Bataan Vet Dr. Ralph Hibbs Dies." *Medford* (Oregon) *Mail Tribune*, October 5, 2000.

Haga, Chuck. "Survivor's Tale: 50 Years Haven't Dimmed Former POW's Memories of Japanese 'Hell Ship.'" *Minneapolis Star Tribune*, October 23, 1994.

Helms, Nat. "The 'Tiger of Malaya,' General Tomoyuki Yamashita, Was Hanged Near Manila in Retribution for Japanese War Crimes." *World War II*, February 1996.

Hogaboom, William F. "Action Report Bataan." *Marine Corps Gazette*, April 1946.

Hull, Michael D. "The Battle for Manila Liberated the Philippine Capital but Cost Thousands of Lives and Devastated the 'Pearl of the Orient.'" *World War II*, November 1996.

Picket, W. F. "Naval Battalion at Mariveles." *Marine Corps Gazette*, June 1950.

Ross, Gloria D. "A Singular Man." *Airman*, January 1982.

Simnacher, Joe. "Veteran Radio Newsman's WWII Exploits Shaped Life." *Dallas Morning News*, July 28, 2005.

"Ten Cigarets a Month, Four Bars of Soap a Year Allotted to Americans Held by Japs." *Charleston Evening Post*, April 23, 1945.

Whitman, John W. "Delaying Action in the Philippines." *World War II*, November 1998.

Wilde, Matthew. "Family Sacrifice." Waterloo/Cedar Falls, Iowa *Courier*, November 11, 2008.

Womack, Tom. "Sword of the Rising Sun." *World War II*, February 1998.

Wynn, V. Dennis. "Massacre at Palawan." *World War II*, November 1997.

Yamamoto, Mayumi. "After 53 Years, Ex-POW Meets His Japanese Guard." *Pacific Stars and Stripes*, July 22, 1998.

Author Interviews

Bill Adair, October 2009
Joseph Alexander, March 2010
Ernest J. Bales, February 2010
Silas K. Barnes, February 2010
Charles Baum, February 2010
Walter Bell, April 2010
Hersheal Boushey, February 2010
Alex Burton, January 2011
Wayne Carrington, October 2009
Henry J. Cornellisson, March 2010
Sonia B. Davis, February 2010
Randall S. Edwards, June 2010
Russell Gill, August 2010
Alyne S. Gray, April 2010
Smith L. Green, October 2009
Roy E. Hays, February 2010
Robert B. Heer, March 2010
Edward Jackfert, March 2010
Charlie James, April 2010
Warren B. Jorgenson, February 2010
Clemens Kathman, March 2010
Paul Kerchum, June 2010
Henry King, March 2010
Ben L. Lohman, March 2010
J. D. Merritt, October 2011
John H. Oliver, February 2010
John E. Olson, March 2010

Cletis Overton, May 2010
Menandro "Andy" Parazo, October 2010
Ken Porwoll, November 2009
Edwin Preston, April 2010
Edwin P. Ramsey, June 2010
Louis Read, October 2009
Richard Sims, January 2011
Henry G. Stanley, October 2009, February 2010
Edgar D. Whitcomb, October 2009, June 2010, January 2011

Oral Histories

Courtesy National Museum of the Pacific War, Center for Pacific War Studies:

Robert A. Brown
Ken Calvit
Arthur Campbell
John Cook
Warren Elder
Harold Feiner
J. S. Gray
Robert Haines
Weldon Hamilton
Bill Harrellson
Sam B. Moody
John E. Olson
Cletis Overton
John Real
Jay Rye
Agapito Silva
Lester Tenney

Courtesy Chuck Hodge:

Russell Gill
Menandro "Andy" Parazo

Web Sites

American Defenders of Bataan and Corregidor: site dismantled, July 2010

Army Quartermaster Museum—Fort Lee, Va.: www.qmmuseum.lee.army.mil/wwII/bataan

China Marines official website: www.chinamarines.com

Defenders of the Philippines: http://philippine-defenders.lib.wv.us/

Descendants Group of American Defenders of Bataan and Corregidor: http://www.dg.adbc.org

HyperWar: U.S. Army in WWII: Fall of the Philippines: www.biblio.org/jhyperwar/usa/usa-p-pi

194th Tank Battalion in Luzon Campaign, 1941–42: www.militaryphotos.net/forums/archives/index

Philippine Scouts Heritage Society: http://www.philippine-scouts.org/history

U.S. Marines in World War II: Western Pacific: www.marines.mil/history

U.S. 31st Infantry Regiment Association: www.31stinfantry.org/history

Miscellaneous

Coleman, Elbert Vernon. Unpublished diary/narrative. Courtesy National Museum of the Pacific War.

Davis, Sonia B. Unpublished manuscript, "My Experiences as a Prisoner of War." Courtesy Sonia B. Davis.

Declassified document instructing security forces at Taiwan POW Camp (entry of August 1, 1944) on "final disposition" of American POWs. Courtesy John Oliver.

Heer, Robert E. Unpublished personal account, "General MacArthur's Escape on PT Boat #41." Courtesy Robert Heer.

"The Japanese Story." Packet No. 10, Publication of American Ex-POWs Inc., National Medical Research Commission. Courtesy Henry G. Stanley.

Pase, Joseph G. Testimony concerning Japanese war crimes, September 15, 1945. U.S. War Department War Crimes Office. Courtesy National Museum of the Pacific War.

Read, Louis. Unpublished memoir, "No Bugles, No Parades." Courtesy Louis Read.

Acknowledgments

Hundreds of people, both living and dead, played indispensable roles in creating the book you're holding in your hands (or the one on the screen of your Kindle), and I owe each of them a debt of gratitude.

This number, of course, includes all the surviving veterans of the Philippines campaign who gave of their time, knowledge, and energy to grant me personal interviews. But it also includes the writers of dozens of memoirs and autobiographies, ranging from those so obscure that only a handful of readers are aware of them to those by well-known authors that have sold thousands and thousands of copies.

Many of these writers are now long deceased, but in recording their firsthand experiences during one of the darkest periods in human history, they helped ensure that what they suffered, and triumphed over, won't be forgotten. I'm deeply grateful to them all.

There are, however, a few individuals whose contributions to the story of *Undefeated* were too utterly irreplaceable for me not to identify them by name.

My friend Floyd Cox, an unpaid volunteer who directs the oral history program at the National Museum of the Pacific War in Fredericksburg, Texas, opened his files to me and provided transcripts of interviews with a long list of Bataan and Corregidor veterans.

Chuck Hodge, another friend and one of the few people in America who holds the distinction of interviewing more World War II veterans than I have, generously shared his videos, provided contact information for veterans I might otherwise have missed, and loaned me a monumental stack of books from his vast collection.

As always, my wife and number one copy editor, Lana Sloan, was the first person to read my rough drafts and offer much needed suggestions for improvement. Thanks, honey, for the long hours you invested in my behalf at times when you were overburdened with writing and editing work of your own.

Thanks, too, to Jim Donovan, my longtime literary agent, not only for sell-ing the book but for helping me track down such key interviewees as Lieutenant Colonel Edwin Ramsey, who led the world's last cavalry charge on Bataan and later served as a major leader of the Philippines guerrilla movement.

In working on my fourth military history with Roger Labrie, my editor at Simon & Schuster, I found him to be as insightful and perceptive as ever, and I'm grateful for his help and friendship all along the way.

Several relatives of deceased veterans offered invaluable assistance in obtaining photographs and key bits of information. These include Alyne Gray, widow of Sergeant J. S. Gray; Richard Sims, grandson of Captain John Coleman; and Jennifer Hibbs Eastberg, daughter of Major Ralph Hibbs.

If I've neglected to mention you here by name, it doesn't mean I don't value your help. My sincere appreciation to everyone who had a part in this one.

Bill Sloan
Dallas, Texas

Index

Credits for the Photographs

Courtesy John Olson: 1

National Archives: 2, 6, 9, 10, 14–20, 22–24, 28, 29, 32–35

Courtesy Edgar Whitcomb: 3

Courtesy Joseph Alexander: 4

Courtesy Peggy King: 5

Courtesy Edwin Ramsey: 7, 8

Courtesy Louis Reed: 11–13, 31

Courtesy Richard Sims: 21

Courtesy Jennifer Hibbs Eastberg: 25

Courtesy Clemens Kathman: 26

National Museum of the Pacific War: 27

Courtesy Cletis Overton: 30

Courtesy Mrs. J. S. Gray: 36–38

About the Author

Bill Sloan is a respected military historian and the author of more than a dozen books, including *Brotherhood of Heroes* and *The Ultimate Battle*. A former investigative reporter and feature writer for the *Dallas Times Herald*, where he was nominated for the Pulitzer Prize, Sloan lives in Dallas, Texas.

"A haunting tale of an island transformed from tropical paradise into the Alamo of the Pacific, and a fitting tribute to the heroes who fought, suffered, and died there."
—JONATHAN W. JORDAN,
bestselling author of *Brothers, Rivals, Victors*

Bill Sloan, "a master of the combat narrative" (*Dallas Morning News*), tells the story of the outnumbered American soldiers and airmen who stood against invading Japanese forces in the Philippines at the beginning of World War II, and continued to resist through three harrowing years as POWs. For four months they fought toe to toe against overwhelming enemy numbers—and forced the Japanese to pay a heavy cost in blood. After the surrender came the infamous Bataan Death March, where up to eighteen thousand American and Filipino prisoners died as they marched sixty-five miles under the most hellish conditions imaginable. Interwoven throughout this gripping narrative are the harrowing personal experiences of dozens of American soldiers, airmen, and Marines, based on exclusive interviews with more than thirty survivors. *Undefeated* chronicles one of the great sagas of World War II—and celebrates a resounding triumph of the human spirit.

"Sloan expertly illuminates the dark, early days of World War II in the Philippines, as well as the savage aftermath, in staggering detail. *Undefeated* cements Sloan's reputation as one of the war's eminent historians and storytellers."
—JOHN D. LUKACS, author of *Escape From Davao*

BILL SLOAN is a respected military historian and the author of more than a dozen books, including *The Ultimate Battle* and *The Darkest Summer*. At the *Dallas Times Herald*, where he was an investigative reporter and feature writer, he was nominated for the Pulitzer Prize. ... llas, Texas.

Scan for more on this author:

MEET THE AUTHORS, WATCH VIDEOS AND MORE AT
SimonandSchuster.com

COVER DESIGN BY DAVID TER-AVANESYAN
COVER PHOTOGRAPHS © ROGER VIOLLET/GETTY IMAGES; ISLAND © 123RF

HISTORY 0613

ISBN 978-1-4391-9965-7 **$18.00 U.S.**/$21.00 Can.

PRINTED IN THE U.S.A.